Comics and Cognition

COGNITION AND POETICS

Cognition and Poetics (CAP) fosters high-quality interdisciplinary research at the intersection of cognitive science, literature, the arts, and linguistics. The series seeks to expand the development of theories and methodologies that integrate research in the relevant disciplines to further our understanding of the production and reception of the arts as one of the most central and complex operations of the human mind. CAP welcomes submissions of edited volumes and monographs in English that focus on literatures and cultures from around the world.

Series Editors:
Alexander Bergs, University of Osnabrück
Margaret H. Freeman, Myrifield Institute for Cognition and the Arts
Peter Schneck, University of Osnabrück
Achim Stephan, University of Osnabrück

Advisory Board:
Mark Bruhn, Regis University Denver, CO, USA
Peer Bundgard, Aarhus University, Denmark
Michael Burke, University College Roosevelt Middelburg, The Netherlands
Wallace Chafe, University of California Santa Barbara, USA
Barbara Dancygier, University of British Columbia Vancouver, Canada
Frank Jäkel, Universität Osnabrück, Germany
Winfried Menninghaus, Freie Universität Berlin, Germany
Keith Oatley, University of Toronto, Canada
Jan Slaby, Freie Universität Berlin, Germany
Reuven Tsur, Tel Aviv University, Israel
Mark Turner, Case Western Reserve University Cleveland, OH, USA
Simone Winko, Georg-August-Universität Göttingen, Germany
Dahlia Zaidel, University of California Los Angles, USA

Cognitive Approaches to Early Modern Spanish Literature
Edited by Isabel Jaén and Julien Jacques Simon

Cognitive Literary Science: Dialogues between Literature and Cognition
Edited by Michael Burke and Emily T. Troscianko

A Prehistory of Cognitive Poetics: Neoclassicism and the Novel
Karin Kukkonen

Poetic Conventions as Cognitive Fossils
Reuven Tsur

Sexual Identities: A Cognitive Literary Study
Patrick Colm Hogan

Expressive Minds and Artistic Creations: Studies in Cognitive Poetics
Edited by Szilvia Csábi

4e Cognition and Eighteenth-Century Fiction: How the Novel Found Its Feet
Karin Kukkonen

Probability Designs: Literature and Predictive Processing
Karin Kukkonen

The Poem as Icon: A Study in Aesthetic Cognition
Margaret H. Freeman

Style in Narrative: Aspects of an Affective-Cognitive Stylistics
Patrick Colm Hogan

Kinesic Humor: Literature, Embodied Cognition, and the Dynamics of Gesture
Guillemette Bolens

Beckett and the Cognitive Method: Mind, Models, and Exploratory Narratives
Marco Bernini

Comics and Cognition: Toward a Multimodal Cognitive Poetics
Mike Borkent

COMICS AND COGNITION
Toward a Multimodal Cognitive Poetics

Mike Borkent

Oxford University Press is a department of the University of Oxford. It furthers
the University's objective of excellence in research, scholarship, and education
by publishing worldwide. Oxford is a registered trade mark of Oxford University
Press in the UK and certain other countries.

Published in the United States of America by Oxford University Press
198 Madison Avenue, New York, NY 10016, United States of America.

© Oxford University Press 2024

All rights reserved. No part of this publication may be reproduced, stored in
a retrieval system, or transmitted, in any form or by any means, without the
prior permission in writing of Oxford University Press, or as expressly permitted
by law, by license, or under terms agreed with the appropriate reproduction
rights organization. Inquiries concerning reproduction outside the scope of the
above should be sent to the Rights Department, Oxford University Press, at the
address above.

You must not circulate this work in any other form
and you must impose this same condition on any acquirer.

Library of Congress Cataloging-in-Publication Data
Names: Borkent, Mike, author.
Title: Comics and cognition : toward a multimodal cognitive poetics / by Mike Borkent.
Description: New York, NY : Oxford University Press, 2024. |
Series: Cognition and poetics series |
Includes bibliographical references and index.
Identifiers: LCCN 2023022529 (print) | LCCN 2023022530 (ebook) |
ISBN 9780197509784 (hardback) | ISBN 9780197509807 (epub)
Subjects: LCSH: Comic books, strips, etc.—Psychological aspects. |
Cognition. | Modality (Linguistics) | LCGFT: Comics criticism.
Classification: LCC PN6714 .B669 2023 (print) | LCC PN6714 (ebook) |
DDC 741.5/9—dc23/eng/20230808
LC record available at https://lccn.loc.gov/2023022529
LC ebook record available at https://lccn.loc.gov/2023022530

DOI: 10.1093/oso/9780197509784.001.0001

Printed by Integrated Books International, United States of America

For Sara

CONTENTS

List of Illustrations   ix
Acknowledgments   xiii

1. Introduction   1

2. How to Talk about Comics and Not Fear Them: Literacies, Fallacies, and Modalities   5
    2.1 Modalities and the Battle of the Books: *Essex County*   5
    2.2 Literacies and Fallacies   13
    2.3 "Literacies Are Legion:" On Multiple Literacies, Multimodality, and Disciplinarity   18
    2.4 A Cognitive Approach to Comics and Multimodality   29

3. Multimodality and Cognition: Perception, Knowledge Networks, and the Construction of Meaning   32
    3.1 Cognition and Textual Experience   32
    3.2 Perceiving Comics   38
    3.3 Cognitive Topology   50
    3.4 Dynamic Cognitive Processes   57
    3.5 Conclusion: The Power of the Multimodal Mental Image   67

4. Paneling Construal and Viewpoint: Abstractions, Bodies, and Synesthetic Forms   69
    4.1 Viewpoint and Construal: From the Body to the World   69
    4.2 Abstraction and Viewpoint Construal: Interpreting Genre and Style   70
    4.3 Agentive Bodies and Emotions   76
    4.4 Materialized Sounds and Viewpoints: Synesthesia, Typography, and Balloons   98
    4.5 Spatial Strategies and Viewpoint Orchestration   105
    4.6 Conclusion   108

5. Expanded Viewpoint Networks: Metonymies, Metaphors, and Other Blends 110
   5.1 Expanding Networks 110
   5.2 Multimodal Metonymies 111
   5.3 Figurative Metaphors and Other Blends 119
   5.4 Woven and Extended Viewpoints 130
   5.5 Conclusion: Expanded Networks of Presentation and Viewpoint Construal 136

6. Temporalities: Metaphors, Modalities, and Arrangements 138
   6.1 Comics, Time, and/or Sequentiality 138
   6.2 Cognition and Space/Time 146
   6.3 Temporal Shifts: Timeline Manipulation and Blends 154
   6.4 Designed Layouts and Temporal Multiplicity 168
   6.5 Conclusion 180

7. Spatial Conceptualizations: Layout as Viewpoint and Narrative Strategy in *The Underwater Welder* 183
   7.1 Introduction 183
   7.2 Visualizing Metaphors of the Self through Layout 185
   7.3 Salience and Materialized Narrative Anchors 194
   7.4 Conclusion 197

8. Abstraction and Experimentation in Comics: Improvisation and Meaning 198
   8.1 The Problem of Abstraction and Simplicity 198
   8.2 Dynamic Forms and Narrative Potentialities 200
   8.3 Abstraction and Cognition 204
   8.4 Experimentation as Metacommentary: Possibilities and Refusals 215
   8.5 Conclusion 227

9. Conclusions and Extensions: Expanding Multimodal Cognitive Poetics through Digital Comics 228
   9.1 Conclusions 228
   9.2 Digital Alterations and Expansions of Multimodality 229
   9.3 Toward a Dynamical Multimodal Cognitive Poetics 240

Notes 241
References 251
Index 277

LIST OF ILLUSTRATIONS

FIGURES

2.1. From Jeff Lemire's *Essex County* (2009, 126)   8
3.1. Joseph Jastrow's version of the duck-rabbit illusion (1899, 312). Public domain   39
3.2. Most common terms for basic elements of a comics page layout, based on Groensteen (2007) and McCloud (1993)   43
3.3. "Who hasn't fantasized . . . ?" (1997) editorial cartoon by Aislin (alias Terry Mosher), accession number M2000.79.59. With permission of McCord Museum, Montreal   46
3.4. Reversed reconstruction of Aislin's "Who hasn't fantasized?"   49
3.5. Mental spaces diagram illustrating how cross mappings, blending, and backward projection build composite meaning   65
4.1. Selection from *The Photographer* by Lefèvre, Guilbert, and Lemercie (2009, 48)   73
4.2. Yorick's execution scene in Vaughan and Guerra's *Y: The Last Man: Cycles* (2003, 89)   77
4.3. Selection from Rob Guillory's *Farmhand* (2019, n.p.), showing variation in figuration within a short scene   84
4.4. A panel from Julie Doucet's *My Most Secret Desire* (1995, n.p.)   85
4.5. Two of Scott McCloud's facial expressions of "emotional primaries" (2006, 83)   89
4.6. Selection from Guy Davis' *The Marquis: Inferno* (2009, 73)   92

4.7. Part of Will Eisner's illustration of text interactions with facial expressions (Eisner 2008a, 113)   93

4.8. Selection from Eisner's "micro-dictionary of gestures" showing examples of anger (2008a, 105)   97

4.9. Typographic manipulation in Mike Mignola's *Hellboy: Conqueror Worm/Strange Places* (2009, 64). Colors by Dave Stewart   102

4.10. Common balloons, left to right: speech, whisper, thought, and scream or electronic voice (by author)   103

4.11. My rendition of the general shapes of "Kiki" and "Bouba" that varied subtly among several studies   104

4.12. A panel with narratorial adult commentary located outside the frame while depicting a recalled event in Alison Bechdel's *Fun Home: A Family Tragicomic* (2006, 15)   106

4.13. Art Spiegelman's layered presentation of panel spaces to reflect different narrative spaces in *Maus* (1997, 16)   107

5.1. Matt Madden's "A history of American comic books in six panels" (2012)   113

5.2. Selection from Moore and Gibbons' *Watchmen* (1986, 4.19)   115

5.3. An early scene with the protagonist, Gus, from Jeff Lemire's *Sweet Tooth* (2010, 23)   122

5.4. Bombing panel from Marjane Satrapi's *Persepolis: The Story of a Childhood* (2003, 103)   125

5.5. "Never Do This" from *xkcd* (Munroe 2011)   126

5.6. Depiction of Agent Mason Savoy and his cibopathic ability in *Chew: The Smorgasbord Edition* (Layman and Guillory 2013, n.p.)   127

5.7. A singular and ominous shift in Savoy's mental imagery (Layman and Guillory 2013, n.p.)   129

5.8. Two panels from Moore and Gibbons' *Watchmen* (1986, 8.25) illustrating uses of visual style and language presentation to weave two stories together   131

5.9. Full-page summary panel from *Soupy Leaves Home* by Cecil Castellucci and Jose Pimienta (2017, 58)   134

6.1. Scott McCloud (via his cartoon persona) explains the space-time synergy of comics with a clock metaphor (1993, 100)   *139*

6.2. Selection from Stan Lee and Jack Kirby's 1965 *Captain America* comic, "Among Us, Wreckers Dwell!" (reprinted in Eisner 2008b, 131). © 1965 Marvel Comics   *142*

6.3. Diagram of temporal construal for panels in Figure 6.2, contrasting the duration implied by the pictorial and indexical modalities of the figures and actions (grey box) and the verbal modality (white box)   *144*

6.4. From *Calvin and Hobbes* © 1986 Bill Watterson. Reprinted with permission of Andrews McMeel Syndication. All rights reserved   *155*

6.5. "Hike" in *Super Mutant Magic Academy* by Jillian Tamaki (2015, 91)   *158*

6.6. Jeppard kills an antagonist in *Sweet Tooth* (Lemire 2010, 92)   *161*

6.7. Gus kills in the same style as Jeppard, a year later in the series (Lemire 2011, 65)   *163*

6.8. Learning to fight in *Soupy Leaves Home* (Castellucci and Pimienta 2017, 34)   *165*

6.9. Temporal marking and encapsulation in *George Sprott, 1894–1975* (Seth 2009, n.p.)   *167*

6.10. Visual blends and domain transformations in *Baddawi* (Abdelrazaq 2015, 84)   *169*

6.11. Final panel of poster board in *Building Stories* (Ware 2012)   *173*

6.12. Complete mural-layout, including story content, of *Red: A Haida Manga* (Michael Nicoll Yahgulanaas (mny.ca) 2009). Image credit: J. Litrell   *178*

7.1. Initial fragmentation at the doctor's office (Lemire 2012, 41)   *186*

7.2. Underwater fragmentation (Lemire 2012, 112–13)   *188*

7.3. Multiple selves moving atypically (Lemire 2012, 123)   *192*

7.4. Viewpoint reorientation and coherence (Lemire 2012, 196–97)   *193*

8.1. James Kochalka's untitled comic, included in *Abstract Comics* (Molotiu 2009, n.p.). Copyright: Kochalka 2009   202

8.2. Untitled comic by author   213

8.3. "Allegory #7" by bpNichol (1970b, n.p., used with permission of the Estate of bpNichol)   216

8.4. David Garneau's "Aboriginal Curatorial Collective Meeting" (2012. Oil on canvas, 152x122 cm)   224

9.1. Screen shot from *Hobo Lobo of Hamelin* by Stevan Živadinović (2011)   235

TABLE

2.1. Overview of modalities and sign types as typically employed in comics   25

ACKNOWLEDGMENTS

I am indebted to many who have contributed to the development of this book.

The seeds of my interest in multimodal literatures, like many, began in childhood with *Calvin and Hobbes* and *Spy Vs Spy*, but did not germinate until Stephen Scobie introduced me to the experimental visual poetry and comics of bpNichol. Ever since then, my interest and enthusiasm for comics have only grown.

Barbara Dancygier introduced me to the cognitive frameworks that helped me engage with multimodal literatures in new ways that aligned with my interests in reader responses and meaning. This book would not exist without the opportunity to take a few courses with her and for her ongoing enthusiasm, support, and many conversations with her as my supervisor. I cannot thank her enough for the many years of mentorship and friendship.

I am grateful to Alex Bergs, Tom Hoffman, and Peter Schneck who facilitated a visiting-scholar position and subsequent visiting professorship at the University of Osnabrück, which provided me with significant time and many experiences researching and lecturing on visual poetry and comics, and lots of laughs and great conversations along the way, including with Jens Bonk and others too.

I was also very fortunate to enjoy a postdoctoral fellowship, which began the development of this book, with Bart Beaty, whose own broad ranging and rich works and ongoing conversations supported and expanded my work.

My thanks for many instances of inspiration, advice, support, interest, and encouragement along the way from my teachers, supervisors, mentors, colleagues, and friends: Frederick Luis Aldama, Mary Chapman, Margery Fee, Raymond Gibbs, Rick Gooding, Sherrill Grace, Frederik Byrn Køhlert, Donato Mancini, Paisley Mann, Laurie McNeill, Kevin McNeilly, Mara

Moen, Laura Moss, Vin Nardizzi, Eleanor Nichol, Shweta Narayan, Jeffrey Nordstrom, Jonathan Otto and Rebekah Kartal, Eve Preus, June Scudeler, Jeff Severs, Michael Sinding, Ted Slingerland, Nick Sousanis, Kashmiri Stec, Peter Stockwell, and Eve Sweetser.

My thanks to my parents, Art and Annette, for their ongoing interest in my research. It is also a joy to share a love of comics with my daughters, Madeleine and Zoë, who keep me and the library very busy finding and discussing all things comics arts!

I have been fortunate to be the reader, listener, student, peer, or teacher of many who have encouraged and expanded my thinking about multimodal literatures and cognition, at conferences, in seminars, in journals and books, and in the classroom. Many of these influences are cited throughout this book. Many more have surely and unfortunately been lost to my terrible memory for names. I remain grateful to the supportive academic atmosphere in which I could test-run and nuance my thoughts. Any errors and omissions in scholarly approach or conclusions reflect solely on me, of course, despite the many voices along the way who have informed my thinking.

This work could not have been accomplished without the inspiring work of comics creators, many more than could have been included in one book. Many creators have graciously extended permission for me to include their works. Many figures have also been included under fair use for academic purposes. Where necessary, permissions were secured from copyright holders. Whether or not permission was required, I am grateful to all creators and publishers for being able to include the figures in this book, and copyright remains with them.

My gratitude is extended to the editors of the *Poetics and Cognition* series at Oxford University Press for their patience and support.

Some of the research that was conducted in the writing of this book was supported by the University of British Columbia. Most of this work was supported by a postdoctoral fellowship, and to some extent a doctoral scholarship prior to it, from the Social Science and Humanities Research Council of Canada.

Finally, this book would simply not exist without the enduring and patient love and support of my wife, Sara, who has made everything possible.

CHAPTER 1
Introduction

In this book, I seek to isolate and elaborate upon the significance of core competencies of human imagination and communication that the comics form, and its possible interpretations, so productively showcases and exploits. Theories of art and literature have focused in different ways on the meaningfulness of works, with a long history of productive debate and trends. I take up some of these concerns in the next chapter, but will not rehash them for long. Rather, I have sought to build on productive connections among several traditions of inquiry, bridging literary, educational, and artistic criticism through their shared alignment with recent research in cognitive science. I seek to provide an empirically responsive critical framework that showcases how readers navigate the multimodal complexity of comics to build comprehension.

Comics harness the reader's imagination to produce a range of felt experiences of the text. For other literary forms, Peter Stockwell (2009) describes the reader's experience as the "texture" of a text, and Margaret Freeman (2007, 2020) similarly calls this "poetic iconicity," in which a poem builds up real-world resonances with rich conceptual and affective meanings. What these concepts focus on is the way that the meaning of a text is richly immersive and sensual, not just conceptual. I lean most heavily on the field of cognitive linguistics to unpack how this is possible, because, despite the field's name, it brings together a range of interdisciplinary insights from studies of perception, intersubjectivity, development, culture, and philosophy, as evidenced in Barbara Dancygier's edited handbook (2017) and some other key texts in the field (see especially Lakoff and Johnson 1999; Langacker 1990, 2008; Oakley 2009). I expand on these interdisciplinary resonances and draw in other relevant insights, such as from visual psychology and elsewhere, in order to develop an approach that contributes to literary, artistic, and cultural analyses of comics. Showing how the structures and processes of cognition inform the comprehension of comics can present a clearer understanding of how multimodal communication prompts the rich texture that makes reading comics so engaging to readers and critics alike.

In critical theory, Jonathan Culler (1981, 2007) has repeatedly called for the reunification of poetics and hermeneutics to bridge the analysis of literary forms and the wide-ranging potentialities for their interpretation. The field of cognitive poetics (and others by similar names, although sometimes with inconsistencies about what they mean by "cognitive"[1]) attempts just that, since a central premise of recent cognitive research is that perception and conceptualization are intrinsically linked, and that to separate form from meaning does not reflect the rich, contextualized, and embodied nature of different types of communication.

Multimodality has recently come into the field of cognitive poetics, especially through the work of Alisson Gibbons (2012a, 2012b), Karen Kukkonen (2013a, 2013b, 2013c, 2017), Dancygier and Vandelanotte (2017a, 2017b), and others. Nick Sousanis' brilliant comic about comics, *Unflattening* (2015), draws strongly from the same and complementary traditions to explore how multimodality harnesses reader perceptions and experiences to "unflatten" conceptualization and open up opportunities for creative thinking. This creativity operates at multiple levels at the same time, from in-the-moment constructions of a "storyworld" (Herman 1997, 2003, 2009a; 2011) that also harness universal patterns and tropes (Hogan 2003), from unconscious predictions and inferences to the conscious experiences of the text. This research has shown that much of comprehension operates at the unconscious level of cognition, and that meaning is "more than words and deeper than concepts" (Johnson 2007, ch. 2; cf. Oakley 2009, 61–62). Multimodal communication is also deeply situated and contextualized in social usages (Kress 2010),[2] which I discuss in terms of intersubjective, human-scale, and perceptual biases in cognition. In this book, I seek to add to this array of emerging interest in multimodal forms and cognition by expanding on these many levels of cognitive engagement and their role in the comprehension and texture of the multimodal literature of comics.

My approach to the comprehension of comics tends to focus on the "reader," although I occasionally also refer to them as a viewer. I consider these synonyms because of the "visual thinking" involved in perception (Arnheim 2015) and the ways that comics encourage different "ways of seeing" (McCloud 1993, 31). Yet, commonplace understandings might dismiss viewing as simple and naïve (despite the opposite), and consider reading to be more complex. To harness this common notion, I lean toward using "reading" to reflect the complexity involved in integrating and interpreting multimodal cues, and typically in ways that align with narrative aims. "Reading," in my view, has also expanded well beyond the logocentric notion of all communicative cues as equating to linguistic marks (i.e., "linguistic imperialism" [Bateman and Wildfeuer 2014, 181]), which is still quite common, to a sense of interpretive potential that varies well beyond linguistic parameters brought through the affordances of each modality. In Chapter 2, I unpack more of the impoverishments of terminology and engagement that comics expose through their multimodality, nuancing further this notion of reading through a focus on definitions of literacy and metaphors of communication. I make the case for a more robust understanding of multimodal communication through cognitive science and my proposed multimodal cognitive poetics.

In Chapter 3, I outline the key insights from cognitive science and multimodal analyses to offer a general multimodal cognitive poetics. I discuss embodied cognition (shorthand for "4E cognition," which I explain), focusing on key cognitive parameters and processes of knowledge structure, activation, and transformation, as it relates to a simple cartoon. I show how perception connects to conceptualization as part of the rich array of largely unconscious processes of knowledge activation that build the readers' experience of the multimodal text. The cognitive processes of attentional guidance, prediction, inference, metaphorical and domain activation, mental simulation, and blended constructions all lead to comprehension and interpretation. All of these elements are required to produce the reader's sense of texture and meaning. I elaborate on the conceptual overview of the multimodal cognitive poetic approach presented in Chapter 3 in all subsequent chapters, which traverse a range of features of the comics form.

In Chapter 4, I focus primarily on the multimodal composition of panels, exploring questions of abstraction, viewpoint, construal, depiction, and material conventions. In it, I seek to show how key features of figures, their language, and their contextualization within the panel lead to the construction of complex multisensory mental scenarios. Chapter 5 continues to expand how viewpoint and construal function in relation to more "figurative" meanings, through a discussion of metonymy, metaphor, and other blends. I show how pictorial, verbal, and structural modalities offer creative opportunities for meaning construction, and how conspicuous depictions can launch creative figurative interpretations.

The next two chapters expand on questions of sequentiality and segmentarity, particularly focusing on the challenges of temporality and its relationship to space in terms of both strips and layouts. I begin in Chapter 6 by focusing on how comics and time are commonly theorized, and how this relates to different mental metaphors about time that are incompatible and lead to inconsistencies in space-time theorization. I then show how modalities carry different temporal inferences, which lead to asynchronicities between modalities that need to be overcome in order to construct a coherent mental scenario. I show how cognitive biases, material anchoring, and creative processes account for the construction of coherence, and I emphasize how temporality is a complex emergent property of multimodality and creative cognitive processes that does not follow formulaic models of space-time, but strategically flip between them.

I pick up on the notion of material anchoring in Chapter 7 to elaborate on how layout can be creatively employed to build complex character viewpoints and build links across longer narratives through narrative anchors. To unpack the significance of these ideas, I analyze complex viewpoint constructions through links between layout and metaphors of the self in the graphic novel *The Underwater Welder* by Jeff Lemire.

In the final two chapters, I shift to focus on areas of exploration and transformation in comics and multimodal communication. In Chapter 8, I examine abstract and experimental comics (also called art comics) to illustrate how their seemingly simple presentations challenge readers to improvise meanings through perceived connections, patterns, and implications. I show how mental processes produce fictive transformations that suggest temporal, agentive, and narrative qualities to abstract forms. This range of possible meanings invites readers to improvise a wide array of interpretations, including exploring metacommentaries about the self and about colonial viewpoints in communication.

I conclude the book in Chapter 9 through a brief examination of the transformations to composition and interaction offered by digital and webcomics. I show how their elasticity and interactivity productively expand the cognitive framework, inviting ongoing analysis of the cognitive implications of the many changes to the comics form through their digital expansion. This leads to the possibility of an even more expansive *dynamical* multimodal cognitive poetics.

CHAPTER 2
How to Talk about Comics and Not Fear Them

Literacies, Fallacies, and Modalities

2.1 MODALITIES AND THE BATTLE OF THE BOOKS: *ESSEX COUNTY*

North American dominant culture has long had a vexed relationship with comics. To unpack this relationship, I begin with an instructive story from 2011. It involves a book, *Essex County* by Jeff Lemire, which was one of the entries in the popular contest *Canada Reads*. This radio (and more recently television) program, launched by the Canadian Broadcast Corporation (CBC) in 2002, seeks to popularize books for the general Canadian populace through a "literary title fight." Through this riff on the game-show contest form, *Canada Reads* "showcases Canadian writing, promotes Canadian writers, encourages literacy, and supports the publishing industry in Canada" (Moss 2004, 7). In the show, Canadian celebrities debate and judge a group of books surrounding a yearly theme or type of work. In 2011, the theme was "what is the essential Canadian novel of the decade?" The books included a variety of genres, including satirical, historical, and semiautobiographical fictions. By this time, CBC had also integrated digital feedback to inform the development of the program by having online polls for the public to select the books for the competition. At the end of the show, readers again voted online to give "The People's Choice," which *Essex County* won in 2011 by a landslide (CBC 2011b).

Comics and Cognition. Mike Borkent, Oxford University Press. © Oxford University Press 2024.
DOI: 10.1093/oso/9780197509784.003.0002

The show is quite popular among Canadians, evidenced not just through online polling numbers, but also in the fact that all of the selected books typically launch onto Canadian bestseller lists in the weeks prior to the airing of the show, and winners have gone on to become international bestsellers (CBC 2016). So, while a fun radio and television contest, it is also a high-stakes competition for publishers and authors. To have a book selected for inclusion in *Canada Reads* likely means instant success. *Essex County* has certainly had such success, having won awards and been optioned for a movie. But the conversations surrounding *Essex County* in the competition itself speak volumes about the vexed relationship between comics and literary culture. It also opens up a necessary conversation about literacy and comprehension.

Each year, five celebrity judges advocate for one book at a roundtable presentation and engage in debate over the relative merits of each in a "battle of the books." In 2011, the judges included a range of Canadian cultural figures: a politician, actor, journalist, musician, and television personality. Over the course of several episodes, the judges debate and then summarily vote off books, much like contestants get voted "off the island" in the reality TV show *Survivor*. Each judge familiarizes themselves with each book, so that they can compare and contrast the different works effectively and strategically. Typically, a lively debate surrounds each book, and viewers can expect to gather a good sense of the content and style of each work from this discussion. In the case of *Essex County*, the judges roundly lauded its powerful storytelling, its engagement with different generational concerns, its transformation of Canadian values and experiences, and its incorporation of the Ontario landscape. One judge "loved the characters" that "tugged at the heartstrings" (CBC 2011a).[1] Another "didn't want to read it" initially, but in the end "found it very moving." Others found it "stunning," "remarkable," "beautiful," "haunting and heart breaking." Everyone agreed that it is a very good book.

The musician Sara Quin was the book's advocate. She suggests that the strength of *Essex County* comes from its "comic book qualities," which make it more relatable for many readers. She argued that "the graphic novel ushers in a new way to view caricatures that we've grown used to reading about in Canadian literature, and it reframes the lives of Canadians in a contemporary form." In this way, "it transcends the graphic novel genre [. . .] and has a well-deserved place amongst the more traditional literature included this year." Through this presentation of *comics as literature*, Quin attempts to start a conversation around the graphic novel as a storytelling medium and to focus on the stories as such, rather than debate what constitutes a novel and how it should be told. After all, the wide range of genres on offer during the 2011 search for the "essential novel" already played loosely with the category, and Quin sought to engage the graphic novel as just another genre in the mix.

Despite its award-winning status and popularity with the wider public, and notwithstanding the fact that the judges unanimously enjoyed and commended it, *Essex County* was summarily dismissed in the first round of the contest (only Quin voted to keep it in the mix). Quin blamed this dismissal of the graphic novel on a generational discrimination against younger people who have a more open view of literature, rather than the "traditional" view she suggests motivates the other, older judges. One judge expressed the traditional perspective on literature, for instance, when they noted that "it's too early for a book like that." Another judge stated simply that it was not a novel because of the "lack of writing," or, as another noted, its "lack of words." As such, over the course of one debate, the judges offer a contradictory position of both admiration and dismissal of the book.

To contextualize this discussion, it is helpful to briefly examine an example from Jeff Lemire's *Essex County* (Figure 2.1) for a better sense of the storytelling, which the judges found both evocative and out of place because of its "lack of words." This example is a transitional page that is composed of a single panel—often called a "splash page"—that highlights a character in a particular moment, and might be what the judges had in mind. Here the character, Lou Lebeuf, is shown at two moments in his life. This section of the book is told from the perspective of his older self, who now struggles with taking care of himself while his mind slips into memories about his former hockey days with his younger brother, Vince. Their hockey careers began on the backyard creek together and moved on into the professional realm. Here he looks back at a memory of himself as a child out on the creek playing hockey with his brother. On the previous page, old Lou has just walked into the springtime creek, but as he submerges, he is carried away by a stream of thoughts that turn back into a winter memory of his childhood. The memory continues on the following page in a more typical comics grid layout of panels, in which Lou helps Vince with his skates so they can start a game. Then the imagery returns to old Lou on the edge of the creek. This splash page is significant since it introduces this brief memory and it highlights specific qualities not found in the content of the memory itself. Furthermore, it shows how much is communicated through both pictures and words. As Quin argued, the "lack of words" should not be considered a slight against the storytelling.

In this example, Lemire exploits several commonplace metaphors about time and identity to construe a childhood memory (I will go into more details about the cognitive functions of metaphors in subsequent chapters). For

Figure 2.1 From Jeff Lemire's *Essex County* (2009, 126).

instance, time is shown in particular through the contrast between the two characters who are the same person in the same environment but separated over many years. This contrast of figures establishes a metaphor of identity that distinguishes the essential self (the same self through time) from the temporally distinct subject (our changeable natures over time). Splitting the self across time naturally introduces a perspective on personal history, which might offer the criticality of hindsight and resonances of nostalgia.

Moreover, the shared location of the creek anchors the two characters together, while hinting at the common metaphor of time flowing past, like a river (more on temporal metaphors in Chapter 6). Thus, Lou is standing in the creek watching from a different point in the flow of time, looking back at his former self. The creek reinforces the sense of time, while also giving some more pictorial features for manipulation. For instance, it is salient that ice separates old Lou from his younger self, since this depicts how time works with memory by separating events from action. The character is no longer able to play with his brother, except in the distanced space of memory, and yet that space is also fallible because of its inaccessibility and brittleness, frozen and perhaps distorted by time. Furthermore, locating old Lou in the inhospitable, cool depths of the water construes his present position as equally unsettling and uncomfortable. This presentation is not quite a simple re-experiencing of the liveliness of youth, despite us knowing he is standing in the springtime creek thinking of skating in winter. The discomfiting elements further heighten the ominous sense behind his memory. The juxtaposition of the two figures suggests a static, frozen quality to the memory, along with nostalgia for a happier time, inverting the coldness of a winter game with the coldness and fragility of old age and brittle memories. The frozen tears, which reinforce his gaze toward his past self, also reinforce a sense of somber reminiscence and loss. This image, therefore, raises questions about what is being mourned (childhood, his brother, or something else?) while also constructing a clear personal viewpoint for old Lou. He is presently full of nostalgic reminiscences about a time of physical prowess, relationship, and joy, while simultaneously imbuing these with a sense of his current fragility around not just his body, but also his mind and its memories that are distorting and slipping away from him. This section of *Essex County* explores all of these ideas, which this splash page develops primarily through a rich visual metaphor.

Notice how I have yet to mention the language of the panel. The picture builds complex metaphorical and character-specific content. However, the brief statement "You ready yet Vince?" from young Lou also presents important details that push the action and social dynamics of the memory along onto the subsequent page. The statement shows how Lou is waiting on Vince to get ready, and in the context of such statements, the "yet" indicates a sense of both expectation and exasperation. It turns out on the next page that Vince still has trouble tying his own skates, even while playing hockey better than Lou. This brief statement sets up the older-brother ethos of Lou, who waits on his brother (in both senses). Lou is shown throughout this section of *Essex County* looking out for Vince throughout his hockey career. As can be seen, sparse language adds to the affective and conceptual qualities of the panel, and much emerges out of the pictorial and verbal cues separately and in conjunction with each other. These evocative aspects of storytelling are likely what made all of the judges enjoy the book, even despite themselves in some cases. And yet, the judges relied on the quantity of words as evidence of good storytelling, despite the rich qualities added by the images that weave memories and metaphors. Importantly, the words or the images would be lesser if they stood alone. They build together.

This togetherness of modes is in fact the crux of the issue for the judges. One sympathetic judge observed that it is "hard to nominate a book like that to Canada" and "I don't think that now is the time yet though, or ever, to nominate a graphic novel [...] to inspire people to read by comics" (CBC 2011a). Another judge noted that he "didn't have to use any arguments" to disqualify the book, presumably because it naturally disqualified itself by being a comic. After all, as another judge suggested, "We need people to read books, so we need to read," and the "most essential novel" therefore needs to "inspire people to read." What these comments suggest is that reading a graphic narrative is not considered *proper*, *real* Reading. In other words, by having images contribute to the storytelling, *Essex County* did not count as proper Literature or an avenue to true literacy. Being a comic, being made up in part by images, marks the story as lesser than other works of fiction. What this criticism lacks is an engagement with the book on its own terms, as a composite or hybrid art (i.e., the terms that Sara Quinn argued make it the essential novel of the decade because it reflects a contemporary approach). To the judges, the pictures in *Essex County* seemed to distract from the necessary skills of reading. While Quin argued that because the book included images, "that doesn't make it less of a novel" or less worthy of careful reading, the general consensus among the judges was that in fact it did.

2.1.1 What Is Reading?

The debate over the merits and pitfalls of *Essex County* highlights two understandings of the notion of reading. One solely focuses on the verbal construction of meaning, which reflects the traditional and still dominant *linguistic model of literacy*. Such a view led the popular anti-comics figure Fredric Wertham to state that "comic books are death to reading" (Wertham 1955, 121) and "the enemy of education" (qtd in Dorrell, Curtis, and Rampal 1995, 232). The other understanding looks more broadly to storytelling practices, including both language and other modes of communication, which has been called the *multiple literacies or multimodal* approach.

For the judges of *Canada Reads*, there was a distinct difference of opinion between which model to apply, with the dominant, language-focused model of literacy winning out. This is not surprising, since this model has long been the most pervasive approach in Western education systems (Dorrell, Curtis, and Rampal 1995). There are several beliefs about language and images that inform these models, which in turn impacts the reception of comics more broadly. These models of meaning also explain the marginalization of comics over the past century, a marginalization that is rapidly disappearing, thanks to a shift toward the multimodal view of literacy, which this book works to contribute to. This ongoing shift in perspective has recently been evidenced again in the *Canada Reads* contest, with the graphic memoir *Ducks: Two Years in the Oil Sands* by Kate Beaton (2022) winning in 2023, albeit with a divided vote of 3-2 (CBC 2023).

There are several reasons for the marginalization of comics in the realms of literary culture, several of which align with models and values of literacy. As Beaty and Woo (2016) discuss in *The Greatest Comic Book of All Time*, the appreciation of different works of art and culture rely on different socio-cultural value sets. They show how a range of differing criteria can make a wide variety of exemplar comics the "greatest." Many of these different values are established through the training offered by different social and cultural institutions, including families, religions, schools, government policies, and media outlets.

One way in which comics are often marginalized by critics is through their designation as "low" or "popular" culture in contrast to the "high" culture of, capital L, Literature. Literature, in this view, only includes "serious" novels, poetry, and plays. Similar high/low distinctions are made on the Visual Art side of the equation as well (Beaty 2012). Thus, their popular and accessible nature makes comics somehow too simple to be taken seriously. Furthermore, their "hybrid" qualities are at best considered gateways to "serious" works, with the assumption that with further education and refinement the reader/viewer will naturally progress up to true appreciation of *real* Art and Literature. The assumption of progression from low (popular) to high (serious) arts, often assumed to be from simple to complex works and ideas, misses the fact that these different types of cultural artifacts reflect different socio-cultural, economic, and communicative roles and values. Human cultures have a wide diversity of communicative forms, and to be popularly accessible and constituted out of hybrid cues does not necessarily take away from the cultural and intellectual value of comics, and may in fact add to it by presenting opportunities for diverse means of expression and engagement.

One way that the high/low paradigm is instantiated is through the belief that comics are a literacy-training form that should be left behind as people gain in linguistic proficiency, as they move to the preferred model of communication only through language (Dorrell, Curtis, and Rampal 1995). As such, "teachers have been educated to consider the movement from pictures to words largely as a matter of intellectual progression" (Millard and Marsh 2001, 27). This is a fundamentally flawed and reductive view of communicative forms and language use. Children learn language in conjunction with a wide array of prompts from other modalities in everyday life, like gestures and intonations. Similarly, visual cues and artifacts like picture books aid comprehension and lead to linguistic concretization (Nodelman 1988), but other crucial communicative forms continue to maintain strong multimodal linkages, such as in film, textbooks, blueprints, advertisements, and so on. Language acquisition occurs in association with a wide array of non-linguistic modalities and in a range of contexts (Gibbs 2006a; Tomasello 2008), and these continue to inform communicative forms in society. Within a traditional view of literacy, this multimodal background is viewed as a necessary evil that is then cast off for pure literacy, a type of Platonic ideal. This logocentric perspective considers multimodality a distraction from ideas, rather than a contributor to conceptualization. Of course, this view also ignores the fact that visuality still informs our interactions with language, since part of reading and writing is seeing printing, seeing *visible language*, which can add meaning through design choices like font type and adjustments like italics and bolding, and through structures like headings and paragraphing (see McGann 1991, 1993). As W. J. T. Mitchell (2002, 2008, 2012) has repeatedly asserted, many media are *visual media* or "mixed media," because they materialize and manipulate communicative modes in ways that must be seen to be understood.[2] There is more to be said about modes and media, which I will turn to shortly. Despite these multimodal features, the more traditional view of literacy maintains the superiority of language over other modes.

The fact that other modalities add to the meaningfulness of many different artifacts and experiences has led to the development of an alternative approach to literacy that broadens its terms of reference beyond language proficiency to engage with other modalities of expression and the forms they take. This other position asserts the need for a model of *multiple literacies* that promotes the careful and critical engagement with a variety of modes of communication that work together, rather than focusing only on reading and writing and the idealized and culturally sanctioned sphere of high Literature. It was such a model that Sara Quin was suggesting the other judges explore.

Essex County's speedy dismissal from the *Canada Reads* show may seem low stakes. The book has clearly been successful, and *Canada Reads* helped give it a brief moment in the public spotlight. Its very presence in the lists also shows how comics are becoming an increasingly accepted form of contemporary storytelling. However, the fact that *Essex County* was so easily and summarily dismissed because it was a comic is significant. It signals an ongoing bias against the form grounded in ideas and concerns about literacy, which supports Fuller's (2007) argument that *Canada Reads* tends to reinforce fundamentally traditional and normative literary values. Sara Quin's suggestion that there is a generational distinction between two perspectives on literature, with one valuing only *language* and the other valuing broader forms of *communication*, reflects an associated debate between these two positions on literacy or multiple literacies in general. While these positions are not determined by generations per se—since they have both been argued about for the past century, especially in educational philosophy—the linguistically governed model has been dominant in education for a long time and has only recently been nudged out by the multiple literacies approach, which includes interests in media literacy, numeracy, and visual literacy.

Moreover, comics have grown in popularity and cultural legitimacy in part due to their increasingly diverse and mature stories seen especially in "alternative comics" (Aldama 2010; Hatfield 2005), including fictional and non-fiction works (like graphic memoirs like *Ducks* which recently won *Canada Reads*). Academic circles have also increasingly accepted graphic narratives as an area of research, although not commonly a complete expertise associated with a professorship or area of graduate research, with conferences and journals now dedicated to the form. Nonetheless, the recent dismissal of *Essex County* shows that old ideas continue to hound the form and limit its reception in some circles. This reluctance to adjust views about literacy and literature stems in part from pervasive ideas and fallacies about modalities and communication.

2.2 LITERACIES AND FALLACIES

2.2.1 The Problem of the Visual

Without taking away from the benefits of linguistic literacy, the idea of literacy also comes with a host of assumptions about language. One particularly influential idea is the conflation of language with thought, in which literacy becomes the only way to express oneself and build meaning accurately, whereas other forms are simply inadequate or, worse, corruptive of this pure transmission of thought from one user to another (I return to this fallacious notion of thought transmission in the next section and later chapters).

In the context of comics and the moral panics around images, on the surface it seems that words are simply better and safer than images. For instance, it is instructive to consider the moral panic around comics as leading to delinquency, as led by such cultural and political figures as Fredric Wertham in the United States and E. Davie Fulton in Canada in the 1940s and 1950s (Wertham 1955). For them, there is a distinct problem with images. One can read "Literature" about murder and mayhem (*Hamlet*, say) and presumably be fine, but to read a comic book about the same thing is somehow corruptive because it shows the actions and cruelties. They were particularly concerned about such materials in the hands of children (and to some degree, rightly so). The concern with comics about such content led to criminal legislation (in Canada) or industry codes (in the United States) and even comic-book burnings across North America (Bell 2006; Nyberg 1998; Purvey and Belshaw 2011).[3] It is the *showing* rather than *telling* that seemed to be of particular concern.[4] Such a perspective presumes a power to the image that outstrips and even corrupts the written word because of its immediacy and ease.

If this sounds familiar, it may be because it reflects long Western cultural traditions of iconophobia in Judeo-Christian views of idolatry. The juxtaposition between word and image is nicely encapsulated in the biblical story of Moses' return from Mount Sinai with the Ten Commandments inscribed on stone tablets, only to find his people worshiping a statue of a golden calf. This story enacts a stark contrast between the sacred written "Word of God" and idolatrous "graven images" (Exodus 20:4). The story directly ascribes a truthfulness to language and a falsity to images; an Ideal imbedded in words that material expression in other arts simply cannot compete with. The distrust of images over words, until very recently, had a strong intellectual and social presence. As W. J. T. Mitchell notes, a common distinction associates words "with law, literacy, and the rule of the elites" and associates images "with popular superstition, illiteracy, and licentiousness" (2008, 15). In this view, language breeds civility, while pictures breed anarchy and savagery, which reflects the notion and concern with the "visual turn" (19).[5] As in the days of Moses, so too in the early days of comics. While in decline, the fear of the visual turn remains a common frame of reference for many in the West, either consciously or unconsciously, by having informed disciplinary and educational approaches if not cultural and familial backgrounds.

As W. J. T. Mitchell shows, putting literacy and imagery in opposition is a fallacious dualism, since cultures have long been instantiated multimodally across various types of artifacts and media:

> Media are always mixtures of sensory and semiotic elements, and all the so-called visual media are *mixed* or hybrid formations, combining sound and sight, text and image. Even vision itself is not purely optical, requiring for its operations a coordination of optical and tactile impressions. (2008, 15)

The anxiety about a visual turn is based on the assumption that pictures are problematic, superficial, distracting, and yet pervasive and all consuming, leading people to engage within a simulacrum of reality rather than with reality. In contrast, language is deemed the sole source of rich and critically informative meaning that is only by necessity materialized in sound or visible text. Yet all modalities are informative in their own ways, so, while they are different, they need not be treated preferentially or antagonistically. The preference for language runs deep, and the fear of the visual turn propels other fallacious ideas.

Perhaps the most commonly correlated ideas with the visual turn are the contradictory notions of pictorial totality and pictorial transparency—that is, that pictures are both all consuming and seductive and yet easily explainable and self-evident. For instance, images are often considered to be obvious, clear, and singular illustrations, in contrast to the depth, nuance, and segmented elements of language, a distinction heralding back at least to Gotthold Lessing's *Laocoon* (1874) in which he distinguishes between pictorial immediacy and verbal narrativity. However, as art critic E. H. Gombrich (1977, 1973) and visual psychologist Rudolph Arnheim (2004 [1969]; 2009 [1974]) among others have argued, pictures are complex compositions, and their deliberate representations breed intricate interpretations of what is shown and hidden, of reflections and illusions, that require an active engagement by the viewer. While many pictures seem to be grasped immediately in a glance because of their similarity to the source, they also invite meditation and interpretation on what they represent, how the subject matter is construed, and whether it invokes scenic and event structures that move toward action and narrativity. Thus, some critics build analogies between language and image, to accent their compositionality as requiring careful attention, like a form of reading (Cohn 2013; Kress and Van Leeuwen 1996). The distinction between static immediacy and compositional development and narrativity does not reflect how the modalities function, but is predicated on ideas about them instead.

The idea of pictorial immediacy highlights the notion that images seem to transmit their subject matter clearly and without complication or qualification; it instantiates the common phrase that "seeing is believing." But, as will be discussed in more detail in the next chapters, seeing is so much more complicated than that. Seeing is better thought of as doing, searching, and thinking (Arnheim 2004; Noë 2004). As Michael Newall (2011) argues, seeing is a complicated engagement with pictorial depictions, including engaging how the representation resembles the real world, how the viewer processes what they perceive and recognize as well as elaborate on, how conventions and social values guide comprehension, and how stylistic choices build a material experience of the artwork itself. As such, a theory of comics must engage all of these variables, each of which emphasizes different qualities of artistic expression and reception.

As I will show in subsequent chapters, the acts of representing, highlighting, and orchestrating features are practices that are employed by various modalities, and these can align together through a clearer focus on how they link to the construction of mental imagery. For now, it is crucial to recognize that images, just like writing, constitute a complex mode of communication that should not be broken down into easy truisms. Rather, images offer an array of features that can be creatively engaged to uniquely construe subject matters and offer new insights to readers. It is how these components are used, within the contexts of their histories, conventions, and material qualities, that expression occurs. The immediacy of the image is in fact not static, but rapidly becomes dissected and mobilized by the complexities of thought.

2.2.2 Problematizing Literacy: The Conduit Fallacy

The transmission model or immediacy fallacy of pictures parallels a similarly reductive model of language conceptualized through the *conduit metaphor* (Reddy 1979; Lakoff and Johnson 1980), and is a common folk philosophy that informs the traditional model of literacy and likely plays a role in its ongoing perseverance in the face of the multimodal model. This pervasive metaphor presents language as operating like a conduit or tube through which meaning passes from one person to another. It sees individual words as discrete objects or containers that carry this meaning through the conduit to the receiver. The metaphor can be seen expressed in common sayings like "Did you get what I said?," which construes meaning as an object that is transported between the two people, and suggests understanding as the ability of the receiver to grab and hold onto it.[6] While this metaphor helps us visualize the intersubjective quality of language, it is better understood as the *conduit fallacy* (Dancygier 2012, 203–4) for several reasons. For instance, it ignores the social, cultural, and even material contexts that impact how language is used and interpreted, thereby ignoring how form and context alter meaning. It also ignores how various discourse and media conventions and values surround and inform communicative forms and their reception. The metaphor also largely ignores that both senders and receivers have different intentions, perspectives, and interpretations of both the surroundings and the subtleties of the words themselves. In short, the metaphor obscures the formal and contextual elements that impact meaning, in terms of language use as well as the other modes and media that surround and carry it. This means that language is never a pure system, but one that subtly changes based on where and how it is used, and by whom and for what purpose.

The conduit fallacy attempts to make a dynamic and flexible communicative system into a static model. The outcries of language purists over changes to dictionaries and usage patterns fail to grasp this dynamicity, but rather assert that language is being corrupted from its static ideal. Their approach attempts to maintain what Amy Devitt (2004) calls "linguistic hygiene," an unrealistic and impossible state of static systemic purity (see also Shea 2014). The conduit fallacy supports the traditional model of literacy by ignoring the complex contexts and materials that make up communication—something that the multiple literacies model engages.

In the context of comics, these fallacies about language and images obscure a more dynamic reality. Pictures cannot totalize or overwrite the meaning of verbal cues, but function in fundamentally different ways from them, presenting contexts for the language use, all while the language refines interpretations of stylistic choices of depiction. Thus, there is not a simple, fixed relation between pictures and language, but rather an array of interpretive possibilities .

As this book shows, comics are more than just images plus language, or language plus images (depending on your preference). They are also often sequentially and schematically laid out through strips of panels. They are designed much like architecture, to be navigated and used in (usually) a clear manner and to promote specific effects. The panels braid meanings through resonances between and across many pages (Groensteen 2007, 2013). Barbara Postema (2013) rightly argues, along with other scholars, that it is the separation, spatialization, and sequentialization of images and texts that make comics a unique form of expression (see also Drucker 2008). But it can be difficult to account for the meaning-making of these aspects of comics compositionality. Each panel offers a nuanced picture, but it also gains meaning through its relationship to the language within and surrounding the panel, and other surrounding panels, layouts, and pages. Sometimes things are silent, and at other times explosions of sound and dialogue pervade the textual experience. Panel borders can also construe content by being ornate, plain, or even invisible. I will discuss the meaningfulness of such features in detail in subsequent chapters. For now, it is safe to assert that images and language are coordinated in a wide variety of ways in comics through this range of modes and conventions. Comics are a *multimodal* network, whose strategies for combining modalities must be navigated and analyzed, and this requires a dynamic model of meaning-making for analysis, one that the traditional model of literacy insufficiently addresses. A better account of how meaning is constructed through diverse communicative modalities is required.

2.3 "LITERACIES ARE LEGION:" ON MULTIPLE LITERACIES, MULTIMODALITY, AND DISCIPLINARITY

2.3.1 Multiple Literacies

Pushing beyond language to include other forms of communication prompts alternative definitions for literacy and communication. Influential literacy scholar Jay Lemke begins a widely anthologized article with the phrase "Literacies are legion" (2004, 71). He argues that "critical interpretive skills must be extended from the analysis of print texts to video and film, to news photos and advertising images, to statistical charts and tables, and mathematical graphs" (78). To him, the focus on interpretation is the realm of literacy education, which means that new types of interpretive (or "reading") practices are needed to deal with the different types of media. Graphic novels like *Essex County* fall nicely into his model of areas that require new skills for interpretation. No longer is reading just about the words, but about *multiple literacies*. For instance, the complexity of images in *Essex County* requires engaging with the notion of "visual literacy," or better "multimodal literacy," which might include spatial, pictorial, and material literacies that include an awareness of the institutions, conventions, and practices that inform how representations are made and received (see Elkins 2008; Mitchell 2008). Lemire's use of brush and ink to develop more crude depictions than, say, the clean lines of action comics by Jack Kirby leads to particular inferences about the artwork itself, giving it a moodier, emotive quality. In a way, this perceptual quality makes the images' line style slightly less realistic, but more evocative by adding emotional valences that contribute to their overall meaning (Lefèvre 2016). The images also sit within broader cultural frames of reference and evaluation, including traditional theories of literacy that led to its expulsion from *Canada Reads*. Furthermore, the art work of *Essex County* circulates outside of the book as well, as it is featured in promotional materials, book displays, and news stories, which served different cultural, social, and economic functions. Developing just visual literacy requires developing a sense of a work's place in art history, modes and techniques of book production, major expressive traditions, genres and styles, visual perception and reception, and so on. And that is just for visual literacy—one among many types of knowledge that people draw upon to varying degrees depending on cultural, social, educational, and other experiential backgrounds.

The reception of comics, therefore, can be affected by many variables. As Aaron Meskin (2007) argues, comics are assessed from many different perspectives and with different value sets, depending on the reader's background. Meskin considers comics a *hybrid art* because of the way in which they activate art historical, literary, and cultural knowledges in order to be meaningful. Pierre Bourdieu (1990) calls this web of background knowledge that is socially and culturally situated as a person's *habitas*. Beaty and Woo (2016) draw on Bourdieu to show how different forms of evaluation are leveled against comics depending on their content, distribution, and the audience that is examining or receiving them. They present a series of short chapters each arguing for a particular comic as "the greatest comic book of all time" (their book title) to illustrate how different value systems impact reception. These value systems play a significant role in how readers make meaning of such works, and either laud or fear them. Arguably, in the case of *Essex County* in *Canada Reads 2011*, the *habitas* of most judges included the more traditional educational perspectives and conservative social values about the role of reading in society, and it was the enactment of their largely shared education and political *habitas* (not a failure in any way on the part of the book's advocate, Sara Quin) that led to its dismissal. Background values bias perceptions and evaluations. Thus, Barbara Herrnstein Smith (1995) argues that statements of value always include an evaluative element. As such, background knowledge (*habitas*) positions different types of cultural artifacts and practices, building hierarchies of value, and this informs how a given artifact or even action is interpreted. The multiple literacies approach adds a range of further communicative artifacts and spaces beyond the prioritization of language, and a critical approach must include how these different forms are evaluated as part of their contribution to meaning construction and cultural production. To discuss comics then as a form of communication includes the awareness that *habitas*, background knowledge, and socio-cultural experiences play a significant role in how or which comics are read, by whom, and when. Neil Cohn (2021) has recently analyzed a range of socially and culturally diverse groups of readers to show how varied comics reception can be, and that the form is not universally understood but situationally nuanced. Cultural backgrounds play a significant role in guiding understandings and interpretations of comics, and part of that background includes educated perspectives on literacy.

I have, in a way, played up the antagonism between narrower, language-focused views and wider, communication-based approaches to literacy. Of course, this antagonism exists, since it is still impacting the reception of works like Lemire's *Essex County*. However, these models of literacy can also be seen in more compatible ways, since the multiple literacies approach simply widens the view to include other communicative forms as requiring evaluation. These can be aligned as simply different levels of engagement with the details of communication, and they prioritize different aspects of it. To take the multiple literacies approach does not devalue the traditional notion of language literacy, but recognizes that language is always found in conjunction with other non-linguistic modalities. This model returns us to Mitchell's (2008) argument that all media are hybrid media, composed of multiple modalities in some way or another. Many critics of publishing and design (see Bringhurst 2004; Levenston 1992; Lupton 2004) show that the structure of books and other forms of communication add much to the words they present and are associated with. Such visual textual qualities of production can contribute substantially to meaning, including in experimental literary works (Borkent 2010, 2014; Gibbons 2012a, 2012b). The presentation of language changes with time, due to changes in technology and production as well as in socio-cultural values. Rachel Malik (2008) describes these changes as emerging from shifting "horizons of the publishable," and these inform or create opportunities to develop new technologies, beliefs, and abilities about and for communication. As Malik notes: "Publishing as a set of processes and relations form a sequence or a range [. . .] which govern what it is thinkable to publish within a particular historical moment" (709). Thus, language use (as well as of other modalities) is always contextually informed, both in everyday conversation and within different media, including through technological and cultural shifts. The diversity of communicative horizons continues to grow, with multimedia technologies and cultural values changing and expanding in many directions. The idea of "multiple literacies" engages with such changes, in particular the contextual needs of communicative forms, to open up many different contributing factors to the reception of texts by teaching critical engagement or assessment skills from different perspectives. Subsequent chapters of this book present a cognitively robust approach to multiple literacies that can account for the situated and material nature of meaning construction within a cohesive framework. However, to get there, further refinement about key features of comics as a form of communication is required.

2.3.2 Multimodality, Media, and Disciplinarity

The focus on multiple literacies highlights that meaning can be constructed through many different communicative resources or, more specifically, semiotic modalities. Multimodality is the construction of meaning through multiple modalities in a given medium of communication. Multimodality features in communication in both its natural state—in conversations between people, which typically include cues like gesture, gaze, and intonation—and through mediated forms and artifacts like mosaics, books, and films. Several approaches, informed by semiotics and linguistics, have tackled areas of multimodality, in particular to show their social qualities and conventional patterns (Bateman 2014, 2017; Bateman and Wildfeuer 2014; Jewitt 2008; Kress 2009, 2010). Following in part from Marshall McLuhan's (1964) notion that media reify and extend the senses and create opportunities for innovation and new communicative and conceptual realities, scholars have generally shared the notion that modalities are perceptual channels for communicating various types of signs, and these signs are often mediated or presented in material cultural products with specific constraints on and conventions around expression. Since most media include multiple modes, scholars like W. J. T. Mitchell have popularized the definition of media as "mixed, hybrid media" (2002, 174), which can lead to more nuanced analysis. Hayles (2004) similarly argues for "medium-specific analysis" that is also inherently multimodal. Bateman (2017) has synthesized these positions to suggest that a medium is a specific presentational space (television screen, book page, computer interface, etc.) that constrains through its material qualities the particular modes (such as image and text) that creators might use to communicate in a chosen form or genre and social situation, all of which have discrete conventions.

For comics scholars, there has been some confusion and competing ideas about how to define comics in relation to media, with some comics scholars following McCloud (1993) in considering comics as a medium unto itself, since it has a relatively circumscribed form of presentation that combines image and texts as "sequential art" (after Eisner 2008). However, as Marc Singer (2018), among others, has observed, to call comics a medium is to erroneously conflate a communicative form (with its set of possible genres and conventions) with the space that materializes it (the medium that prescribes particular modes that encode the form). Comics are a form of print (and more recently digital) media. The heightened use of multimodal composition in comics does not separate them fundamentally as a new medium; rather they are a form of expression within a given materialized space of expression. To conflate the form communication takes with the medium that materializes it introduces fuzziness and imprecision into analysis.

One suggestion that at first glance appears to resolve the debate of whether comics are a medium is to define media subgroups as a "family of media" under a broader media type (Bateman 2017, 169). For instance, Bateman includes graphic novels, infographics, written language, and illustrated documents as separate media within print media. This approach maintains the definition of media as materialized parameters for modes of communication and creates room for breaking up the dominant forms of expression within them. One concern with this approach is the use of the same term, medium, for separate levels or groupings of analysis. Moreover, this approach integrates aspects of historical, social, and conventional usages as part of the schematic, which introduces some potential for confusion. For instance, it may not be clear to readers or analysts how an infographic is substantially different from a comic as a distinct form of materialized expression, since they can have strong similarities in styles of depiction, segmentation, and so on. In fact, some infographics use comic strips to communicate, such as seen on some airline emergency-response infographics. Thus, I prefer to separate sociocultural usages from the medium that materially circumscribes and delimits the types and affordances of modalities, recognizing that all sociocultural contexts play a formative role in how users communicate in a given medium. To borrow a term from ecological psychology, a medium can be said to present a delimited group of modalities that themselves present a specific set of "affordances" (Gibson 1979; Greeno 1994), which are opportunities for interaction or expressive action restricted by the material qualities of the space (here mediated rather than environmental). As such, comics are a conventionalized form of expression that can include many genres (such as superhero narratives, journalism, autobiography, infographics, and so on) but which is presented in print or digital media, and which has a discrete set of modalities.

While the affordances of media are materially constrained, conventions and style vary across socio-cultural traditions, and as such the expression through a given medium varies according to context. Socially, culturally, technologically, and historically informed aspects of expression within a given medium are better accounted for in definitions of genre and form. Genres are defined as contextually responsive compositional choices within given parameters of expression in a discourse community (Bazerman 2012; Devitt 1993, 2021), since the medium and its modalities provide opportunities for social action through a range of forms and genres. Similarly, there are universal patterns of narrative, but their compositionality varies in response to socio-cultural contexts as well (Aldama 2009; Hogan 2003, 2008). Maintaining the definition of a medium as solely a materialized space for specific modes that can be leveraged in different forms and genres of communication allows for clear analysis of how these features align with patterns of conceptualization, evaluation, and socio-cultural reception, and helps isolate changes that occur within the field of comics studies due to changing technologies and especially the shifts that occur between print and digital media and between social contexts. This distinction, which at first glance seems to reductively separate form and meaning, does not in fact elide the fact that the meaningfulness of a text is the summation of the pragmatic and situated readerly processes and experiences of engaging, evaluating, and interpreting the medium and its modes, as well as genre conventions and innovations of a given text all together. Rather, this separation allows for clear analysis of the roles each of these elements play in meaning construction.

Within the materialized space of a medium, a wide array of communicative signs in different modalities can be used to prompt meaning construction, with modes serving different communicative roles (supportive, co-constructive, or dominant in the construction of the message) depending on the conventions associated with the medium, form, and genre that they are working in. While a given modality may be prioritized in a medium or genre, such as a traditional novel's focus on the verbal modality, even then it is always in conjunction with other modes, including the use of visuality of font to indicate emphasis, tonality, and modulation (reflected in uses of bolding, underlining, and italicization), the material and spatial qualities of the page (which can impact the pacing of the reader), as well as the inclusion of images (such as author photos or illustrations). To be clear, with comics, nearly all of the modalities are developed within or in conjunction with the visual modality, since language, images, sequences, layouts, and even the material limitations of the page are all coordinated and engaged predominantly by visual means. However, within this visual presentation there remain clear contributions from different modalities and with particular types of representational function. For instance, while not a dominant communicative modality, even the materiality or tactility of the book and page can inform subtle perceptual inputs to conceptualization. The slight pause associated with a page turn may serve to add suspense by cutting off and then revealing new information. Or, expectations about plot structure may be informed by the comparative weight or depth of how many pages have been read and remain in the work, with genre and format expectations contributing to this assessment (i.e., the feedback is different for a short, episodic floppy versus a long hardbound graphic novel). Thus, multimodality raises questions about communication that must include thinking about the orchestration of a range modalities and their associated types of signs, even if one modality is prioritized in the communicative form.

Types of signs vary in commonality and functionality depending on the modality. The Peircean sign system (1940), which categorizes semiotic signs as either icons, indexes, or symbols, as the three meaning-making functions of semiotic resources, helps address the communicability of multimodal texts, including comics (Magnussen 2000). This model has informed some pragmatic approaches to media studies (Bateman 2017) and has been corroborated by research in cognitive linguistics as well (e.g., Hiraga 2005; Taub 2001; Zwaan and Yaxley 2003). By definition, the icon is a sign that shares a resemblance to its referent, such as an image that reflects what it depicts. Broadly speaking for comics, the dominance of images that reflect recognizable things suggests they are operating primarily as icons, within which there is a wide range of abstraction possible from realism through to emojis and beyond. An indexical sign indicates a causal connection or "existential relation" (Hiraga 2005, 30) between elements. For instance, smoke indexes the existence of fire, even if the fire itself is not perceived. Finally, a symbol functions by convention to build a connection between sign and meaning, and is especially obvious with written language. More details about these sign functions are outlined in Table 2.1.[7]

The typical reader experiences most modalities and sign types in comics visually, and with a wide array of conventionalized knowledge informing the construction of meaning. For instance, speech balloons are a conventionalized means of connecting a speaker (depicted iconically through the pictorial modality) to their words (presented through the symbolic signs of the verbal or linguistic modality). The speech balloon is neither of these types of representation, but is an indexical sign, which sets up a causal link between the other two modalities. All together, these three modalities and signs present a particular character's voice to

Table 2.1 OVERVIEW OF MODALITIES AND SIGN TYPES AS TYPICALLY EMPLOYED IN COMICS.

Modality	Sign Types and Features
Pictorial, imagic	Typically dominated by iconic signs. • Includes a wide range of types of abstraction in image depiction and figuration. • Can include indexical and symbolic signs, based on convention or experience.
Verbal, linguistic	Most often expressed through symbolic signs to reflect speech, thought, and narration. • Can include iconic signs, such as through onomatopoeic sound effects. • Often inset into images through indexical signs like speech or thought balloons and text boxes that relate to their role.
Diagrammatic, schematic	Generally establish causal and correlational relationships and meanings, using typical structure of an indexical sign: • Includes speech balloons, thought bubbles, and narration boxes, all of which align or index the contained signs with a character, storytelling role, or function. • Includes also conventionalized motion paths (action lines) and emotion marks ("runes"), which index prior actions or internal states. • Includes panel ordering in sequences and layouts to suggest causal or event structure.
Material, tactile	Does not necessarily use the three-part sign function system, but can work in conjunction with them, especially where the page grip, movements to navigate in digital comics, or other cues add to the meaningfulness of other cues. • The materiality of the medium of expression constrains how much can be placed or perceived at once on a page or screen, which in turn functions as a subtle input into communication, especially when cartoonists use page turns or have images bleed off of the edges of the page to highlight a moment in the story. For instance, experimental comics creator bpNichol mimics the likely hand placement of the reader with handlike imagery in one comic to emphasize the notion that readers are co-creators of meaning, that they are an important part of the text (Borkent 2019b).

the reader. Thus, a panel with a character speaking is a multimodal complex of three sign types working together to convey a speaker and their words to the reader. All of these sign types function to direct the reader to salient aspects of a scene and build a rich textual experience.

Importantly, a single sign can have multiple types of function (Magnussen 2000). Some examples of multifunction signs include:

- The iconic face of Guy Fawkes takes on symbolic meanings of resistance through masks in *V for Vendetta* and for the hacker collective Anonymous.
- Onomatopoeic sound effects are linguistic symbols that also operate as iconic signs, since they directly mimic the experience of sound.
- Indexical speech balloons take on symbolic meanings when David Garneau uses them as components of a colorful painting to reflect a conversational experience as well as decolonial resistance (their emptiness functions as a symbolic sign). I discuss this painting in more detail in Chapter 8.
- An image of smoke iconically representing itself and indexically references combustion, which does not need to be perceived to be understood.
- The conspicuous line styles of particular artists might be said to indexically foreground a creators' act of creation, referencing the artist's hand moving as part of the meaning-making experience of the text.

As these examples illustrate, different modalities serve different communicative functions at different times, and can act as composite references through these different sign function categories. Readers must navigate and synthesize this multimodal and multifunction composition into a coherent communicative construct.

Comics highlight the complex multimodal webs of meaning construction and present an opportunity to unravel the different challenges and questions of studying this network. Questions that arise include: What do individual modalities offer, or fail to offer from a communicative perspective? How do they shift when presented in conjunction with other modalities? How do readers navigate these different and disparate cues to build a comprehensive understanding of mixed modes, such as in a cartoon or page of panels? Comics are relatively ubiquitous in Western culture, from newspaper strips, online jokes, and library stacks, and so most people are able to recognize at least some basic comics conventions when they see them. Such conventions include presenting information through a series of images, or using speech balloons to give voice to the associated image. Many Western readers already have a sense of how to interpret such cues, but how do these interpretations reflect the strategic usage of specific modalities and their compositional opportunities? And how does this knowledge help analysts explain why readers respond in particular ways or develop particular readings of the composite cues?

For quite some time comics researchers have attempted to isolate the communicative value of comics, and particularly the network of modalities, by trying to develop comprehensive definitions of the form. These definitions are revealing, but reveal more about the interests of the researchers than of the modalities in question. Some critics have favored seeing comics as part of visual art history by emphasizing them as "sequential art" (see Eisner 2008; McCloud 1994), others have presented more egalitarian definitions by highlighting them as a mixture of pictorial art and language in "hybrid art" (Harvey 1996; Hatfield 2005; Kunzle 1973; Meskin 2007), and others focus more on comics as "visual literature" or "graphic literature" (Chute 2008, 2010; Kuipers 2011), which emphasize their storytelling or literary qualities. Each position tends to reflect the disciplinary backgrounds of the critics and can lead to blindspots in criticism (Singer 2018). Some terms also serve more pragmatic than descriptive needs to market and circulate these multimodal texts: using the term "graphic novel," rather than comic book, helped legitimize their contributions to literary scenes (high culture) rather than to popular culture, while also potentially signaling differences in storytelling aspects, with comics books offering more episodic stories and graphic novels offering longer contained stories, though these distinctions do not necessarily hold up under close scrutiny. This is especially notable in the application of "graphic novel" to *nonfiction* works like Joe Sacco's comics journalism or Allison Bechdel's autobiographies.

The definitional challenges of comics studies arise from disciplinary differences and assumptions (Hatfield 2008). A truly interdisciplinary approach must take on all features of comics, without necessarily allowing disciplinary values to direct interpretations completely. Disciplinary expertise play a significant role in developing knowledge due to their differences in focus and level of analysis (Becher 1994), but these perspectives should not bias against other features of the text. That is a tall order, when expertise and interest will always guide inquiry. For instance, a visual arts critic might emphasize the line style, caricature, perspective, visual allusions, and possibilities for analyzing gesture and expression, as do Carrier (2000), Groensteen (2007), and Grennan (2017), but this may come at the expense of verbal cues. A literary critic, on the other hand, might emphasize the generic conventions of the language employed in the narrative boxes and dialogue, as does Miodrag (2013), or focus more on the narrative and thematic connections to literary and critical theory, as does Chute (2008), but this may miss nuances of visual or diagrammatic execution. Finally, cultural historians like Gabilliet (2009, 2010) might focus on how the production values of the comic book reflects a particular moment in the history of mass market printing or how a particular cultural moment leads to different perceptions of the form. Other cultural critics might note how comics inform and are informed by political codes and socio-cultural values of their time (Beaty and Woo 2016; Cohn 2007; Murray 2000), and how fan culture has developed around these particular developments (Woo 2011).

Each of these perspectives offers important insights into how comics function as a form of communication that is culturally and socially reflexive. I am not discrediting any of these critics; I have learned much from them. Their work is important, and reflects the strengths of the different knowledge traditions that they represent, and they are not necessarily biased against other approaches. But as Marc Singer argues in the aptly titled book *Breaking the Frames* (2018), disciplinary approaches can limit or even misconstrue what is being analyzed by applying a disciplinary frame or approach to comics and their makers and fans, rather than building an interpretive frame up from the comics themselves. Aaron Meskin similarly argues that need to "get beyond the definitional project" by understanding any given comic "on its own terms and by reference to its own history" (2007, 376). Arguably, at the most basic level, taking comics on their "own terms" and from the ground up means addressing the readerly process of navigating and constructing meanings from the forms' multimodal, composite qualities, putting these qualities in dialogue with their historical, cultural, and social contexts.

Since there are several dominant modalities in comics, any given comic uses different opportunities for expression from each of these modalities. Comics have been called *visual narrative*, *graphic narrative*, and *visual literature*. All of these names reflect an emphasis on their visuality, but this generalizes too far what is actually distinctive about comics, since it lumps several modes that communicate differently under the common umbrella of visuality. To be somewhat facetious, even a regular novel could be called a visual narrative, since it published in the visible written language mode for others to read. A more comprehensive name that reflects comics on their own terms is to include them with children's picture books and artists' books as a form of *multimodal textuality* or multimodal narrative (if there is a clear story), since they use pictorial, verbal, and other modes of communication together as a hybrid art. Of course, some comics emphasize pictorial content over language, and some are even "silent," in that they completely avoid the verbal modality, while others are word rich and pictorially sparse. Nonetheless, they are all multimodal, and the typical comic requires attention to orchestrated images and texts laid out in segmented sequences. Disciplinary methods of analysis and critical traditions offer powerful tools or entry points into engaging carefully with a creative work. They should not be revoked just because they are incomplete. Rather, putting these different areas of emphasis together into a coherent theory of the multimodal form and its construction of meaning is the main interdisciplinary challenge. In this book, I take up part of this challenge by offering a cognitive model of multimodality through which to ground discussions of meaning construction.

2.4 A COGNITIVE APPROACH TO COMICS AND MULTIMODALITY

The emphasis on meaning is of central interest to each of the aforementioned disciplines, and yet there is very little consensus on how to define it, since what is meaningful to each discipline varies by its methods and assumptions (Becher 1994), including how each defines and analyzes communication. Charles Hatfield (2005) argues that comics communicate through four types of tension between ways of representing and experiencing textual meaning (word vs. image; panel vs. sequence; sequence vs. layout; text world vs. materiality of media). These tensions reflect the various features of the print medium, the general form of comics, specific modalities, and the reader's experience of these features in use. In other words, the modalities are always in dialogue with a reader who navigates the tensions and makes them meaningful. As such, they always need a reader to interpret them as a communicative act.

The role of the reader in developing meaning is often either lauded—for their co-creative role (e.g., McCloud 1993; Postema 2013)—or simply assumed in much of the comics studies research, with limited acknowledgment of meaning construction processes that inform the reader's engagement with the text (although this is growing, as I discuss and integrate in subsequent chapters). Moreover, often meaning is assumed to be contained in cultural artifacts, but the question of how a text becomes meaningful in specific ways to specific readers is often glossed over in favor of statements about what is communicated, as though the textual meaning is relatively self-evident to any given reader or viewer. Thus, in literary studies, one might present a "reading" of a text by analyzing what different themes contribute to an overall perspective, but not delve into how readers might develop and know those themes to be significant in the first place, and what opportunities might have also been present for alternative interpretations. What is it about the orchestrated multimodality of the text that makes the critic notice certain features over others, and why is it that most readers experience texts in subtly distinct ways (based on background knowledges, assumptions, etc.), but in broadly similar ways (such as the general enjoyment of *Essex County* shared by all of the judges of the *Canada Reads* contest)? The processes of how readers engage with the modalities, navigate tensions, and come to conclusions about what a sequence or story might mean within the comics form remains relatively under-analyzed.

This book seeks to provide a practical framework derived from recent research into visual, verbal, social, and developmental cognition, to buttress the many important ongoing discussions of comics across the disciplines. While variation among readers clearly impacts understandings (Cohn 2021), in order to develop an applicable multimodal theory of cognition for comics studies, I will emphasize the range of features that generally fall into the category of "comics" in the Western anglophone tradition, despite there being potential for debate about whether there are comics that do or do not include such features, or whether other traditions use other conventions. Here, and particularly in the next few chapters, I will generalize to focus on *typicality* for the sake of illustrating crucial reader cognitive capacities and processes for navigation and interpretation, assuming that variation exists within examples and interpretations. In later chapters I engage with some more diverse examples, still admittedly from my area of expertise in the Western anglophone tradition, to expand on how the cognitive patterns and processes remain relevant even in spaces of experimentation. Studies have also shown how the cognitive parameters and processes I discuss are largely consistent cross-culturally (and I try to gesture to key areas of variability where necessary), but I have focused the analysis on one major area of production to illustrate the cognitive approach in addressing variations across styles and conventions. I leave it to scholars of other comics traditions and specialties to apply or contest the cognitive approach as it may be applied in those other spaces.

Any model of multimodal communication must reflect the dynamic interactions between the comic's features and the reader's abilities and backgrounds, which will in turn clarify what is at stake in particular textual features and their interpretations. In this book, I seek to present a framework that can help bridge literary, cultural, and historical approaches to materiality and meaning by grounding them in core insights regarding reader comprehension processes. As such, I hope to add to the work of others by presenting a multimodal cognitive poetics that is responsive to both insights from cognitive science and literary and artistic scholarship.

My approach to applying cognitive research to cultural artifacts seeks to present a core theory of *how meaning is constructed* in response to multimodal texts in order to ground analyses of features and interpretations within evident cognitive parameters and particular social and cultural contexts. The guiding questions that I pursue throughout this book are: How do readers navigate multimodal textual cues? How do these navigational processes and cues in turn activate, derive from, and inform the reader's knowledge and comprehension? And, how do these different processes combine modalities and culminate in novel multimodal meanings? This cognitive approach, thus, seeks to unpack the processes behind the experience of multimodal reading to show why readers understand the works in question as they do (for literature, see Dancygier 2012). Furthermore, understanding cognition can help add nuance to particular interpretations of works—and so I will model many short "readings" throughout this book and ground them in knowledge of cognitive processes as a form of multimodal cognitive poetics. Crucially, this approach shows how comics are perceived (as in looked at, broken down, and reassembled) and how this connects to meaning-making processes. In a way, I offer in the remainder of this book an account of how Hatfield's tensions reflect clear interpretive practices and biases of cognition, to show both why comics are evocative forms of storytelling and how knowledge of cognition sheds analytical light on their enticing and insightful approach to communication.

CHAPTER 3
Multimodality and Cognition

Perception, Knowledge Networks, and the Construction of Meaning

3.1 COGNITION AND TEXTUAL EXPERIENCE

As I discussed briefly in the previous chapter, there are competing perspectives on how modalities communicate, how cultures value these various communicative practices, and how these ideas relate to ongoing challenges and changes to how readers engage with multimodal communication. Comics, as a specific form of multimodal text, require a theoretical framework that unpacks how readers navigate and combine different modalities like pictographic depictions, structured panels, and abstract symbols like words or punctuation to construct complex meanings and interpretive possibilities. Analysts of multimodal texts must be sensitive to the ever-shifting relationships between modalities across a text as well as to how a reader's socio-cultural and educational experiences might inform how cues are perceived, valued, assessed, and interpreted. This chapter presents several key cognitive processes that inform how readers engage such works. These processes ground the analyses in all subsequent chapters and provides a means of accounting for why comics are so evocative as communicative forms.

3.1.1 What Is Cognition?

Cognition has come to mean a wide range of things, grounded in a variety of epistemic systems across religions, philosophies, the sciences, and the arts. In Western traditions, debates have developed around the commonly recognized distinctions between what people sense with their bodies (perception) and what they consciously know (conception), which have also been popularly inscribed through the Cartesian dualism between the feeling, unconscious, reactionary, bestial body and the rational, logical, thinking mind.[1] This dualism, along with the conspicuousness of human language, has led many to promote the "first cognitive revolution," which developed ideas about thought based on ideas about language (and especially the formal properties of grammar and syntax), asserting that there must be universal linguistic abilities that govern the mind, sometimes called mentalese or Universal Grammar (see Chomsky 1965; Pinker 1994).[2] These ideas were also informed by early brain imaging and studies of anatomy to develop the idea of brain modules with prescribed functions (Fodor 1983), which was further influenced by technological ideas of computation and mathematics. This developed a computational view of mental processes.

However, the evidence for a universal language of thought as well as modular and computational models of cognition simply do not hold up under recent research and scrutiny (Barsalou 1999; Casasanto 2011; Tomasello 1995, 2008; Shimojo and Shams 2001). For instance, the few universal aspects shared by languages, and that, therefore, could be said to reflect universal aspects of mind, relate to broader social, perceptual, and physiological constraints and abilities of the human creature, rather than presumed higher-order mental computational features ascribed to grammar and modules in the brain (Evans and Levinson 2009). The first-generation approach to cognition attempted to separate forms (as universal features) from meaning (which is culturally grounded) in order to present an idealized model of thought. However, cognition is more complex than language and computation, and separating form from meaning is a false dualism. Cognition is much more dynamic than this sanitized and formulaic first approach.

A second generation of cognitive science, which informs this book, is now building an account of how thought, action, and communication are informed by much more dynamic interactions between human senses and experiences of the world (perception), including the workings of short- and long-term memory, predictive and inferential processes, and specific social, cultural, and material contexts (broadly speaking, the environment). Embodied experiences of the world are now significant inputs into how scholars understand the development of abilities, reasoning skills, and concepts (Gibbs 2006a; Johnson 2007; Lakoff and Johnson 1980). This approach continues to recognize aspects of research under the previous model (such as the arbitrariness of some symbolic forms with regard to meaning), but recognize that form and meaning are quickly paired as constructions in the mind through processes of conceptualization that include responses to broader contexts of use (see Hoffmann 2017, 2018). As such, the new approach strongly emphasizes studies in the fields of semantics, rhetoric, and pragmatics—all of which focus on connections between forms and meanings in context, rather than a decontextualized universal structure to language and meaning.[3] As Menary (2015) shows, there is a consistent through-line in pragmatist philosophy that focuses on how embodied experiences inform thought, which recent cognitive science has come to extensively analyze and affirm.

This new focus contrasts with the first-generation emphasis on grammar and syntax as the dominating formal architecture of meaning by emphasizing a wider array of contexts and experiences that inform meanings and contribute to how grammar and syntax are often interpreted. In the new approach, syntax and grammar have been re-conceptualized through the development of "cognitive grammar" or "construction grammar," which show how even grammatical and syntactic forms are imbued with specific and often embodied meanings that inform the inferences and projections that language users make about representational choices and how they contribute to the trajectory and emergent meaning of the text (see Hoffmann and Trousdale 2013; Langacker 2008). As Hart and Queralto note, the radical aspect of this cognitive approach is that "the difference between lexical and grammatical constructions lies only in the degree of abstractness or schematicity which they encode in their semantic structure" (2021, 532). As such, semantics is interwoven throughout the levels of schematicity, with lexical and grammatical aspects operating synthetically with other levels as enmeshed meaning-prompting components. This contrasts with approaches to multimodality in comics that separate lexical or grammatical aspects from their semantic embeddedness, such as some of Neil Cohn's work.[4]

The second cognitive revolution has prompted several decades of research that analyzes the ways that cognition and communication are informed by embodied or experiential inputs (Chemero 2009; Rohrer 2007; M. Wilson 2002), including the environments in which people are situated and act and related specific processes of embodied activation (Gibbs 2006a; Hutchins 2005, 2010). Under this revised cognitive perspective, researchers consider the mind and its concepts as emergent properties of underlying experiences and processes, such that conscious experience is a process of activating and blending cues from the brain, body, and environment. Karen Kukkonen (2019) helpfully summarizes and mobilizes the general features of this view as "4E cognition" for the purposes of literary historicism. Her 4Es describe cognition as "embodied" (as part of the physical sensations of self and movement), "embedded" (since it is situated in social, cultural, and material contexts), "extended" (through technologies and practices, like writing, drawing, and reading), and "enactive" (since perception is informed by assumptions and predictions about actions and environments). These general features of 4E cognition inform my work as well, but I will continue to refer to this as embodied cognition (but as broadly conceived to include all aspects of the 4E summation), for ease of reference and since this widened usage is common in the ongoing scholarly conversation. Embodiment is now broadly considered to be more than just the body-mind network, expanding to include the environment or niche in which the body-mind acts. I have called this an "ecological approach" to cognition (2015), since it places cognition as part of an emergent property of a wide array of networks established between environmental and organismic factors such as perception, anticipation, prediction, memory activation, reaction, and response adaptation. Meaning is grounded in this web of embodied experiences, established through both the human internal and external sensorium, and is informed endlessly by expectations and engagements with the environment, be it real or mediated.

The embodied perspective has revolutionized cognitive science and offers much to the humanities as well. Lakoff and Johnson (1980, 1999) were some of the earliest promoters of the approach in philosophy and linguistics.[5] They argue that this approach reformulates or refutes many older dualistic and deterministic ways of analyzing human experience.[6] Edward Slingerland (2008) makes an extensive case, in light of more recent research, for the ways that this embodied approach changes how critics study culture by locating meaning in the networks of knowledge activated through perception and action (see also Johnson 2007; Noë 2009). He argues that this approach provides an opportunity to "vertically integrate" the arts and sciences through evolutionarily and psychologically reflective discussions of meaning-making. Embodied constraints, broadly conceived, can provide some universal parameters and connections while remaining flexible to the variabilities of human cultures and individuals, in particular by illustrating the incredible fluidity of cognition to repurpose experiences, to reformulate perceptions, and to develop diverse conceptualizations of the world.

The fields of cognitive poetics (see Stockwell 2002, 2009), cognitive literary studies (see Zunshine 2006, 2010), and other related subdisciplines expand on these interests as they pertain to studies of culture, art, and literature, although there is a fair degree of confusion created through the indiscriminate use of first- and second-generation cognitive science. As such, I focus in this book on relevant insights from the psychological disciplines that inform an embodied (4E) understanding of cognition and aligned studies in cognitive poetics (and related approaches), and direct them toward the multimodality of comics. This work contributes to recent developments in multimodal cognitive poetics as well (see Gibbons 2012; Kukkonen 2013a, 2013b), recognizing the multimodal and multisensory complexity of communication and cognition.

3.1.2 Text and Texture

The recent shift to an integrated embodied approach locates and highlights the critical processes behind how perceptual experiences are stored, activated, recycled, and combined to build meaningful, conscious effects and understandings (Gibbs 2006a; Johnson 2007; Rose 2005; Stockwell 2009). Such an approach sees communicative artifacts (including comics) as multimodal cues that prompt and anchor cognitive processes that in turn draw on prior perceptual and cultural knowledge to build meanings (Hutchins 2005). Embodied communication is naturally composed of multimodal experiences (through gesture, intonation, interaction, etc.), and mediated contexts leverage aspects of these experiences. A cognitive approach to meaning in comics requires careful attention to the specific ways that modalities engage cognitive processes, biases, and constraints, as well as how these integrate and reflect variations in cultural, social, and individual experiences.[7]

Rather than divide perception (form) and conception (meaning) as distinct entities, as Cartesians and formalists do, the embodied approach sees concepts as the emergent multimodal properties of dynamic, unconscious engagements of perceptual experiences that prompt processes of conceptualization or meaning construction (Barsalou 1999; Fauconnier and Turner 2002; Talmy 1996). Put another way, textual comprehension, much like everyday experience, is grounded in embodied and distributed experiences, such that texts activate multisensory background knowledge to prompt meaning development through strategically invoked mental imagery and conceptual development (Bergen 2005, 2012). A text's specific means of perceptual activation (which includes aspects of attention, prediction, memory, and inference) is what makes it unique and allows it to offer specific types of information and connotations. The strategic uses of a modality's representational resources and affordances (such as the image's ability to show, or a word to tell) construes the subject matter by highlighting some features of a multimodal source in memory over others. For instance, an image can present a distinct perspective on an object that makes it seem tiny and innocuous or big and imposing, or can render it either familiar or unfamiliar. Thus, representational choices (color, perspective, etc.) offer particular perceptual experiences to the reader, which in turn prompts a particular type of mental access and activation of the subject (I expand on forms of construal more in the next chapter). Multimodal communication becomes even more complicated, since every modality presents unique opportunities to construe a subject, while also creating complicating interactions with other modalities. Furthermore, feedback loops among textual cues, background knowledge, and the emerging mental imagery all add to and adjust the predictive and interpretive inferences about a text as readers progress through it. In short, readers learn from a text as they interact with it, much as people do in natural environments, which changes how they respond to and interpret various textual choices going forward.

Cartoonists work hard to build up and mobilize a repertoire of multimodal skills and resources to communicate about a given topic, including perhaps training with writing guides like those by Jessica Abel and Matt Madden (2008, 2012) or by Will Eisner (2008a, 2008c, 2008b), and often working collaboratively as writers, illustrators, colorists, and letterers, all of whom have also studied the works of others. That being said, many creators may not be fully aware of the cognitive impact of their choices, preferring to do it by feel, but are aware of the resultant message they are striving to invoke and the specific background information upon which they draw.

What a cognitive perspective offers this complicated analytical scene is the ability to show how these modalities function and synthesize in the ways they do for readers, thereby offering an explanatory (not prescriptive or determinate) model of how meaning emerges for readers. By noting the predictive, inferential, and interpretive possibilities the text offers, and linking these to cognitive processes, I hope to show how various construals and developments of the subject matter emerge for readers from specific textual features. Conscious textual comprehension, the generally referred-to "meaning" of a text, is a late emergent stage in a series of largely unconscious dynamic interactions among visual perception, activation processes of biases and stored knowledge, and mental imagery development that builds meaning incrementally, non-linearly, recursively, and opportunistically in response to multimodal textual cues. Understanding this dynamic "cognitive unconscious" and how it leads to meaning gives insights into the emergent conscious sense of texts, of what readers may have understood, enjoyed, and felt. Stockwell (2009) describes the transformation from a verbal text's representation into the more personal readerly experience of it as the shift from text to "texture." This term nicely suggests the imbuing of a text with more personal levels of nuance and feeling through the activation of embodied knowledge. Comics add further complexity to this idea, by showing the central role of multimodality in texture as well.

The embodied approach I take to the texture of comics weaves together a range of common human cognitive processes and biases, which are further informed or adjusted by cultural and social contexts. In this chapter, I focus on several central concepts that I consider most helpful in bridging disciplines and engaging in a more robust multimodal cognitive poetics, with subsequent chapters expanding on aspects of this overview. These concepts recognize common pragmatic influences over all forms of communication, not just comics. Nonetheless, the ways that comics integrate the multimodal resources of images, texts, layouts, and other conventionalized signs often complicate these concepts and render them a crucial resource for thinking about theories of cognition as well.

3.2 PERCEIVING COMICS

3.2.1 Training Perception

As I have noted, perceptual cues and embodied experiences inform how readers conceptualize and interpret a multimodal text. Perception is a complex cognitive operation informed by processes of selection, identification, prediction, inference, and abstraction. Humans all share biases and "gestalt" patterns in perception that facilitate comprehension (Arnheim 1999, 2004, 2009; Chandler 2007, 151–52; Gibbs 2006a; Johnson 1987, 2007; Slingerland 2008). For sensorial experience to be meaningful it must be categorized, generalized, combined, and even projected into the future through connections to past experiences.[8] Such processes led the visual psychologist Rudolf Arnheim to emphatically and persuasively argue that "visual perception is visual thinking" (Arnheim 2015), since the ability to comprehend an artwork and other communicative forms requires the navigation and integration of a range of cues based on subconscious processes of attentional selection, gestalt impressions of forms, and the integration of responses from past perceptual experiences. Similarly, art historian and visual psychologist Ernst Gombrich shows repeatedly how the notion of "the innocent eye" ignores "the beholder's share in the reading of images, his capacity, that is, to collaborate with the artist and to transform a piece of coloured canvas into a likeness of the visible world" (1959, 246). As he rightly shows, seeing involves learned processes of identification and response that build an "illusion" of immediate recognition. Gombrich refers to illusion as a process of "projecting meaning into" an image across a range of types of perspective and abstraction (203–41).

Through the notion of illusion, Gombrich highlights that viewer perceptions can build conscious experiences that are not necessarily synonymous with what is shown in a work of art. He suggests that "[t]here is no rigid distinction, therefore, between perception and illusion" (Gombrich 1959, 29). For instance, he refers to the famous example popularized in psychology by Joseph Jastrow of the duck-rabbit (Figure 3.1),[9] which is a representational paradox but a perceptual certainty: it is either perceived as one or the other creature, but never as both at the same time (1959, 3–8). Karen Kukkonen, following the analysis of this image by Wittgenstein, refers to this feature as "multistability" that involves "switching back-and-forth between two different, coherent percepts on the basis of the same image" (2017, 343), a concept she also ascribes to a range of aspects of comics, such as complex perspectives or divergent reading paths. Similarly, Arnheim affirms Wittgenstein's analysis, summarizing that "this is not a matter of two different interpretations applied to one percept, but of two percepts . . . derived from one stimulus" (2009, 95). The representational togetherness is a certainty, but a tension arises in perception and conceptualization. Thus, perception is more than the passive receiving of "pure sense," and it requires the integration of background knowledge (of animal forms), inferences (is it one or the other), and interpretations (this is a multistable illusion) in order to become meaningful or comprehensible.

The active nature of perception counteracts naive structuralism in comics studies, which can assume an immediacy and clarity to pictorial cues. For instance, McCloud assumes that images in comics are generally passively received rather than interpreted (McCloud 1993, 49), and it is

Figure 3.1 Joseph Jastrow's version of the duck-rabbit illusion (1899, 312). Public domain.

only in their sequential interactions that the reader begins to participate in meaning construction (67). However, as I have discussed, perception is active rather than passive. Rather than being a simple input, perception is meaningful because it interrogates cues by activating relevant background knowledge to make predictions and inferences about relevance and potential meaningfulness, which prompts further interpretations as predictions are confirmed or amended, all of which inform comprehension and analytic responses.

Cognition is strongly biased toward use and interaction (Noë 2004, 2009), which informs what people perceive as meaningful and how they engage or respond with it. For instance, as a social species, faces and face-like features are major attractants of attention because they are sources of intersubjective connection through gaze and expression (Dukewich, Klein, and Christie 2008). Similarly, as active creatures in dynamic environments, people are more attentive to moving or altered elements than static or repetitive ones. Finally, perception is goal directed, such that one can become focused on tracking one element of a scene (because someone told you it was important, say) and miss other salient details because of this fixation. This is called attentional blindness or change blindness (Simons and Chabris 1999). Such processes and biases are multimodally integrated across all perceptual systems by linking visual perception with the other senses (see Barsalou 1999, 2008; Gibbs and Colston 2012; Slingerland 2008). The bias toward action and interaction is particularly salient for how multimodal literatures present their subject matter in order to construe, attract, control, and manipulate the perception of cues through stylistic choices.

Past experiences further inform perception, as people are socialized and enculturated to attend to key features or to search through particular environments in strategic ways to find meaningful cues. Such is the case for both natural environments and artificial ones like pages in a book. Perry Nodelman (1988) describes how young children learn ways of seeing and reading through picture books (see especially ch. 1). Children learn such assumptions and skills as recognizing that a range of pictorial styles can still represent the same particular object, that repetition often means causal relations, and that figures may be isolated and float on the page when in actuality the object is situated in a complex environment. Similarly, much of Gombrich's analysis of art and illusion illustrates the historical transformations as artists learn from one another across the Western tradition to build new opportunities for the beholder to engage. Learning to isolate and interpret patterns of representation, abstraction, and connection are crucial skills for a mediated society. Readers and viewers require a certain degree of education in order to recognize the meaningfulness of images and other representational cues, in order to avoid confusion. People must learn to build connections between types of depictions and representations and the world around us, since "the likeness that art creates exists in our imagination only" (Gombrich 1959, 191), and the "recognition of images is connected with projections and visual anticipations" (191). As evidence of this, Nodelman (1988, 11) notes how one study of intercultural depiction found that a Western styled realist drawing of musculature on an arm and wrinkles on a face was interpreted by Bantu viewers as incisions (see Duncan 1973, 9). Relatively realistic depictions can be misinterpreted without exposure to the mode's styles or conventions of representation within a particular community of communicators. The multimodal literacies that weld forms and meanings include socially and culturally developed skills, such that while aspects of visual depiction (especially photo-realistic works) seem universally accessible, there are also aspects that are culturally coded and may diverge depending on cognitive capabilities and socio-cultural backgrounds (Cohn 2021).

The principle of the educated eye also applies of course to variations among readers and viewers within communities (Cohn 2021). Degrees of background education, exposure, and expertise have been shown to impact analysis of visualizations through eye-tracking research by Gegenfurtner, Lehtinen, and Säljö (2011). They showed how expert viewers parse and evaluate relationships within visualizations more quickly than novices because their task-specific knowledge helps guide attention. They have learned where to look for key pictorial information, and this speeds up and directs their visual perception and subsequent comprehension. From similar examples of cultural and experiential grounding in image perception, Nodelman (1988) surmises that "all visual images, even the most apparently representational ones, do imply a viewer, do require a knowledge of learned competencies and cultural assumptions before they can be rightly understood" (17). While the notion of cultural relativity should be hedged somewhat in regard to image recognition, especially for photographic or realistic depictions, Nodelman can be reframed here as recapitulating some of the subtle cognitive biases toward interaction, relevance, and action guided by memory, which informs how readers perceive and interpret mediated communication.

Cultural backgrounds and more discrete discourse communities can also impact perception through multimodal interactions. For instance, English language users tend to scan left to right through sequential cues, whereas Hebrew readers do the opposite, which in turn can impact inferences about directional depictions of time and causation (Fuhrman and Boroditsky 2010). Literacy education also changes how cues are navigated by facilitating "the development of analytic visual processing" (Morais and Kolinsky 2005, 191–92) by drawing more attention to the connections between parts and wholes—with literacy comes an increased facility in parsing differences and in seeing how parts contribute to holistic understanding. Importantly, such research shows that learned patterns of textual engagement can become inscribed in perceptual biases with multimodal and conceptual implications.

There is a tension then, between universal attention-grabbing elements, such as gaze attraction to faces and figures, and how those features are then conventionalized and interpreted in particular discourse communities (such as the emergence of house styles of depiction for Marvel and DC superhero comics). There are also obvious degrees of accessibility based on representational style, where photographs are much easier to recognize and interpret than more abstracted visual forms. The notion of embodied cognition discussed above, and unpacked throughout this book, acknowledges and assumes this cultural and social context-dependent malleability as part of all levels of thought, while at the same time noting common processes that work through them as well. Perception then is a complex engagement with modalities that is driven by how attention naturally is drawn to particular features (faces, movements, etc.) while it has also been trained in a particular multimodal discourse community to navigate texts in specific ways (left to right, top to bottom for English readers).[10] Reader perceptions have been crafted to navigate images and texts through exposure to various reading practices through education systems, and exposure even at home to picture books, magazines, and other types of multimodal texts. From such experiences, multimodal perception becomes a trained instrument of meaning construction.

3.2.2 Perception and Attentional Guidance in Comics

The multimodal orchestration and design of elements on the comics page guides attention as part of the semantic dynamics of the page. When readers examine a typical comic, the initial feature they likely notice is the layout of sequences of panels that cover the page (see Figure 3.2) and encompass a variety of communicative modalities with varying degrees of detail, all of which inform the initial perceptual processes that I discuss in this section. Panels come in a variety of sizes and arrangements that can prioritize particular images or cues (by making them bigger or bolder), or can equate all panels evenly (through shared structural features). Likewise,

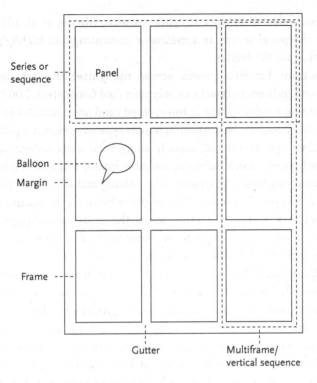

Figure 3.2 Most common terms for basic elements of a comics page layout, based on Groensteen (2007) and McCloud (1993).

various visual attractants might override the bias to start reading at the top-left (for the English reader), and present moments to pause or prioritize particular pieces of information based on size, color, figuration, and location (typically perception is trained in the West to prioritize the first and final panels, as well as the central one, if available). The frame of a panel and the margins of the page (the "hyperframe": Groensteen 2007, 30–31) might be ignored as conventionally static elements of presentation, while the contents of individual panels then become the objects of attention. At the same time, bleeding images off of the edge of the page, breaking figures through panel borders, or aspects linking across wider sequences all draw attention briefly to these features as participants that not only enclose content, but also can serve to foreground the power or significance of a particular cue (see Borkent 2017). For instance, a superhero may be presented as breaking out of the panel frame, so as to construe their movement as particularly fast or powerful. Moreover, the presence of words and characters can shift reading patterns within and between panels, including skipping environmental cues, in order to prioritize content that seems most relevant to the emerging narrative (Kirtley et al. 2018). Thus, typically the panel serves as a means of presenting and highlighting key information for the reader.

Interactions between panels across the gutter through sequences, layouts, and indirect networks of relations (see Groensteen 2007) further complicate how information is interpreted (and are discussed in detail in subsequent chapters). Nonetheless, panels typically present a picture with a particular style and detail, usually along with written cues of various types (such as in speech balloons, narrator boxes, and sound effects) and forms (including font adjustments like bolding and size). How readers interpret such features and put them together becomes the meaning of each panel, and as they accrue together across the sequence and page, they aggregate and adjust in relation to one another to form the more complex meanings of the comic strip or comic book.

Neil Cohn helpfully refers to panels as "attentional windows" (Cohn 2013b, 56–59), by which he means that they offer readers a snapshot of visual perception focused on something in a given scene. These attentional windows develop into sequences of content that are blended together to develop more complex connections between content. The notion of attentional windowing aligns well with research in visual perception, since cognitive systems are designed to work with broken pieces of perception in order to build up coherence. As I discuss shortly regarding eye tracking, attention and perception are complex processes of meaning construction, and the panel crucially frames (literally) the content to guide the reader.

Panels help direct the reader's attention by windowing or constraining it while presenting an image (and often text) with varying degrees of detail. These windows offer particular perspectives—can be up close and personal, distant and aloof, and looking directly, downward, or upward upon whatever is represented. As such, they offer not just a picture of something, but they also position the viewer in relation to it, while providing limited degrees of access and engagement. This directs the reader's attention to the content but also construes the content through specific constraints on how readers might engage it, which adds to its meaning. For instance, presenting the image as though the reader is looking up toward a figure might construe that figure as powerful, awe-inspiring, or terrifying because the viewer is positioned in a subservient position (Eisner 2008a, 92), or perhaps construes the viewer as crafty in advancing toward or sneaking away from the figure. Of course, the story context plays a significant role in prompting the reader's interpretations of this positioning.

Panels can also direct attention through qualities of representation, ranging from photorealist to heavily caricatured figures, and can orchestrate the presentation of other modalities, such as how it integrates language as sound effects, or through speech balloons that fill up the scene, taking up presumably insignificant perceptual spaces in the storyworld. This multimodal orchestration of pictures, language, frame borders, and other conventions aid in but can also suppress different types of perception and comprehension. All qualities of representation play an important role in construing the content; their particular orchestration, gestalt impressions, visual style, and so forth interact to inform reader interpretations. All modalities have various specific capacities to construe their subject matter.

3.2.3 Tracking Perception and Conceptualization

The strategic use of the different modes of communication compose the content of the panel. Cartoons are great snapshots of the effectiveness of strategic manipulations of modalities in single panels, and political cartoons are especially focused on construing their subject matter for social effects (Bergen 2003; El Refaie 2009). While not comic strips or longer graphic narratives, which integrate more temporal and narrative qualities through juxtaposition of panels in sequence, cartoons are close cousins to comics because they employ many of the same multimodal discourse conventions. The cartoon's relation to a comic book is much like the postcard short story to the novella. Thus, I join many scholars who include cartoons as part of the category of comics, including philosopher Aaron Meskin (2007), historians Robert Harvey (1996) and Thierry Smolderen (2014), and communications scholars Charles Hatfield (2005, 2009) and Bart Beaty (2012), among others. In light of these qualities and consensus, I turn to engage the complexity of cognition in relation to the multimodal strategies of an editorial cartoon.

In the following editorial cartoon (Figure 3.3) by Canadian cartoonist Aislin,[11] I examine the interplay between linguistic, pictorial and orientational cues in a single panel cartoon (in the next few chapters, I focus on complicating these patterns while analyzing the impact of sequential paneling). I show how Aislin employs key features to offer a darkly humorous cartoon, while unpacking the cognitive patterns and processes that go into how readers likely understand it.

This particular cartoon directs the reader's attention in several ways that likely prompt a series of stages to the conceptualization process. Eye tracking helpfully shows how readers parse and integrate communicative cues, since how the eye moves through cues aligns with how information is processed. It reflects the order of attention to that work and can

Figure 3.3 "Who hasn't fantasized . . .?" (1997) editorial cartoon by Aislin (alias Terry Mosher), accession number M2000.79.59. With permission of McCord Museum, Montreal.

indicate where people leap forward and backward in order to clarify or reinterpret their predictions and inferences as they develop comprehension (Duchowski 2002, 2007). What the eye looks at, and in what order, gives clues as to how the features (of an image, of a text, or of an environment) are being engaged with and processed, which in turn reveals how meaningful percepts and conceptualizations are being constructed by readers and viewers. In terms of embodied cognition, eye tracking allows a literal glimpse into how attention and perception informs conceptualization.

Eye-tracking studies of visual art show that viewers initially generate a gist impression of the work prior to more detailed engagement (Locher 2015). Similarly, readers typically engage with cartoons in three steps: first, readers take a general quick glance at the image, and especially focus on character's faces and general action spaces to get the gist of the subject matter and gestalt patterns as part of "preparatory" processing (Carroll, Young, and Guertin 1992, 450). For this cartoon, they likely focus on the figure on the ski-doo. Second, they read the textual content, while occasionally attending to the relevant related element in the image; here integrating the caption into the image. And, finally, they may return to the image for more careful scrutiny (see Cohn 2013a; Foulsham, Wybrow, and Cohn 2016; Holsanova, Holmberg, and Holmqvist 2009; Kress and Van Leeuwen

[46] *Comics and Cognition*

1996), such as here to clarify details of the fantasy. For more complex works and sequences, there are even more back and forth glances between text and image to relate the contents as they develop (see Duchowski 2002, 2007), which reflects how readers update their predictions and inferences as they navigate a text. There is also a strong processing bias toward verbal text because it typically takes longer to parse and contains more detailed information (Carroll, Young, and Guertin 1992; Kirtley et al. 2018; Loschky et al. 2018).

Furthermore, spatial contiguity of elements develops meaningful relationships by grouping information (a feature of gestalt perception), such as uniting the skidoo rider with his machine as a compound agent in the cartoon above. Grouping is important for relating details within panels, but also facilitates bridging sequential connections between panels in comic strips by perceptually prioritizing contiguity over other types of relations, such as vertical sequences or other patterns that may emerge in the perceptual and conceptualization process (Holsanova, Holmberg, and Holmqvist 2009). A bias to build relationships based on contiguity is further reinforced by conventions in comics, such as by having balloon tails show connections between depicted speakers and their words, or aligning sound effects with actions (Forceville 2005; Forceville, Veale, and Feyaerts 2010). Such connections show how context-specific relevance (in both prediction and inference) is also crucial to parsing relationships between contiguous elements, especially in the confined multimodal spaces of panels. Generally, in the case of comics, the image and text components are relatively sparse, to help develop clear relationships between elements, but they can become quite complicated. Strategic orchestration of interactions between cues within panels allows cartoonists to help direct the reader's attention to salient elements in order to try and prompt specific interpretations of the cues.

The design or presentation of paneled information also impacts perception by guiding attention through the exploitation of visual salience or through gestalt impressions like pattern recognition, figure/ground effects, or object completion. For instance, the dominant placement and bright box of the caption in Aislin's cartoon at the top-left of the dark panel helps prioritize it as necessary information, and it might draw the reader's eye more quickly away from the cursory glance at the image of the jet-skier. Being in the top left is also the dominant position for English-language readers to start reading a text, which is further reinforced by the diagonal arrangement of first the caption, then the picture, then Aislin's signature. The three boxes group together within the wider black box of the cartoon to make a complete presentational space. The diagonal linear alignment also facilitates scanning patterns to follow the predicted motion path of the jet-skiing figure. These different features guide attention and orchestrate cues to make for a directional valence to the content and may help to reinforce or strengthen the punch line.

While no eye-tracking study has analyzed this particular cartoon, it is likely that the described general biases and processes of attention are involved for readers and that representational choices strategically construe the subject matter for them. For instance, the pictographic cues are composed of two distinct parts, with the central image of the man on a jet-ski dominating as a focal point, while the modified or stylized frame of a rifle scope contains the figure through figure/ground gestalt and perspective effects. Based on the attentional research, readers likely glance briefly at the figure to assess his activity, go back and read the caption, then return to the figure to consider how the caption and figure relate. A reader may recognize on the initial scan both the figure and the frame, or may only notice the frame on the subsequent review, since the cross-hairs are a more subtle element within the composition. Either way, the implied path of motion of the figure helps guide the reader's attention directly to the frame's cross-hairs of a rifle's scope and its implications for the jet-skier. At the same time, the constructedness of the image keeps the possible actions of a sniper as a future potential action, not actually realized.

All of these perceived elements and possible inferences happen very quickly for readers, and the back-and-forth relations of image and text elements are largely unconscious. The compositional qualities help the reader perceive content in a subtly ordered manner that develops a multimodal punch line as a response to the title. Importantly, the effectiveness of the composition is informed by acculturated patterns of semiotic decoding, since the reading path of the English-language reader informs how readers respond to the image. The picture is more dynamic because the man is moving from left to right, rather than the other way around, and elements become highlighted along that reading path, as the readers combine the title with the figure and the scope.

To highlight the effects of how these features direct attention, I have reconstructed a flipped version of the general features of the cartoon (Figure 3.4). In the original cartoon, each component functions as part of an orchestrated hierarchy of cues from top to bottom, left to right. Reversing that order subtly alters perceptual engagement with the components, by foregrounding the cross-hairs first, rather than the rider, which decreases the saliency of the cartoon's overall meaning. The original exploits diagonal groupings and motion cues to guide readers through the

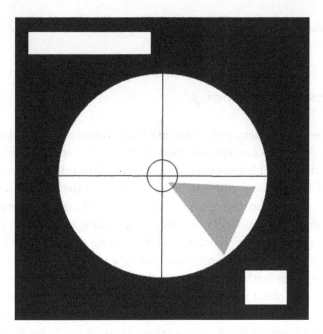

Figure 3.4 Reversed reconstruction of Aislin's "Who hasn't fantasized?" (by author).

image, leaving the cross-hairs as a final (and potentially surprising) revelation and future action. The reversed version weakens the visual punch line by potentially envisioning the potential shooting sooner and to contemplate the figure less. These differences are significant, because the cartoon positions the reader in the role of the sniper, which is likely (and hopefully) a shocking position to be in for most. In the original, the jet-skier and his movements are prioritized, followed by the revelation or clarification of the full meaning of the reader's positioning as viewer and potential actor. Furthermore, the consistent motion across the cartoon feels more natural for a Western readership, which renders a clearer motion path for the figure and reinforces a causal relationship with the reader. It also reinforces a stepwise reading, from caption to jet-skier to rifle scope, which puts the emphasis on a fantasized murder at the end of the cartoon, which makes for a more salient political point.

As I have shown, the perceptual process of attentional guidance through compositional choices surrounding the modalities of language, pictures, and layouts subtly impacts the overall meaning of the cartoon, and any other attentionally windowed panel. Over the next few sections, I will unpack further the cognitive parameters and processes that offer a more comprehensive engagement with how meaning or texture is constructed in response to this cartoon, as well as to add more background information to nuance why such a shocking murder fantasy was editorialized in a popular publication.

3.3 COGNITIVE TOPOLOGY

Because perceptual cues, such as attentional guidance and gestalt patterns, inform processes of conceptualization and overall comprehension, recent theories of mental processes have incorporated the role of several levels of mental imagery and embodied experiences into the understanding of meaning construction. Reading and viewing go well beyond a simple process of decoding one modality or another. Processing information requires selecting, predicting, inferencing, and integrating the possible meanings of a cue by activating elements and building a mental scenario, a simulation, to facilitate further prediction and inference making and to develop interpretations about event structure, characters, viewpoints, and the environment, be it fictional or real (Zwaan 1996, 2004, 2009; Zwaan et al. 1998). Significant evidence from various areas of cognitive science, including neurology, developmental and visual psychology, psycholinguistics, and cognitive linguistics, shows that embodied experiences and perceptual processes structure mental scenario and conceptual developments (see Bergen 2012; Coulson and Matlock 2005; Gibbs 2006a). Moreover, these experiential structures are stored in long-term memory and activated for in-the-moment use in working memory (Hoffmann 2017). Thus, to perceive and understand the world or a text, mental models guide predictions and percept development, such that enculturation, education, and personal experience all play a crucial role in perception and response (Fabry 2017; Fabry and Kukkonen 2019).

Experiences are often categorized through several levels of abstraction and similarities across levels of generalization that range from basic assumptions about roles and intentions, objects and locations, and interactive dynamics, up to more complex cultural and ideological concepts. Cognitive processes integrate these elements into different types of knowledge networks, including categories surrounding prototypical features, domains of knowledge that build around experiential associations, and through metaphorical relationships based on various types and levels of resemblance or connection. Furthermore, abstract patterns of sensorimotor actions and perception called schemas facilitate inferences about and interconnections between modalities. The term cognitive topology refers to all of these different arrangements of information that structure long-term memory, which I unpack further below and in subsequent chapters.

This cognitive topology provides parameters and structure to cognitive processes of activation and comprehension in short-term memory. It is cognitive topology that helps inform what is activated in processes of perception (such as glimpsed through eye tracking) by informing predictions and inferences, and these continue to develop through short-term, in-the-moment conceptualization processes. Thus, to analyze the construction of meaning requires that I first outline some significant cognitive topological structures, and second, in the subsequent section, unpack specific activation processes that draw on these structures to build meaning.

3.3.1 Schemas and Mental Metaphors

The previous discussion of Aislin's cartoon and attentional guidance already indicates how the constructed and multimodal nature of representing information allows for some degree of control of the reader's perceptual and interpretive processes by exploiting attentional and predictive responses to text cues. Underlying these general patterns are a host of cognitive structures and processes. Here I briefly describe two basal structures that play an important role in many connections between form and meaning across modalities.

The previous sections describe attentional guidance through perceived motion of the figure and the orchestration of representational cues along a reading path. These patterns relate to schemas, which are recurrent perceptual or gestalt-like structures of embodied experience. Often referred to as "image schemas" in the embodiment research, I prefer simply the term schemas to clarify that they are not necessarily "imagic" but perceptual in a wider range of ways. As Mark Johnson (1987, 2007) defines them, they are "organizing structures of our experience and understanding at the level of bodily perception and movement" (Johnson 1987, 20), and as such "they transcend any specific sense modality, though they involve operations that are analogous to spatial manipulation, orientation, and movement" (25). He argues that

> In order for us to have meaningful, connected experiences that we can comprehend and reason about, there must be pattern and order to our actions, perceptions, and conceptions. A schema is a recurrent pattern, shape, and regularity in, or of, these ongoing ordering activities. (29)

Examples of schemas include MOTION, PATH, BALANCE, EMANATION, VERTICALITY, SCALARITY, and DIRECTIONALITY.[12] Such multimodal experiences can be thought of as basic perceptual logics that apply wherever they are perceived. For instance, beyond the motion, path line, and center/periphery characteristics of the cartoon discussed above, the schema of the CONTAINER also plays a role in creating a sense of compositional unity of different elements of the cartoon. Thus, the dark frame of the cartoon acts as a container that holds the title, image, and signature within itself as distinct but connected elements. Within the container, elements can still be preferentially treated due to size and orientation, which include their own schemas, such as the reading line from top-left to bottom-right using a modified version of the UP-DOWN schema. Furthermore, the CONTAINER schema may also play a role in grouping the man and his skidoo together as a singular agentive unit on the water. This perceptual unit-making allows readers to think of him and his machine as one entity contained within the sights of the gun scope. Furthermore, the inside/outside logic of the container may help reinforce the insider-outsider dynamic that is part of the shooter/jet-skier antagonism in this cartoon. Finally, the schema of containment also informs the concept of fantasy from the title, as something that is outside of reality, which further modifies the perceived antagonism of the image.

As this description shows, schemas, while seemingly simplistic, are significant abstract parameters that inform perception and conceptualization. These basic sense experiences can inform how readers categorize and connect objects, actions, and interactions by suggesting a logical, inferential pattern to abstract reasoning and interpretation. These basic bodily knowledges inform inferences about representational cues and are a part of the specific roles and values of particular areas of experience (more shortly), but also operate at a more basic level to structure categories or cultural scripts that include rote actions. As such, schemas underscore the human-scale perceptual reasoning that applies to a range of multimodal cues and inform all areas of cognitive topology to some extent.[13]

One particularly important way that schematic knowledge couples with basic experiences and builds meaning is through what have variously been called conceptual metaphors (Gibbs 2006a, 2011; Kövecses 2010), mental metaphors (Casasanto 2009, 2013, 2017), or cognitive metaphors (Dancygier and Sweetser 2014). I prefer and employ the term mental metaphors throughout this book (mostly to avoid the overuse of the term cognitive), though these are all largely analogous terms that serve to encapsulate a range of unconscious metaphorical reasoning patterns that develop specific connections and concepts based on schematic and experiential correlations. These metaphorical types include primary metaphors (Grady 2005), that focus on early developmental concepts like UNFEELING

IS COLD (grounded in an infant's feelings of proximity to a care provider) and ontological and orientational metaphors (Lakoff and Johnson 1980), such as GOOD IS UP (which is grounded in the experience of feeling more capable of agentive action when upright). As their names suggest, each type of metaphor focuses on a specific category that relates to different types of embodied experience.[14]

Returning to Aislin's cartoon above, mental metaphors about morality and action, such as DOWN IS BAD, may be invoked by the downward trajectory of the jet-skier, implying that either he or the shooter are heading into a space of dubious moral action. Similarly, an ontological metaphor like CONTAINMENT IS CONTROL reinforces the sense that the reader/sniper has control over the situation by containing the jet-skier in their sights. Another common containment metaphor—CONTAINER IS CONTENTS— also reinforces the trope of fantasy (rather than of actual assassination), by focusing on the cartoon as an enclosed space of fictional action that is contained and kept apart from the world. Each of these schematic structures invokes metaphorical connections to experiential and cultural knowledges that add depth to how cues might be interpreted and operates as an unconscious structure rather than a conscious invocation of specific content, such that there is not a jet-skier schema, but a PATH schema that informs how that skier is perceived in motion. Mental metaphors can operate at a range of levels of conceptualization, adding or reinforcing basic inferential details about control or movement, or by linking to more culturally complicated moral valences. Various metaphors help structure thought and inform how readers connect experiences and knowledge to interpret communicative forms. While I have only touched on schemas and conceptual metaphors here, they continue to be developed in detail in the following chapters.

3.3.2 Domains and Categories as Knowledge Networks

Domains are multimodal, interwoven networks of embodied experiences, cultural information, and other forms of learned knowledge stored in long-term memory.[15] For in-the-moment, "online" understanding, domains of knowledge are accessed to contextualize and interpret communicative acts and experiences (Cienki 2007; Croft 2002; Fillmore 1982). In other words, selected elements of long-term memory are activated in short-term working memory as circumstances require (see Schweppe and Rummer 2014), and these inform predictions, inferences, percept formations, and interpretations. Moreover, the activation of domains is not unilateral and direct, but often recursive and adaptive, such that readers and experiences check inferences against background information repeatedly so that they can corroborate assumptions about a cue, or update them as needed, modulating and adjusting responses and interpretations along the way (Barrett 2017). As such, cognitive processes attempt to minimize prediction error in order to facilitate rapid and accurate comprehension of cues (Fabry and Kukkonen 2019), and structuring knowledge in networks of relevant and interwoven knowledge can support this process.

The networked structure of domains is crucial for how they function in cognitive processes. Charles Fillmore describes domains as

> any system of concepts related in such a way that to understand any one of them you have to understand the whole structure in which it fits; when one of the things in such a structure is introduced into a text, or into a conversation, all of the other things are automatically made available. (Fillmore 1982, 111)

A common example of a domain is the basic economic transaction domain in which terms like "buy," "sell," "goods," "retailer," and "customer" are understood in relation to one another. Different elements of a domain highlight particular things, roles, and values (see also Oakley 2009, 139–51; Zwaan 2008), and each of these can be access points into the domain.[16] As embodied, multimodal, interactional networks, these knowledge structures are not limited to language (see Cienki 2007, 173; Oakley 2009, 140–41), and can include a range of cultural scripts (Herman 1997). Moreover, as I have shown in relation to anarchist comics (2019a), multimodal cues and storytelling practices can seek to update a reader's domain assumptions as they move through a text by redefining or questioning aspects of the network. This relies on the plasticity of cognitive networks, which can grow and adjust over time. As such, domains aggregate new information into relevant domains, concretizing or renovating aspects of the network, or even adding subnetworks, depending on the expected or novel nature of the experiences.

Because domains are networks, how domains are represented can activate their content in a way that highlights and promotes particular inferences and connections and with varying degrees of granularity. Croft (2002) employs the notions of figure and ground to show how a representational cue highlights (figures, profiles) a particular piece of information within a domain, thereby facilitating access to the broader base (background) of that domain without necessarily requiring equal access to all details (see also Barcelona 2002, 2003). This is an economical approach to working memory (and prediction), which is focused on the goal of context-relevant comprehension (Gibbs and Tendahl 2006; Wilson and Sperber 2004). As will become important in subsequent chapters, which examine links across a range of cues in comics, highlighting primes a domain to ease access and interpretation of subsequent references to it through domain evocation and decompression, while simultaneously constraining other inferences and mappings to other domains through this focalization (Fauconnier and Turner 1999; Sweetser and Fauconnier 1996).

Because of the experiential grounding of domains, they network concrete and abstract information, including schematic logics (Clausner and Croft 1999), that can be activated and combined for a range of literal, metaphorical, and metonymic connections, which I discuss in more detail in the next two chapters. These connections are facilitated by how domains organize and categorize information, including based on roles, values, and so on. Domain-specific or categorical information can build metonymic connections within domains, or metaphorical mappings between them. The orchestration of schematic, concrete, and abstract information allows for creative elaborations and connections in inferential thinking. Likewise, how a domain is activated by a prompt, such as the degree of specificity and what is focused on, can produce quite different interpretations or construals of both the information being communicated and how it relates to the domain (Lakoff 1987). For instance, if a reader described the Aislin cartoon above as being about a person riding a toy on some water, the commentary about the specific type of toy (the jet-ski versus others like inflatable rings), the type of water (a lake versus a swimming pool or river), and the gender or other information about the man are lost. By removing different aspects of the imagery inherent in the fantasy, this reflection of the cartoon shows how degrees of abstraction impact access and impoverish comprehension. It also shows how typically categories are most useful at a lower scale of abstraction to maintain perceptually and conceptually significant qualities (Gibbs 2006a, 82–86), which link to other contextually and experientially significant information.

Finally, contexts play a significant role in how domains and particularly categories are accessed and employed. Experiential as well as communicative contexts provide parameters for domain activation by helping to prime and guide predictions and perceptions. For instance, the relevance of cues is gauged against expected contexts and usage patterns (see Wilson and Sperber 2004). Usage of a cue or category marker in a particular context, if expected, streamlines prediction and comprehension or, if it is atypical or unexpected, can become salient or noteworthy because it disrupts predicted patterns. Context, be it a given scenario or even a type of genre, primes particular domains (and even provide genre patterns) prior to engagement to facilitate comprehension, and as contextual and domain knowledge grows, so do the nuances of understanding (Kukkonen 2013a, ch. 2).

Aislin's cartoon offers notable examples of how several domains and categories are activated in conjunction to make its point. First, the written caption, which is placed in a titular position (itself a categorical or genre convention to signify text that encapsulates a subsequent work), invokes the domain of fantasy, of envisioning something unrealized yet desired after in some way. The words leave the actual content of the fantasy undetermined, prompting the reader to turn to the picture to figure out what it entails, to answer the reader's likely question, "fantasized about what?" To generate this question, the language has prompted the activation of the domains of fantasy, with its specific roles and values related to the fantasizer, object or person of attention, potential actions, a fictional realm of action, and so on. The fantasy domain is then applied to the pictographically represented domains of specific water sports or more general summertime activities, attempting to guide the applicability of the fantasy domain and to align its roles and values accordingly to the imagery. Finally, the domain of hunting or sniping is added through the pictorial element of the view-finder of a rifle's scope, which as a cue also highlights a particular agentive role within those domains. Readers are required to put all three major domains together to comprehend the cartoon in some way. How they align these domains will inform their interpretation of the fantasy and the various roles and values of the different figures depicted and inferred in relation to it. If the reader misses any one of these cues, they might conclude that Aislin promotes actual murder, or is wistful about summer coming soon, or fantasizes about hunting. The composite is much more nuanced and complex. Most notably, the fantasy domain substantially reconstrues the potential violence of the image by removing its enaction and instead focuses on the emotional tenor behind the act.

As an editorial cartoon, which as a genre typically responds to recent issues or events, context also plays a significant role in guiding interpretations of Aislin's work. Even without any specific context for the cartoon itself, readers might consider it a hyperbolic reflection of anger or irritation at the jet-skier's loud presence. Importantly, an annotation by Aislin at the McCord Museum gives more historical context for this cartoon's message. The note states that the "cartoon was drawn in reaction to the death of two small children in a Sea-Doo accident" on July 12, 1997, in the Chambly Basin in Quebec (Aislin 1997, n.p.). This annotation suggests that readers at the time would be particularly attuned to this context, which adds specific details to the domain of jet-skiing and the desire for justice or retribution. This context shows how Croft's notion of domain highlighting applies to cartoons, since within the Quebec social context of July 1997, the focus of the image on the rifle scope becomes a much more pointed outcry about the event, specific dangers of jet-skies, and potentially also a call for regulations (as retribution), rather than a more general comment on their presence. Contextual knowledge transforms this cartoon from a general situational concern to a more nuanced personal and socio-cultural comment that adds to an ongoing public conversation and seeks to even update domain knowledge about jet-skis.

3.4 DYNAMIC COGNITIVE PROCESSES

As I have discussed, attentional guidance, schemas, mental metaphors, and domain knowledge all play a crucial role as background cognitive guiderails for readers as they engage with Aislin's cartoon, and with comics in general. However, this cognitive perspective is incomplete without a clear understanding of how these multimodal elements activate and synthesize throughout the reading process, or, put another way, how short-term memory works through dynamic unconscious activation, prediction, inference, and conceptualization to build conscious comprehension and texture. Here I focus on the two most helpful insights in recent modeling of mental processes that align with and mobilize these features—mental simulation and mental space blending. These two insights succinctly illustrate how background perceptual and conceptual processes coalesce through cascades of meaning construction to build comprehension.

3.4.1 Mental Simulation

Research into mental simulation has unearthed a range of dynamic processes that expand in more detail on how people make inferences about environmental, social, and communicative cues to build conceptual understanding of a situation or a text. Lawrence Barsalou, a major early developer of the theory, offers this helpful synopsis:

> Simulation is the reenactment of perceptual, motor, and introspective states acquired during experience with the world, body, and mind. As an experience occurs (e.g., easing into a chair), the brain captures states across the modalities and integrates them with a multimodal representation stored in memory (e.g., how a chair looks and feels, the action of sitting, introspections of comfort and

relaxation). Later, when knowledge is needed to represent a category (e.g., chair), multimodal representations captured during experiences with its instances are reactivated to simulate how the brain represented perception, action, and introspection associated with it. (Barsalou 2008, 318–19)

Lisa Feldman Barret (2017) expands on this model to include emotional states and prediction. These inferential and predictive processes of object, intention, and pattern recognition inform a wide array of how people make experiences meaningful by mapping them into mental simulations of expectations and knowledge. Barrett summarizes the process as such:

> Your brain continually predicts and simulates all the sensory inputs from inside and outside your body, so it understands what they mean and what to do about them. These predictions travel through your cortex, cascading from the body-budgeting circuitry in your interoceptive network to your primary sensory cortices, to create distributed, brain-wide simulations, each of which is an instance of a concept. The simulation that's closest to your actual situation is the winner that becomes your experience, and if it's an instance of an emotion concept, then you experience emotion. [. . .] This is how brains and bodies create social reality. This is also how emotions become real. (151)

As such, she surmises elsewhere that "the human brain is a cultural artifact" (144) because it is informed by the acculturated buildup of concept simulations from the socio-cultural context in which and through which brains form meaning-constructing patterns.

Importantly, for mental simulation to function effectively in the ways described, a key requirement is that mental action becomes separated from bodily action, so that things can be manipulated and combined in mental imagery. Langacker refers to this as the subjectification and attenuation of cognition (2008, 528, 536–37). The abstracted nature of cognition also means that mental simulation functions opportunistically and incrementally (Bergen 2012), since it only builds a piecemeal mental image to suit the situation, or in the case of media, in response to textual cues and contexts. The activation of background knowledge and experiential information to build meanings unsurprisingly also reflects processes of memory formation, which include building more abstracted mappings between shared elements, but also more abstracted reflections of the experiences themselves. As such, activation and structure are always interwoven. As Adele Goldberg notes, memory is

> necessarily partially abstract insofar as the experience is not recorded completely. We might remember seeing a kumquat but we have abstracted away

from the color of the kitchen table upon which it sat; we also may have not noticed the tiny scratch or the exact length of its stem. So our mental representation of an experience, no matter how vivid, is partially abstracted from actual experience. (Goldberg 2013 in Hoffmann 2017, 4)

Thomas Hoffmann (2017) argues that the multimodal nature of experience and memory informs how meaning is made by activating common connections and patterns of experience as multimodal constructions, building up connections between similar experiences that can inform concept and category formation. Sociocultural and other background experiences serve an important role in enculturation and developing multiple literacies to facilitate clarity in communication through multimodal constructions. Nonetheless, despite these commonalities in reader cognitive processes, the variation of background knowledge between readers always leads to some degree of variation in comprehension and texture due to differences in how cues are simulated and their associated predictions and recalibrated prediction errors. Thus, for Aislin's cartoon, reader backgrounds will certainly influence how they simulate both the actions and intentions behind the text, since varied knowledges inform the predictions made about both the sniper and the jet-skier.

Mental simulation has also been suggested to play a crucial role in developing viewpoints and empathy (Freedberg and Gallese 2007; Mar and Oatley 2008; Zunshine 2006), since seeing bodily cues of someone else's mental state (such as through agitated gestures, tears, or smiles) or physical state (such as with a limp or blood) gives viewers clues to make inferential assessments and sympathize with the other's situation. As such, it is the cognitive process behind Theory of Mind (ToM), the ability to "recognize the thinking or feeling of others in order to predict their behaviors and act accordingly" (Megías-Robles et al. 2020, 2).[17] Moreover, sociocultural experience impacts how actions and interactions are assessed. Activating embodied experiences plays a crucial role in building rich connections with depicted subjects, including establishing a sense of empathetic vulnerability (Szép 2020). These are crucial features of intersubjectivity and sociality (Oberman, Winkielman, and Ramachandran 2010; Zwaan 2009), of which communicative artifacts play a significant role as extensions of minds (Hutchins 2005, 2010; Menary 2013).

Simulation also extends beyond this intersubjective attributional quality of ToM, since it allows people to also assess objects in various mediums for their interact-ability and to develop a sense of things and possible meanings and responses to them, including how and why others might access them in particular ways (Barsalou 1999, 2008; Freedberg and

Gallese 2007; Gallese 2003, 2005; Gallese and Lakoff 2005; Gibbs 2006). Thus, simulation extends to both people and the environment to facilitate action and comprehension.

These details about simulation in cognition allow for more specific observations about Aislin's cartoon and how it constructs salient and contrasting viewpoints, and how this leads to broader social functions as a sociocultural and cognitive artifact. Aislin's cartoon powerfully positions the reader in the role of the shooter of the jet-skier, locating the reader as an active participant considering the act of killing. For readers to feel as though they are inhabiting this viewpoint, they actively animate the perspectives and actions associated with the textual prompts to build a textually specific simulation. Simulation activates the general movement of the jet-ski along with more minute details of the figure's facial expressions, and the potential actions of the sniper, linking these to their relevant domains and possible meanings. These activations develop particular viewpoints and inferences about actions and fantasies. For instance, the unsympathetically caricatured facial expression of the rider suggests a laissez-faire, unconcerned attitude. The rider seems to be unaware of the potential for irritation or harm in his actions and is more interested in being, as he is labeled, a "hot dog," an ostentatious show off. This viewpoint contrasts with the presumed state of someone who is fantasizing about shooting him, which would either be that of a stoical sniper or, more likely in the historical context, an enraged avenger. Moreover, the cartoon could have presented the scenario in a different manner, such as by showing the jet-skier and sniper individually, but this would substantially alter the simulated qualities of the cartoon. However, such a presentation would weaken the message, making it feel less personal, because viewers would not align themselves in their mental simulation with the sniper's viewpoint. The alignment of viewpoints takes a clear position on the situation while also highlighting the relevance and significance of the caption about fantasy.

By positioning the reader as the sniper, the imagery presents a very clear revenge fantasy to illustrate the cartoon's title, and simulation makes the situation emphatically one-sided and personal. The modalities are orchestrated together to direct attention in several ways: by presenting a clear, active figure, a position in relation to him, and a question about how to engage from that position in contrast with the jet-skier's viewpoint. By simulating these contrasting viewpoints, and construing them through the framework of fantasy, the reader engages with the political positions around jet-skis. This includes, if they are historically engaged, connecting the position to the original scene that this cartoon reflects upon, that of the deaths of two children and the public calls for more justice and more safeguards in the future. In this caricature, Aislin emphasizes the obliviousness of the inconsiderate rider to contrast with the wider public outrage, acknowledging the powerful feelings of the public for revenge and control through his cartooned fantasy.

As readers simulate and predict their way through the cartoon's structured cues, they likely go through a cascade of textual experiences, correcting predictions as they build meaning. For instance, the fantasy might briefly seem to be about enjoying a care-free ride on a jet-ski until one recognizes the sniper's scope framing and re-construing the action, noting the prediction error that this cartoon is not just about jet-skiing. That initial emotional engagement with jet-skiing, at the same time may subtly inform how the reader simulates the actions of the sniper, and how repulsive or not they might find the act. Even at just these general levels of simulation, personal preferences and experiences, social and cultural values, acculturated concepts and historical knowledge, all play a role in simulating the active and affective meanings of the cartoon.

Importantly for a discussion of multimodal meaning, simulation is also essential for understanding metonymic and metaphorical expressions (Bergen 2012; Gibbs and Matlock 2008) and many other inferential processes in both literal and figurative language and art comprehension (Bergen 2005; Gibbs 2006b; Matlock 2004). In Aislin's case, the cartoon seems to operate primarily through metonymic rather than metaphoric forms, since it continues to comment upon the same domain of jet-skiing and to construe it through a caricature of the rider. However, it also blends the scene with a particularly militaristic or revengeful response. This antagonistic fantasy likely reflects the tenor of public debates, therein drawing on the metaphorical notion of ARGUMENT IS WAR, in which there are winners and losers based on different styles of argumentation, including perhaps editorial cartooning. On this metaphorical level, the cartoon also purposefully activates (through fantasy) a particular view of public discourse that is emotionally valanced and divorced from direct retribution. Thus, metonymic and metaphorical qualities blend together to inform how readers might interpret the cartoon.

No matter which types of response the reader might be inclined toward for the cartoon and the tragedy it responds to, it is clear that images and words prompt complex simulations that present connections between elements with unique structure and content in order to develop a dynamic scene with emotional, social, and political valences (see also Mar and Oatley 2008; Oatley 1999; Prinz 2004). The ability to make predictions and inferences across modalities at varying levels of abstraction shows how simulation is at the core of meaning construction by activating multimodal, embodied, acculturated, and intertextual knowledges. While mental simulation articulates how modalities activate prior knowledge to make predictions and connections through simulation, this concept does not fully describe how inferences and projections combine into coherent mental imagery, conceptualization, and global comprehension. This combinatory apparatus at the core of cognition is clarified through the theory of mental space or conceptual integration, often referred to as "blending."

3.4.2 Blending as Online Assemblage

Aislin's cartoon shows how a single panel can present information strategically, through the presentation of various verbal and visual cues, the perceived positioning of the reader, and the use of framing techniques that impact gestalt connections. The most comprehensive approach for showing how these complex types of cues build, extend, or transform into meaning is the theory of mental spaces and conceptual integration—also called blending. While there is still ongoing research and debate about some aspects of the process (Gibbs 2000; Barrett 2017, 151), there seems to be general agreement that conceptual integration operates along these lines as the engine of meaning-making. Understanding the blending model, therefore, helps analysts articulate how meaning is most likely being made by integrating central observations about cognitive topology and activation processes. In particular, blending helps to document how specific combinations of information from different domains and across levels of embodied experience (including both metaphorical and metonymic conceptualizations) can meld together in the dynamic, in-the-moment processes of meaning-making and comprehension.

Mental spaces, the foundation of the blending model, are "small conceptual packets constructed as we think and talk, for purposes of local understanding and action . . . [and] can be used generally to model dynamic mappings in thought and language" (Fauconnier and Turner 2002, 40). Mental spaces are in essence the cognitive building blocks that result from the abstracted and domain-organized nature of long-term memory being activated through mental simulation as predictions and inferences are developed. Mental spaces are highly restricted, economical, malleable, and context-specific, drawing on relevant information from across the spectrum of embodiment and with the goal-oriented and context-dependent biases of cognition. These spaces reflect mental simulation making pieces of relevant information accessible in short-term memory, so that readers can predict, assess, combine, reject, and infer or interpret as part of the largely non-conscious process of meaning-making.

Blending takes mental spaces a step further to articulate how these spaces combine, often in cascades of meaning-making, to develop elaborate meanings with internal and emergent logics distinct from the original mental spaces and background information activated by a given cue. In short, it shows how incremental activations and simulations of cues develop into more detailed mental scenarios, conscious textural experiences, and interpretations of a text. As a model of meaning construction, it incorporates the mapping principles attributed to metaphorical, metonymic, and analogical processes (Grady 2005), thereby positing a consistent cognitive "model of creativity" (Fauconnier and Turner 2002; Turner 1999, 2014). Blending can operate within or between modalities and the principles remain essentially the same. Much of the blending process is unconscious, but understanding the different parameters of blending helps readers and critics unpack the processes that gave a text a given texture.

To build a composite blend of information, two or more mental spaces selectively project salient information into a combined mental space, the blend, that has its own emergent structure. The emergent structure can remain the end product, can be projected back into the input spaces for the purposes of reassessment, or can be further blended with other mental spaces. Thus the process of blending fulfills the purposes of composition, completion, or elaboration (Fauconnier and Turner 2002, 345). Furthermore, blends regularly compress aspects of input spaces in order to highlight their critical features and to facilitate their subsequent use (Fauconnier and Turner 2000; Turner 2006), much as Croft (2002) describes domain activations discussed above. Blending offers a means of distinguishing how communicative cues strategically activate synergistic responses that inform meaning construction and interpretive processes.

Connections between mental spaces are facilitated by how they are presented (such as Aislin's orchestration of cues), the topological structure and detail of the reader's background information stored in long-term memory, and how this information is activated in relation to the text. Projections and cross-mappings between mental spaces occur through vital relations, such as shared roles, values, space, time, change, analogy, properties, similarity, and category (Fauconnier and Turner 2002, 92–102). In other words, mental spaces connect either through shared cognitive topological features or experientially and textually informed patterns, such as Hoffmann's multimodal constructions. Vital relations play a significant role in particular in the discussion of sequentiality and temporality in subsequent chapters, since the vital relations of roles and figuration, for instance, help readers connect repeated images together as a single character in action. Thus, vital relations guide in-the-moment blends in response to cues. Blending thereby integrates the earlier discussion of perception, attention, and prediction into a model of conceptualization and interpretation.

As discussed above, the meanings of Aislin's cartoon are constructed through the strategic engagement with the main domains of jet-skis (and within it a more specific domain about the accident at Chambly Basin), of shooting or killing, and of fantasy. A blending analysis articulates clearly how reader engagements with the cartoon and the activations of domain knowledge build mental spaces and contribute to the texture of the cartoon. While much of what I have discussed already has elements of blending behind it, it can be beneficial to comprehensively diagram how readers likely navigate the cues to construct meaning (see Figure 3.5). While such diagrams will not be a common feature of future chapters (as I tend to write out the blending process instead), they can be an important analytical tool. The following diagram illustrates the core principles of vital relations mappings and blending processes described above, including employing the blending framework's concept of backward projection, which illustrates a final prediction error testing and assessment process by using the blended composite meanings to consider the role of fantasy in response to a real-world problem.

This diagram shows how mental spaces are often established in hierarchical or embedded relations according to different domain roles and values, in particular a distinction between two kinds of agent that align with distinct social values. Modalities help establish and anchor these relations through their orchestration in the source text. For the cognitive processing of the cartoon, each prompted domain (fantasy, jet-skiing, the recent accident, and the sniper) is established as its own mental space at a strategic time, with specific connections to the others through their ordering (starting with the framing of fantasy) and through to the actions embedded in different agentive viewpoints. These interactions establish contributions to the resultant blend and overall meaning.

The beginning caption sets up an alternative mental space of fantasy, in which all actions visualized are not real and may even be considered socially unacceptable. The statement is presented as a truism from a commentator, establishing the domain of fantasy to construe the depiction as non-factual or viable, such that the caption both establishes and simultaneously negates

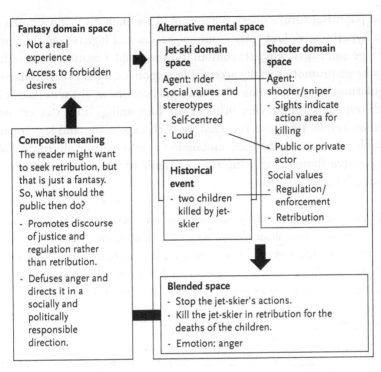

Figure 3.5 Mental spaces diagram illustrating how cross mappings, blending, and backward projection build composite meaning.

the depiction of a potential murder. As Dancygier and Vandelanotte summarize, "negation may be used to reject a viewpointed understanding of a situation, rather than negating the truth of a fact" (2016, 17), such as acknowledging the tragic events while also rejecting a particular response to it. In this case, this inherent rejection promotes alternativity, which "profiles an alternative epistemic stance" (Dancygier and Sweetser 2014, 149). The opening caption establishes a global mental space for enactment and assessment, thereby acknowledging through negation that it is a common feeling to want to seek revenge for the death of innocent children, while also not supporting a violent reaction. The powerful simulation of the subsequent blend of the domains of personally killing the freewheeling jet-skier serves to acknowledge the public anger and potential desire for retribution for the tragic event in Chambly Basin.

At the same time, the framing of the entire cartoon in terms of fantasy negates the violent reaction, serving to acknowledge the desire and redirect it at the same time. The resultant backward projection to the domain of fantasy that encloses the blend builds inferences that might be put as this question: "If we cannot actually kill the negligent rider

MULTIMODALITY AND COGNITION [65]

(and potential future ones), what should we then do?" The simulation of a hyperbolic violent retribution expresses and legitimizes the public outrage and anger, while its combination with the negation space of fantasy helps promote socially acceptable responses, such as discussions of regulations or prohibitions of jet-skis and how one might seek justice for such tragedies and prevent others from happening. Thus, this editorial cartoon fulfills its social function by both expressing and legitimizing a public sentiment and then mobilizing it in a call for alternative and progressive thought, shifting the epistemic viewpoint on the tragedy. Elisabeth El Refaie notes,

> Political cartoons generally operate on two distinct levels: on one level, they tell an imaginary story about a make-believe world, while on a second, more abstract level, they refer to real-life events and characters. [. . .] A viewer who understands a cartoon on the level of its fictional narrative may nevertheless struggle to discern its real-life referents, since this kind of interpretation requires some interest in public affairs and knowledge of politics. (El Refaie 2009, 186)

As I have diagrammed here, documenting the blending process, combining perceptual and conceptual content, reveals how the two levels of meaning in this political cartoon are established. It can also isolate where variations in interpretation arise. The cartoon will obviously vary in its meaningfulness to different viewers, depending on their own social values around jet-skis, their historical background knowledge around the events that inspired the cartoon, and how they attend to and integrate the different elements of the cartoon.

This seemingly straightforward cartoon demonstrates how many layers of complexity can exist within a single panel. Importantly, the presentation of cues helps establish relationships that guide inference patterns in important directions and for emotional and political effects. If the fantasy domain was included in a different relation, such as through a thought bubble for the jet-ski rider, the resultant blend and backward projections would shift dramatically, perhaps to make a case for the rider's innocence because of distraction or for criminal charges because of a murderous daydream showing intent. The patterned orchestration of modalities—the attentional guidance that activates knowledge in strategic ways—is crucial to their interpretation because it fosters specific cascades of simulations and blends that establish positions, combinations, and extensions of the source domains and backward projections.

3.5 CONCLUSION: THE POWER OF THE MULTIMODAL MENTAL IMAGE

As I have shown through the example of Aislin's cartoon, such multimodal works prompt a range of responses in readers by directing attention through textual cues and highlighting particular aspects of their content through the affordances of modalities, and in turn how readers make inferences through mental simulations and creative combinations that rely on background knowledge. While I have focused here on a single cartoon, the following chapters develop the complexity of cognitive interactions across longer sequences and layouts of panels. Importantly, how modalities are orchestrated and presented within panels (such as this cartoon) and in longer texts informs how readers parse, unpack, interpret, and reinterpret them. While readers may prioritize one mode over another—most typically words over images, or images with characters over images without them—such perceptual engagements also adapt to the structure, content, and generic and pragmatic goals of the text as it begins and as it unfolds. Thus, there are general patterns of engagement, but there is no definitive hierarchy or fixed relations within or between images, words, and layouts.[18] Rather, analysts must be sensitive to specific textual features, and the range of potentialities or affordances for engagement and interpretation.[19] Tracking the cognitive topology and potential activational processes helps ground textual interpretations in the medium-specific qualities of the text and possible responses or texture.

Because of this idiosyncratic complexity, Bateman (2014) makes a strong case for engaging with image and text relationships in medium- and context-specific ways (see also Bateman and Wildfeuer 2014) that focus on their semantic and pragmatic qualities. As Bateman (2014) notes, there are a range of interactions between pictures and text that inform their contributions to the emergent meaning, often anchoring one modality in relation to the other so as to extend, elaborate, enhance, contest, contrast, or explain the other, which Aislin's cartoon evinced with the framing action of the title for the image. Bateman argues that this range of interactions gives different types of signs different functions (such as placing text in a speech balloon or outside the panel as narration), and that these combinations complicate the model of meaning construction. Understanding mental space blending helps shed light on how these varied combinations work. As such, I follow Bateman in focusing on the emergence of composite meaning (115), within which modalities work both separately and synthetically toward particular textual aims, including narratological and rhetorical goals.[20] Thus, interactions within and between modalities need to be contextualized within the discursive forms and functions and pragmatic aims of a text (cf. 205–11, 234–38), which a focus on mental simulation and blending helps elucidate.

The cognitive model I have begun to develop here accounts for these needs by isolating types of knowledge (schemas, domains, metaphors) that structure cognitive topology, how they are activated through mental simulation, and how they develop into novel meanings through blending. This cohesive set of cognitive parameters and processes link perception to multimodal conceptualization to show how personal texture emerges from engagement with a multimodal text. Crucial to this process is the piecemeal responsive and predictive construction of novel and creative mental scenarios, no matter how serious or absurd, truthful or nonsensical, that are continually checked against the mediated communicative context and updated whenever new information, or alternative interpretations, are required.

CHAPTER 4
Paneling Construal and Viewpoint

Abstractions, Bodies, and Synesthetic Forms

4.1 VIEWPOINT AND CONSTRUAL: FROM THE BODY TO THE WORLD

How bodies and spaces are presented in a comic impacts how readers construe the content and attribute viewpoints to various aspects in panels and across stories. As discussed in relation to simulation theory in the previous chapter, viewpoint is broader than character-level attributions of Theory of Mind, and includes attributions of agency and intention to the epistemic stance of narratological choices and storyworld comprehension, the construction of which rely dominantly on stylistic choices associated with bodies and spaces. Construal refers to these different choices that build viewpoints, and it is especially helpful at highlighting broader narratological stances that can fall outside of character-level attributions of intent (Kukkonen 2013, ch. 3). In this chapter, I remain focused largely on singular panels or short sequences to engage the development of viewpoint and construal of content at their initial compositional construction and take on longer sequences in later chapters. This approach helps to isolate a number of important features and conventions that build from the previous chapter's discussion of attentional guidance and simulation in a cartoon. The focus on panels shows especially readerly connections between perception and simulated blending processes in the construction of viewpoint and construal of content based on stylistic choices surrounding the depiction of bodies and scenes. These construals and viewpoint attributions are the opening volleys in storyworld construction, since they offer the first hints of "blueprints for a specific mode of world-creation" (Herman 2009a, 105).

To engage with aspects of construal and viewpoint in style and composition, I have chosen three interwoven aspects that highlight the importance of cognitive processes. Abstraction is always a part of communication and cognition, since it interweaves history and enculturation in memory with attention and prediction in perception and the attribution of meaning to often incomplete forms. Abstraction serves as a helpful stepping-off point into a discussion of construal of subject matters, since it highlights the active role of cognition in developing meaning, and how stylistic and generic choices can impact simulative and blending processes, at both the concrete levels of the multimodal text and how these link to higher-order generic domains. I begin by linking genre and abstraction, to show how cognitive activations of viewpoints and construal are always situated in discursive concerns. I then go on to show how more specific communicative choices around abstracted bodies highlight the role of simulations and biases in cognition to develop more nuanced character viewpoints and emotional depths. Finally, I show how more conventional cues leverage synesthetic qualities of indexical signs to construe and viewpoint verbal information. By linking abstraction, embodiment, and convention, I seek to highlight the interwoven levels of viewpoint and construal that pervade multimodal compositionality in comics.

4.2 ABSTRACTION AND VIEWPOINT CONSTRUAL: INTERPRETING GENRE AND STYLE

The multimodal cues in a panel are fragments of a storyworld, fictional or actual. As such, they are always incomplete and somewhat abstracted and separated from experience. Such perceived components do not pose a problem for cognition since all of perception is piecemeal and continually stitched together. This is an energy-efficient approach to engaging and assessing the significance of information, prioritizing some aspects over others and integrating them into meaningful actions and experiences (see Barrett 2017; Barsalou 2009; Fabry 2017; Kukkonen 2020). This is why gestalt impressions are so important, since they guide this stitchwork. Moreover, creators of mediated forms of communication like comics can harness this capacity for working with fragments and abstraction to be strategic in construing how readers might engage their subject matter and imagine a very particular kind of storyworld.

Modalities offer a range of possible stylistic choices which allow for different construals of a subject, while also giving readers opportunities for personal engagement with a work by requiring them to in-fill around and unpack the significance of such choices. As art psychologist Rudolf Arnheim observes, "images are pictures to the extent to which they portray things located at a lower level of abstractness than they are themselves. . . . Pictures are not mere replicas. . . . Abstractness is the means by which the picture interprets what it portrays" (Arnheim 2015). Similarly Robert Solso asserts that "all art is abstract, more or less" (1994, 233), ranging from the realism of "representational art" to the conceptual interests of "abstract art" (see also Medley 2010). As such, this range of abstractness from realism to conceptualism lead Medley and Haddad (2011, throughout) to argue for the concept of "the realism continuum," wherein a representation shares an affinity with what it represents to a greater or lesser degree. Much like language, which is much more abstracted from experience, pictures and other modes and qualities of representation are also distanced from experience by how they select and present cues that strategically activate embodied knowledge. How something is presented, even in pictorial form (and including what Gardner 2011 calls "line style"), contributes substantially to the meaningfulness of a panel. Meaning emerges through the many opportunities for interpretation that fragmentation and abstraction provide.

The multimodal complexity of most panels complicates how elements may be interpreted by a reader. Representation is the use of a modality (signifying form) to highlight or profile particular qualities of experience through abstraction and presentation within a particular system of codes and discourse contexts. For instance, how people draw varies (beyond differences in ability) by contextual and pragmatic concerns: the same artist would create differently for a game of Pictionary than for the court room since these contexts provide distinct constraints and communicative or generic aims. Similarly, each of the abstracted choices of a panel's content contributes to its meaning on a number of levels from orchestrated connections to intertextual links, including its construal of the subject matter and the addition of metaphorical and metonymic connections.

The variability of representation means that readers develop different inferences and interpretations based on subtle representational cues, including in visual styles, such as types of caricature or shading that add perceptual qualities to the storyworld that can heighten associated mental imagery and blends, even if they are less realistic from an objective perspective. For instance, each of the bodies included in figures in this book, drawn by a wide range of artists in many styles, is similarly simulated as a living body in an active space, despite varying substantially in terms of perspectives, details, or abstracted features (more on this later). Moreover, their bodies may range in typicality from the teenager to the cyborg to the animal or even plant, and yet aspects of body-ness continue to be activated and blended as part of readerly engagement. Such diversity can be accounted for in terms of how readers naturalize the degrees of veridicality exhibited by a work to their own understanding of experience. E. H. Gombrich (1959) describes this as "the beholder's share" in meaning-making. Gombrich notes that by focusing on "likeness" or objective mimicry in art (and arguably in most other modes of representation) analysts may miss out on valuable layers of possible information and textual experiences—on what Peter Stockwell (2009) calls the "texture" of the reader's experiences of texts. Gombrich suggests that analysis should include a deeper look at experiential equivalences imbedded in forms and functions that prompt textual experiences of veracity and stasis, illusions and dynamicity, and more, through the viewer's construction of specific relationships. Karen Kukkonen (2013a, 2014, 2016, 2020) expands on this by examining how the fragmented and open nature of communicative cues and genres relies on the reader's or viewer's capacity to in-fill key aspects of content and personal nuance through predictive and inferential reasoning, including regarding fictionality and genre conventions. Kukkonen links this capacity to both viewing art (connecting to Gombrich's crucial research) and reading (connecting to Iser's reader response theory).

Mental simulation and blending theories outlined in the previous chapter confirm these arguments. As I will continue to explore, the blending framework helps showcase the communicative value of these mappings at various levels of relation, from complex domain knowledge about roles and values, down to more categorical or prototype markers, structural patterns, and nuanced inferences. The experience of a text or work of art is constructed in part by equivalence mappings across many different levels of granularity or abstractness to populate mental imagery that is itself abstracted and malleable in nature. Moreover, complex blends go beyond equivalence to project or elaborate on meanings as well through novel constructions beyond our experiential domains, into the fantastical.

4.2.1 Abstraction, Genre, and Construal in *The Photographer*

The non-fictional account of *The Photographer* by Didier Lefèvre, Emmanuel Guibert, and Frédéric Lemercier (2009) offers an helpful example of how different types and qualities of representation can construe and nuance perspectives and interpretations. This graphic narrative presents Lefèvre's experiences traveling in 1986 as a French photographer documenting a *Doctors Without Borders* (*Médecins Sans Frontières* [MSF]) mission to Afghanistan during the first Afghan War. The text combines Lefevre's photographs and writings with Guibert's drawings and adapted text as a form of collaborative memoir.[1] The following selection (Figure 4.1) offers several noteworthy elements that show how a comic can develop multimodal resonances between different visual styles in the pictorial modality to develop a richer textual experience of the subject matter. First, note the stark contrasts between the two types of images that present the story, the detailed, black-and-white photographs taken by Lefèvre on his trip, and the simply colorful abstract line drawings by Guibert and Lemercier that fill in the story. Second, the stylistic contrasts are heightened by the fact that the vast majority of narration and dialogue occurs in the drawings, leaving the photographs silent. Furthermore, there are multiple viewpoints and perspectives taken that develop contrasts and nuance to the story. I will examine each of these features in more detail below.

First, the contrast between black-and-white photographs and colorful line drawings gives two types of images with different associated senses of realism that develop two contrasting viewpoint simulations. The photograph presents exactly what the photographer sees through

Figure 4.1 Selection from *The Photographer* by Lefèvre, Guilbert, and Lemercie (2009, 48).

PANELING CONSTRUAL AND VIEWPOINT   [73]

the camera and specifically chooses to record. The drawings, on the other hand, present the photographer in a wider dynamic context, including the surrounding people and conversations. In reading both of these images, readers likely simulate in much the same way the movements and activities of the child riding the donkey, the people walking, and so on, which blends them together as a unified reality. Yet, the photograph gives substantially more detail, presenting a more realistic view of a specific scene at the given moment, which aligns with its documentary function. However, somewhat ironically, while rich in detail, there is a paucity of information within in it about the photograph's context, which the drawings instead contribute. This contextualization includes populating the reader's mental imagery with colorful scenes and characters' voices, motivations, and actions. In a way, by adding more perceptual and viewpointed details, the drawings make the photographs more real than if they were presented alone. On the other hand, the photographs, as documentary artifacts, anchor the expressive drawings in a specific moment in history.

Both types of image offer different qualities of experience and senses of realism through their unique representational choices, grounding aspects of interpretation in genre expectations of each form as either documentative or expressive. As Hoffmann and Bergs (2018) show in their application of cognitive grammar to genre theory, genre is an experiential construction that is formed at multiple levels of granularity in order to link form and meaning while also remain responsive to new expressions and uses (see also Kukkonen 2013a). As such, genres act like crucial abstract domains that texts are aligned with, which guides interpretations, since the domains activate specific inferential logics and entailments. The documentary or journalistic genre of the photograph helps readers interpret them as a silent, factual record, whereas the drawings are conceived of as post-hoc personal narration (journal, memoir, autobiography) that adds the subjective qualities of the dynamic context surrounding the photographs. While journalistic in nature, the photograph should not necessarily be taken as a neutral, objective fact, but as another form of strategic recording with qualities of focus and framing informing what the viewer sees and responds to (Lopes 2016). The graphic narrative foregrounds this subjectivity, by including strips of camera film with multiple shots and only one circled in red, showing how the photographer sought to capture or construct a particular image and selects only one among many that matches a particular aspect best. Thus, both types of image highlight viewpoints and narrative spaces, but in subtly different ways that align with different generic domain logics and intentionality.

While being distinct in terms of their abstractedness or realism and their genre affiliations, the photographs and drawn images both work together to develop the narrative. For instance, each of the photographs in this example develops the narrative by framing the drawings. In the first panel readers likely focus on the faces of the child and parent and simulate their gaze as joint attention, which lends the photograph an intersubjective interactivity, which might include aspects of seeking out intentions and actions regarding both the refugees and the photographer's group. When joint attention is broken, as the refugees pass by, the photographer must turn to others to query the actions of the travelers, not understanding what they are doing. The drawn panels fill in details about the refugees, expanding on the questions raised by the intersubjective hint in the opening photograph. Thus, the simulation of gaze and motion from the photographs establishes a human-interest scene that then becomes populated with intentions and motivations from the drawings. The attribution of these more subjective qualities in the middle panels, which are developed in the dialogue between the photographer and his companion, are complemented by the sparse drawings, which in a sense remove the outer details of the figures to heighten attention to their potential inner motives as agents in a dynamic world. Contemporary Western assumptions about photographs (as documentary records) and drawings (as personal, intentional expressions) support these inferences, since each uses its function to establish and construe its content, while also collaborating with and nuancing the other style.

As this short example shows, abstraction in, and genre expectations for, representational style functions to focus attention on different viewpoints and values within a narrative and to drive the development of specific mental spaces that can elaborate upon or decompress cues (see Pedri 2011 for a more thorough engagement with the larger story). Choices in representation impact mental simulations by focusing the reader's attention on particular features over others, through abstraction and framing, and by building from associated domain-specific assumptions about types of representation and genres. Here, the photographs emphasized a silent journalistic witness to the details of a specific moment. The drawings and dialogue work together to expand on how others interpret those moments and the viewpoints of those involved, especially the photographer's subjective perceptions and experiences of this world and the figures he encounters. In this example, simulating the singular viewpoint of photographic details, and then populating them with the colorfulness of both exterior environments and intersubjective intentions, gives this sequence its rich power as both documentary history and personal story, as readers develop a viewpoint for the photographer, his knowledgeable companion, and to some extent a projected understanding of the Afghan refugees.

The potential for viewpoint development and complication, including through assumptions about genre and style, is crucial to the function of both images and text and becomes more complex as they develop multimodally and sequentially in comics. While I focus on aspects of it here, viewpoint will also pervade the discussions in this book, because it pervades communicative modalities and human experience.

4.3 AGENTIVE BODIES AND EMOTIONS

4.3.1 Figure-ground Configurations: Interwoven Schematic, Literal, and Metaphorical Meanings

So far, character and narrative viewpoints have been considered through the lens of pictorial abstraction and its connection to genre values, as well as briefly through character interactions and joint attention or shared gaze. I turn now to expand on these bodily cues that add nuance to actions and interactions. Readers make many inferences about interactions and intentions by simulating how bodies are represented, based on bodily cues like their spatial positions, postures, gestures, gazes, and expressions. All of these cues contribute to viewpoint and action comprehension, including by often clarifying or adding to the meaning of dialogue and narration. For instance, Mittelberg (2013, 2017, 2018) shows that gestures often encode meaningful schemas and force dynamics that serve semantic and pragmatic functions in communication. These dynamic aspects of gesture can also be approximated in a static form like comics, and reactivated through mental simulation. I examine the construction of what Will Eisner (2008b) calls "expressive anatomy" (which includes facial expression, gaze, posture, and gesture) to represent bodily states of being, interaction, and motivation. I show how mental simulation and blending of these cues draw on embodied mental metaphors about identities, intentions, and ideas to build character viewpoints and even narrative world epistemology.

When viewers see a figure, no matter how photorealistic or abstract in depiction, they generally simulate the represented bodily state in order to understand and interpret it.[2] This is particularly important in comics, in which many panels often include active figures from a range of perspectives and distances. How readers simulate these figures is predicated on prototypical assumptions about how bodies and objects function in space. Cognition tends to bias toward what one might consider normative inferences, unless

[76]   *Comics and Cognition*

a reader's background knowledge and experiences or other textual cues shift that inferential process toward alternative interpretations.

How figures are simulated is also informed by visual depictive and compositional strategies that guide perception (as discussed in the previous chapter), like the orientations and weights of cues prompting gestalt patterns and assumptions about viewpoints and interactions, including power dynamics. For example, in a scene in Brian K. Vaughan and Pia Guerra's *Y: The Last Man* series (Figure 4.2), two consecutive panels present two different perspectives on a central antagonist, Victoria, the leader of the "Daughters of the Amazon." The first panel focuses on Victoria's face, speech, and gun. The panel focuses in on her face and emphasizes her words by placing the speech balloon at the top of the panel. Readers likely focus first briefly on her face (because of the intersubjective perception bias toward gaze connection and interaction), which is also nearly centered in the panel, lightly colored, and framed by the dark shadow on her cheek and the dark gun. Readers then likely turn to read her spoken words (another gestalt and literacy bias discussed in the previous chapter) before turning back to the whole image and connecting the speaker to her words and the gun. The layout of the language creates a string of words that lead down to her face, reinforcing the indexical link between speech balloons and the character. Her term, "observe," seems to invite the reader to examine the

Figure 4.2 Yorick's execution scene in Vaughan and Guerra's *Y: The Last Man: Cycles* (2003, 89).

gun, which appears to be offered to them, reaching almost out of the panel toward them.

Tracing likely readerly movements around the modalities in this panel sheds light on the orchestration of speech and objects that form a multimodal and experiential loop within the panel. Interestingly, readers likely end up focused on the gun at the top-left of the panel, which creates a break in the flow of reading from left to right, in particular since the gun and her face point left. This circular and bifurcated perceptual experience within the panel likely creates a slight pause for the reader, as the reader builds up their own momentum to move their attention back in the right-ward direction to keep reading the next panel. This contrasts to the conventional pictorial encoding of actions to align them with the reading path, such as having a figure walking in the direction of reading, which creates a textual momentum that can be used and manipulated for various effects (Borkent 2017). This slight pause builds both a hint of suspense and lends weight to Victoria's words, which aligns with the sense of superiority or authority granted her by the slightly upward perspective toward her face, and her looking down her nose at the reader. The panel orchestrates each cue to position the viewer in a passive position, as one of the "sisters" perhaps, from which to respond to the powerful figure's statement.

The second panel picks up on the same focus on Victoria as a powerful figure, but repositions the reader as a more distant observer. This shift in perspective and intimacy reinforces the power dynamics of the initial panel with a clear hierarchy among three sets of characters, while contextualizing her words in a broader scene in which the reader becomes aware of the crowd of "sisters" (her gang of "Amazons") observing the impending execution of the story's protagonist, Yorick. Whereas the first panel focuses on the leader, the second positions her in relation to others, zooming out to contextualize her actions and statement. The high-contrast darkened figures at the center of the image again draw the reader's attention as a unit, which also serves to highlight the evocative postures of the executioner and the captive Yorick. The third dark character on the right is Yorick's sister, Hero, who has just captured and turned him over to Victoria. Yorick's lower position matches the perspective of the previous panel, allowing the reader to connect them together. The reader might feel an affinity with or empathy for Yorick in this case, as they have just inhabited his physical position in their simulated scenario for the previous panel. Furthermore, the lower center of perspective in the second panel maintains this subtle affinity with the captive, rather than with the crowd, as the reader simulates Yorick's lower perspective and continues to experience it with him. These visual cues help the reader simulate and blend an empathetic character viewpoint.

Readers will also simulate the bodily states and language of the other characters in relation to Yorick. For instance, by simulating the executioner's collected and focused stance, which has aligned her eye and gun with Yorick's head, a reader likely infers her intentions very quickly by activating domain knowledge about guns and executions, surmising that death is imminent. This reveal follows nicely from the slower, circular display of the gun in the previous panel to build more emphasis on the focus and purpose of the leader's actions. Likewise, readers will recognize and simulate the shared attention of the crowd on this scene. Nobody is distracted. These viewpoint-aligning parameters create a very linear, focused, and dualistic antagonism between the man and the group of women. This singular focus also allows for a surprise twist to occur from outside the panel shortly thereafter to allow Yorick's escape. All of these aspects involve controlled framing of perspectives and bodily actions to guide the reader's attention and to build up suspense. Even this cursory focus on how multimodal orchestrations of bodies and objects inform perception and mental simulation to blend elements together shows how viewpoint qualities of power dynamics, intentionality, and empathy are subtly constructed throughout a scene. But this only scratches the surface.

Further cognitive features and functions scaffold a reader's engagement with this scene. The perceptual emphasis on schemas and perceptual gestalts (presented in the previous chapter in connection to mental metaphors) is helpful here to clarify interpretations of figuration and pictorial orchestration. For instance, in the first panel, a reader's gestalt process of object completion allows them to assume and simulate Victoria as having a complete body connected to Victoria's represented talking head. Object completion functions as a form of perceptual metonymy to allow people to respond to an object as whole even when only catching a glimpse of part of it. This process includes activating prototypical and schematic notions of the *body schema* (Gallagher 2005), that is, the network of sensorimotor perceptions tied to our bodies, including movements, postures, and so forth. Body schemas operate primarily at an unconscious level and include biomechanical constraints (Bonnet, Paulos, and Nithart 2005). Encoded in the body schema is the assumption of the surrounding, manipulatable environment (called peripersonal space) in which the body acts. The body schema, therefore, helps build mappings among domain knowledge, categories and prototypes, and other embodied experiences to promote simulations and blends, in particular ones that relate to specific inferences and interpretations about agent and object states and relations

(Abdel-Raheem 2017). The body schema supports conceptualization in the first panel, which focuses on just a face and hand, by prompting the assumption that the head is attached to a body in space, and that this is the same body that is holding the gun. The color of Victoria's jacket helps maintain the body schema integrity by mapping together her wrist and torso. Proximity of the cues also help maintain this connection. In this example, readers employ a generic placeholder from the body schema to construct a basic mental space for a singular character and viewpoint, which the next panel then populates with more specific details, intentions, contexts, as well as other viewpoints associated with other characters. The body schema helps readers interpret the posture of the leader, as well as integrate this with her peripersonal space and the other characters. The body schema further builds action, since it helps readers form a blended simulation of her movements through shifting force dynamics between the panels, since the bodily posture changes from displaying to aiming the gun. The body schema plays a crucial role in helping build these connections through mappings among key features of figures, movements (cause and effect), and expressions, and helps readers interpret the change as a dramatic gesture.

Specific domains and mental metaphors are also evoked by pictorial and verbal cues that further elaborate on the significance of the bodily gestures and power dynamics. The broad domains of gender dynamics, execution, and Judeo-Christian stories help readers interpret the actions and underlying concerns about patriarchy and heroism that are major themes in the comic series (Khng 2016; Mellette 2021) and which are glimpsed in these panels. Mental metaphors can provide shortcuts and assumptions that direct simulations and blending patterns around these domains regarding orientations, viewpoints, roles and values, and broader social commentaries. Górska (2018, 2019) shows how schemas facilitate the blending of metonymic and metaphoric functions in cartoons to build multimodal expressions. Such schematic constructions include primary metaphors like UP IS GOOD, KNOWING IS SEEING, or BODY IS SELF, all of which add to the meaningfulness of this scene. For instance, the orientational hierarchy of the leader and the captive reinforces a clear power dynamic based on the UP-DOWN schema and its conceptual associations with power and morality through the UP IS GOOD and UP IS CONTROL mental metaphors. While readers might not accept Victoria's position as morally acceptable, her group looks up to her as a leader, and so her powerful figuration reflects their group viewpoint. The different proximities of the characters in the second panel creates clear insider-outsider dynamics, since the distant group of women are closely interconnected through similarities in features, orientations, proximity, and gaze. The group contrast to the lone captive in the foreground, which uses CONTAINER, FIGURE-GROUND, EXPULSION, as well as UP-DOWN schemas to reify polarized social dynamics. The shared vectors of gazes (a collective gaze) from the group against the sole captive (and the reader behind him) further builds a schematic perception of this antagonistic viewpoint dynamic that aligns opposing moral values and power relations.

The mental metaphors of SEEING IS KNOWING, BODY IS SELF, and OBJECTS ARE ABSTRACT ENTITIES are especially helpful for structuring and guiding inferences about complex character viewpoints and narrative world epistemology within and across modalities in comics. In this example, as discussed, the leader entreats her followers to "observe" as she makes a new reality unfold, which invokes the mental metaphor of SEEING IS KNOWING. Witnessing here is as much a conceptual development as a perceptual phenomenon. The group's witnessing of the execution affirms its meaningfulness in establishing a new world order. Thus, the metaphor ABSTRACT ENTITIES ARE OBJECTS also plays a role in readers reinterpreting the gun as both an object as well as the vehicle for transformation, conceptually compressing cause and effect into a singular item.

The execution domain, which connects to moral purity in the second panel, also reflects the BODY IS SELF metaphor, since the killing of the body is the killing of an individual self, a unique entity. This metaphor is further connected to the mythic domain of Judeo-Christianity when Victoria refers to "the fall of man," which is a reference to the biblical story of Adam's betrayal of his promise to God in the Garden of Eden, after which God expels Adam and Eve from the Garden to suffer in the world. The orientational dynamic connects to domain knowledge about the religious story to guide mappings between the roles and values of the characters. Here, the leader presents herself as morally justified, like an agent of God, in executing the captive, thereby expelling him from the world much like God expelled the people from the Garden. Yorick's death is here conceptualized as a part-for-whole metonymy, a cognitive shortcut that stands one person in for all of humanity, expanding the BODY IS SELF metaphor into something more religiously inflected like BODY IS COMMUNITY.

The irony, of course, is that the land in which they live is not an idyllic place like the Garden but a dystopia, which re-construes Victoria as a villain, whose powerful position is in fact a misappropriation of perceived moral hierarchy. In this moment, Victoria's act seeks to transform the religious origin story, which reflected the spread of humanity across many lands into a dystopian future, since she is seeking to literally execute the last man on earth, thereby ending the reproductive future of the human species. Thus, the typical metonymy of one man standing for humanity becomes a literal truism rather than a figurative cognitive shortcut for religious failing. Victoria's religious fanaticism comes through in this conflation and inversion of literal and figurative interpretations of the religious and perhaps patriarchal domains. She believes that the plague that killed most men was divine judgment, and that the execution of Yorick is completing this work. The complicated metonymies and metaphors that swirl around this act develop a complex antagonistic viewpoint in juxtaposition to Yorick's life, but one that does not solve the dystopic and gendered conflicts that direct the story, but potentially expand them further.

As this example illustrates, the process of interpreting bodies in action involves situational and metaphorical blending of objects, people and domains to construct viewpoints. The interactions between modalities and domains draw on key schemas and mental metaphors to develop salient blends that include schematic, literal, and figurative layers of conceptualization that clarify the oppositional viewpoints.

4.3.2 Embodied Biases and Assumptions in Perception: Blindness and Oversight

How readers perceive and conceptualize the stylistic presentation of figures involves cognitive patterns like the body schema presented above, as well as biases and assumptions that can constrain how interpretations are developed. A relatively realistic representational style is not necessary to build active and rich comics. The body schema is activated as much for a stick figure drawing in an *xkcd* comic (such as the one discussed later in this chapter) as for the figures discussed above. Thus, there is a wide degree of abstraction afforded a figure before the body schema can no longer be applied to make inferences about its composition, orientation, and potential actions (see, e.g., Bonnet, Paulos, and Nithart 2005). Abstract comics, on the other hand, activate other dynamic qualities for inference building about agentive action, and I discuss those in Chapter 8. The body schema serves as a common topological feature that helps construct discrete character viewpoints across the range of abstraction in many comics.

The body schema facilitates many predictive and interpretive aspects of reading that in fact biases perception against nuance by guiding attention and cognitive energy toward coherence and interpretive validity. As such, as Cavanagh (2005) shows, unexpected or irrational elements of art, such as impossible shadows or perspectives, are often not initially perceived by a viewer. This relates to a cognitive phenomenon called attentional or change blindness, which is produced by the cognitive bias to focus attention only on elements that are deemed significant for action or response (Simons and Levin 1998, 1999; Noë 2004; O'Regan 2011). While research on these cognitive blindnesses tend to focus on real-world experiences, I follow Cavanagh to note how they apply to mediated experiences in comics as well. Such blindness is experienced frequently by comics readers, evidenced through a blindness to variations in representational cues, such as slight variations in form, color, shape, and style of figures and spaces that occur regularly between panels, especially in long-form comics. Blindness is less prevalent in shorter forms, like in comic strips, since there are fewer opportunities for variation. However, significant differences in character presentation can be seen in comparisons of older and newer versions of the same strip, such as changes to the presentation of the characters in older and newer *Garfield* or *Peanuts* strips. Recognition of characters between older and newer versions relies in part on a blindness to their irregularity in relation to each other in favor of conceptual viewpoint coherence.

While this bias delimits perception to some extent, the blindness helps to create a seamless reading experience and connects to the body schema as well through the minimization of variations in figuration. For example, in Rob Guillory's *Farmhand* series, notice how the hair of the protagonist switches direction frequently, often even on one page and in the middle of a conversation (Figure 4.3). I certainly did not notice this on the first read. This blindness to a very clear fluctuation in bodily presence illustrates how readers cognitively locate viewpoints and bodies in more abstracted ways to populate mental spaces in order to build a model of the scene and interpret it effectively. It is only through closer analysis and attention to representational cues that such fluctuations are made obvious. These blindnesses show the power of predictive and inferential processes to select and inform how information is processed. Of course, variation in readerly interests and backgrounds will significantly impact how blind a given reader is to different features. Regular readers of comics have trained their perception to navigate the form more effectively than non-comics readers. Increased familiarity may decrease blindness, but that is not necessarily given.

Moving through different levels of abstraction, there are of course other more specific embodied, sensorimotor experiences that help readers simulate texts. For instance, readers will generally assume the presence of peripersonal (close contextual) and background spaces, even if they are not depicted, as part of substantiating a storyworld. This pervasive assumption means creators can manipulate its composition, either by including or deleting contextual details, such as by removing the background in all but the first panel in the previous example. Such

Figure 4.3 Selection from Rob Guillory's *Farmhand* (2019, n.p.), showing variation in figuration within a short scene.

choices focus the reader on the actions and interactions of characters. Conceptually, the storyworld is maintained as a mental space in which the conversation is ongoing, which allows it to be obscured. Similarly, Marjane Satrapi's graphic memoir *Persepolis* (2003) includes only rudimentary representations of peripersonal space and backgrounds, which focuses the reader on the sparse and emotive qualities of the figures, but perhaps also thematizes the limited viewpoint of the child protagonist who often is baffled by things happening around her. On the other hand, some comics include many details, such as Warren Ellis and Darick Robertson's *Transmetropolitan* series (1997–2002), which strategically includes detailed, gritty backgrounds that add qualities about the cyberpunk storyworld, many of which are often not directly relevant to the plot. However, these details align with the story's focus on the actions of the protagonist, gonzo journalist Spider Jerusalem, who, particularly in the first year of the series, seeks to document the many different characters and political forces that influence the City.

In all of these brief examples, the peripersonal and background spaces of characters typically align with the pragmatic and epistemic interests of the scene or the overall story. For Ellis and Robertson, the journalistic fiction includes many details that create the City as its own character, while for the science fiction of Guillory the storytelling style focuses on personal interactions. Interestingly, *The Photographer* example discussed above utilizes the differences in peripersonal space as presented by simple drawings and detailed photographs to complicate how readers understand the documentary genre. On the other hand, the *Y: The Last Man* example maintains relatively unencumbered peripersonal and background spaces to maintain the ease of interpretation of its evenly paced dystopian narrative. Other genres of comic use figure-ground effects in other ways. For instance, Jack Kirby rendered superheroes more dynamic by removing backgrounds and emphasizing the actions of characters with action lines, which stylize schematic cues for force and motion (see Potsch and Williams 2012; I analyze this further in relation to temporality in Chapter 6). Such representational strategies strategically manipulate peripersonal space and backgrounds to promote the general discursive interests of the comic, and readers move through and interpret such texts differently based on these complex contextual cues that inform character and narrative viewpoints.

Embodied expectations and biases can also be actively or strategically complicated in order to develop reinterpretations of peripersonal and background spaces, in a way disrupting the ease of comprehension facilitated by these spaces in the previous examples. For instance, in the following example (Figure 4.4) from her semi-autobiographical collection *My Most Secret Desire* (1995), Julie Doucet purposefully thwarts expectations about

Figure 4.4 A panel from Julie Doucet's *My Most Secret Desire* (1995, n.p.).

figure-ground effects, motion vectors, speech balloons, and the domestic domain in order to develop a nuanced character viewpoint. The scene is rendered in a flat, undifferentiated depiction of the author's kitchen, which forces readers to actively search for the protagonist. Doucet's difficult style invites a "reading protocol of inversion" (Chaney 2011, 132), as a surreal effect that asserts her necessary presence as a focalizer of the story while requiring the reader to still actively seek to see her. This aspect of Doucet's style serves as a feminist resistance and subversion of masculinist tropes by disrupting the presumptions of the gaze (Køhlert 2012).

As a snapshot into the protagonist's life, this single panel presents a complex web of possibilities for interpretation. Firstly, visual chaos makes many objects and the protagonist hard to distinguish. The protagonist is intentionally obscured through her off-center position and her housecoat pattern that further blends her into the chaotic clutter. Furthermore, attention seems to be drawn to the fridge, as the central dominant feature, yet also break across it, since its left-hand side acts like a panel frame, almost breaking the panel in half. Finally, the inanimate objects yell disconcerting and negative comments like "Destroy!" and "Kill," which make each take up personal space as an actor with a viewpoint in the storyworld, rather than being simple household objects in peripersonal space. As I have previously shown, attentional guidance is crucial to building comprehension in comics. In this example, attentional distraction or maladjustment is perhaps a better description. Doucet purposefully obfuscates attentional direction to develop a perceived sense of confusion or difficulty.

The perceptual confusion becomes actively antagonistic through the animate gesticulating and yelling containers and appliances, armed with cutlery, which present a clearly fantastical quality to the domestic domain: presumably most people would not expect a ketchup bottle to yell "Bitch!" nor others to conspire to "Kill! Kill!" As such, these conspicuous and unreal objects present a puzzle to comprehension: What do they mean? Why are these objects presented as animate in this purportedly autobiographical scene?

This panel comes shortly after the protagonist awakens from a bizarre, misogynistic dream, so initially readers might infer that the scene reflects her blended state of consciousness between dream-sleep and wakefulness, wherein the sexist hostility she experienced in her dream bleeds into her domestic physical reality. However, in a subsequent panel, the character reflects on her cacophonous kitchen as her "reassuring reality," which suggests that something more is going on here. This textual cue invites another round of mental interrogation. Perhaps, the text is also inviting readers to interpret the wrathful environment as an expression of the character's viewpoint, as a reflection on her gendered experience of an always antagonistic world. Another inference from this conclusion is that the objects might be a projection of self-hatred (including a culturally constructed one) that informs her perceptions. As such, the vocal objects materialize the character's internal viewpoint to reflect a range of experiences and values. Blending non-factual external features with internal viewpoints potentially develops a mental simulation that is deeply personal while recuperating its fantastical qualities into the genre of autobiography as expressions of the self.

It could be argued, therefore, that Doucet is presenting a darkly humorous visualization of her experience of gender objectification and masculine antagonism, inviting the reader to explore and question these issues by experiencing the difficulties of her lived experience. Perhaps her chaotic kitchen reassures her because, there, inanimate threats cannot cause harm because of their fictional aggression, whereas even in her dreamscape, the intersubjective abuses and potential violence inherent in gendered discourses and power dynamics continue to make explicit the real potential for abuse and trauma. Doucet breaks expectations of presentation and genre in order to develop a complicated blended viewpoint in which gender dynamics inform perception, and brings the reader into that space of confused and antagonistic perception. Perhaps the comic shows a hint of freedom from oppression, even if that is still a frighteningly inhospitable place, simply because the objects cannot actually hurt her, which is somewhat reassuring, even if the aggression remains a part of her lived experience. But her message may also be that the objectification of women is a bad dream that never ends, and it slowly works itself even into the perceived spaces and safety of one's home. As El Refaie (2013) argues, inconsistencies between modalities or within storyworlds often prompt metaphorical interpretations, which happens here through the reinterpretations of everyday objects as expressions of the character's viewpoint (this constructs underlying mental metaphors like EXTERNAL EXPERIENCE IS INTERNAL EXPERIENCE or ENVIRONMENT IS SELF), which also leads to other inferences about a broader feminist epistemic narrative position. Much more can be said about Doucet's feminist use of surreal and grotesque qualities to challenge normative understandings about gender and sexuality (see Køhlert 2012), but here I limit my analysis to how Doucet's approach creates an inhospitable space for both her self-presentation in her comic and for the reader of it, challenging conventional knowledge about both comics and everyday experience by blending the figure with her peripersonal and background spaces. Just one panel illustrates the complex viewpoint construction established through her stylistic choices.

Note how Doucet's visual cacophony contrasts with the realism of the previous example from *Y: The Last Man* (Figure 4.2), where concepts of the self were contained within bodies (BODY IS SELF), even while they are also exploring ideas about post-patriarchy. Attention to how character viewpoints are constructed, and how prompts construct the reader's relationship with those viewpoints, is crucial to interpreting comics from a feminist perspective. As Mel Gibson (2015) shows for superhero comics, while there are certainly concerning trends in comics which reify a very prescriptive male gaze, there are also opportunities to re-educate the eye through strategies that build cross-gender alignments in viewpoint. The analysis of the role of attentional guidance, viewpoint construction, and mental simulation of both realistic and fantastical environments presented here helps show how such transformational strategies function.

4.3.3 Facial Expressions

While I have touched briefly on gesture and bodily metonymies through the body schema, the analysis focused on interactions between figures and spaces. Bodies themselves offer much for interpretation beyond their general presence, orientation, and coherence. For now, I will also put aside a range of domain-evoking features (i.e., metonymies, discussed in the next chapter)—such as pictorial cues like era-specific clothing or hair styles, technologies (like car types), arenas of action (like gladiators in the pit), and other contextual markers—to focus on body-specific cues that contribute to the viewpoint construction of character personalities, motivations, and intentions.

As discussed in the previous chapter on simulation theory, when it comes to bodies, readers simulate characters from the outside in, using bodily cues to simulate predictions and inferences about internal states, like emotions (Feng and O'Halloran 2012; Prinz 2004) and morality (Kukkonen 2013a, ch. 4; Prinz 2007). People use cues about bodily action, such as what is being grasped for, to develop an intentional viewpoint for a figure (and this works for non-human creatures too, of course, to a more limited extent, and often with anthropomorphized qualities). People use facial expression to gauge emotion, and use gestural cues to clarify both emotive and communicative contents. All of these cues work together, along with other discursive and contextual information (such as speech or thought balloons that give more information regarding potential internal states), to build up mental scenarios of character viewpoints and to gauge subjective aspects like motivations and intentions. For this reason, Will Eisner

(2008b) developed an entire book on "expressive anatomy" to illustrate the complexity of representational qualities associated just with elements of the body in comics, including different types of posture (such as passive, aggressive, and so on). I will focus on only several of these as dominant communicative cues, namely facial expression, posture, and gesture. In particular, I emphasize how these cues establish mental spaces and clarify cross-modal inferences in blends about viewpoints and actions. At the same time, it will also become clear that these bodily cues are extremely sensitive to context. For instance, in the case of emotion, Barrett (2017) persuasively argues that bodily representations of emotion are extremely context and character dependent, such that there are few universal expressions of emotion, just situated and constructed ones. While color-emotion attributions, such as "seeing red," have a fair degree of universality (reflecting proprioceptive universals related to affect), even those have constructional variations based on national and linguistic groups (Jonauskaite et al. 2020). This constructional view contradicts some more universalist discussions of emotional representation in comics, which tend to be more formulaic and essentialist.

Faces are particularly salient for the expression and construal of subject matter and especially for presenting emotions. However, they are not as clear as they might seem. Scott McCloud (2006) draws from the popular, yet problematic, psychological research of Paul Ekman (2003) into facial expressions of emotion. McCloud describes the visual presentation of six major emotions as "emotional primaries" (see Figure 4.5), which are anger, disgust, fear, joy, sadness, and surprise, and which have a wide range of

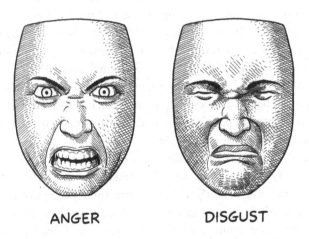

Figure 4.5 Two of Scott McCloud's facial expressions of "emotional primaries" (2006, 83).

intensities and tonal qualities. He follows Ekman to assert that "these are basic emotions which all human beings exhibit, regardless of culture, language or age" (82) and suggests that "emotional primaries [can] be mixed to create many of the expressions we see every day" (83). As such, McCloud (and Ekman before him) presents facial expressions as clear, universal indicators of very specific meanings.

At first glance, the notion of emotional primaries seems clear and uncontestable. However, these essentialist approaches to emotion do not withstand scientific analysis. As Lisa Feldman Barrett shows, interpretations of facial expressions are very socially, culturally, and contextually dependent (Barrett 2017). There is significant diversity in how emotions are constructed, categorized, presented, and interpreted across cultures (Barrett 2006). Moreover, out of context, a face can be read in several ways. For instance, Barrett (2017) shows a closely cropped photograph of Serena Williams appearing to some to scream in terror or anger, when in fact, she is yelling in triumph after winning a tennis match. In context, her emotive expression is completely expected and is perceived as triumph. Taken out of context, using an image typical of those used by universalist research on emotional primaries (like McCloud's above), it becomes difficult to interpret correctly. Thus, a universalist approach has trouble qualitatively engaging her reaction because it assumes that faces clearly display essential or primary categories of emotion. The constructionist approach takes a broader, contextualized view in order to explain how someone might perceive her emotions as triumph. As Barrett concludes, "In real life, we usually encounter faces in context, attached to bodies and associated with voices, smells, and other surrounding details. These details cue your brain to use particular concepts to simulate and construct your perception of emotion. That's why, in the full photo of Serena Williams, you perceive triumph, not terror" (43). As such, the constructionist view attempts to attend to many cues that inform emotion perception. Such an approach aligns well with the science of mental simulation, the previous discussion of body schemas and peripersonal space, as well as other cues to be discussed below. Comics help cue emotion interpretation through the contexts presented in panels and sequences. In comics, the discourse context impacts the semantics of the image.

As Barrett and other researches note, expressions of emotions are difficult to codify because they are interpreted by others through a range of bodily and contextual cues that inform their perceptions, reactions, and interpretations, all by using mental simulation to build interpretative possibilities from available contextual and background knowledge (Freedberg and Gallese 2007; Iacoboni 2009; Prinz 2004). As the phenomenologist Maurice Merleau-Ponty affirms: "It is through my body that I understand other people, just as it is through my body that I perceive 'things.' The meaning of a gesture thus 'understood' is not behind it, it is intermingled with the structure of the world outlined by the gesture" (Merleau-Ponty 1962, 216). Because emotion is deeply rooted in bodily sensations and sensorimotor and proprioceptive effects, these simulations are richly embodied, but also prone to error based on experiential differences and limitations on cues. Moreover, cultural concepts and semantic contexts about emotion strongly inform interpretations (Barrett 2006, 2017; Bertoux et al. 2020). These cognitive realities of emotion as bodily, discursively, and contextually-dependent align well with the theory of embodied meaning I use throughout this book. It also aligns with how images represent emotion, which tends to place particular emphasis on the face, as well as bodily orientation and touch (Feng and O'Halloran 2012). The face is a crucial location for the depiction of many emotions because it is a core site of expressivity and intersubjectivity in people, and therefore most viewers fixate on it. In fact, mutual gaze and shared, joint attention are crucial steps in cognitive development and language learning (Tomasello 1999, 2008). Many comics reflect this focus through regular close-ups on faces followed up by contexts and actions, such as the scene from *Y: The Last Man* discussed above. Through contextual and interactive cues, comics present complex emotionally salient character viewpoints through these multimodal and sequential qualities.

Before I turn to the multimodal constructions of facial expressions and viewpoints, I will examine an evocative depiction of a single facial expression created by Guy Davis that illustrates how faces can be manipulated and abstracted to prompt powerful affective responses. Davis uses masks and distorted faces and bodies to develop a sense of horror at the supernatural in *The Marquis* series (1997–2009), collected in *The Marquis: Inferno* (2009). For example, in Figure 4.6, a grotesque figure with an almost human figure and a face with extra teeth, hollow eyes, and variegated skin attacks the protagonist, an investigator intent on solving a series of murders. The terrifying scene derives its sharp emotional quality through the simulation of dynamic action and the perception of immediate danger. The perspectival choices seem to place the reader, as much as the shadowy protagonist, in harm's way, exposed to the grotesque demonic figure hurtling out of the panel. The facial expression of the demon matches quite well McCloud's depiction of "anger" in Figure 4.5, but I would suggest that it is better described as aggression in this context, perhaps harnessing elements of domain-specific animalistic information regarding dogs or other vicious animals that align with other images of the figure in the comic. Moreover,

Figure 4.6 Selection from Guy Davis' *The Marquis: Inferno* (2009, 73).

the dominant emotional quality for the reader is likely not focused on the aggression of the demon's viewpoint, but rather aligns in empathy with the protagonist and may even react in self-protective revulsion. Since the reader cannot see the face of the silhouetted figure, the figure's reaction is unknowable, which limits the direct simulation of the protagonist's viewpoint in this moment. Likely, the reader would perceive the demonic figure as a terrifying threat to the protagonist and experience some degree of terror, fear, or a related emotion as the dominant emotion ascribed to the panel in general, including possibly ascribing it to the protagonist. As such, the depicted aggression is interpreted and responded to in order to build a secondary affective layer to the panel, locating two viewpoints and empathetically and personally aligning the reader with one of them. As this example shows, the context dependency of emotion construction adds complexity to interpretations.

Underpinning this readerly texture are several embodied cognitive capacities that add to the horror. Most immediately is the simulation of an impending aggressive impact from an antagonist. Importantly, the body can also be read as horrific because of its perceived deformities, its lack of adhesion to prototypical or normative expectations about human bodies and faces that often ground reader simulations about actions and emotions (the simulation would be different if it were a different type of body, of course). Lack of connection to prototypes and body schemas can create discomfort, generally, and in this case, the aggression increases a sense of horror and revulsion. Davis' crude, sketchy line style adds to these emotional constructs, since it slightly inhibits object recognition, on top of the atypicality of the figure. The context of this interaction, during a dismal evening hunt for a murderer, further heightens the experience of foreboding and fear. The facial and bodily configurations of this particular panel develop a rich array of embodied and conceptual meanings about this storyworld in which demons are on the prowl.

The previous example may still seem to suggest that facial expressions, even presented through atypical depictions, are easily interpreted. I will turn now to another example that showcases the importance of multimodal and contextual cues for seemingly transparent depictions of emotion. This example comes from Will Eisner's guide for comics creators, *Comics and Sequential Art* (Eisner 2008a), in a section focused on bodily and facial expressions. Eisner provides a full page of strips that repeat the same set of facial expressions but include different phrases in the speech balloon, such as "Goodbye," "I love you," or as seen here, "You're fired" (Figure 4.7). The examples illustrate a wide range of construals that are picture dependent, such that the nature of the boss's emotional engagement with the firing is construed respectively (left to right) as being something like unconcerned, wily, upset, smug, or despondent. The faces employ an abstracted form of emotional representation that is also culturally and convention dependent for interpretation, such that increased familiarity with caricature and art styles from different social and cultural contexts may influence how a reader will interpret such emotive depictions (Cohn 2021). Nonetheless, each of these faces builds a different character viewpoint, in which readers draw on the same domain knowledge of employment, but develop different inferences about the personality of the boss and their relationship to the employee and motivations for firing them. It is perhaps also significant that the reader is positioned or aligned somewhat with the viewpoint of the employee being fired, looking into the face of the manager rather than witnessing the firing of someone else, since this might create a sense of personal emotional responses to such a situation, especially based on the intersubjective weight of eye contact and facial expressions of happiness or sadness.

Figure 4.7 Part of Will Eisner's illustration of text interactions with facial expressions (Eisner 2008a, 113).

The limited contextual information in these panels, with no peripersonal space beyond cross-hatched shading in the lower background, also limits the interpretive possibilities for the reader. Perhaps the first panel's disinterested dismissal makes sense as a simple one panel scene, wherein readers can assume there to have been a very brief meeting with the boss. However, the other examples provide inadequate context to interpret exactly why the boss is hysterical or pleased with the decision to fire the employee. Moreover, is the firing happening in an office or out in some other space, such as in front of other employees or customers in a store. Likewise, the domain of employment could be actual or fictional, perhaps only invoked as part of a conversation between friends, where one is pretending to fire the other for something they said or did, thereby leveraging the power dynamics of employment as a humorous relational metaphor. These broader contextual possibilities show how the panels seem to offer a coherent and easily intelligible presentation of emotion, with language giving some crucial informative cues, but they still leave the reader with only a rudimentary impression of the situation based on background domain information about employment and cultural and conventional readings of facial expressions. The reader needs further details, such as from other adjacent panels in a sequence, to build a more comprehensive understanding of the character viewpoints and associated emotions. As these examples stand, they remain an evocative but very limited presentation of emotion since readers cannot fully ascertain the intentions or motivations of the character expressing them.

Another quandary, which I explore in more detail in Chapter 6, is the temporality of the panel. The examples illustrate a brief duration in time (the time it takes to say "you're fired") in which the facial expression and phrase are collocated. The phrase is brief, but it is unclear when the facial expression is made in relation to it as part of a multimodal enunciation. Only one face actually has its mouth open, which suggests that several of the faces are being depicted either before or after the statement. It is hard to say exactly how this might alter the mental simulation of this moment, but there are likely slight variances in inferences that occur. For instance, the disinterested face may seem to best preface the dismissal, while the smirk may seem more fitting as a final, figurative punch, and the sobbing face may pervade the entire statement. Moreover, as I discuss in more detail in Chapter 6, these variations or asynchronicities in the temporality of modalities (pictorial immediacy and linguistic phrasing) nonetheless unite into a singular multimodal expression through mental simulation and blending. As such, the facial expressions can act like gestures to enhance verbal content.

4.3.4 Gestures

Facial expressions and gesture may be separated for analysis, but often they work together as a composite of bodily expressivity. Other gestures beyond facial cues can include head tilts, arm and hand gestures and movements, and so on. Irene Mittelberg introduces gesture in a way that applies well to comics when she writes:

> Gestural communicative acts are inherently embodied and indexical. So, in principle, they can only be fully accounted for by viewing them through a pragmatic lens, and thus by considering aspects of multimodal discourse pragmatics and the physical, contextual, and sociocultural anchoring of human cognition and situated meaning-making. (2017, 203)

While Mittelberg is writing about everyday gestures, her description can translate to the mediated space of comics well because it highlights the importance of the situated and physical properties of gesture while also noting their embodied (for comics read pictorial) and indexical qualities. Drawing on research by Kendon (2004) and Müller (incl. 2007), Mittleberg goes on to highlight how gestures are "discourse integrated" (204) and, thereby, always serve a communicative function. Culturally conventionalized forms of gesture called emblems (such as crude angry gestures seen frequently in rush-hour traffic) fit into this wide view. Research into gesture typically focuses on embodied rather than mediated depictions of communication, which limits the complete applicability of this research to comics, but several observations are particularly relevant to how readers likely engage with bodily postures and gestures in comic. As a large research field, I will not engage in a systematic analysis of different types of gestures and meanings (for instance, rhythmic gestures that are common with everyday speech do not feature in comics). Rather, I will focus on the major theoretical parameters that align with the interests of this book, which will hopefully serve as a bridge for others interested in developing more detailed analyses. Moreover, because bodily cues include a range of other meanings, including non-gestural intersubjective interactions and environmental engagements, a higher-order approach helps locate gestures in an analytical framework of mediated bodily representation that has informed this chapter so far.

Co-speech gesture—when gestures accompany spoken language (mediated in comics form through a figure and a speech balloon)—require a complex web of simulation and blending that predicts, integrates, and interprets different multimodal cues. Like facial expressions, readers simulate and integrate the gesture at a point in the discourse that seems appropriate to its communicative effect, in a way rebuilding a mental equivalent of what viewers experience with natural gesture usage. As such, they come with the same temporal challenge as interpreting Eisner's facial expressions discussed above. Gestures can be used for a variety of purposes, such as for pointing (deictic clarification), emphasis and emoting (gesticulation), as well as for reenacting (pantomime) and diagramming spatial or conceptual content, including to spatially isolate different viewpoints (Dancygier and Sweetser 2012). Importantly, Wilson and Gibbs (2007) have shown that gestures enhance comprehension of both real and imagined actions and ideas.

Furthermore, the peripersonal spaces around the speaker (including both interpersonal spaces and those above and around the dialogists) has different functions, and gestures employ space in a wide variety of communicative ways, such as to locate information, reenact actions, add emphasis, and so on (see Kendon 2004; McNeill 1992, 2005; Müller 2007). For instance, pointing across the interpersonal space at the other person may be considered accusatory, while gesturing into it may pantomime or reenact another figure pointing at something in the story being retold. Likewise, a gesture upward may be used to interject or to emphasize a point, and using both hands together can develop patterns of relation aligned with elements in the verbal expression that are realized in the gesture ("on one hand . . . On the other . . .)"). More directly related to the arts, gesture can also evoke schemas and force dynamics in artworks (Mittelberg 2013, 2017, 2018). These gestures can even help others understand artworks they have never seen, so much so in fact that the unseen work can be analyzed in ways that helps the person describing and gesturing about it to better interpret it (Narayan 2012). As such, co-speech gesture is a powerful tool that uses spatial, iconic, diagrammatic, and symbolic cues as contextually and discursively required. Gesture in comics has very little research focused on it, but it can safely be claimed that mediation limits the range of possible types of gesture since it renders the dynamicity of co-speech gesture static, and requires mental simulation to animate and integrate it. Such instances of static gestures might be better conceptualized as part of a range of co-text images that may be interpreted to have similar conceptual valences as other forms of gesture (Hart and Marmol Queralto 2021). Importantly, some research has focused on emblematic gestures in comics, of which comprehension rates parallel real-life gesture examples (Fein and Kasher 1996).[3]

Beyond the varied work of co-speech gestures, lone gestures and postures tend to be emotive, emblematic, or conventionalized. As seen in

Figure 4.8, which selects one of several emotion examples, Eisner offers a range of postures that he considers to be clear pictographic depictions of anger. For each of Eisner's figures, readers simulate the posture and action, particularly the balled fists and forward-leaning stance, not only to interpret what might be being expressed about how the character feels, but also to draw up reasonable associated intentions, motivations, and other qualities that build a generic scenario in which such expressions occur. Such meanings are grounded in simulated activations of embodied schemas and mental metaphors of emotion (Forceville 2005, 2011; see also Kövecses 2010, 2013), which add opportunities to enrich viewpoint constructions. For instance, balled fists are often associated with domains of tension, hostility, or fighting (such as boxing). These domains also include mental metaphors that suggest emotions are explosive, hot, or energetic, all of which may be inferred from the depicted bodily states.

At the same time, as with the facial expressions, arguably these postures are much more open to interpretation than originally presented. Despite how convinced a reader might be about their internal simulation of the figure's viewpoint, research into the emotive communication of static postures reviewed and elaborated on by Coulson (2004) shows that interpretations of body postures are highly variable, with lower agreement about expressions of disgust, fear, and surprise, but higher agreement about expressions of anger, sadness, and happiness. Confusion between different attributions (such as between surprise and happiness) cloud the results further. Coulson notes that context markers likely play a significant role in interpretations, and the recent research into emotion discussed earlier confirms this. Such research suggests that posture is less deterministic of interpretations of simple emotion categories and should be considered more in terms of construal, showing a gradient of affective meaning within context. Thus, simulation and domain knowledge develop active mental imagery that imbues and construes figures with viewpoint-aligned content, but interpretations are still quite open.

Figure 4.8 Selection from Eisner's "micro-dictionary of gestures" showing examples of anger (2008a, 105).

4.4 MATERIALIZED SOUNDS AND VIEWPOINTS: SYNESTHESIA, TYPOGRAPHY, AND BALLOONS

Visual demarcations of sound, through the typography of written language (how it looks, rather than what it says) and speech balloon structures, function like gestures by invoking embodied processes aligned with viewpoint and environmental interpretation. Writing, as "visible language," offers important attentional and perceptual guidance to simulations, and can imbue words with emphasis or other viewpoint construals through typographical choices (Gibbons 2012b). In comics, linguistic communication is further elaborated on through the indexical and iconic structures of speech balloons and thought bubbles. Narratorial boxes can also reflect reported speech, but in a less direct manner that depends much on the style of storytelling and the role that the narrator takes within it. All of these levels of reported and indirect speech and sounds, and how they are orchestrated within and around panels, develops viewpoints and environmental cues that correlate to a hierarchy of roles and values within the text's discursive space (see Dancygier 2012, 2019; Dancygier and Vandelanotte 2016, 2017). Here, I focus primarily on the comics-specific aspects of these various features for presenting and orchestrating language, showing how their functions connect to cognitive processes. Importantly, typographic cues and balloonic innovations blend forms and meanings across sensory categories in what I suggest is a media-induced form of synesthesia that adjusts common mental metaphorical beliefs about language.

4.4.1 The Conduit Metaphor

Interpretations of sound effects, balloons, and boxes derive from important aspects of cognitive topology and processes. The blend of indexical and iconic meanings of space are driven by mental metaphors that inform understandings of these conventions. As briefly discussed in Chapter 2, often language is discussed in terms of material objects, like when people say "I can't quite grasp what you're saying" or "Did you get that?" These expressions (and many others like them) reflect the mental metaphor IDEAS ARE OBJECTS, and as such ideas can be passed around, manipulated, transformed, or broken. Thus, people talk about "building" an argument or idea, which builds through metaphorical materials that give it value. This metaphor informs a common folk theory of language that Michael Reddy calls the *conduit metaphor* (1979). This metaphor treats words as objects that contain meaning and moves this meaning between people through conversation or other forms of communication. This is a slightly more complicated metaphor than just IDEAS ARE OBJECTS because containers have extra schematic structures, especially insides and outsides. For instance, meaning can also be difficult to package or unpack. For instance, one might have trouble "putting an experience into words" or "getting at what is being said." In his reconsideration of the conduit metaphor, Joseph Grady (1998) shows how it blends together several schemas and mental metaphors, which makes it a powerful and flexible system (even if it is somewhat fallacious, as I discussed in Chapter 2 and unpack further here).

The conduit metaphor is further complicated when talking about media, including comics. Books are material objects that contain words in specific forms and with various conventions that all connect to different kinds of meanings. For the conduit metaphor, material culture acts to double the container or object of meaning, since books contain words that contain meanings, which could be called the *extended conduit metaphor*, since it reinforces the object-and-container-ness of communication. Readers typically compress the assumptions of containment for both words and books to focus primarily on the meanings, unless a work takes a particularly conspicuous material form that accents the constructed nature of such containment, such as Jonathan Safran Foer's *Tree of Codes* or other experimental texts (Gibbons 2012a, 2012b). Word balloons work in a similar way to books, in that they are also "containers" or objects for words and meaning (Forceville, Veale, and Feyaerts 2010, 67), but, because of their visually conspicuous nature, balloons and boxes also resist, to varying degrees, the easier compression of book and word to meaning. Often, as I will discuss here and in the next chapter, balloons and boxes use their material, formal, and conventionalized qualities in creative ways that add to meaning construction, thereby, not allowing the formal qualities to disappear into compressions. So, at the level of language representation, the conduit metaphor may seem intact to some degree, but at the material level, comics resist it.

Of course, meaning does not reside in words at all, but in the activation of background information—be it personal, acculturated, socialized, standardized, and so on—all of which contributes to the variation in responses to and interpretations of all texts. Literary criticism flourishes in the fractures of the conduit metaphor. While communication requires some degree of tractability between language users, the variations show that the conduit metaphor is in fact a fallacy, since a word does not equate to a fixed meaning, but is in fact much more flexible in how it is interpreted based on users and contexts (Dancygier 2012, 203). While there will be a fair degree of agreement about linguistic meanings, the variations in reader cognitive topology will inherently lead to variation in reception.

This is particularly noteworthy when attempting to isolate the meaningfulness of formal manipulations of typography and balloon forms, since how they are simulated and blended to construct meaning may be challenging to locate, and interpretations may also vary. In what follows, I will isolate several cognitive aspects of how readers assimilate formal manipulations into a coherent meaning.

4.4.2 Typographic Manipulations and Onomatopoeia

Typographic choices play an important role in how readers navigate a text and build comprehension.[4] Readers simulate and blend the visual aspects of represented language with aural qualities to construe the linguistic meaning, updating the conduit metaphor since adjusting the object modifies the idea. Visual construals of language include reading visual emphasis through bolding or italics as tonal emphasis, and reading fractured sentences, such as by adding full stops between words, as an emphatic or clipped or terse tone. Similarly, size of font can align with magnitude of sound, with bigger words aligning with louder sounds. Such mappings of different sensory forms together align based on syncopating more abstract perceived affinities in attentional guidance, fluidity, dominance, and so on. Cross-sensory or synesthetic mappings based on analogous perceptual experiences rely on parallel simulations of multisensory experience at an abstract, schematic level to align embodied experiences of both mediated textuality (such as reading conventions) and intersubjective or environmental experiences (such as of how people generally speak in a given context). In terms of the conduit metaphor, the form of the container aligns analogically with other multisensory experiences to construe the contents.

Similarly, language can be presented in clean type or more idiosyncratic handwriting, which suggests aspects of a more technical or personal expression, respectively. Handwriting often adds interpretive possibilities, such as erratic or scratched-out forms suggesting a more distressed character viewpoint (see Borkent 2017). It can also offer a general sense of closeness to the writer, as readers simulate the execution of writing as a background domain, while reading the language as well. This explains the popularity of handwritten texts in autobiographic and dramatic genres by presenting an "autographic style" (Fischer and Hatfield 2011).

Synesthetic blends are particularly noticeable for more conspicuous usages of typographic manipulations. Sound effects, which are onomatopoeic iconic symbols, often mobilize several features of typographic form, word, and context to construct meaning. These cues are typically embedded into a scene, often mobilizing font size to indicate the magnitude of the sound, while using word placement to draw attention to where the sound is located. In this sense, the word functions to communicate both the nature and location of the sound as an environmental feature. Some artists embellish on typographic aspects of sound effects to add to the texture of the work. Figure 4.9, for example, shows how Mike Mignola creates a dramatic punch for his popular character Hellboy that breaks both his opponent and the rocks on which they are fighting. As Scott Bukatman notes of the page from which this panel comes, "The page works as narrative; it also works as design. It hums with kinetic energy while also maintaining a formal stasis" (2014, 113). The simulation of the movements of characters and rubble creates a dynamic moment, even while the balanced and minimalistic presentation offers a sense of designed stasis. The tension between form and action is particularly evident through the use of specific typographical choices. The jumbled formal manipulation of the letters of the sound effect, "BOOM," builds affinities between the letters and the rubble, since the letters are similarly falling apart, highlighting the letters as objects. However, the font color and size demarcate the letters as separate, as not-rubble, which maintains the language-sound synesthetic blend for the onomatopoeic word. The size and alignment of the letters with the rubble show also how sonically as well as physically substantial the rock fall is. The word-rubble blend reinforces the power of Hellboy's punch, developing a percussive and destructive moment. The tension between word-object and word-sound blends to form a synesthetic icon of Hellboy's power.

4.4.3 Balloons and Boxes

Speech and thought balloons typically use language to present the voices and thoughts of characters, and boxes often imbed narratorial content in or around panels. The structure of the word balloon typically uses an indexical "tail" to indicate who speaks or thinks, to maintain clarity about each character and their viewpoint. Moreover, if there are multiple balloons in one panel, readers will typically follow the layered patterns of their source language: for instance, in English, balloons and text boxes are typically read left to right and top to bottom, to maintain clarity about the flow and interactive aspects of the information. Multiple balloons may also be separated and staggered in the panel to indicate the different voices and their order in a conversation. As a written text, the cues are relatively straightforward to parse as direct reported speech (as spoken words or internal thoughts). Narrative boxes can act as an indirect speech balloon, but lack a tail in order

Figure 4.9 Typographic manipulation in Mike Mignola's *Hellboy: Conqueror Worm/Strange Places* (2009, 64). Colors by Dave Stewart.

to maintain the distinction between the narratorial discursive viewpoint and the character viewpoints as expressed in language. The lack of a tail makes perceptual sense, since the narrator is often not directly present in the experiential spaces of the storyworld, but operating in a broader orchestrating, commenting, and storytelling role, depending on the type of narrator and their associated viewpoint construction.

Balloons and boxes take up space within the panel, obscuring aspects of the represented storyworld to embed information that readers simulate from a different sense modality, adding sound to the image. Balloons materialize non-visual modalities, orchestrating different voices and viewpoints that readers simulate within a coherent, multimodal scenario. As such, the imagic cues discussed above play a significant role in interpretive processes of the language in the speech and thought balloons, even while the balloons obscure areas of the image. Perceptual processes of object completion allow for visual coherence in the image despite this intrusion. A novice reader might wonder if the speech balloons are material objects in the storyworld, such as a billboard. However, familiarity with discursive conventions and intersubjective norms around conversations (and, with some explanation of comics-specific conventions from an expert like a parent, teacher), readers will quickly assign these visual objects their conventional meaning as an iconic container for sounds. Generally, while embedded in the image of the panel, the conventional speech balloon (along with other balloons, captions, and narrator boxes) is conceptualized as a non-pictorial space reserved for the visual presentation of the verbal modality, for writing. Simultaneously, the visual structure of balloons can also vary to add meaning, such as to indicate the difference between the tone and volume of a whisper and a shout.

There are two particularly important ways in which the formal qualities of balloons harness cognitive processes to prompt meaning and interpretive possibilities. The first is the specific visual qualities of their forms and how they present their content. The following simple illustration (Figure 4.10) shows four common types of balloons with distinct conventionalized boundaries. These shapes align with particular meanings, acting as a comics-specific "construction," a specific form-meaning pairing. These formal meanings are not accidental, but motivated from embodied schematic and synesthetic cues. Most readers likely barely need the caption to guess which is the whisper versus the scream. As discussed with sound effects, readers isolate perceptual analogical qualities that map between visual and sonic forms, such as the more tentative or hesitant qualities of

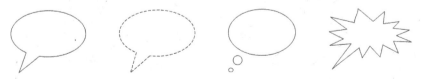

Figure 4.10 Common balloons, left to right: speech, whisper, thought, and scream or electronic voice (by author).

the whisper, which are visually analogous to the softness or broken line of one speech balloon, which facilitates the blending of form-meanings. Sometimes whispers are presented also in a lighter hue for the balloons and words, or in a smaller font, for a similar perceptual analogical mapping. The thought bubbles also function like speech balloons, but illustrate that their qualities are not direct speech, but separated or broken from the thinker by imbuing the tail of the balloon with the perceptual brokenness of the bubbled tail. One might infer from the form that this voice has no direct sonic quality directed out from the subject, and is therefore mental speech. Likewise, the jagged outline of the scream suggests an abrasive quality that creates a synesthetic blend of visual or material (as in a jagged object) and sonic modalities, becoming an icon of harsh sound. There is a range of other ways that the outlines of speech balloons offer emotional and other cues (see Forceville 2013; Forceville, Veale, and Feyaerts 2010), all of which function in similar synesthetic ways to analogically integrate abstracted aspects of sensorimotor and intersubjective experience into formal choices.

Gestalt psychology and simulation studies support the argument for embodied motivations or groundings for meaning by showing strong perceptual and conceptual connections between sight and sound. First studied in gestalt psychology (Köhler 1929) and reconsidered recently in psycholinguistics (Ramachandran and Hubbard 2001), the bouba/kiki effect suggests that resonances can be elicited between abstract linguistic forms and visual forms. In these studies, participants are shown two images that resemble those in Figure 4.11 and asked to guess which one is "bouba" and which is "kiki." An astounding 95 percent of Western participants mapped "kiki" to the jagged figure and "bouba" to the smoother one. Ramachandran and Hubbard (2001) posit that this almost universal mapping suggests that perceptual analogies among how the word is voiced, how the figure looks, and how the word sounds all contribute to a sense of similarity, which they ground in "sensory-to-motor synaesthesia" (19). Research into

Figure 4.11 My rendition of the general shapes of "Kiki" and "Bouba" that varied subtly among several studies.

the multimodal integration of sight, sound, and touch in language and culture continues to affirm the conclusions from the bouba/kiki studies (Fryer, Freeman, and Pring 2014; Slingerland 2008). This research includes interests in iconicity in which emotional and psychological qualities are connected to forms in meaningful ways (see Burke 2001; Hamburger 2011; Hiraga 2005; Nänny and Fischer 1999; Taub 2001).

The shapes of speech balloons function through perceptual analogies, as synesthetic blends that add tonal and emotional qualities to the language presented in them (see Forceville 2011, 2013). Such synesthetic mechanisms in fact harness mental metaphors at low schematic levels that support the conduit fallacy and its associated mappings for IDEAS ARE OBJECTS. Comics mobilize multiple layers of this concept through formal and conventionalized structures, and particularly through the conventionalization of different balloonic qualities.

4.5 SPATIAL STRATEGIES AND VIEWPOINT ORCHESTRATION

As visual presences, balloons and boxes can function as objects in space, acting as a layer imposed into, on top of, or around an image. Such layering can be used creatively in both regular and experimental comics (see bpNichol in Chapter 8). Balloons and boxes orchestrate and align information in a way that influences how readers connect, interpret, or construe the language. For instance, Alison Bechdel, in *Fun Home: A Tragicomic* (2006), uses common comics conventions to include narrative boxes outside of the comics panel or in small, visibly distinct boxes nestled within, while integrating dialogue as regular speech balloons within the scene (see Figure 4.12). This example comes from a series of panels in which Bechdel contrasts salient qualities of herself and her father, here contrasting her utilitarianism to his aesthetic interests (with a hint of irony here too, since she, as a cartoonist, is obviously interested in aesthetic choices as well). Notice how the narratorial commentary is outside of the scene, which clearly distinguishes between her past-tense memory of a conversation within the panel and her present-tense adult interpretation of that moment. This organization of past and present viewpoints is used across the graphic memoir or "autographic" (Whitlock 2006), in which past-tense experiences are shown within the panel, in combination with her adult narration, literally surrounding the panel with context and commentary.[5] The narratorial adult perspective overtly re-construes the meaning of the memory through extra commentary, thereby modeling how memory blends the experiential and narrative senses of self, in which experiences are interpreted later in

Figure 4.12 A panel with narratorial adult commentary located outside the frame while depicting a recalled event in Alison Bechdel's *Fun Home: A Family Tragicomic* (2006, 15).

terms unknown to the experiencer at the time of memory formation. These two types of selfhoods align with the dual child and adult viewpoints, one simply moving through experiences, the other reflecting on how these experiences connect to broader questions and themes about the nature of the relationship between Bechdel and her father.

Another text that uses spatial qualities of comics to engage with the nature of memory and storytelling, but in a way that complicates further the roles of recollection and interpretation, is *Maus* (1997), Art Spiegelman's classic comic auto/biography. In that work, Spiegelman directly integrates perceived layers of content into the narrative to tell the story of his father as well as the story of the comics' creation. Spiegelman often weaves the present-tense process of interviewing his father about his Holocaust experiences, and of his own experiences creating the comic itself, with the more central depictions of his father's past experiences, the focus of his biography. Unlike Bechdel's more structured orchestration of viewpoints,

Figure 4.13 Art Spiegelman's layered presentation of panel spaces to reflect different narrative spaces in *Maus* (1997, 16).

Spiegelman plays with the layering of cues in a way that relies on the reader to interpret the embedded viewpoints.

In a particularly salient example of multimodal orchestration, spatialization, and construal (Figure 4.13), Spiegelman interrupts the flow of the historical story with a frame-less panel that seems to reside in the space behind the other panels. Note how Spiegelman presents himself as using an interruption gesture with his question, a gesture that also seems to point directly into a previous panel, highlighting content he finds confusing (the name Lucia). Moreover, the moment construes the son's viewpoint with a hint of uncertainty at the veracity of his father's memory, despite relying on it for the story. His father in turn responds both spatially and emotionally. He also directs the reader's attention back across the story panels, looking toward his son to angrily clarify the confusion and to reassert his veracity and authority over his memory. The compositional choice to frame some events and not others places the future characters within the space of composition, literally on the blank page, where the father and son can interact around and clarify details of the historical story that is the main focus of depiction.

This multi-layered structuring of dialogue and characters within the story also creates a circular aspect to reading, in which the reader's gaze is encouraged to cycle back and forth around the historical content as well. At the same time, the forward-facing activity of the father on his exercise bike (the location of his interview) also creates a forward-facing (despite ironically self-effacingly immobile) momentum that maintains the reading path back into the history. This combination of storyworlds and spatial practices creates perceptual layers on the comics page, with the past and present narrative spaces rising or falling in visibility to the reader as the dialogue interrogates it in a different discourse space. This skillful use of presentational spaces allows for a self-reflexive integration of the past and present, as stories that are being both carefully orchestrated and composed by dual storytellers, the father and the son, as co-creators. Spiegelman's spatial strategies regularly reminds the reader that this is a story about a story about the Holocaust, being filtered through multiple perspectives, familial dynamics, artistic interests, and other drivers and values that influence how the story is told and received. Such strategies present a richly personal and interpersonal story of the Holocaust, offering a glimpse into the deep impacts that the Holocaust had on individuals and on their families both during and following its atrocities. Spiegelman's spatial strategies, along with other storytelling techniques, reinforce the challenges of recollection and representation associated with this traumatic history, and the viewpoints that tell it.

4.6 CONCLUSION

As I have shown through these previous examples, the presentations of bodies in space, including a variety of postures, orientations, and peripersonal spaces, help build complex mental scenarios through simulation and blending that can facilitate or obscure viewpoint construction. Here, ideas about attention and simulation have been further expanded to include the body schema, and other complicating features of environments, to show how readers might make predictions and inferences about characters and storyworlds in order to interpret the range of cues. Background domains and associated mental metaphors add to these interpretative possibilities. Viewers read pictographic representations of bodies by simulating them as bodies that are self-contained and are actors in the social and physical world, despite a variety of different ways of representing them.

The presentation of figures and environments in panels is layered on top of with visualized sounds that take on physical qualities in order to add meaning through sound effects that harness synesthetic sense analogies. These synesthetic qualities are further conventionalized and visually manipulated through balloons and boxes whose features add a range of construal and viewpointed qualities. The conduit metaphor of communication is synesthetically expanded through these choices that act as salient embodied anchors for mental simulation and blended elaborations of viewpoints.

The combined effect of these bodily, peripersonal, and synesthetic qualities in a panel is to build a complex space of subjective, intersubjective, and environmental information that allows readers to predict and develop viewpointed and interpretive possibilities for figures, their actions, and the broader story. An embodied approach to these features provides a cohesive explanatory framework for how these different modalities and types of expression coalesce into a coherent mental scenario with multisensory vibrancy.

CHAPTER 5
Expanded Viewpoint Networks

Metonymies, Metaphors, and Other Blends

5.1 EXPANDING NETWORKS

This chapter follows closely on the material developed in the previous chapter, in which I focused primarily on how stylistic choices surrounding bodily depiction and balloons construe content and develop viewpoints. I showed how basic figures in space are depicted to focus attention on features through their strategic composition that configures, orients, and builds interactions in space, exploits expressive anatomy and gesture, and visually enhances and structures linguistic cues to develop mental images that are rich with viewpoint details like emotions, intentions, and so on. The examples generally aligned with typical embodied experiences in a way that lends them a degree of factuality or expectedness, which facilitates more direct predictions and inferences in mental simulation. As such, readers likely align the cues with embodied expectations of how people and things work in the world, abstracting and separating them from lived experience enough to construct new construals of subjects and viewpoints.

Beyond subtle construals of the subject matter, representational choices can add what in literary studies might be considered "figurative" meanings, such as through metaphorical or metonymic associations. While communication studies have often considered figurative meaning to be ornamental or peripheral rather than central to acts of communication, Dancygier and Sweetser (2014) show how recent cognitive linguistic research finds that figurative qualities pervade language and thought and reflect different strategies for accessing and manipulating embodied knowledge. Recent research in visual and multimodal metaphor supports this argument as well (Abdel-Raheem 2017; Bergen 2003; El Refaie 2013; Forceville 2008). Knowledge of cognitive processes of meaning-making is particularly helpful for unpacking how readers may develop and interpret pervasive figurative meanings, generally considered under the guise of metonymy and metaphor, and especially in comics (Kukkonen 2008). In this chapter, I show how visual metonymy, metaphors, and material conventions can build complex blends that expand the meaning potential of depictions of characters and their viewpoints, further complicating how readers might interpret cues.

5.2 MULTIMODAL METONYMIES

Barbara Dancygier and Eve Sweetser define the concept of metonymy as "the use of some entity A to stand for another entity B with which A is correlated" (2014, 100). They go on to helpfully synthesize the scholarly literature to define two dominant forms of metonymy based on categorical or domain-based[1] correlational relationships. Categorical metonymy "is based on a relationship between a larger category and a smaller subcategory which is part of the larger category" (101) and is often linked to language changes, such as the term "dog" once referring to a specific group being generalized to a much broader group, thereby further abstracting the term within the category. Another example might be a specific artist's style or work becoming almost synonymous with a particular art movement, such as the artist Andy Warhol as representative of the pop art movement, in this way also reflecting the influence of one artist's style on a wide category of works. Domain metonymy is different, since it "refers to all usages where one reference to an element of a [domain] is used to refer to either the [domain] as a whole or to other associated elements of the [domain]" (101), such as describing sailboats as "sails on the water," which in fact refers conceptually to the whole boat through reference to a perceptually salient element. I will discuss these two forms of metonymy in more detail below. While these forms of metonymy show differences in association based either on more abstract categorical properties or on specific domain relations, these forms can interact as well at higher levels of abstraction, wherein categorical elements of a more abstract domain can be metonymically activated.

Crucial to my focus in this book on the roles of attention and perception in meaning construction, Dancygier and Sweetser note that metonymic correlations across modalities derive from the basic perceptual ability for pattern completion that pervades cognition (2014, 102). Pattern completion is one of the key components of gestalt perception discussed in the previous chapter, through which the panel, as a unit of attention, is always incomplete and references a broader storyworld, which is a metonymic function (Kukkonen 2008). While gestalt psychology tends to focus on visual perception, a multimodal approach to metonymy shows how this same perceptual process in fact aligns with deeper conceptual processes. As such, Dancygier and Sweetser suggest that this metonymic capacity for correlational, expansive mappings means "it has even deeper cognitive roots" (100) than metaphors, which blend domains. With metonymic activations, readers are given a hint of an aspect of a category or domain, and they complete the associated pattern of embodied knowledge by simulating other relevant connections to fill in the gaps or expand upon its associated qualities as seems relevant to the context. This also reflects an important aspect of learning, by which domains and categories are expanded through associations that then allow for more nuanced predictions, inferences, and actions. Effectively mapping between elements of a domain or category from just an element has clear advantages. For instance, recognizing the general domain of snakes from a glimpse of a tail can allow one to employ appropriately cautious reactions, until identification can rule out whether or not it is poisonous at least. That metonymy is a basic cognitive function should not be surprising, then, since it is a key mechanism for guiding perception and action in a dynamic world.

Either form of metonymy can be described through a mental space blending analysis by looking at how knowledge networks are decompressed into emergent understanding, such that the part is decompressed to give access to the whole of its associated background. In terms of blending theory, metonymy is constrained to a single domain or category, but within this constraint it "changes the way in which its roles and relations are filled" (Dancygier and Sweetser 2014, 93) by strategically activating parts for wider connections.

The two types of metonymies vary in their associations with modalities and in their use in comics. While domain-specific metonymies are often easily connected to experiential domains, categorical metonymies are most often found in symbolic transformations over time, such as in polysemy, where one word can mean multiple things, and other kinds of language changes (Dancygier and Sweetser 2014, 101). Categorical metonymies are less commonly associated with pictorial cues, because they tend to be less symbolic in nature, and therefore are less common in comics. Nonetheless, as I show in the following example, categorical associations can provide important content for critical analysis. Domain-specific metonymies are most common in comics, as they are generally across modalities. Domain metonymies are common in political cartoons (Bergen 2003) and advertising (Cohn 2010); for example, a figure may allude to political entities, such as by referring to the "White House" or by using the Uncle Sam figure, to reflect the wider domains of political institutions and propaganda in the United States. Similarly, the costumes of popular superheroes, like *Captain America*, metonymically reflect the flags of their nation or other characteristic associations that can be decompressed to activate core roles, values, and concepts that layer heroic capacities with nationalist meanings (I discuss such an example in the next chapter; see also Borkent 2017). As such, metonymies are not necessarily just hints of straightforward content that sit more in the background, but can add significant construal and viewpoint content to comics, expanding access to networks of meaning and presenting further opportunities for interpretation.

To better present how metonymies work in more complex ways in comics, I turn to Matt Madden's short comic, "A history of American comic books in six panels" (2012), reproduced in Figure 5.1. Each panel mimics a popular

Figure 5.1 Matt Madden's "A history of American comic books in six panels" (2012).

and representative comic from a historical moment, building a web of intertextual connections.[2] Madden begins with Siegel and Shuster's original rendering of Superman (beginning in 1938), the first popular superhero. This panel activates domain knowledge about comics to metonymically exploit a specific comic to reflect the birth of a genre category, the superhero comic. The language in the panel further highlights popular thematic content, here the superhero's association with American patriotism and moral values of protection and authority. Subsequent panels metonymically reflect (as outlined in Madden 2012): (Panel 2) Harvey Kurtzman and Wally Wood's parody of Superman, "Superduperman" in *Mad* magazine #4 in 1953; (3) Robert Crumb's iconic characters from the "keep it truckin'" strip in his underground classic magazine *Zap Comix* in 1968; (4) a memorable flashback scene in Alan Moore and Dave Gibbon's classic antihero series *Watchmen* (1986–87; collected as a "graphic novel" in 1987); (5) Art Spiegelman's Pulitzer Prize–winning biography/memoir *Maus* that was serialized from 1980–91, and reprinted in many editions since (mimicking specifically 1997: 201); and (6) the protagonist of Chris Ware's collected series *Jimmy Corrigan* (2002), with the background reflecting the style of Daniel Clowe's 1993–97 series *Ghost World* (collected edition, 1998). Each of these panels reflects a specific work from a specific time by mimicking their visual depictions and adding speech and narration that paraphrases their content and tone as well.

In terms of the types of metonymy, this comic activates both types in different ways. By reflecting a specific work in a part-for-whole relation, each panel operates initially as a domain metonymy. Most of these works that Madden metonymically evokes have won awards, hit bestseller lists, inspired movie adaptations, and feature prominently in the popular imaginary around comics. Their wide recognizability facilitates their metonymic activation and decompression of domain knowledge of themselves.

But each panel also functions in this comics "history" to invoke a work that is popularly associated with a transformative moment in the style and content of American comics: the birth or popularization of (1) superheroes, (2) satirical comics, (3) underground and adult comics, (4) revisions of superheroes, (5) non-fiction comics like biography and journalism, and (6) alternative (non-superhero) and avant-garde comics and graphic novels. The specific connection of each work to moments in comics history, and their presentation in a specific historical order and with dialogue, also helps to conceptually unite them to build a historical metanarrative about developments in topics, styles, and approaches to content in a variety of fictional and non-fictional genres. Each panel encapsulates key category markers of a particular moment, thereby providing even uninitiated readers with prototypes or canonical exemplars that prompt genre knowledge for each historical moment (see Solso 1994, 236–39, 251–53). The novice comics reader can read this short strip and go on to likely recognize the sources and perhaps other members of these different artistic movements or genres, whereas a more experienced reader will see more of the subtle connections. Thus, the comic strip is a domain-specific delight for experts, who recognize the specific source texts, and a categorical education for novices who gain insights into the styles of different genres and their historical unfolding. This is the power of domain and categorical metonymy in each panel.

To aid the reader's construction of domain metonymies, Madden adds details and typical features of the visual style and characters of the key comic that are worth unpacking. Each panel is a composite of cues that often blend key features or content from different places in their source text to aid recognition and comprehension. He also adds iconic signs on their shirts that highlight their motivations or values connected to their thematic content (e.g. being chill, making money, asking questions). For instance, the likely source, the original panel, showing the character The Comedian from Moore and Gibbons' *Watchmen* (Figure 5.2) varies from

Figure 5.2 Selection from Moore and Gibbons' *Watchmen* (1986, 4.19).

EXPANDED VIEWPOINT NETWORKS [115]

Madden's version, which focuses more closely on The Comedian's face, adjusting his expression to match the contemplative nature of his caption. Madden also adds The Comedian's characteristic cigar, which he smokes regularly throughout the comic but *not* in the scene Madden replicates. Furthermore, The Comedian's iconic happy face pin includes some drops of blood, which reflect the cover imagery of the graphic novel as well as the most common representation of it in the comic, although *not while being worn* by The Comedian, including not in the source panel. These adjustments prompt domain-specific metonymic mappings to the wider narrative and its popular imagery of the blood-stained happy face pin, a pin that takes on a multi-layered, aggregated meaning across the story (Kukkonen 2008, 95). Through this pastiche of elements, Madden presents a summative caricature of The Comedian, rather than replicating him, by compressing several characteristics and features of the graphic novel into one presentation. He even includes the dollar sign on The Comedian's shirt, which reflects his self-serving motivations expressed throughout *Watchmen*.

Furthermore, Madden uses language in a way that mimics the source text. Again, in this panel, his narrator box reflects the original panel by Moore and Gibbons and seems to comment on The Comedian's actions. In the original, the narration is provided by the character Dr. Manhattan, who reflects on how The Comedian is well suited to a climate of madness and butchery. In Madden's version, he generalizes the commentary to highlight a concern with the nature of heroes and the hypocrisy of power, which is a broader theme throughout Moore and Gibbons' graphic novel. Here, the figure and the narrative caption metonymically blend key elements of the source, to paraphrase a transformative text in comics history when action comics became more self-reflexive about characterization. Coming out in 1986–87, *Watchmen*, along with Frank Miller's reformulation and problematization of the character of Batman in 1986 in *Batman: The Dark Knight Returns* (2002 [1986]), attempted to revise how mainstream comics presented the values and motivations of their main characters, thereby turning the genre toward darker and more psychologically mature themes. Madden nicely encapsulates that genre shift through carefully constructed metonymic cues from a core text.

This panel also includes another anomalous or non-metonymic alteration by changing the color of The Comedian's shirt to red. Several other panels also include this same color change, which, along with the linked content of the speech balloons, serves a pragmatic and epistemic rather than metonymic function by helping the reader to nominally blend the characters with each other. While their features and actions change, the character viewpoints of Madden's comic become enmeshed on a narrative level. The linked language and shirt color between panels, therefore, helps connect the diverse figures, generalizing them to highlight Madden's metacommentary on the growth of comics through genre developments rather than have the reader focus too closely on the characters themselves. In this way, by strategic uses of metonymy and misrepresentation, Madden opens the opportunity for readers to unite the characters into a singular figuration of history, as a figural conceptualization of a multimodal literature developing through time.

Moreover, the red shirt acts as a category metonymy for the protagonist (established especially by the first panel with the superhero). The consistent metonymic mapping to a key role through a simple repeated cue supports textual cohesion, but it also layers on a category metonymy for heroism that is not necessarily a key feature of several of the comics referenced. In this way, the figuration of history may also become inflected with a heroic construal. Because several texts are not heroic in nature, readers might shift this notion to a more abstract level, to see all of these works united as a singular, heroic figuration of genre interventions into the history of American comics. By way of metonymic attribution, then, the creators of these works were artistic heroes, revolutionizing the form.

As I have shown, Madden's comic functions metonymically on several levels, with each panel functioning in similar ways to the one from *Watchmen* discussed above. Each panel maps characters to works, works to artists, works to genres, styles to genres, and comics genres to broader narrative traditions. Each panel blends together features from a transformational work that is indicative of changes in representational styles and narrative genres, highlighting an ongoing self-reflexivity involved in comics innovations. More specifically, from the perspective of metonymic mappings, each panel mimics a recognizable panel in a well-known comic as a domain metonymy: panel for specific comic. It also compresses a range of cues from the wider context of that comic as another intra-textual domain metonymy: a set of details evoking a whole character or story. Finally, through the specific comic reflecting shifts in genre or artistic movement, this presentation prompts a category metonymy that is further clarified through the verbal statements: each offers an exemplar of an artistic movement. Through this multimodal compilation of metonymic cues and stylistic adjustments (including blending together two comics in the final panel), Madden delights those who know, and educates those who do not, about some key developments and figures in American comics history, not by naming them, but by metonymically highlighting key multimodal features of their works and movements. As such, Madden's comic functions as an intertextually rich meta-commentary on the historical development of various styles and genres of American comics.

Beyond its entertaining and educative qualities, this comic also showcases the selective, evaluative, and pragmatic nature of metonymic composition (Littlemore 2017). By focusing on particular examples and features within comics at the expense of others, Madden isolates something specific for the reader's attention. For instance, he focuses on Spiegelman's self-reflexive authorial moments, rather than engage too directly with Spiegelman's father's experiences of the Holocaust, or family turmoil, or other specific aspects of the interwoven memoir and biography. Thus, Madden assesses *Maus* in terms of what it offered the history of the development of the form and a genre of comics, rather than engaging with the details of what the text tells about survivors of the Holocaust. This is not a critique of Madden's comic, since his purpose is to tell a history of comics. Rather it shows the selective and evaluative quality of metonymic constructions because of how they highlight specific features of domains when activating them. They direct attention to key features, giving them rhetorical weight toward the purpose of the text.

Similarly, this foregrounding function also serves to support specific viewpoints that may align with social values and other intersubjective aims. For instance, a critique could be leveled at Madden's comic for its preference for white male authors and their male protagonists. For instance, Alison Bechdel's *Fun Home* (2006) or Lynda Barry's *One! Hundred! Demons!* (2017 [2002]) could have replaced Spiegelman's panel representing the self-reflexive author, and thereby reflected another significant award-winning innovator in the memoir genre in comics while metonymically glimpsing more of the diversity in the comics industry. While Western Anglophone comics still have a predominantly white and male authorship, there are many diverse voices in that publishing space, especially in alternative genres (see F. Aldama 2009, 2010; Hatfield 2005). In this sense, the metonymies employed in Madden's comic may support a more homogeneous perspective of the medium than in reality. However, the significant influence of each of the examples cannot be ignored. Moreover, the pragmatic and discursive needs for textual cohesion between panels also supports the use of a singular gender. Alternating between genders in the middle of six panels might distract from the connective mappings within the text by prompting a category shift in readers, thereby impeding its communicative function as a unified text. As such, a gendered critique is valid in terms of literary history, but also runs up against issues surrounding the internal pragmatic communicative functions of textual relevance and cohesion.

As I have shown, while metonymy may seem like an innocuous means of compounding and linking information, it does so subtly, strategically, and multimodally toward a communicative goal. Categorical metonymy helps readers to put the six panels together into the historical narrative about genres, while the domain metonymy isolates specific features of works from each moment that contributed to the developments of the form. There are clear implications for the kinds of inferences readers might make, through simulation, mental space decompression, and blending, based on what qualities the metonymic element highlights about the source domain or category, and how familiar the reader is with the source inter-texts. By mapping these metonymic and non-metonymic aspects of textual comprehension, analysts (and teachers) can better understand how readers might interpret or become confused by this variety of cues.

5.3 FIGURATIVE METAPHORS AND OTHER BLENDS

In the previous two chapters, I discussed how mental metaphors are embodied concepts that inform how readers build meaning from textual cues. As pervasive components of cognitive topology, mental metaphors can inform interpretations of any form of communication. Here, however, I shift focus to more overt, textually constructed metaphorical patterns that fall into the more traditional sense of metaphors as builders of "figurative meaning," in contrast to literal meanings. Rather than relying on pervasive cognitive scaffolding for blending processes, these metaphors are unique textual constructs. At both the cognitive and textual levels, metaphors are typically defined as instances of mappings of content *between* two separate domains rather than within a domain (thus, in contradistinction to metonymy). However, there are cases where metaphors are grounded in or integrate metonymies, which can make the distinctions somewhat slippery (see Barnden 2010; Fauconnier and Turner 1999, 2008; Radden 2003). This slippery quality emerges in several analyses in this section. For this reason, I rely on the terminology of blending theory, since it allows for a whole range of mappings within a single process, thereby locating the metonymic contributions to metaphorical understandings in a singular framework and explanation of mental scenario construction.

To return to the definition, metaphors often build connections between domains by projecting structure and content from a more concrete domain (the *source* domain, such as a spatial cue) onto a more abstract domain (the *target* domain, such as about time): the TIME IS SPACE mental metaphor mapping is instantiated in expressions like "the past is *behind* us" or "look *into* the future" (this is very common crosslinguistically, but not in some languages: see Núñez and Sweetser 2006). This metaphor will be discussed in more detail in the next chapter on temporal construal. Like with metonymic mappings, for a metaphor to be constructed, features of a domain are highlighted to facilitate selective, partial mappings of structure and content onto another "target" domain (Barcelona 2002; Gentner and Bowdle 2008). It occurs commonly both within and between modalities (Forceville 2008; Gibbons 2012). For space and time, perceptual experiences of time are highlighted through how they are spatialized, such as by placing the agent into the flow of time as they "press on into the future" or in a more passive sense as they watch "time slip by." As these examples show, source and target elements of metaphors can reflect viewpoints and construe and highlight aspects of the different domains, and how these metaphors are constructed and interpreted can vary depending on cultural contexts as well as personal intentions and intersubjective goals.

George Lakoff posits the "invariance principle" to account for the cognitive structures (such as schemas) that constrain what can or cannot be connected through shared topology based on embodied parameters: "What the Invariance Principle does is guarantee that, for container schemas, interiors will be mapped onto interiors, exteriors onto exteriors, and boundaries onto boundaries . . . and so on" (1993, 215). Karen Sullivan (2017) expands on this principle by helpfully documenting the different mapping possibilities of the KNOWING IS SEEING metaphor (discussed in the previous chapter in relation to the conduit metaphor), in which she shows how different forms of the metaphor take up different structures, roles, and values in one domain and maps them to corresponding qualities in the other. For this metaphor, the mappings represent the viewer as the thinker, the object as the idea, visibility as intelligibility, the light source as the source of knowledge, and light emission as intelligence. In this way, Sullivan goes beyond Lakoff's structure focused approach to develop the "extended invariance principle" (404) to emphasize how broader aspects of domain knowledge, including roles, values, and processes, can all build correspondences in metaphor construction.

The blending framework helps isolate contributions to metaphorical meanings through principles that align closely with Sullivan's extended invariance principle, through what Fauconnier and Turner call "vital relations" (presented briefly in Chapter 3). Vital relations facilitate mappings between a wider list of perceptual and experiential features, connecting mental spaces through qualities or patterns of experience including links based on figure or identity, role, cause-effect, change, space, time, category, intentionality (read: viewpoint), and other basic experiential grounds for making inferences and connections (Fauconnier and Turner 2002, 93–102). Importantly, structure and content mappings can occur from the most basic mental metaphors up through to elaborate networks, all of which rely on the same principles of selective domain highlighting, decompression of domain knowledge, and compatibilities based in various affinities and invariances in cognitive topology (see Fauconnier and Turner 2002; Lakoff 1993; Lakoff and Johnson 1980). As such, blending can account for metaphorical constructions as "double-scope blends" (combining domains) in contrast to the "single-scope blends" (working within single domains) of metonymy. As a model of mental processing, these blending principles all apply to multimodal cues as well, since they rely upon embodied topology and activation processes in perception and conceptualization. In this section, I present a range of pictorial and multimodal metaphorical (or metaphor-like) blends that transform how figures and spaces are read and interpreted through creative construal and viewpoint developments.

5.3.1 Figure Blends

As I discussed previously, figures can often be presented in ways that metonymically highlight their roles and values within a domain. Metonymy functions by decompressing salient, domain-specific content to enrich mental space simulations based on text- and context-relevant connections. The same principles of activation, decompression, and elaboration of domains apply to the development of metaphors as well, except those connections align based on structural affinities or vital relations that prompt integration networks between domains rather than within them. Metaphorical constructions can occur in many ways, including within or between modalities. For instance, Gus, the protagonist of Jeff Lemire's limited series *Sweet Tooth* (2009–13), is a pictorial blend of human and deer features, a fact explicitly highlighted in a scene where he meets a deer face to face in the forest in the first issue of the series (Figure 5.3). This builds up a metaphorical relation that blends human and non-human domains through elements of shared features or figuration. The blend of the domains includes noticing differences between them with regard to cultural assumptions about viewpoint, intentionality, and cognitive acuity. The blend also raises questions to some extent about which way to map content, from the person to the deer, or vice versa, unsettling the assumed directionality of metaphorical mappings. Lemire's story explores the experiences of genetic "hybrids" like Gus (a.k.a. "Sweet Tooth") in a post-apocalyptic world, which reveals cultural assumptions about animals, such

Figure 5.3 An early scene with the protagonist, Gus, from Jeff Lemire's *Sweet Tooth* (2010, 23).

as that their doe-eyes indicate stupidity, and often subverts these viewpoint assumptions through the hybrid characters.

At the outset, the blended figure of Gus adds to his characterization, by emphasizing the sense of him being potentially dim-witted (because of his vacant doe-in-the-headlights stare that affirms his deer-ishness, further cued by his horns and similar ears). This projection of bodily structure onto cognitive performance, from deer outside to deer insides, is grounded in the CONTAINER image schema and the related mental metaphors of CONTAINER IS CONTENTS and BODY IS SELF. What is on the outside is also on the inside. This blend of pictorial cues projects significant information from the

[122]   *Comics and Cognition*

deer domain onto the person, which develops Gus' viewpoint metaphorically, since it brings together two disparate domains, altering the domain of the "boy" through the projections of "deer" domain content. In traditional metaphorical analysis, the dominance of boyish characteristics of the figure make it the target domain, onto which the deer source domain is projected. In terms of blending theory, the emergent, metaphorical structure emerges from projecting content primarily onto the subjectivity of the boy, and backward-projecting assumptions about this to qualify or amend assumptions about his character viewpoint. The deer domain projects character qualities like low acuity, stun-ability, as well as sprightliness and other qualities, which are already a part of the multimodal construction of his character in earlier scenes in the comic, but reinforced through this encounter.[3]

Gus' hybrid nature is explored at length throughout this powerful series, and is especially noteworthy when he interacts with "normal" humans who are often hunting hybrids like himself. Importantly, the contrasting qualities of his physical features at times renders him less than human because he is combined with an animal, which is lower on the cultural hierarchy. At other times, he seems more than human in his perceptions of the relationships around him and as he comes to bridge the human and other-than-human worlds. But his "lower being" status in the storyworld, further exacerbated by his lower status as a child, transforms him conceptually into a pathetic creature. Thus, there is an implied viewpoint ascribed to Gus by his simple, hybrid composition (which he goes on to prove wrong).

Importantly, as Katherine Kelp-Stebbins (2012) argues, the hybrid qualities of the comics medium make Gus' story especially compelling and nuanced in its engagement with questions of animality and humanism:

> The body of Gus, like the narrative body, is caught in webs of speculation and information, which do not resolve into easy answers. Similarly, the sketch-like quality of the lines further attests to the situatedness and partiality of the knowledge they afford. Beyond the hybridity of word and image, comics' hybrid relation to representation and presentation makes ambiguous any distinctions between pure human and other. [. . .] In their artifice, comics motivate critical examination of what sort of 'knowledge' is produced by scopic regimes and just how transparent the lines between perceived and received information may be. (345)

Putting aside the problematic assumptions in this quote about the reception and transparency of modes, the ability of comics to blend different forms, both within modalities as seen in the case of Gus' blended body, and between modalities throughout, gives them powerful capacities for complex figural and figurative construals and conceptualizations. Gus' hybrid body is an actual as well as metaphorical body in the story, which raises questions about the nature of human subjectivity, perception, and action through what at first glance seems a simple metaphorical construction that opens up multiple interpretative entailments. Such subtle metaphorical prompts through figural blends are very common in comics.

5.3.2 Environmental Blends

Another powerful metaphorical type of blend is seen in environmental manipulations, here illustrated by Marjane Satrapi's graphic memoir, *Persepolis: The Story of a Childhood* (2003). This example (Figure 5.4) shows the effects of bombings in Tehran through a combination of visual flashes or sound or impact lines that pervade a packed room with small windows and a single light fixture. The light fixture also invokes an impressionistic resemblance to a wrecking ball in the middle of things, prompting a metaphorical elaboration on the scene that complicates the childhood viewpoint.

The sense of the lightbulb being a wrecking ball helps connect the sonic experience of the terrifying bombs and the vibrations in the building to a more general sense of purposeful demolition (metonymically evoking the domain by the wrecking ball), aligning more directly with the intentions behind the bombings. That demolitions are typically done to empty, condemned buildings is also an important facet, since it suggests that those in charge are unconcerned with what or who is destroyed. The somewhat erratic motion of the light/wrecking ball also suggests that the destruction is unpredictable and unfocused, which makes the scene far more anxious. This metaphorical elaboration on a simple feature of the setting metaphorically invokes important broader aspects of the wartime experience, well beyond that of the protagonist's childhood viewpoint. Highlighting the intentional yet erratic and demolitional focus of destruction shows how the activities of war erase the individuality of citizens in favor of the aims and ideologies of those in charge. The bombs are disconnected from the specific people on the ground, and yet it is these people who are faced with the wrecking ball of historical events. This construal of war refocuses the power of ideology as an act of simple brutality: loud, ruckus, destructive, impersonal, and deadly. The loss of individuality under war is also reflected in the silhouettes, rather than detailed presentation, of figures along the bottom of the image.

Figure 5.4 Bombing panel from Marjane Satrapi's *Persepolis: The Story of a Childhood* (2003, 103).

As this example shows, a well-crafted and abstracted environmental metaphor can pack worlds of meaning into the construal of a simple scene, adding contrasting viewpoints with different roles and values in the story. Through this metaphorical embellishment through the art style, the viewpoint of the narrator is complemented by a broader storyworld viewpoint that includes commentary on powerful people whose choices can deeply impact the everyday person.

5.3.3 Viewpoint-environment Blends

Environmental cues can also more directly integrate with character viewpoints through metaphorical viewpoint projections. The following examples show how environments can reveal subjective qualities of character's experiences (see also Borkent 2017). While the Satrapi example above captured elements of this, they were experiences that were still a part of a shared reality, as part of a wider storyworld viewpoint, which is more "objective" and epistemically expected. The following examples are much more subjective.

"Never Do This" (Figure 5.5) comes from the popular, award-winning web comic *xkcd*, created and continually updated since 2005 by Randall Munroe. The first three panels offer a fairly straightforward sequence involving two (stick) figures investigating things around them with a pocket microscope. This does not seem like cause for laughter, yet the overly dramatic final panel is amusing, in large part because of the shifts in the background cues.

In the first three panels, through the metonymic association with microscopes and through their dialogue, the two figures exhibit the roles and values of wonder and scientific discovery as they "look at stuff!" The light-hearted quality of the first three panels changes abruptly, with the room darkening, and their interactions and shared desire to discover dissolving into singular, monotonous murmurs and static, self-protective postures. The vital relations of figures, change, and cause-effect help readers interpret the change, recognizing that the examination of their fingernails has prompted a dramatic change from action and conversation to incoherence and stasis. The transformation emerges by blending the panels into an event structure and then answering the question that the final panel prompts: what caused the change? Decompression of specific domain knowledge about fingernails suggests that neither of them realized just how dirty and gross their fingernails really were. Such knowledge only emerges out of interrogating the inputs to the causation blend. This sequence also establishes both the cause and effect of revulsion, which is the subject, the "this," of the title.

Figure 5.5 "Never Do This" from *xkcd* (Munroe 2011).

[126]   *Comics and Cognition*

What is especially interesting about this comic, as the section title suggests, is the cognitive work behind interpreting the final panel's dark background, which heightens the emotional impact of the revlusion. The switch in lighting could depict a turn toward nighttime; however, the narrator box tells the reader that this is just "minutes later…." This cue requires the reader to reinterpret the background as non-veridical, as a depiction of something other than the natural background in the storyworld. The background must be interpreted figuratively. A metaphorical viewpoint elaboration is initiated by the characters' postures and language. Their perceptions and desires have been subsumed into darkness. This panel reflects and plays with the SEEING IS UNDERSTANDING metaphor mentioned above. The comic suggests that some things, like what is under fingernails, should not be seen, and therefore, known. One might infer that the background projects their negative internal subjective viewpoints onto the storyworld, projecting a visual metaphor and summary of their perceptions and reactions. Their world has not literally darkened, but their emotional state has. The immobile and darkened aspects of the final panel end the strip on a static note, with the recovery of the characters from their shock but a hoped-for future. By blending and simulating this panel to make sense of the changes in actions and character viewpoints, readers build a complex mental model of the event and its emotional impact that lingers because of the static perceptual qualities that subsume the characters.

The next example (Figure 5.6) functions similarly to "Never Do This," by projecting the internal viewpoint of the character onto subsequent and stylistically distinct panels, but in a more complex manner that elaborates solely on the mental simulations of the character rather than integrating viewpoint cues into the environment. This viewpoint elaboration draws the

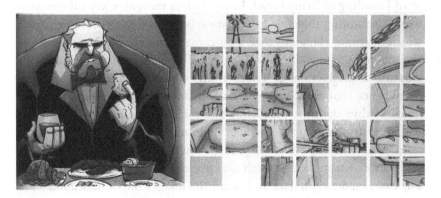

Figure 5.6 Depiction of Agent Mason Savoy and his cibopathic ability in *Chew: The Smorgasbord Edition* (Layman and Guillory 2013, n.p.).

reader into the internal visions of a character rather than along with them in their physical storyworld. This visualization of subjective viewpoint plays with the underlying SEEING IS UNDERSTANDING metaphor. It comes from the fantastical cop-thriller series *Chew* (2009–16) by John Layman and Rob Guillory. The character, Agent Mason Savoy, fits the same set of skills as the series protagonist Tony Chu, who is described as "cibopathic. That means he can take a bite of an apple, and get a feeling in his head about what tree it grew from, what pesticides were used on the crop, and when it was harvested. Or he could eat a hamburger, and flash onto something *else* entirely" (2013, n.p.). This ability is consistently represented throughout the series with a visual shift in panel color scheme, rendering all cibopathic information in an orange-sepia tone. The obvious disjuncture between the character setting and the images facilitates the consistent mapping of this content into an integrated yet separate mental space network that presents the character's internal mental imagery, as defined by the comic as the character's cibopathic ability.

The externalized projection seen here reflects Savoy's mental simulation of information residing in his food. This strip of panels comes from a several-page sequence that tracks his process of eating and visualizing the associated information. In this example, in the opening panel, Savoy is shown eating bread at a dining table. Subsequent panels shift dramatically in visual style to present images of wheat growing, dough kneading, and bread baking in a somewhat fractured manner. These silent panels elucidate for the viewer the specific evocations of the domain network associated with the bread, including a visualized feeling of history and agency surrounding it, while also construing this information that is fractured and that the cibopath must sort through to comprehend as a coherent mental image. The gestalt impressions of singular images, such as of kneading or firing bread, helps readers recognize key information, while also noting that this information is fractured and missing panels, which suggests elements that may come into existence at random, as the cibopath eats more. These panels illustrate clearly the cibopathic masticular production of information, while illustrating the sensory intelligence that must be applied to organize and interpret a coherent image within the bits, paralleling the comics structure with the act of eating, of fragmenting in order to build meaning. From this composite strip, readers might even interpret the multitude of panels to map to his multitude of taste buds, which also present overlapping sensations. In any case, readers simulate and blend the images into a multimodal scenario that reflects the historical and agentive information Savoy gleans from his meal.

Having evocatively established his abilities to metonymically encapsulate the history of an object by eating it, subsequent strips and pages have Agent Savoy turn to a piece of a human ear, working bite by bite to visualize a range of associated events and characters. This horrific meal allows him to solve a mystery. Over these pages, the main panel and associated mini-strips shift in focus. Slowly the main panel focuses on Savoy's serious face, while the cibopathic visualizations become more numerous while also focusing increasingly on only one character's face. By the end of the sequence (Figure 5.7), it becomes very clear that Savoy's ability to deduce information from the ear has led him to a crucial character, Olive, the daughter of the series protagonist. The contrast between the opening strip and this later strip illustrates a significant transformation in Savoy's viewpoint. While the opening sequence shows his cibopathic perception through the innocuous and pleasant things of his meal, the scene becomes increasingly ominous through stylistic and pictorial shifts, which reconstrues his abilities and viewpoint to that of perceptual acuity and a focused threat.

Understanding what is happening across these pages requires an allocation of different values and viewpoints to specific mental spaces. The different types and colors of panels present cues that suggest a sense of the character's synesthetic experience by prompting several parallel paths of mental imagery simulation that must be blended to form a coherent sense of the character's viewpoint. This cohesion is facilitated by expanding on or complicating the structure of the SEEING IS UNDERSTANDING mental metaphor discussed above. The SEEING IS UNDERSTANDING metaphor is also closely related to another mental metaphor, GRASPING IS KNOWING, exhibited in expressions like, "I don't get what you mean" wherein ideas are treated like objects to be held in order to be comprehended. In this comic, another sense is added to the metaphor for knowing by constructing the

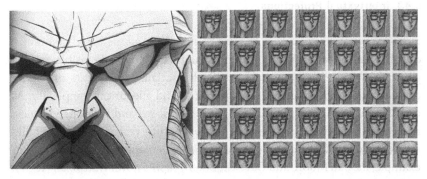

Figure 5.7 A singular and ominous shift in Savoy's mental imagery (Layman and Guillory 2013, n.p.).

metaphor, TASTING IS KNOWING. This new metaphor is, ironically, only accessible through visualization that constructs a synesthetic metaphorical blend between taste and sight to helps readers build a more generic mental metaphor like PERCEIVING IS UNDERSTANDING, through which any sense perception or feeling can contribute to knowledge. *Chew* wonderfully illustrates the principle of embodied cognition that perception and conception are united.

This comics page, and others like it, shows a creative instantiation of the use of multisensory experience for meaning-making. Furthermore, it supports Edward Slingerland's argument that metaphors (and I would suggest, blending in general) are a form of "voluntary, partial, and optional synaesthesia" (2008, 160), such that mappings between senses inform meaning construction. In this case, light and vision metaphors for knowledge, which are extremely common in Western philosophy and culture (Vasseleu 1998),[4] are leveraged to develop a multisensory blend. Moreover, the multisensory nature of perception includes metacognitive aspects in its predictive and inferential qualities, such as social and abstract reasoning (Deroy, Spence, and Noppeney 2016). In this comic, multisensory reasoning is mobilized to build a perceptual viewpoint blend. Such a blend that profiles the senses thus alters how readers simulate the page by encouraging readers to simulate a *robustly multisensory experience* of Savoy's meal and investigative eating, blending metonymic and metaphorical connections into a complex experience. This pushes well beyond the reader's experiential grounding for simulations when engaged in interpreting embodied actions throughout comics. Here, synesthetic simulation is foregrounded and made resonant, as part of a character-specific viewpoint and skill.

5.4 WOVEN AND EXTENDED VIEWPOINTS

5.4.1 Intertextual Projections

Selective synesthesia serves an important role in all mediated communication, wherein language and other cultural cues are made visible and organized in material representation. Such spatialized elements of comics can also take on metonymic, metaphorical, and allegorical complexity. As discussed in the previous chapter, narrative boxes and balloons visualize and structure verbal cues. They can also weave intertextual content to build resonances and direct commentary between elements in storyworlds. For example, in Alan Moore and Dave Gibbons' graphic novel *Watchmen* (1987), a shipwreck horror comic embeds another storyworld within the story to

Figure 5.8 Two panels from Moore and Gibbons' *Watchmen* (1986, 8.25) illustrating uses of visual style and language presentation to weave two stories together.

allegorically highlight the emotionally charged concerns and growing chaos on the city street. The graphic novel initially introduces the shipwreck comic with a surprising shift in style in the opening panel (see Figure 5.8), before the next panel contextualizes it as the first panel on a page being held by a character reading it beside the local news stand in the *Watchmen* storyworld. The speech balloons are also revealed to be a conversation between the newsstand clerk and some neo-Nazi punks, wherein they voice their fears about nuclear apocalypse and Dr. Manhattan, a superhero character.

The structural and stylistic choices of these panels help build intertextual resonances between the two storyworlds while keeping them distinct. The first panel reflects the page of the shipwreck comic's world being read at the news stand, while the dialogue intrudes from the surrounding world of *Watchmen* (notice how the balloon tails go out of the panel, "off-screen"). The visual style of this panel mimics the style of a mid-1900s genre popular during the Red Scare, which helps build metaphorical parallels to the *Watchmen* world with its similar concerns (Kukkonen 2013b). The next panel flips the visual location and sources of dialogue, which clarifies the sudden shift in storyworld and dialogue in the first panel, but maintains the blending of verbal cues from both storyworlds through the distinctively stylized narration box from the pirate comic. The narration of the first panel presents the shipwrecked protagonist's ruminations about the bloated bodies of his fellow sailors that are buoying him up and reminding him of his own imminent death. However, the intrusion of the dialogue from the neo-Nazis thematically aligns with the pirate narration, in which they too could be said to be literally offering their "bubbling dialogues" (dialogue in speech bubbles), but in their case revealing their obsession with nuclear destruction rather than shipwrecked deaths. Since the bubbling is coming from decomposing bodies in the source text, this intertextual development adds an ominous tone to the potential apocalypse threatening the chaotic city and metaphorically assesses the quality of the neo-Nazis as well, building a metaphorical resonance between the two storyworlds.

The story-within-a-story builds up thematic or allegorical resonances through several important cognitive mappings. The intertextual weaving operates through visual categorical metonymy that activate the genre of horror comics from the 1950s, as well as specifically mapping the narration boxes between storyworlds as a domain metonymy. The second panel also repeats the first panel in a more gestural monochrome style, illustrating its context, reinforcing that the first panel is only part of a larger whole. Similarly, domain metonymy is relevant in activating the atomic anxieties reflected in the punk's statements about "this big flash" and "this terrible noise," while the other punk's statement about "it's his fault" locates the conversation in the *Watchmen* story. All of these category and domain metonymies help develop resonances between the two worlds, setting up the intertextual relationship.

As visual style and categorical and domain metonymies build intertextual alignment, a metaphorical relationship emerges between the two storyworlds, using the pirate story as an allegory that highlights the anxiety and terror felt by characters in the *Watchmen* world. The narration highlights (including literally bolding the key terms) features for dialogue and actors in the main story, foregrounding the "pandemonium," "damnation," and later death's "deliverance." Each of these elements are terms from the narration in the pirate story, but foreground statements and actions amid the growing chaos in the *Watchmen* storyworld. This short intertextual interaction highlights how the simple stylization of narratorial boxes, balloon tail orientation, and distinctive visual depictions helps keep the two narrative strands distinct but allows one to speak allegorically into the other (see Kukkonen 2013b). As such, the distinctive visual styles of each comic maintain a clear domain metonymic connection to their sources, while allowing their details to metaphorically blend and inform the epistemic viewpoint of the broader narrative of *Watchmen*. Using an embedded horror comic as a spotlight on thematic content construes the original storyworld as even worse than originally perceived, since the horrors of two different dystopian existences resonate and reinforce each other, heightening the dread and tensions within the broader epistemic and narratorial viewpoint that informs associated character viewpoints embedded within the *Watchmen* storyworld.

5.4.2 Narratorial Projections

As the examples from *Fun Home* and *Maus* in the previous chapter and *Watchmen* here show, different visual spaces in the panel are assigned different narrative and narratorial functions, and conventions for balloon and caption types as well as modality-specific cues help maintain these distinctions and allow them to work in multimodal and synesthetic conjunction to develop rich stories. However, sometimes the distinctions between cues and conventions are less overt, and their narrative functions must be inferred from conspicuous and anomalous elements imbedded within the visual cues of the panel itself. In some cases, the change in cues can prompt the reader to build new interpretations of aspects of the character or the storyworld (such as the shift in light to dark backgrounds in the *xkcd* comic earlier), but in a way that moves beyond character viewpoint construal. For example, in Cecil Castellucci and Jose Pimienta's *Soupy Leaves Home* (2017), open areas of storyworld objects and spaces are used as locations to compress background narratorial content (Figure 5.9). While these are similar to the metonymic character projections of internal states discussed earlier, they serve further narrative functions and require a bit more disentanglement.

In this example, the protagonist, Soupy, narrates her excitement about learning the pictographic signs that "hobos" (Depression-era homeless people) use to communicate to others in order to stay safe and find resources as they moved around. While narrator boxes clearly reflect her commentary, the signs themselves are incongruously written and annotated on the road in front of her and her friend and teacher Ramshackle. As the story shows, typically such signs are written inconspicuously and less frequently on fence posts and other objects. Yet here, the characters walk and clearly engage with the very conspicuous signs that Ramshackle's deictic gesture highlights, perhaps capturing him in the process of explaining their meanings. The symbols on the road are laid out like a glossary or

Figure 5.9 Full-page summary panel from *Soupy Leaves Home* by Cecil Castellucci and Jose Pimienta (2017, 58).

cheat-sheet and suggest that Ramshackle is teaching Soupy the meaningful annotations located with them.

The anomalous, conspicuous, and over-abundant presentation of the signs arrayed on the road invites readers to reinterpret the road as being both the material location as well as a metaphorical presentation space, on which the characters both walk and read. To understand the function of this page within the broader narrative, readers must first disentangle it from the more straightforward travel or adventure narrative, to see it as a different type of narratorial space. It functions much like a dream sequence, with the effusive visual style adding to this effect, pulling back from more immediate experiences in the moment-to-moment narration to offer a different presentation of the story. This requires a cognitive shift in mental space formation, since the reader must interpret this page differently from previous ones.

The narrator boxes introduce the page in summative terms, listing features of the terms that aggregate experiences of signs being everywhere and providing different types of information. This conclusive presentation of the signs sets up an interpretive mental space for the details embedded within the image, engaging their over-abundance and conspicuousness as part of a summary presentation of a longer locative and educative experience. While this seems like a straightforward blend of domains (travel, writing/reading, education), there are important metonymic compressions at work in how readers must combine information in order to interpret the road as summary presentation of an education space. Readers must perform multiple compressions of time, events, and cultural and social values and domains into one space whose epistemic viewpoint is more global rather than episodic.

The image presents the road as the location along which these signs are encountered and blends it with the specific variety of signs and their annotations that may be encountered. This blend compresses disparate parts into a whole representation, having each sign serve to metonymically invoke a separate location in which a sign may be experienced and links to domain-specific knowledge (including about camping or the police, or more broadly about intersubjectivity or action). It also compresses many instances of Ramshackle's explanations into a singular instance, since Ramshackle likely teaches many of these signs while the two characters pass them. The postures and expressions of the characters also construes the teaching and learning as a joyful and lively experience. Importantly, each sign invokes a separate location of learning about signs, and compresses them into the same panel, to give a global view of Soupy's development. The presentation of all of the signs blends them together from multiple instances to give a comprehensive perspective, and also backward projects the generally warm affect of this panel back across those many instances.

The page also utilizes mental metaphors to support this educational blend. Roads are often employed as metaphors for timelines and processes (more on temporal construal in the next chapter), such as when someone talks about their future being "further down the road" or of them "heading toward retirement." Such statements reflect the LIFE IS A JOURNEY and more broadly the TIME IS SPACE metaphors. Here, space and time assumptions might suggest that Soupy has already learned the signs behind her, but is still learning the ones in the foreground, as she is oriented toward the future of her learning journey. Understanding the road and the symbols as an educational experience also relies on mental metaphors about knowledge such as the previously discussed mental metaphors IDEAS ARE OBJECTS and SEEING IS UNDERSTANDING, which connect to the overt depiction of Soupy and Ramshackle gesturing to the signs on the road's surface. The combinations of these metaphors through both the narratorial boxes describing the signs in general, and the specificity of them on the road, document a much longer learning experience with clear temporal and ideational logics. These mental metaphors facilitate the blending of road and its associated experiences to be read as both material and figurative space.

I call such a blend an example of narratorial projection because it takes over the storyworld with an epistemic presentation of Soupy's broader experience, rather than a more episodic, in-the-moment subjective experience of her character viewpoint. While the whole story is told from Soupy's perspective, this panel shifts registers into a more abstracted, narratorial viewpoint, shifting away from the more direct representation of her character viewpoint throughout much of the graphic novel. This is but one example of how anomalies or changes in multimodal depiction can prompt viewpoint shifts, and it shows how blending, metonymy, and metaphors can all function on multiple levels of abstraction to build global insight.

There are of course many other ways to employ speech balloons, narration boxes, and narrative projections than those discussed in these sections. Rather than attempt to be comprehensive in terms of stylistic variables, I have chosen to highlight how choices align with the cognitive topology and processes that underpin comprehension and interpretation, focusing on developing these as an analytical toolkit.

5.5 CONCLUSION: EXPANDED NETWORKS OF PRESENTATION AND VIEWPOINT CONSTRUAL

The material, perceptual, and conceptual layers of comics panels facilitate a range of both literal and figurative blends that inform interpretations of both a character's subjective viewpoint and broader narratorial and epistemic viewpoints and events within a storyworld. The meaningfulness of figures, language, balloons, and boxes, and all of their associated manipulations, comes through the simulation and blending of iconic, indexical, metonymic, and metaphoric mappings that imbed attributional qualities of communication within pictorial contexts to build novel compressions and combinations of domains and mental spaces. Importantly, it is their use in a specific discursive context that clarifies how multimodal properties are functioning in the wider network of signs and meanings.

This chapter has analyzed fundamental features that at first glance might appear largely transparent to the reader, but in fact rely upon rich cognitive structures and processes that activate metonymic and metaphoric qualities to give the comics nuance and depth, especially regarding construal and viewpoints. Readers do a wide array of predictive, inferential, and interpretive work while simulating and blending multimodal cues, perceiving, navigating, and assessing each panel and series to build coherence in the most relevant and economical way. Focusing on the role of metonymies and metaphors shows how a range of embodied domain activations can develop nuanced readings, both realistic and fantastical, in a way that highlights the multimodal and emergent realities of the readerly experience. Similarly, the structural and presentational spaces of panels contribute to this experience through their own schematic and synesthetic qualities. Each of these levels of complexity has shown the dynamic nature of the reader's interpretive processes that rely on cultural, social, intersubjective, personal, and contextual nuances to simulate and construct a wider range of viewpointed meanings.

CHAPTER 6
Temporalities
Metaphors, Modalities, and Arrangements

6.1 COMICS, TIME, AND/OR SEQUENTIALITY

So far in this book I have tended to focus on the wealth of meanings that panels and short sequences of panels prompt, prioritizing the multimodal compositional qualities of panels over wider spatial and sequential interactions (what Thierry Groensteen (2007) calls arthrology). Now I turn to the question of temporality, which is typically associated with the specific role of how panels in sequences, grids, and layouts break information down into discrete units and deliberate patterns that contribute to meaning development.

Barbara Postema (2013) rightly argues, expanding on Scott McCloud's work, that the "gap" between panels (the gutter) plays a significant role in the medium, since it is there that the reader participates most crucially in constructing narrative comprehension by making sense of the differences between panels and stitching them together into a unified whole. The focus on the gutter (this gap, fracture, blank space, and so on) appears in various guises across comics studies, including in McCloud's earlier structuralist work in which he notes that "despite its unceremonious title, the gutter plays host to much of the magic and mystery that are at the very heart of comics" (1994, 66). McCloud also argues that the gaps make the medium inherently participatory, since "the audience is a willing and conscious *collaborator*" (65) through the process of bridging the gaps that he calls "closure": "Comics panels fracture both time and space, offering a jagged staccato rhythm of unconnected moments. But closure allows us to connect these moments and mentally construct a continuous unified reality" (67). In this chapter, I expand on the creative cognitive processes discussed in previous chapters to show how they inform how readers navigate the interactions between panels and build temporal interpretations of sequential meanings as part of constructing this unified textual meaning.

Comic strips have traditionally been treated as reflecting temporal construals with relatively clear durational qualities, acting somewhat like a fragmented film strip. However, as I discuss in this first section, readers make a wide range of inferences about temporal cues in response to their perceived understandings of narrative and character viewpoints, actions, and goals. Temporality is a widely varied and nuanced experience of a text, and it operates within as well as between panels. Panels do not just reflect points on a ticking clock, as McCloud visualizes it for readers (Figure 6.1), and as did Eisner before him (2008, 27). They offer much more temporal complexity, as McCloud also admits. So, even while he presents a clock in which "*time and space* are *one and the same*," McCloud subsequently disclaims that "the problem is *there's no conversion chart!* . . . So, as readers, we are left with a *vague sense* that as our eyes are moving through *space*, they're also moving through *time*—we just don't know *how much!*" (1994, 100, emphasis in original). Thus, while a sense of time seems self-evidently crucial to storytelling, it is difficult to account for.

This "vague sense" of time being directly related to space is a product of cognitive capacities to activate embodied temporal meanings from spatial

Figure 6.1 Scott McCloud (via his cartoon persona) explains the space-time synergy of comics with a clock metaphor (1993, 100).

cues (Gallagher, Martínez, and Gastelum 2018). Moreover, as I show, temporal duration plays a supporting role in a range of storytelling aims, providing an organizational logic to events and interactions. More importantly, temporality is an emergent property of cognitive assumptions, inferences, and projections from multimodal cues (such as the direction of movement of McCloud's character in the clock), not just spatial arrangement, and as such, character and narrative viewpoint construction and readerly assumptions, predictions, and interpretations about actions and the order of events and interactions guide how temporal meaning is made. Sequentiality is crucial to developing a range of subjective inferences about character interactions and event structure, from which temporal clarity emerges alongside other storytelling goals, but duration and other temporal qualities are also part of the constructed mental scenario that is not at all formulaic but dynamic and multifaceted in its temporality.

The central conflation of temporality and spatiality in discussions of comics have distracted scholars from the conceptual and perceptual negotiations that inform how panels blend together into comprehensible strips, scenes, and stories and what role the modalities and the medium play in the construction of meaning. McCloud and others are not wrong to focus on the contributions of space to discussions of time in comics, but the conversation should look much deeper to see how cognitive parameters and processes engage with the medium to build textual experiences like temporality and narrativity, which are emergent understandings of sequentiality and multimodality, rather than generalize too quickly to equate time and space as one. While there is a long Western tradition of treating time in such monolithic terms (Cooperrider and Nunez 2013, 225), such a perspective does not correlate well with the cognitive research into embodied experiences of temporality and its expression through multiple modalities.

In this chapter, I continue to develop an embodied approach that shows how sequential meaning is motivated and constrained by panel contents and arrangements in conjunction with embodied assumptions and processes. I show how temporal inferences vary by modality, and how their asynchronicities blend into narrative coherence. I go on to discuss central mental metaphors that inform how readers interpret space, time, and events, which unpack in more detail McCloud's space-time clock metaphor and how it both helps and hinders the conversation. I show how different mental metaphors inform simulated prediction and inference patterns, expanding on the cognitive parameters and processes described in previous chapters. This analysis reveals how the spatial relations of comics panels act as "material anchors" that motivate interpretations by directing improvisational qualities of gap-filling that occur through simulation and blending. This microprocess expands to wider narrative interests through salient features acting as "narrative anchors," which I develop in more detail in the next chapter as well. As such, the conventional form of comics functions on several levels through a variety of what I would call generically "cognitive anchors." Through this analysis, I show how temporal cues are significant mostly as subjective construals of depicted experiences rather than the more formulaic approach espoused by early theorists in which comics compose a more static time-space matrix. Much more important to meaning-making is the simulated projection of domain knowledge about spaces, actions, and events that order experiences and give them human-scale meaning and predictability.

6.1.1 Temporal Asynchronicities: Reading and Reconstructing Temporal Cues

While comics are spatially complex, their material organization is but one modality that contributes to temporal understandings. In short, time cannot be assumed of the sequential presentations of panels (as evidenced by anomalies in McCloud's discussion of transitions: see Cohn 2010), but functions as a secondary property emergent from blends of multimodal cues within and between them. Moreover, temporal inferences vary between modalities and panels, as illustrated by a short example from a 1965 *Captain America* comic, "Among Us, Wreckers Dwell!" by Stan Lee and Jack Kirby (Figure 6.2). At first glance, this comic seems to fit McCloud's description of space-time unification, since the consecutive panels offer a clear presentation of a brief event in which Captain America (CA) and Bucky fight two villains. The event structure seems straightforward. However, careful examination of the temporality of the multimodal cues suggests a less-than-clear presentation that readers navigate, largely unconsciously. Recall that simulation is incremental, context sensitive, opportunistic, and ephemeral (Bergen 2012, 132), which means that modalities can simulate in parallel (Kuzmičová 2014, 277–78), and the blending process integrates these streams of simulated content into a meaningful whole. Examination of the temporal qualities of these panels shows how context sensitivity, viewpoint construction, and a degree of temporal flexibility are crucial for this meaning coherence.

Beginning with the first panel, temporal analysis of the parallel simulations of the modalities shows how much information needs to be connected in order to interpret the scene. Simulating the visual depictions of mid-motion figures requires building backward and forward in time to

Figure 6.2 Selection from Stan Lee and Jack Kirby's 1965 *Captain America* comic, "Among Us, Wreckers Dwell!" (reprinted in Eisner 2008b, 131). © 1965 Marvel Comics.

understand their postures and the actions. The indexical motion lines map onto the movements of the figures to help show the trajectory of motion, reinforcing that the man's fall is directly related to the force of CA's punch. These simulations have a fairly clearly associated temporal duration, since readers know roughly how long such actions would take to perform. The verbal modality offers a different temporal quality to the panel. Speech and auditory pathways are simulated as part of verbal rehearsal, even for silent reading (Kuzmičová 2014, 277),[1] so CA's statement encodes with it the time it would take to speak it, which is substantially longer than the punch itself (say around 5 seconds). While a comics panel prompts parallel simulations, this asynchronicity in temporality between modalities raises the question of how readers then synthesize the temporal diversity within the multimodal composition. For instance, when during CA's statement does he punch the villain, if one modality happens experientially (and, therefore, in simulated mental imagery) much more quickly than the other? However, most readers likely did not stop to ask such a question. The asynchronicity of modalities occurs in analysis of individual modalities, but not in the multimodal texture of the reading experience, which reveals that unconscious cognitive processes have quickly accounted for and moved beyond these asynchronicities.

On one level, actions and language can be blended through assumptions about intersubjective communication. The bold font of "free men" and "too" suggests points of emphasis in speech. Emphasis often aligns with gesticulation or other gestures in natural conversation, and so perhaps in this case with a well-placed punch. In this way, readers likely integrate the verbal and visual simulations as a co-speech gesture, aligning the punch either midway or at the end of the statement.

Whether or not the punch occurs at the middle or the end of CA's statement may be irrelevant, since its emphatic role and the consequence to the villain is more important to the pragmatic aims of the panel, which showcase CA's power and identity. Broader cognitive goals likely override differences in temporal qualities of modalities to help build a coherent mental scenario that accounts for and integrates more of the cues. Cognition is primarily biased toward goal-directed action (recognition of objects and dynamic interactions in an event structure) and viewpoints of characters (to ascertain motivations and to predict subsequent actions). Domain knowledge, in this case about American political ideals, fighting, and villainy, helps nuance the viewpoint dynamics to develop clear roles and values. This information clarifies why the two figures are fighting, with CA fighting for political freedom (rather than totalitarianism), and the fact that CA seems to be winning (a point for democracy) is far more significant than when in his statement he hits the villain. Overall, the temporal asynchronicities within the panel are likely ignored by the reader in favor of highlighting the content of CA's statement, his physical dominance, and the villain's incapacity. Thus, at the panel level, interpretations of character viewpoints (roles, values, motivations), their interactions (who is doing what to whom?), and the overall qualities and order of events inform how modalities are processed, with temporal qualities of modalities playing a secondary role at most (see Borkent 2017 for more analysis of this panel).

Temporal asynchronicities abound and compound throughout this sequence of panels. I will not examine the subsequent panels in quite the same degree of detail as the first, since similar temporal asynchronies and pragmatic shortcuts occur within all of them to develop both character-specific and broader narrative viewpoints. Put in sequence, further observations about temporal inferences surround transitions and alignments between panels. Continuing with the previous example, the durational qualities of

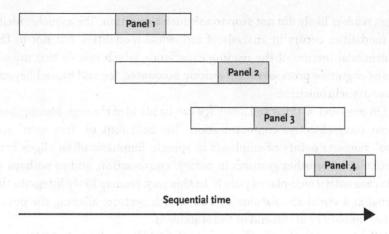

Figure 6.3 Diagram of temporal construal for panels in Figure 6.2, contrasting the duration implied by the pictorial and indexical modalities of the figures and actions (grey box) and the verbal modality (white box).

the represented thoughts and statements consistently chafe against the depicted rapidity of the actions across panels. For example, the second and third panels depict nearly simultaneous time frames in the event structure, but offer diametrically opposed perspectives on the action, one presenting the viewpoint of the villain, the other of the heroes. At the same time, the verbal cues again overrun the individually depicted panels as well as their sequential connections. In Figure 6.3, I diagram the entire sequence to show how the temporal construal of the verbal modalities (as white boxes) far exceed that of the depicted actions of figures (embedded grey boxes), even when including their elongated duration with indexical motion lines.

Without reading the words, the simulated duration of these action-packed four panels would likely not exceed five seconds long in actual experience, but to read (and silently vocalize) the dialogue and thoughts takes longer. The verbal modality seems to slow down or even pause the action, especially in the third panel, by having the reader engage with statements and thoughts that reinforce and expand on the interactions and motivations behind the depicted actions, such as to highlight the teamwork of the heroes and the failure of the villains. By the end of these four panels, in large part due to the framing of the opening line from CA, the failures of the villains in the fight are political and moral failings as well. Again, like in the first individual panel, these wider narrative goals of understanding the subjective experiences of characters and their environments as well as broader themes override any formulaic or rigid view of temporality, while still maintaining a clear event structure with temporal logic. The temporal asynchronies disappear in deference to the goal of generating coherence for the multimodal text. In the end, the experience of temporality is smoothed out and more subjectively nuanced, becoming what Conard and Lambeens (2012) describe as the reader's experienced duration of a panel and cumulatively of a comic, becoming temporal texture.

6.1.2 Sequences and Temporality

The analysis thus far suggests that there could never be a singular version of McCloud's missing "conversion chart" for the temporal qualities of comics, because the sequences are simulated and interpreted in relation to a range of textual features that direct temporal inferences that may generate different temporal rhythms (Conard and Lambeens 2012), with some panels feeling quick and active, and others more static and timeless. These experiential and interpretive variables reflect the incremental, context-dependent, and human-scale biased nature of mental simulation and blending that synthesizes different temporalities across modalities. At the same time, the consistent event structure of the sequence maintains a more objective sense of temporal linearity, despite varied durational qualities within and between panels. As such, sequentiality, while durationally opaque, remains an important temporal marker that also guides comprehension.

As a sequence of attentional units, comics often depict event structures that develop incrementally in a linear progression, as is evident in the scene analyzed above. Similarly, breaks in linear progression negatively impact or slow comprehension (Cohn 2014), which is further facilitated by somewhat predictable or relevant transitions between sequential panels (Hagmann and Cohn 2016). Temporal assumptions about sequential ordering helps build causal connections, as simulations incrementally blend together (Kukkonen 2013c). As Cohn suggests, "'time' is a mental extraction from the causation/change between [panels]" (2010, 134). This does not mean that readers only move unidirectionally through a sequence, but that relevant causality and viewpoint coherence between panels guides reader comprehension. As Cohn (2010) discusses, transitions are not a forward-driven process, but one that goes back and forth assessing the juxtaposition between panels, and composites of panels, that build and update inferential patterns about characters, events, and temporal relations. The construction of temporal comprehension is constrained by assumptions of causation, wherein the presented order of events will even be reconstructed to match causal assumptions in everyday human vision (Bechlivanidis et al. 2022). Eye-tracking data shows this recursive pattern of engagement with texts (Foulsham, Wybrow, and Cohn 2016), and that strategic segmentation, alignment, and arrangement of multimodal elements, including into sequential units, significantly helps guide reader attention and facilitates comprehension (Holsanova, Holmberg, and Holmqvist 2009). Readers regularly reverse and skip around about the sequence for the sake of assessment and re-cognition, checking back on initial predictions and inferences as new information is encountered through backwards projection. Furthermore, layouts also build patterns of interaction that extend beyond linear juxtaposition (Bateman, Beckmann, and Varela 2018). Thus, temporal inferences emerge through conceptual application of content to the sequence (i.e., backward projection of blends), including its logic of proximity and juxtaposition, which is guided by the property of sequentiality.

How readers interpret sequentiality and build connections is guided by a range of cognitive features and processes that include both objective and subjective construals of temporality. In what follows, I will discuss how temporal construal relies on assumptions about space and event structures through mental metaphors and experiential knowledge. I then go on to discuss a range of temporal construals that strategically mobilize cognitive abilities and comics conventions to build creative temporal blends and opportunities for interpretation. This analysis affirms Cooperrider and Núñez's conclusion in relation to a range of cross-linguistic data—and in language that evokes comics no less—that "Time, as conceptualized everyday by humans, is not a monolith so much as a mosaic" (2013, 227).

6.2 COGNITION AND SPACE/TIME

To clarify how temporal construal emerges from spatial cues requires that analyses step further back into gestalt experiences of the spatiality of the comics form prior to importing information from different modalities. While there are complex construals of time through a range of spatial, bodily, textual, and other perceptual cues, broader spatial logics and metaphors inform how this information is blended together. Mental metaphors play a crucial role in how people understand time. Mental metaphors, as discussed in previous chapters, are abstractions derived from embodied experiences. In the case of temporality, such experiential grounds include embodied engagements with space, objects, intersubjective dynamics, and the durational experience of events.

Analysis of mental metaphors shows how the earlier problems in McCloud's accounts of time and space are grounded in a slippage between two dominant and incompatible metaphors that ground objective and subjective construals of temporality. As I argue in this section, both metaphors for temporal conceptualization are relevant to the medium of comics, but in fundamentally different levels of readerly engagement, with one dominating the experience over the other. I then proceed to show how blending theory explains the emergent textual experiences as mobilized by these metaphors and integrates them through viewpoint transformation, thereby isolating how this slippage and confusion about temporality came to be.

6.2.1 Cognitive Structures of Time: Metaphors and Temporality

Perceiving space and temporal duration as they relate to actions and event sequences crucially informs how people operate as creatures in an environment. Perception of the environment is fundamentally viewpointed in two ways, focusing on objects (what is out there) and action (how can I interact with it, including where and when), which are separate yet deeply integrated aspects of the visual perceptual system (Goodale and Humphrey 1998). As such, it should come as no surprise that the most dominant concepts about time integrate these viewpointed visual systems as well. For instance, when people observe something in motion, such as a bird flying, it is recognized as a thing, but also interpreted from an ego-located (deictic) center: a person typically sees a bird flying toward, away from, or past them. To dream of being a bird is a wonderfully novel experience, in large part because it is so atypical to this viewpoint normativity. The general viewpointed understanding of the bird also carries temporal cues about the duration, quality, and proximity of that motion, such as how quickly and nearby the bird flew and how this impacts the perceptual experience. Similarly, experiences of mobility and interaction with objects carries durational inferences, such that people can even conceptualize a location in terms of how long it takes to get there, rather than the physical distance, seen in a phrase like "I live ten minutes from school," or "It's just a short walk away." From these pervasive experiences of temporality, Lakoff and Johnson conclude that "all of our understandings of time are relative to other concepts such as motion, space, and events" (1999, 137). These embodied experiences are primarily encapsulated by a single primary metaphor that supports two related yet incommensurate metaphorical concepts that reflect the two-part visual system.[2]

Lakoff and Johnson observe that all temporal concepts appear to derive from a shared, or primary, mental metaphor that they call the "time orientation metaphor" (1999, 139–41). This metaphor spatializes time and events in a linear manner, with the location of the perceiver or observer as the present location, with the past typically located behind them and the future in front of them.[3] While it can be represented as ORIENTATION AND LOCATION IN SPACE IS ORIENTATION AND LOCATION IN TIME, TIME ORIENTATION metaphor is more concise. In practice, this mental metaphor is seen when people say that they are "*looking forward* to the birthday party" or that they have "20/20 *hind*sight." Comics mobilize this metaphor of time by generally orienting events along a timeline in paneled sequences. McCloud reflects this metaphor when he states, "wherever your eyes are focused, that's now. But at the same time, your eyes take in the surrounding landscape of the past and future" (1993, 104). While examples like Lee and Kirby's above illustrate that there is temporal complexity within comics, it is also clear that the mental metaphor affirms aspects of this basic space-time modeling of the medium. This experientially grounded metaphor also assumes a logic of event structuring that allows the pruning of temporal asymmetries between modalities in panels in favor of event ordering, which also supports narrative goals. The basal assumptions in cognition provide a predictive and inferential logic about representations of events, such that the spatialization of events will generally be assumed to progress from the past toward the future, unless otherwise indicated.

While the TIME ORIENTATION metaphor provides spatial logic for temporal inferences, it in fact grounds two incompatible mental metaphors about time: the MOVING TIME metaphor and the MOVING OBSERVER metaphor. One metaphor has events move past the observer, embedding them within the experience of the event, moment by moment, while the other places the observer outside of the temporal order, viewing the whole sequence of events as a singular timeline. These two metaphorical versions of the primary mental metaphor reflect the two streams of the perceptual system, which focus on either object- or action-related aspects of events and environments.

For the MOVING TIME metaphor, the perceiver (the ego or viewpoint center) is "a lone, stationary observer facing in a fixed direction" (Lakoff and Johnson 1999, 141), as events move toward and past them. In this metaphorical structure, the temporal locations or events act as objects with fronts and backs oriented in relation to their direction of motion toward the immersed experiencer. This metaphor can be seen in expressions like "live in the now," "the time will come," and in a more discrete statement like "Christmas will be here in two weeks." Such examples conceptualize temporal qualities as objects that move toward the observer, with a range of vague to discrete durational qualities, event features, and temporal markings as well. Despite this variation, temporal units consistently move as objects through space toward the stationary observer, with the observer holding the present (as a perceptually singular moment of the present), while the times move past in a consistent direction (see Lakoff and Johnson 1999, 141–45; Cooperrider and Núñez 2013), building an accumulated sense of the future and the past event-objects. This metaphor grounds some inferences about panels as readers engage them in sequences, since the reader can conceptualize each panel as an event-object, as an attentional unit, moving past their present experience of reading, immersed in the story. This reflects the first part of McCloud's description of comics in which one's focus is always the location of "now."

While, people more typically conceptualize the egoic center (usually the self) as immersed in the motion line of temporal events, as just described above, a less common variation, the MOVING OBSERVER or "time's landscape" metaphor (Lakoff and Johnson 1999, 145–48) moves the ego outside of the stream of time-objects to view time as a timeline as it moves past them (Coulson and Cánovas 2009). From here, people can watch the "flow" of time. This "time-substance variation" (Lakoff and Johnson 1999, 144–45) more strongly conceptualizes moments as objects with directed motion and removes the ego as a participant in the events. This metaphor reflects the second part of McCloud's statement about looking over the "landscape of past and future."

Cooperrider and Núñez distinguish this landscape view as "external diectic time" from the more prevalent and emersive "internal diectic time" (Cooperrider and Núñez 2013, 223). Lakoff and Johnson note that the contrast between metaphors is a "figure-ground reversal" that reveals a duality within the general TIME ORIENTATION mental metaphor through which time or the observer can be foregrounded (1999, 148–49). In terms of comics, one metaphor accounts for the more immersive experience of reading through panels, while the other accounts for moments when the reader's attention shifts to the comic as a materialized timeline, which accounts for other meaningful gestalt experiences of layout and other interpretive moments that step beyond the sequence. This reflects a core "tension" in readerly engagements with comics (Hatfield 2005).

Cultural factors especially relating to literacy also influence interpretations of the external perspective as well, showing that space-time metaphors are situated, rather than purely abstract.[4] For instance, English language readers typically map temporal relations left to right, whereas Hebrew readers would typically map from right to left (Fuhrman and Boroditsky 2010). Therefore, stylistic choices in cultural artifacts that prompt alternative reading paths can alter temporal inferences through manipulations of entailments of this mental metaphor (Casasanto and

Bottini 2014). As such, research is showing how cultural technologies influence space-time concepts, but under these variations remain consistencies in terms of metaphorical structures that inform predictions and inferences.

The MOVING OBSERVER metaphor informs aspects of how readers interpret comics structure, especially in light of the less typical *external time-substance, landscape* view. The associated TEMPORAL SUBSTANCE metaphor underscores the notion of panels being discrete temporal objects, as event moments that readers experience as moving in relation to each other as a temporal stream, timeline, or calendar.[5] The panel functions as a temporal container that holds a specific moment, which is different than conceptualizing them as attentional units, which connects to the immersed experience. There are some important entailments to this instantiation of the MOVING OBSERVER metaphor, in particular the notion that the amount or size of the substance or container may equate to durational qualities, since duration or time span is often "construed in terms of spatial magnitude, be it linear extent or amount" (Cooperrider and Núñez 2013, 223). Therefore, when considering the comic as a timeline, readers might infer different temporal qualities to a long, wide panel (which might seem more like a pause of longer duration in the event structure) than to smaller panels (which might seem to offer a staccato, high-frequency rhythm to the event structure). The TEMPORAL SUBSTANCE metaphor would seem to support the reading experience that formal manipulations of panels and sequences contribute to temporal interpretations outside of the contents of the panels themselves. Of course, reading panel size in terms of time is only part of the equation, since panel contents drive much of the reader's predictive and interpretive processes, but size may play a role in setting up aspects of the predictive architecture during the early stages of scanning the page in order to navigate it, or later as readers step back from the panels to rescan the broader connections as part of later recursive and interpretive reflections.

I would suggest that the distanced, landscaped MOVING OBSERVER metaphor may more directly inform conceptualization or comprehension surrounding the initial and summative scanning processes, which could potentially also inform more fine-grained interpretations as readers switch to conceptualizing spatial and temporal relations through the enmeshed MOVING TIME metaphor as part of more immersive reading experiences of panel details. In the end, both metaphors play a role in conceptualization, but with varying degrees of influence based on the structure and content of the comics. Thus, space does not directly equate to time, but is much more conceptually and contextually nuanced. Spaces are not neutral but compositionally loaded, and space-time metaphorical conceptualizations are opportunistically harnessed for rhetorical and pragmatic storytelling aims, with readers likely oscillating between them as they blend and predict and check inferences throughout the reading process. While it may be difficult to separate these two processes, understanding how each metaphor functions can help disentangle their role in comics conceptualization and shows how formal and communicative choices lead to the experience of texture.

Distinguishing between what is presented and how it is comprehended helps articulate the cognitive work behind experiences of comics (Cohn 2010). The MOVING OBSERVER metaphor, and its association with timelines, provides the basal architecture for interpreting connections between sequences in comic strips, helping to develop a global, narrative viewpoint, while the MOVING OBSERVER metaphor informs engagements with narrative experience as these connections unfold, more closely aligned with character and scenic viewpoints. Isolating how these metaphors function in the moment of reading through a timeline helps show how readers cognitively flip between more global and local activations of organizational and compositional cues in order to interpret panels. At the same time, I should note that non-temporal concepts like "order" share representational resources with temporal construal, but can serve different conceptual purposes (Cooperrider and Núñez 2013, 227). For instance, distinguishing between presentational order and temporal sequence contributes crucially to the analysis of the "architectural" postmodern storytelling of writers like Chris Ware, discussed later in this chapter. But first, I turn to how timelines function in the moment of reading to show how sequences develop conceptual depths.

6.2.2 Timelines, Material Anchors, and Vital Relations

The processes of simulation and blending offer a means of analyzing the material forms of timelines and mosaics by tracking the activation and transformation of cues through conceptualization processes. Such a model can clarify how the gaps between panels in the timeline are "closed" through the creative participation of the reader as they develop textual comprehension or texture.

The materiality of timelines anchor specific relations between elements. Their structure invites comparison, interaction, and integration. Readers are encouraged by textual conventions and modalities to interpret spatialized relations in temporal terms by mobilizing the time-substance and time-orientation metaphors. For instance, the most common everyday timeline of the calendar takes the repeated experience of the day/night and compresses them into a singular temporal concept of the cyclical day (Fauconnier and Turner 2002, 195–95). This concept is visually encoded as a unit that can be ordered in lines and grids to form sequences of weeks and months, which can themselves take on a sense of repetition, if not circularity as seasons and years. The formal mosaic of the calendar makes it particularly apt as an example when looking at comics, and it may have been the commonplace artifact that was in the back of McCloud's mind when he erroneously asserted that "time and space are one." While, as the *Captain America* example illustrated, comics tend to emphasize subjective rather than objective construals of temporality, calendars nonetheless give a good starting place for tracking the cognitive work of sequentiality and layout. For instance, they show how events can be presented in relation to temporal conventions (each unit is a day: "The birthday is on Sunday"), is given duration ("the camp went all week"), and is organized in relation to other events. The presentational and organizational qualities of timelines are particularly important for reading sequences of panels in comics, which are then added to or complicated by other compositional and generic inputs.

Coulson and Pagán Cánovas (2009) show how timelines, as material artifacts, employ the mental metaphors of TIME IS SPACE and EVENTS ARE OBJECTS to support the use of particular spaces as temporal units with locations as an extension of the metaphorical systems. Such metaphorical constructions produce conceptual entailments like "Proximity in time is proximity in space" and "temporal duration is spatial extent" (201). They show, however, that timeline meanings are not simply a matter of metaphorical mappings, but include more complex blended structure, through which domains are compressed, aligned, and integrated (202–3) by anchoring the material object on the timeline. As such, a mark on a timeline compresses the details of an event and locates it in relation to other compressed events. Each mark is a "material anchor" that develops inferential structure in relation to other anchors, which can be integrated or decompressed as needed. Edwin Hutchins (1995, 2005) developed the notion of material anchors to explain how cultural artifacts and practices employ features of an object or environment to offload cognitive work. For instance, he analyzes shopping-market queues and time pieces like clocks to show how they anchor concepts of temporal order or duration onto locations and devices. As Coulson and Pagán Cánovas (2009) show, timelines, in both infographic and literary texts, function in the same way (see also Cánovas and Jensen 2013), presenting temporal information in a specific form to ease inferential processes.

While this is helpful for describing basic visual displays, comics complicate the situation since the temporality of the timeline is only partially rather than systematically employed, and each paneled moment contains temporal asymmetries or even atemporalities that inform inferential and interpretive processes. While panels should be considered as material anchors, and page layouts as a composite of anchors with schematic interactional cues, as I have shown, the content of panels plays a significant role in temporal construal. Comics only emerge as a form of timeline through inferred temporal relations between the anchoring functions of panels, and this temporality is inconsistently experienced since not every transition between panels includes clear temporal changes.

To better isolate how transitions between panels blend into emergent understandings, including with temporal qualities as well as character, environment, and event specific construals and interpretations, I turn here to how the metaphorical and conceptual mappings are directed. As discussed in Chapter 3, Fauconnier and Turner (2002, 92–102) show how mappings between mental spaces rely on vital relations. Vital relations are recurrent qualities of experience that are mobilized to build connections and include change, identity, space, time, cause-effect, part-whole, role, property, similarity, category, and intentionality (101). The selective perception of vital relations develop consistencies that ease mappings and are crucial for efficient blending across the spectrum from basic object comprehension through to complex analogical and metaphorical networks (see Coulson and Oakley 2003, 60–61). For instance, people compress multiple past experience to comprehend the round shape of an apple in order to grasp it properly, and this experience of the fruit also gets mapped onto other representations of it, such as the popular notion of the apple being the fruit of evil in Eden or perceptual obstruction in René Magritte's surrealist self-portrait "The Son of Man," which produce different mental scenarios leveraged off of and combining different domain knowledges. As such, vital relations build from experience, but representational anchors allow for increasing complexity of mappings and creative opportunities for interpretation.

Vital relations reflect cognitive perceptual patterns that inform the structuring of domains and mental metaphors and especially inform the ways comics readers process them through specific cues and modalities. For instance, a series of panels representing a character relies on the vital relation of identity and role, which support the blending of different pictorial and verbal cues surrounding a figure into a singular character's body, viewpoint, statements, and experience. In this way, vital relations facilitate predictions about fictional agents or characters across a timeline.

The space-time vital relations, associated with the temporal metaphors discussed above, further align with event-related vital relations like cause-effect, change, and intentionality, to help build character- and event-specific details in a temporal sequence. Returning to the earlier *Captain America* example, the vital relations of identity and role are important in domain activation surrounding the hero/villain dynamic and in blending the different figures together as individual agents interacting, and cause-effect and intentionality help solidify how readers interpret the punches, shots, and movements of the characters. The sequentiality of the panels reinforces the order of event specific cues, which fosters particular temporal interpretations as well. Thus, vital relations serve an important role in supporting the integration of information between panels through blending along a timeline. This model gives a clearer view of Scott McCloud's famous notion of "closure," which produces a "unified reality" (1994, 67), or analogously what Thierry Groensteen vaguely refers to as "iconic solidarity" (2007, 2013), which rightly presumes a perceptual quality that unifies comics.

As I have shown in general, there are several key cognitive aspects to temporal construal in comics. Metaphors play a foundational role in guiding interpretations of the material anchoring of panels, and vital relations help guide simulation and blending processes to prune asynchronies and weave these into a coherent whole. I now turn to several examples to show how different vital relations and blending phenomena correlate to a range of temporal understandings of event structure and duration, to show in more detail how these cognitive features connect to the rich texture of comics.

6.3 TEMPORAL SHIFTS: TIMELINE MANIPULATION AND BLENDS

6.3.1 Decompressing and Elaborating Temporal Cues

The following example (Figure 6.4) comes from Bill Watterson's comic strip *Calvin and Hobbes*. In it, readers move through a conventional four-panel strip, which exhibits a range of temporal qualities that inform its humorous conclusion. In terms of temporal duration, the first three panels appear to operate smoothly together, offering a brief exchange at night. While it is unclear how long the silence of the second panel lasts, domain knowledge about sleep suggests that it would not be too much longer after saying goodnight. However, the temporal experience of the final transition between the third and final panel suggests a

Figure 6.4 From *Calvin and Hobbes* © 1986 Bill Watterson. Reprinted with permission of Andrews McMeel Syndication. All rights reserved.

much longer temporal expanse. While the paneling structure itself shows a clear event structure, which in other contexts might present a timeline with relatively consistent temporal structure, this comic strip is notable in how it dramatically shifts temporalities to make its point. I will walk briefly through how this unfolds in relation to the cognitive processes discussed above.

The initial two panels activate the camping, nighttime, and sleep domains to set up a cozy evening atmosphere with the two friends sharing a tent. These two panels arguably set up an emotional tone of contentment, happiness, and security. The third panel interrupts this comfortable blend by adding the ghost domain, which maps, as a subdomain and through shared vital relations, to the sleep and nighttime domains, but shifts their emotional tone. In another time and place, the question of belief in ghosts might be benign, but while camping in a darkened forest, a space where people may feel out of place and exposed, it becomes something else all together. Moreover, the domain of camping includes the trope of sharing ghost stories around a camp fire. The final panel reveals that in fact, the ghost question reframed the emotional tone of the opening panels, transforming the night into a terrifying experience. Vital relations also help contrast the figures in the opening and closing panels. This is supported by the mirroring effect of the middle of the strip, where the focus of the cues shifts from figures to their environment and back again. The clear change in figuration, and the affective construal of their faces, illustrates that the question broke the sleep domain, transforming the contentment ascribed to the evening into terror. While the four-panel sequence moves quickly to its conclusion, readers would infer that the duration of the character viewpoints is much longer, not just the objective measure of it covering the course of one night, but also the more experientially elongated subjective measure produced by notions of dread and anxiety.

TEMPORALITIES [155]

What is particularly interesting about this comic is the alluded-to content that is missing from the panels and inferred by the reader: the comic does not present a conversation about ghosts, but only shows it being set up and its effects. There are a host of missing panels, if you are interested in who asked the question and what the other responded. There is a huge lapse in both time and content. While the conversation may be of interest, it is also inconsequential to the comic, since the reader likely infers enough to know why the two characters are presented as they are, exhausted and afraid. The inferential process likely includes activating the domain of ghost stories. Since ghost stories around a fire pit are often considered a part of school or youth camps, the characters' repurposing of the sports equipment as impromptu weapons adds a subtle nod to this type of camping. It also infuses fear into an otherwise positive domain. Again, readers do not see where the equipment came from, or when it was procured. None of these specific aspects of the night are shown, but hide in the gap between the panels, transforming the gutter into a "ghost panel," present but unseen.

This comic strip illustrates several important cognitive qualities. Temporal compression and decompression play a significant role in reading the panels in series. The contrast between the nighttime of the opening panel and the daybreak of the closing panel allows readers to clearly locate the duration of the strip. The light/dark imagery also connects to concepts of storytelling and conceptualization, through common expressions of the SEEING IS KNOWING mental metaphor, including statements like "it will come to light," "I see what you mean," and "seeing is believing." It also connects to embodied constructions of mortality and morality, in which light is good, while darkness brings evil and death. In this case, the comic plays with these concepts of belief and knowledge when it comes to supernatural things. Perhaps the truth about ghosts is revealed through the simultaneous terror and survival of Calvin and Hobbes, wherein seeing does not lead to believing, but rather the opposite: the domain of ghosts naturally cannot survive the light of day, but instead live in the unseeing darkness of the mind.

The comic playfully illustrates the power of mental simulation, which prompts an event structure based in the vital relations of change coupled to identity (we see how the characters remain the same while their surroundings change), and through vital relations of cause-effect based on the linguistic content. Readers retroactively infer a range of activities, ideas, stories, and viewpoints to explain the final panel, fitting it into known time expanse (evening to dawn) and common domains. The inferred ghost sequence—silent, invisible, yet content-rich—makes this succinct comic strip insightful and amusing. The characters exhibit naïve and impressionable childhood viewpoints (including Hobbes being a stuffed tiger that only Calvin experiences as animate, another mental simulation compression). Nonetheless, the conceptual work that prompts understandings of this strip relies on common beliefs about the unknowable that work well beyond childhood. Readers will bring a range of interpretations to this missing content, based on their background dispositions, experiences, and belief to unpack the characters' long night of the soul.

A similar, albeit largely silent, example that also strategically employs domain knowledge and gaps between cues to build toward an unexpected conclusion comes from a short comic scene "Hike" (Figure 6.5) from Jillian Tamaki's larger work *Super Mutant Magic Academy* (2015). Unlike the previous example, Tamaki presents a series of largely silent panels that depict two people hiking to view a sunset. The title presents the domain of hiking to encapsulate the various panels, uniting them into a singular agentive experience, a singular hike with unclear duration. To connect the images, readers must recognize and connect the different types of visual information presented. Each panel profiles the hikers in a different environment, developing viewpoints and intersubjective dynamics through space, and therefore through the duration of the hike. Blending the figures into unified characters employs the vital relations of identity, role, space, time, cause-effect, and event structure, which align within the hiking domain, including specific ideas about roles (leaders, followers, assistance), values (journeys, exercise, companionship, shared experiences, etc.), and locations (outdoor vistas, traversals, etc.).

The change in tone of the final panel aligns this example well with the previous one from *Calvin and Hobbes*, as it also retroactively updates or elaborates on the storyworld, requiring the reader to backward project from the conclusion to make additional inferences about previous prompts. In this case, each panel can be reinterpreted in relation to the (likely surprising) revelation that "this isn't working." The dialogue presents a stark contrast to the simulated affection (smiles, gestures, assistance) that populated previous panels. Up until the final panel, readers likely built a relatively positive portrait of a couple, based on pictorial cues and supported by the notion that hikes with just two people are often taken by close friends or lovers. The domain knowledge, along with depicted events, mean that readers likely developed a composite viewpoint for the narrative with positive affect: what a lovely couple. This interpretive process is further supported by the common metaphors about life experiences and relationships being journeys (Forceville 2017) which complements the hike domain.

Figure 6.5 "Hike" in *Super Mutant Magic Academy* by Jillian Tamaki (2015, 91).

The final panel inverts this positive and energetic tone by giving the reader access to a new modality, language, and through it, to the internal viewpoints of the characters. In this case, the truth of the scenario is modality specific rather than multimodally constructed, as in the case with *Calvin and Hobbes*, setting up a positive scenario in one modality and counteracting it through another. With the final panel, readers likely look back over the previous panels to attempt to search out a reason for what might be experienced as a change in tone, to look for a missed hint of discord, in order to rewrite the predictive and inferential blending cascades that built the happy couple. Readers might expect that they missed something.

Notice, however, that the depictive tone of the panels remains constant, even into the final panel. Readers did not miss anything in the visual modality. Rather Tamaki changes the multimodal compositionality of the page, which changes the texture of the readerly experience. On one level, the characters come to a realization about their relationship, and this is vocalized to each other. While appearing together, their language reveals that they are in fact mentally separate. Through this strategic compositionality, the comic also develops a metacommentary on multimodal communication by showing the reader that reliance on visual perception alone may lead to false predictions or superficial interpretations, and that dialogue, or more generally multimodality itself, is crucial in order to ascertain the viewpoint of the Other and a more robust understanding of the whole scenario. Thus, the comic builds an event structure with uncertain duration about the hike and then uncertainty about the relationship that it comes to comment on, but maintains a clear plot and metacommentary.

The examples from Watterson and Tamaki show more than the blending processes of decompression and backward projection in order to blend and reassess cues. The comics also reveal how predictive biases and patterns of thought direct simulations and blends in a particular direction until information shifts how that scenario should be interpreted, at which point backward projections help reassess and build alternative meanings that make sense of the whole. For *Calvin and Hobbes*, the clear temporal markers of night and day heighten the impact of a night spent in terror, whereas for the figures in "Hike," objective temporality is obscured through compressions of an entire relationship and a hike of unknown duration to focus on the significance of a central event, a relational rupture. The obscure temporality of "Hike" functions to also leave it open to interpretation (perhaps the comic is actually a mosaic of multiple hikes, and not a single event structure?), but the end result is clear. The process of building and rebuilding meaning for both examples includes assumptions about actions, intentions, and broader social and cultural patterns and understandings, all of which can bias or slant temporal construals based on reader backgrounds. Fauconnier and Turner summarize biases in blending succinctly:

Composition, completion, and elaboration all recruit selectively from our most favored patterns of knowing and thinking. This makes blending a powerful cognitive instrument, but it also makes it highly subject to bias. Composition, completion, and elaboration operate for the most part automatically and below the horizon of conscious observation. This makes the detection of biases difficult. Seepage into the blend can come from defaults, prototypes, category information, conventional scenarios, and any other routine knowledge. (1998, 162)

Blending analyses helps isolate where biases might inform simulation of background knowledge and the meaningful connections that readers develop in response to textual cues. This makes it a crucial tool for literary and cultural analyses, as well as a teaching tool to help train readers to see their minds in action and to develop more nuanced readings of materials by making blind spots visible and legible, be it in the form of ghosts or unspoken understandings hiding in the gaps and modalities of a sequence.

6.3.2 Embedded Temporality and Stasis: Multi-temporal Compression and Decompression

In this section, I discuss examples of compressions that blend multiple actions or events into a shorter sequence. I also analyze how a couple of these examples also help build intratextual and intertextual resonances that offer opportunities for decompression of domain and textually specific information.

The first example comes from early in the story of *Sweet Tooth* (Figure 6.6), a dystopian science fiction series (2010–13) by Jeff Lemire that tracks the experiences of a hybrid deer-human, Gus (a.k.a. "Sweet Tooth"), and his various companions. I analyzed Gus' hybrid figuration in Chapter 5, Figure 5.3. In this large panel, Jeppard, another main character, beats a hunter of hybrid persons to death so he cannot capture Gus. In this composite panel, the visual perspective reinforces Jeppard's dominance and strength, placing him visually over the reader. The repeated, inset images of his gun's stock reinforces the salience of an object of death within the picture and aligns these elements along a motion line that leads from the raised gun down to the hunter's head.

These imbedded panels function to compress and integrate a series of violent impacts, highlighted by the indexically linked and onomatopoeic sound "thunk." Each inset image shifts subtly in orientation to reflect the angle the rifle would be held at as it came down toward the man's head. This sequence of rifle butts functions like glimpses of a repeated action

Figure 6.6 Jeppard kills an antagonist in *Sweet Tooth* (Lemire 2010, 92).

through time, like a timeline, thereby anchoring and creating a singular representation of a much more extended and brutal beating. Cognitively, this page requires readers to blend a singular reflection of Jeppard's body in action through the vital relation of identity, with a series of repeated actions, through the vital relation of change, as the rifle stock shifts and becomes more bloody as it tracks down the page toward the fallen hunter. This composite panel construes the actions through temporal compression, showing how Jeppard beats the man repeatedly, but with a singular and brutal focus and force. While it is unclear how long the actual murder took to accomplish, this presentation arguably increases the affective resonance of the act. While the imbedded images and the onomatopoeic words reinforce the individuality of each hit and their force, the dominant pictorial presence of Jeppard's angry, shadow-shrouded face behind the repeated rifle butts highlights his vicious and intense character viewpoint, which makes the act appear instant as well as overwhelming.

The scene is traumatic for young Gus to witness, and to some extent for the reader as well. By presenting this scene in a compressed form that highlights the murderous rifle, Lemire asks readers to simulate the scene in a manner that requires decompression and blending, a strategy that encourages a more complex, reflexive engagement with the components that make up the murder. Readers must also witness every murderous hit, as the inset panels anchor the event structure. The repetition of image and sound in a way forces the reader to meditate on the action, rather than quickening recognition and onward reading as might happen with a more straightforward sequential depiction. The process of decompression increases the reading time and attention to the panel's compositionality, which arguably also builds empathy toward Gus' viewpoint, who, despite knowing that the action was necessary, was still deeply upset by it. The emotional impact of the immediacy and intensity of the action endures through subsequent scenes, as it recompresses and combines into ongoing panels. The panel heightens the feeling of the cause, with several effects reverberating beyond the time of the murder.

Lemire replicates the scene with Jeppard ten issues later (Figure 6.7). This time, Gus is now the agent engaged in killing a creature (this time with a brick) to protect others who have been attacked.[6] The repetition of the same number of embedded focal panels, visual perspective, figural depiction (especially mimetic posture and facial obfuscation), build clear affinities between the pages, using the general layout as a narrative anchor that links and blends specific moments across a story (more on this concept in the next section and subsequent chapter). Lemire relies on the salience of the initial forceful composite image of Jeppard to resonate and traverse the many issues until it is repeated. The repetition builds a long-distance blend of qualities of the two characters through the vital relations of role, change, and identity to show how Gus has adjusted to the world around him, transforming from a cowering child into an active protector himself. Through the blend, the characteristics of Jeppard are extended to Gus, showing him to have become more protective and necessarily aggressive, while now also leading other more innocent characters to freedom, just as Jeppard had promised to do for him. Such resonances also suggest a sense of maturation or perhaps corruption, as Gus has come to see and act in the storyworld in particular ways. The repeated pattern of embedded temporality decompresses aspects of the narrative and character viewpoints

Figure 6.7 Gus kills in the same style as Jeppard, a year later in the series (Lemire 2011, 65).

from previous scenes, "braiding" aspects of two key characters and their experiences together (see Groensteen 2007, 21–23).

At the same time, there is a subtle difference between the scenes. The inclusion of a child-like figure within the page is a notable change. The child's perspective, which includes crying from a bite, integrates the innocent gaze that is excluded in the scene with Jeppard. Arguably, this integration of a child victim and witness subtly shifts the construal of the action, by highlighting the protection of the child rather than simply focusing on the brutal action. Here, Gus is actively intervening, whereas that was less clear in the case of Jeppard. Perhaps this allows for a more empathetic construal of Gus' act, because it adds a sense of justification into the composition of the scene.

Regarding the temporality of this composite page, like with the previous example, the duration of the action is less significant than the focus on the act and its effect. It again compresses and integrates multiple strikes of the brick in a rhythmic pattern that suggests a discrete duration, but one that is not necessarily objectively clear. The compression and integration facilitate a slowing down of the reader's experience of pacing and time in the comic to focus on a singularly brutal scene. At the same time, it develops multiple character viewpoints, to focus on subtle construals of cause and effect, motivations, and qualities of experience—all in ways that further the reader's understanding of the characters and their role in and changes through the wider narrative.

Another example of embedded temporality (Figure 6.8), which employs decompressions of cues to construe action that is historically inflected in a different way, comes from *Soupy Leaves Home*, by Cecil Castellucci and Jose Pimienta. Recall from the example about "hobo signs" in the previous chapter, the story focuses on a young protagonist, Soupy, learning "hobo" skills and knowledge from her mentor, Ramshackle. Similar to the other example from this text, this sequence illustrates Soupy's education, here learning self-defense to protect herself while riding the railway and in squatter camps. In this case, the sequence of panels anchor and link together with the language into a smooth event structure. The visual style and content of the sequence of panels change constantly in order to reinforce the domain of fighting, already activated by the previous conversation between the characters. Each panel presents a different categorically prototypical image, respectively: a poster for a martial arts movie like *The Karate Kid*, Japanese samurais, American boxers, Mayan warriors, Medieval British jousters, and Mongolian archers. Like Matt Madden's use of metonymy to depict the history of comics in Figure 5.1, this page uses metonymic invocation of various historical and cultural contexts. However, in this case, the figures maintain hints of the protagonists across the panels through parallels in hat shape and stature. Similarly, the narration boxes maintain linguistic sensibility between the shifting imagery. Thus, the characters map together as Soupy and Ramshackle training in the present, while inhabiting different fighting contexts through the category metonymies.

The narrative incongruity of transforming the characters in attire and context reconstrues how the scene is interpreted, since the characters are not time travelers. Rather, the transformation suggests a mental projection of Ramshackle's background historical knowledge that informs his teaching of self-defense, much like in the example about hobo runes from that graphic novel. His knowledge of history and various styles of combat is metonymically evoked for readers to understand how he incorporates a rich tradition into his approach. As temporal linkages, these decompressions of different moments serve a very different function than in Lemire's murderous meditation, since they import different

Figure 6.8 Learning to fight in *Soupy Leaves Home* (Castellucci and Pimienta 2017, 34).

yet related historical and cultural domains into the scene. The figures are being set up in both a literal educational space as well as a metaphorical space in which elements change to reflect a history of both actions and ideas.

The multi-spatial and multitemporal blends of these panels, which simultaneously depict the present and a past, and in alternative locations, reflects the two characters' viewpoints. The one figure in the role of learner inhabits a time-space blend constructed by the teacher for the purposes of education, or at least reflecting the background knowledge that goes into the actions. While the rhyming sing-song cadence of the language suggests that the protagonists move through the actions swiftly as steps in a singular routine, the images also suggest that the educational process might be substantially longer. It is unclear whether this page encapsulates a single teachable moment for a few key actions, with a nod to the teacher's background knowledge, or encapsulates a much longer educational experience that includes discussions of different combat contexts and historical domains. Nonetheless, the creators' intention is surely not to confuse the reader about who is fighting and why. Rather, decompressing the different elements of the imagery, which traverses many times and geographies, adds to the reader's assessment of Ramshackle's viewpoint and value as a friend, by showing his knowledge as an educator, even while also showing how he is historically ramshackle in his jumbled presentation of the historical order of different domains. Moreover, it shows how multi-temporality and multi-spatiality can coalesce into a meaningful encapsulation of a learning experience and viewpoint construction while remaining ambiguous in duration, highlighting significant historical and scenic temporal valences and rhythms that inform character experiences. This builds character viewpoints without necessarily investing in progressing the plot directly. In fact, violence toward Soupy is not a major element of most of Soupy's story. The dominant temporality of the page, therefore, focuses on developing a temporal event structure for the interactions of the characters, as Ramshackle mobilizes historical concepts in the moment for Soupy.

A final example of metonymically evoked historical cues within a sequence comes from *George Sprott, 1894–1975* by the Canadian cartoonist Seth (2009). The graphic novel documents the life of a fictional television personality (see Marrone 2016). This example (Figure 6.9) presents Sprott signing off from his show with his catchphrase while developing a more expansive timeline by providing an encompassing glimpse of the character's personality and cultural presence.

Figure 6.9 Temporal marking and encapsulation in *George Sprott, 1894–1975* (Seth 2009, n.p.).

The concluding statement and catchphrase are particularly important in blending the panels together the unfinished speech balloons link to build verbal coherence. The language unites and simulates as a smooth, cohesive statement, which prompts the vital relation of (singular) identity for the speaker. This projection of cohesion onto the changing figure suggests that he ages across the panels. Similarly, the embellished frames of the panels vary to reflect technological progress in a manner that aligns with the character's changes. Because of the embodied understanding of aging, a timeline mapping develops that unites the televisions as frames of material (and materialized) anchors, and the changing features of the character imbedded in them reflect successive yet distanced moments in time. Thus, the verbal cues unify the figure and his discrete presence on television at every moment, while the pictographic details of the panel and frame focus on changes to technologies and his body to give a sense of a significant stretch of time.

Much like the *Captain America* example earlier, each modality has a distinct temporality, but with very different construals. The panels thereby align his statement with a compressed temporal location (for instance, readers could decompress each panel frame to make claims about the distinctive quality of television technologies as a temporal location). The linguistic connections between panels also show how his tagline has been consistent through the decades, with each part of the phrase metonymically decompressing to reflect the whole that is spread across the strip (and the ellipses support this metonymic function). Each panel construes a moment and the career in different ways. Overall, the different temporalities of the verbal and pictorial modalities aligned in an expansive yet succinct timeline. The skillful blending of linguistic and visual temporalities constructs a unified and nostalgic overview of Sprott's career. It is no surprise, then, that the subsequent panels in the comic focus on older people relating their affection and nostalgia for the television show and host over time.

6.4 DESIGNED LAYOUTS AND TEMPORAL MULTIPLICITY

One final area of temporality that is more diffuse, but still anchored by the orientation and placement of multimodal elements on the page, comes from cues spread out across layouts, rather than simply in sequence. Hillary Chute notes that "[t]he form of comics always hinges on the way temporality can be traced in complex, often nonlinear paths across the space of the page" (2008, 454). Put another way, Joseph Witek summates that "panels on the page always create narrative meaning both as sequences and as spatial arrangements" (2009, 153). Therefore, a sense of sequentiality, of strings of panel-to-panel interactions, can operate in alternative and even multiple directions. I unpack in the next chapter the use of salient cues to develop narrative anchors that extend and braid networks of meaning across layouts and especially longer stretches of narrative. In this section, I dwell briefly on several examples with more direct strategic manipulations of layouts and panel interactions that develop page specific temporal meanings so as to cover the spectrum of features on the comics page that coordinate and ground cognitive processes. These move beyond material anchors of sequences to complicate and reconstrue timelines and events.

6.4.1 Temporal Parallelism and Metacommentary in *Baddawi*

Leila Abdelrazaq's biographical comic *Baddawi* (2015) tells the story of her father's coming-of-age as a young Palestinian in the 1950s and 1960s.[7] In a moving series of short chapters, Abdelrazaq periodically employs nontraditional layouts to indicate broader relationships and causal forces that inform events. These narratorial interjections offer critical framings of past events, temporarily freezing a complex and dynamic scene to clarify the situation. In a sense, they are a tableau that blends and highlights intersections between everyday life and political life. The following example (Figure 6.10), for instance, interjects into the moment when Ahmad and his family flee to their basement during a bombing campaign and play chess until it is safe. Abdelrazaq exploits the chess game as a domain that grounds visual and conceptual blends that expand the reader's understanding of Ahmad's broader situation. Abdelrazaq's visual strategies help highlight and blend elements of the domains of international politics and chess while clarifying the full range of very different types of actors in and experiencers of the conflict.

Figure 6.10 offers a multilayered visual blend of different political and social actors in the Israeli-Palestinian conflict, which juxtaposes different

Figure 6.10 Visual blends and domain transformations in *Baddawi* (Abdelrazaq 2015, 84).

figures and roles as a unified comment on the situation. The panoramic, full-page spread anchors mappings between actors and concepts by aligning three sections (perceived as gestalt groupings based on shared depictive style), each of which emphasizes distinct figures and interactions, beginning with the main political leaders behind the conflict, the soldiers fighting, and the children playing. The narratorial commentary through the middle highlights how the concept of "war games" unites the three levels of actors, but their viewpoints and motives are substantially different.

The two political leaders loom large over the scene, figured much like puppet-masters over a miniaturized war scene. The large labeled figures of Syrian president Haffez al-Assad, who financed and supported the Palestinians, and Israeli president Ariel Sharon, map directly to the domain of chess by holding what look like game pieces. This pictorial mapping blends the domains by updating the domain of chess with modern-day military equipment, while activating the notions of strategy and competition that are often ascribed to the game players and mapping them to the political figures. Abdelrazaq highlights and exploits this mapping by quickly adding a narratorial comment that contrasts with the

TEMPORALITIES [169]

blend by implying that while the kids were playing a game grounded in logic, the political figures did not appear to be. This narratorial condemnation of the politicians brackets their hands, the central mode of action in chess, to suggest a literal and figural reframing of their work. Al-assad is shown throwing money into the mix, suggesting a direct contribution to the conflict, but also, in the game domain, perhaps suggesting that he is making a wager on the outcome as well. Similarly, Sharon is shown literally controlling the movements of military equipment, as a military leader does, but also in the context of a game appears childish, as though playing with toys. Both al-Assad and Sharon, therefore, construe the leaders as both powerful, meddling, and yet also disengaged to some extent from the full impacts of their acts, with each playing games rather than resolving a significant conflict. The narratorial adjustment toward illogical war games combines with this visual emphasis on economics and frivolity, to construe the leaders as disconnected (here visually as well) from the people whose lives their decisions impact.

Against the backdrop of the playing politicians are two groups of militants and two groups of children fighting each other, with different pictorial styles keeping the groups separate, but with postures suggesting parallels between them. In the foreground, children play at conflict (evidenced by their smiles), while in the more abstracted midground, soldiers engage in battle. Both sets of conflicts simulate quickly as brief snapshots of actions, suggesting an immediacy to their duration. Yet within the context of the politicians and the layout, there is a range of temporal and viewpointed construals that add to this immediacy. There are several interesting features of this page's orchestration and shifting styles. First, it is cut in half by a lazy white line that is fed by the money and tanks of the politicians, suggesting a cause for the divisions that seem to tear apart the ground that the lower figures stand on. The high-contrast, simple, black-and-white imagery for this division and the soldiers that fight across it aligns with the chess domain, but also suggests an overly simplistic or deterministic rationale behind the political and militaristic actions. Moreover, the soldiers are visually identical, rather than contrasting like chess pieces, which undermines the logic of an unavoidable conflict that the pieces support in the game, since it is difficult to visualize the sides without the imposed political barrier. The antagonistic viewpoint construction of the conflict, which the rifles and flags supports, is subtly undermined by the soldiers' synonymity. In terms of temporality, the duration of their fight is immediate but, due to their deeply abstracted depiction, also ubiquitous or beyond any discrete event, acting as icons or tokens of conflict, rather than people.

Below the soldiers, the children shift again the possible construals relating to the conflict, as they become visually more nuanced and distinct. Unlike the generality of the soldiers' conflicts, this could be a depiction of an actual school-yard game, with distinct child viewpoints blending into it. However, the contrast with the more general depiction of soldiers, along with mappings between the postures of the children and soldiers, projects a developmental potential onto the children, showing how they are being enculturated into normalizing the conflict of the adults. Moreover, this potentiality suggests a viewpoint transformation for the children, which hollows out their individuality as they grow up into generic soldiers. They become depersonalized, like a pawn in a game.

There are likely many more entailments to the many connections and stylistic choices prompted by this composite scene, depending on the reader's background knowledge and political disposition toward this particular regional conflict. Nonetheless, as I have discussed, there are several construals of the subject matter that are carefully constructed. The pictorial commonalities between the two sides of the conflict based on ages and roles construes the conflict as one orchestrated for reasons fueled by political aims and is beyond the everyday person's control. In light of the chess domain and the narratorial insertion, the narrator seems to suggest that there are logical solutions to the conflict based on a shared humanity and more personalized viewpoints, but that the politicians would rather play games with each other. Importantly, the visual similarities between the everyday people on the ground suggests that despite the conflict being predicated on ethnic differences within a shared territory, these differences are not so great as to necessitate such deadly conflict.

Abdelrazaq exploits the layout of the page to draw out an extended blend of political and real oppositions in this Middle Eastern conflict, compressing decades of conflict into a single, full-page, layered panel. She isolates different actors on the page through distinct visual styles and frames them through the domain of chess as various game players. The figures at the bottom grow up to become pawns in a politicized space, and her commentary and depictions of everyday people (including both soldiers and children) contrast to the overbearing political and economic wills that seem to control their experiences. Abdelrazaq leverages the layout aligned with the contrasting degrees of visual abstraction and chess domain to develop a temporally compressed view of the region in order to construe a range of viewpoints and temporalities, linking specific people and activities into a historical and political context. At the same time, the soldier-children parallelism adds a futurity to the page that suggests a message of peace based on anti-political sentiments and respect for everyday humanity.

6.4.2 Multi-temporality in *Building Stories*

Another example that further shows how comics can compress or decompress and arrange multiple temporalities comes from *Building Stories* by Chris Ware (Figure 6.11). This example showcases combinations of sequential and diagrammatic relationships between panels and images in Ware's characteristically clean, sparse, and innovative storytelling. Here I will focus on one stylistically evocative element of his broader projects. Ware's exploration of the interaction between materiality and visuality is especially evident in *Building Stories* (2012), which comes in a box and includes the story presented across multiple publication formats (newspaper, flipbooks, board books, standard comic books, etc.). The story places a visual emphasis on buildings and their tenants, and prioritizes pictorial, iconic, and diagrammatic modalities over verbal cues. The artist presents a postmodern, fragmented story, which readers have to literally rebuild from the parts, thereby punning on the title's "building" as both a structure and a readerly process. Such a presentation necessitates the weaving together of disparate cues across the page and throughout the narrative. This interconnecting of content is not wholly ad hoc, but often relies upon stylistic choices and representations drawn from the recent history of Western visual communication and material culture, including styles and icons typically employed in advertising and technical diagrams. By appropriating this abstract and technological aesthetic, Ware educates the reader's eye to engage the multidimensional aspects of comics (Bredehoft 2006), and in a way that necessitates slower, more attentive reading (Banita 2010). Such an approach turns Ware's comics into a multisensory narrative poetry (Kannenberg 2007), and inspires new ways of thinking and building meaning through a range of pictographic and schematic cues (see Ball and Kuhlman 2010; Szczepaniak 2011).

Ware's *Building Stories* offers a range of textual formats and structures, including the employment of innovative layouts to develop alternative and parallel reading paths as well as embedded events and annotations within a larger image. The example shown here is the final panel from a large four-panel poster board included in *Building Stories*. The board acts like a large fold-out multi-page that shows several buildings in a row. Upon inspection, the similarities between buildings, plants, and characters on each panel suggests that it is the same building through the course of four seasons (most noticeably, a central deciduous tree changes to signal these seasonal shifts). I have selected the final panel in spring to focus on some of Ware's diagrammatic layout strategies.

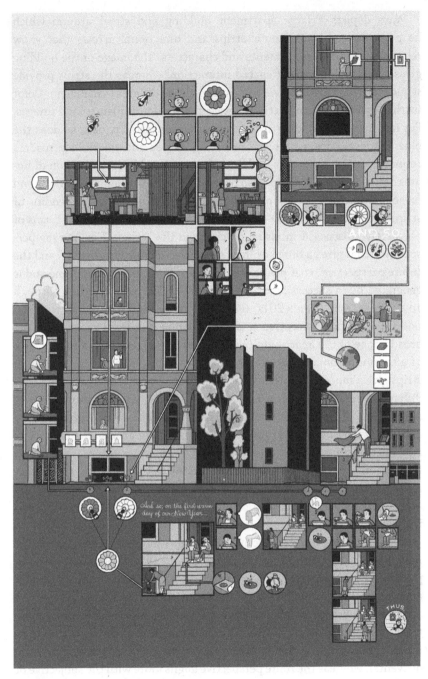

Figure 6.11 Final panel of poster board in Chris Ware's *Building Stories* (2012).

Ware depicts a large apartment building and street around which he presents embedded comic strips and directional arrows that show relationships between elements and characters. The image of the building gives a general domain of spatial interaction, whereas the strips provide sequences that highlight various events about different characters. Color further helps build connections between different sequences and images. For instance, the building appears in several inserted panels, as does the blue window space, where the matching shapes and colors help readers connect the smaller panels back into the storyworld. The repetition of figures between different strips also prompts readers to draw connections and make inferences about temporal order and causation. Ware's imbedding of strips within a wider frame of reference combines two dominant forms of perspective discussed in visual psychology: the "ground" or "survey perspective" that gives a broad or "bird's-eye view of an environment" and the "route perspective" that places emphasis on the figure through time and is generated by "a succession of views taken while one is traveling through an environment" (Denis 2017, 64). These two perspectives align with the notion of gestalt perception and eye-tracking discussed previously. The broad image of the apartment building and the street offers a survey view of a common domain with different agents and spaces. The sequences of strips give a more egocentric route perspective by presenting details about different characters, their emotions and dreams, and relevant histories and events. This combination of perspectives aligns well with narrative and character viewpoint spaces by helping readers anchor the characters and relationships within the storyworld even when there are minimal interactions between the characters. The survey perspective gives a general spatial and cultural domain in which to locate a variety of characters and events, which also gives a combined sense of both togetherness and isolation.

These two types of perspective also align well with the two temporal mental metaphors discussed at the beginning of this chapter, wherein temporal construal locates a subjective and participatory or more distanced and observational orientation for the experiencer. The survey perspective aligns with observational construals of time, because it presents a more totalized perspective in which to locate events and their associated temporal order (such as the many embedded strips of panels that integrate years of events), whereas the route perspective aligns more with the subjective or participatory construal of temporality because it is more enmeshed within sequential cues and arrows as paths. Within this large survey perspective, Ware orchestrates several strips to inject brief narratives about a bee's life, flowers, vacations, and other qualities and backstories of the tenants of the building. He relies on connective lines and arrows and groupings of sequential content to direct the reader around the page, showing the path of the bee in the moment, as well as all of the intersections of other activities and events that precede and proceed from it.

Beginning at the top-left with the bee, Ware employs conventionalized emotion icons of sweat marks to indicate the bee's desire for flowers and its anxiety at being trapped against a window and unable to return to his hive (including thought circles with his spouse mourning his disappearance—thereby also inserting a domestic narrative domain for the "worker" bee).[8] An arrow locates the bee in the window in the strip below it with a lady doing her laundry, with a helpful calendar titled "last year" highlighted next to her. This group of panels is further located with an arrow directing attention to the basement of the building, thereby embedding last year's narrative of the bee's deliverance from the laundry room by the women within the present tense of the building. Notice how in last year's window there are only white and red flowers, but there is another insertion at the bottom of the page of pink flowers and an arrow in the present illustrating that the bee pollinated these to make the hybrid.

With this evident pattern of embeddedness, readers might also notice that other arrows and connective lines all seem to lead to the flowers, and either trace these back to other embedded strips (such as, the old woman, labeled with a calendar titled "long ago," purposefully planting the red flowered plants) or return to the bee's narrative at the top, in which two panels highlight the bee's face and ecstasy at being free. He goes on to gather nectar and return to his family. The bee's story is also linked to the backstory of the white flowers, which are the product of a beach blanket being emptied after "our vacation two years ago" (here, a helpfully captioned photo of a couple on a beach). Other locative lines show the vacation was located in South America, and that the towel was packed by the man and flew back with them. These different backstories about the flowers add several viewpoints and events with different temporal locations and durational construals that align over years to facilitate pollination and the blooming of a new type of pink flower in the spring. Thus, the observational quality of the landscape facilitates a copresence of various past events in order to show how they align.

The story then moves into the underground space, literalizing the grounding of the present in the history of the space, continuing the story with the narratorial phrase, "And so, on the first warm day of our New Year . . ." In the imbedded scene, the woman who saved the bee is shown picking one of pink flowers, a product of the bee's labors. An onlooker, the man whose beach towel made the white flowers, and who sits beside the woman he went on vacation with, fantasizes about the other woman as she bends over. The bee, attracted to the man's spilled drink, laps it up until the man spots and kills him. As the comic concludes, "Thus" the bee's family mourns.

At first glance, the page may appear chaotic for the reader to navigate, but as I have shown, the arrows guide readerly attention around the page to form specific relationships and routes through the cues, such that slowly all of the pieces come together to form a dark and ironic circle of life. Denis reminds us that "[b]ecause they seem particularly suited to show or suggest logical and temporal dependencies, [arrows] are used to make concepts, processes, and theories easier to understand than purely discursive descriptions" (2017, 69). Ware employs them in this exact way, to develop inferences about time, causation, and other logical relations, which combine with other temporal, intentional, and affective cues across panels. For instance, domain knowledge about plants connects the old lady's planting of seeds to the fully flowering plant, the germination process for which is also illustrated for the white flowers through a connected sequence on the right. Ware employs locational arrows and lines to clearly diagram these connections between stories, artifacts, and agents. He also interjects viewpoint details, through the light blue fantasy bubbles at the lower right (mimicking the coloration of the panels featuring the future-projecting fears of the trapped bee at the beginning, and the old lady's thoughts of death on the lower left), to project a potentially desired for future sexual interaction between the man reading on the stairs and the laundry lady picking a flower. Readers must follow the arrows and sequential cues to orchestrate these elements into a temporally logical order based on domain knowledge and temporal cues, noting how the planting of seeds and the bee's liberation and pollination are in the past, the picking of flowers and the bee's demise are in the present, and the fantasy (and the other daydreams and fears) is a possible future. The bee's past fears become reality at the end of the comic, building a sense of irony at coming full circle through a circuitous narrative route.

This example shows just how complex temporalities can become when strategically integrated into a unifying structure, especially in this case when mobilizing the visual discourses of technical drawings and graphic design. The verbal modality played a particularly important role in locating events in time, while design elements organized information in relation to physical location, character viewpoint, and event structure. Ware's orchestrated page draws on an idiosyncratic layout style, but one that, with slower reading and attention, is navigable and intelligible. One might contend that the page is needlessly complex, and that it could be organized as a more traditional layout of strips. However, such a re-sequencing of the page would destabilize the strong sense of space-based and woven interactions provided by the combination of survey and route perspectives and their connections to different experiences of temporality, including switching between the temporal mental metaphors and perspective types, thereby taking away from the pleasure of the puzzle or slow traversing of the various stories imbedded in the composite scene. The global and route perspectives also subtly construe how readers engage the viewpoints. The survey perspective decenters any particular character by emphasizing the location over any given figure. While readers navigate the page, they may emerge to like or dislike particular characters and feel sympathy for the bee, but these are slow emergences of disentangled meaning, rather that abrupt interpretations. Such qualities are a significant part of the texture of Ware's stories.

6.4.3 Carved Time in *Red: A Haida Manga*

The final example of innovation in layout that welds different types of temporality comes from the Haida artist Michael Nicoll Yahgulanaas's *Red: A Haida Manga* (2009). In this graphic novel, Yahgulanaas skillfully presents a traditional Haida hubris narrative that is part of his oral tradition. As Spiers (2014) argues, this comic illustrates a meticulous blend of Haida tradition and innovation. She documents in detail how Yahgulanaas follows the form line and pigmentation rules of traditional Haida art to develop the figures, chronological panel relationships, and the panel layouts. Spiers offers a helpful, detailed analysis of the connections between the historical contexts and traditions, and Yahgulanaas' implementations and innovations throughout his work. Here, I focus on one particular aspect of his innovative layout, the fact that it began as a large traditional mural design (Nodelman 2012; Spiers 2014), similar to those often seen carved and painted on Haida cedar bentboxes and building panels (Borkent 2014a). Similar to the example from Chris Ware, this presentation pulls the reader out of the sequential experience to engage also with a broader survey perspective, but in a way that foregrounds and complicates values and assumptions about comics and storytelling.

The layout for the entire graphic novel uses the black painted lines of this mural as panel boundaries and gutters, with only the occasional rupture for dramatic effect. Yahgulanaas provides a photograph of the complete mural in the back of the book and on the inside of the jacket of the hardcover edition (Figure 6.12), which he invites the reader to use as a

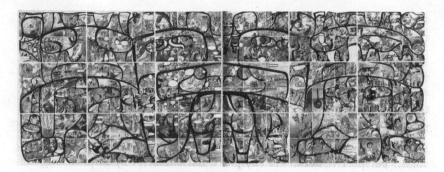

Figure 6.12 Complete mural-layout, including story content, of *Red: A Haida Manga* (Michael Nicoll Yahgulanaas (mny.ca) 2009). Image credit: J. Litrell.

guide to cut the book apart and rebuild the mural. Through the photograph and the invitation, the artist encourages readers to see the wider cultural and conceptual framework that informs the story, while also encouraging readers to rebuild and experience an alternative material view of the text. Reconstituting the mural re-presents it as both story and a traditional building panel; as such, readers are asked to invite Haida ways of seeing into part of their lived reality by putting the mural up in their space. By blending the comic with Haida cultural practices through the integration of carving, painting, storytelling, and building practices, Yahgulanaas prompts the reader to engage with a range of assumptions and values and their associated temporalities.

As Spiers rightly points out, the comics medium, and especially Yahgulanaas' use of particular visual styles and cue, offers an interesting meeting point between orature and literature, since it allows for more types of expressive performance and invites a clearer sense of participation, which aligns with Haida and many other Indigenous oral storytelling practices (51–52). She highlights how this integration of Haida practices into the comics medium carves out a space for resistance of colonial attitudes. Similarly, Harrison (2016) argues that *Red* challenges how Westerners might read time and space, thereby decolonizing the space of comics in particular through how it presents the gutter and relationships among individuals, events, and worldviews in a more holistic manner. Similarly, Clarke suggests that differences in how visual borders are presented in Canadian comics, represented by Chester Brown, Bryan Lee O'Malley, and Yahgulanaas, "serve to reinforce, trouble, and disrupt, respectively, narrative discussions of the same liminal space" (2016, 185). As all of these critics have shown, Yahgulanaas' innovation by integrating and adapting comics to the domains of traditional Haida art and culture challenges how readers engage and comprehend the story. The innovativeness of the layout in *Red* builds a subversive and powerful statement that welds traditional and contemporary storytelling forms and adds a new approach to the comic's reception. Through his attention to different visual and oral communicative practices, Yahgulanaas enacts a powerful quality of Indigenous literatures described by Sam McKengney and Sarah Henzi:

> Indigenous literatures call communities into being. This calling is ultimately rooted in care—care of territory, care of stories, and care of understandings of the world embedded within wider kinship relations among communities, nations, cultures, and languages, as well as with the other-than-human. (2016, 245)

Yahgulanaas presents a way of being that extends and bridges cultural traditions, while building affinities between visual and oral storytelling practices, in a work of cultural ambassadorship and creativity grounded in communal care and kinship relations. Encouraging the reader to cut up the story in order to rebuild the mural aligns with this concept of care and kinship, because it encourages the welcoming of alternative ways of engaging books and spaces that brings Haida expressivity into non-Haida homes, but also only if the reader chooses to. Thus, there is an ethics of both welcome and resistance, revolution and respect, that grounds the work.

Within this discussion, I want to foreground how construals of temporality also shift around this work. For readers first encountering the story, *Red* follows a fairly straightforward sequential storytelling form as it tells a version of a traditional story drawn from the Haida oral tradition. Already, the story is construed as both immediate in telling, but resonant with a longer cultural history. Readers likely expand this sense of historical resonance further when they realize that the story is constrained by a broader architecture informed by Haida material culture, which has renovated and reclaimed the experience of the frame and the gutter. The panel and gutter, as noted, have taken on decolonial and Haida meanings that integrate a sense of history that spans precolonial and colonial experiences, resisting the colonial "white space" while remaining open to the reader's creativity in blending panels together to interpret the sequence. The gutter remains as a separator that requires the reader's participation to connect images, but it also reflects a painted image that encloses and informs the entire comic with a broader cultural and historical frame. Yahgulanaas has integrated a long perspective on cultural history into the contemporary medium, a very different sense of a survey perspective than that seen in Ware's composition. Here, the creator has blended ancient resonances, carving, painting, and storytelling practices into the sequential narrative form, to highlight a specific culturally informed viewpoint on a space of storytelling, and illustrating the ongoing resilience and transformative power of Haida ways of knowing and seeing.

In this section, Leila Abdelrazaq, Chris Ware, and Michael Nicoll Yahgulanaas each employs distinct and innovative visual styles and forms of presentation, drawing from very different cultural traditions and histories, to heighten the experience of the comics page as part of their multimodal storytelling. Each of their approaches orchestrates multimodal cues in a way that requires careful attention to the role of integration and interpretation, in particular around the temporal relations of voices, events, and traditions. Temporal experiences in these works have lengthened through domain decompression to include political, cultural, seasonal, and other historical layers. Abdelrazaq provides a metaphor for rethinking the motivations behind the war games in the Middle East, providing a present-day commentary on the past events. Ware embeds multiple sequences at different points in time (both past and future) and geography into a single short spring-time afternoon at one building, showing the histories, present experience, and future possibilities of the characters. Yahgulanaas interweaves a traditional story and carving practices into a contemporary comics genre, updating and re-presenting orature in this new multimodal form. Each cartoonist makes use of the designed spaces of the page for fundamentally different temporal and conceptual purposes. These strategies orchestrate, manipulate, and transform readerly expectations and responses, requiring reconceptualizations and integrations of multiple temporalities and uses of space on the page.

6.5 CONCLUSION

Temporality is a complex and multifaceted emergent aspect of comics storytelling and does not follow a direct spatial or conceptual formula. Rather, it is a dynamic and constructed experience that relies on significant unconscious biases, mental metaphors, and assumptions that facilitate temporal coherence. Blending different cues typically involves decompression and recompression of different temporal construals, some objectively constrained (such as concepts of the day or seasons), and others that are far more subjectively nuanced (such as the felt duration of a simulated experience). These are further complicated as they intersect in the often asymmetric and disjointed aspects of panels, sequences, pages, and conventions and traditions, but yet generally resolve into a coherent texture for the reader.

In this chapter I have reviewed a wide range of temporal concepts and their instantiation in comics, ranging from single panels to sequences to layouts. I began by showing how the multimodality of comics almost always embed asynchronicities between modalities that must be aligned and assessed in relation to each other and their relevance to the broader textual context. These alignments rely on pervasive cognitive biases that focus on human-scale inferences surrounding pragmatic issues of communication including intersubjectivity and intentionality. These are further nuanced by storytelling aims of event structuring and character and narrative viewpoints and domain activation that are informed by vital relations mappings and other dominant structures of cognition.

Recognizing the multimodal complexity of comics helps to isolate how common statements about space-time relations in comics rely on different and incompatible models of time that reflect the textual form either as a textual artifact or through the lens of the reader's response to their experience of its texture. By recognizing that a sense of movement through time and space reflected the work of reader's cognitive processes rather than the structures of the form itself (because space does not equal time), it became possible to focus more clearly on what is presented and how it is interpreted, without confusing the two. The range of examples proceeded to illustrate that time is an emergent property of cognitive blending to build connections between successive as well as more disparate panels, from single panels up to complex page layouts.

Comics function as complex arrays of material anchors that can instantiate moments on a timeline, but can also be arranged for other conceptual purposes. Different types of cognitive blending, including especially compression and decompression, allow readers to unpack and interpret these cues. Through a blending analysis that approximates the reader's processes of perception and integration, it becomes clear how subtle changes to compositional qualities can prompt dramatic differences in understanding, governed by common biases toward temporal and narrative coherence, character-level viewpoints, and culturally significant contributions to domain knowledge. Viewing the comics page as a composite of material anchors supports analyses of how different cues are orchestrated to contribute to simulated inference patterns, including based on their sequential, orientational, and proximal valences. Such a model works for short sequences of panels anchoring interactions throughout a sequence, right up to more complex patterns and groupings of anchors, such as those seen in the complex layouts toward the end of the chapter. As I discuss in the next chapter, patterns of anchoring give salience to storytelling features that can also reverberate throughout narrative structures, acting as narrative anchors that braid together more disparate meanings and events.

Through the many concepts and examples discussed in this chapter, I have shown how temporality is a complex emergent property of multimodality and relates primarily to subjective construals of depicted experiences and background knowledge and how these relate to a more global narrative structure with or without more objective and static time-space mappings. Much more important to meaning-making is the projection of domain knowledge about spaces, actions, and events in response to the spatialized relationships on the page that order storyworld experiences and give them human-scale meaning and predictability as subjective experiences. These experiences integrate multiple kinds of temporality, including personal perception, affective implications, social and political activities, cultural practices, and historical events, all of which contribute to the experiences of time in comics.

CHAPTER 7

Spatial Conceptualizations

Layout as Viewpoint and Narrative Strategy in The Underwater Welder

7.1 INTRODUCTION

As the previous chapter illustrated, the layout of panels helps establish a range of relational links, in particular suggesting a causality to sequences that helps equate comic strips with timelines through their ability to materially anchor, orient, and build proximal (and sometimes distal) connections between panel positions. However, as I illustrated, asymmetries of temporal construal between modalities, and complications from stylistic choices and domain knowledge, show how temporality is much more an emergent property of textual properties and goals than a dictate of the comics form. As I presented in the final examples, layout can play an important role in aligning and complicating temporal inferences and character viewpoints. In this chapter, I expand on these observations with a particular focus on creative uses of layout choices within a graphic novel, Jeff Lemire's *The Underwater Welder* (2012).

In their review of the comics form, Pederson and Cohn (2016) argue that layout is perhaps the most fundamentally salient feature of comics and can reveal much about changes in expressivity and genre over time. A preliminary study of cross-cultural variation in layout design also indicates systematic uses of features within discourse communities, both culturally or generically defined, and the role of writing systems in guiding layout designs vertically and horizontally (Cohn et al. 2019). Bateman et al. (2021) offer a thorough review of the empirical research of comics layouts and show that inter-panel relationships are fundamentally guided by layout patterns, which align with my presentation of attentional guidance and causal relationships discussed in previous chapters. They also note that broader interconnections within a text are harder to systematically analyze. It is here that the cognitive theory of blending helps bridge corpus analyses like those performed by Cohn and Bateman and others with broader aesthetic and narrative analyses.

In more aesthetic terms, Bukatman (2014) and Molotiu (2012) have described spatial complications through layout innovations as reflecting tensions between action and stasis, or sequential dynamism and iconostatic perception, respectively. The tensions between dynamic and static qualities that emerge from aesthetic choices that exploit the affordances of frames and other structures of the comics page can prompt an awareness of the constructedness of a comic's message, even prompting "ruminative," slower reading experiences (Bukatman 2014), similar to those described of Chris Ware's work in the previous chapter (including the alternating between gestalt or ground perspectives and the path or eye-tracking perspectives). This attention to the textual form as overt rather than invisible participant in the composition helps raise a range of questions about the role of stylistic choices in communicative goals. Comics set up relational networks that direct and also transcend sequentiality, in ways that might align with narrative epistemology, character viewpoints, or other conceptual developments. Overtly unconventional or playful uses of the form can prompt inferences and blending patterns that extend well beyond the individual panel or the page.

In this chapter, I examine Jeff Lemire's graphic novel, *The Underwater Welder*, as a helpful and succinct case study that shows how creators can mobilize connections between stylistic uses of the spatial logics of the page to elaborate on character viewpoints in the moment and across a story to develop conceptual and narrative depth. As of yet, little scholarly work has examined Jeff Lemire's graphic novel *The Underwater Welder*. Previous scholarship on the author's works has analyzed aspects of his popular realist graphic novel *Essex County* (featured as an example comic in Chapter 2)—focusing particularly on depictions of adolescence (Malaby and Esh 2012), the embodiment of elderly memory (Mullins 2014), and the Canadian mythos of hockey (Jacobs and Paziuk 2016). Others have examined his dystopic and posthumanist series *Sweet Tooth* (2010–13), focusing on the construction of empathy (Cardoso 2016) and posthuman hybridity (Heimermann 2017; Kelp-Stebbins 2012). I have briefly examined

Lemire's use of conflicting modalities in *The Underwater Welder* to develop contrasts between past and present character viewpoints (Borkent 2017, 551–56), but not the wider character and narrative developments that are reflected in frequent and conspicuous layout choices discussed here. The prior scholarship on Lemire's oeuvre highlights his skill at constructing nuanced personal narratives, but typically takes a literary analytic approach that focuses on character and narrative developments and generally pays much less attention to the aesthetic and spatial choices that inform how these are constructed.

Lemire's manipulations of modalities develop complex resonances through a variety of stylistic choices, such as parallelism, repetition, blends, and allusion, which add nuance to his storytelling. To unpack the evocativeness of creative layouts in Lemire's book, I elaborate on visual and spatial representations of metaphors of the self as they pertain to character viewpoint development. I then draw on Barbara Dancygier's (2012) helpful concept of narrative anchors, as salient features that prompt recursive connections that build narrative comprehension, to align blending theory with Thierry Groensteen's (2007) concept of braiding, and in a way that elaborates on the material anchors of the comics form presented in the previous chapter. I analyze Lemire's development of particularly salient layouts as narrative anchors, showcasing the use of the comics page as a prompt for broader cognitive processes that support comprehension of character viewpoints and their transformations across a text. Lemire's graphic novel provides a clear example of how layout can play a crucial role in mobilizing visual metaphors and mental space anchoring for narrative aims, braiding crucial insights about character viewpoint changes across a story.

7.2 VISUALIZING METAPHORS OF THE SELF THROUGH LAYOUT

The Underwater Welder tells the story of Jack Joseph, a thirty-three-year-old welder for an oil rig in Nova Scotia, Canada. His father went missing when he was a boy, and Jack has not come to terms with the loss. As he and his wife expect a child of their own, Jack suffers a slow mental breakdown in the weeks prior to the due date. It becomes clear that his own impending fatherhood has triggered unacknowledged childhood questions about Jack's father's disappearance, and he struggles to come to terms with his past in order to embrace his future. While, in some respects the story is quite straightforward and at times a little repetitive, Lemire excels in mobilizing the affordances of layouts to depict internal turmoil and changes. The story utilizes repetitions of pictorial cues of water and a pocket watch, along with associated metaphors surrounding knowledge and consciousness—such as surfaces and depths, access and distance, order and chaos—in conjunction with layout manipulations, to develop the reader's understanding of the protagonist's mental struggle. As such, the graphic novel offers an informative example of some formal possibilities of comics storytelling that promote salience and narrative development, by visualizing mental states through pictorial and structural cues.

To begin, I focus on the use of page fragmentation as a salient means of depicting character viewpoint. Early on in the narrative, Jack hallucinates while welding underwater. He hears a voice and sees an old pocket watch on the seafloor. He then blacks out and awakens in the rig's infirmary. The narrative style of presentation of Jack's conversation with the doctor is particularly revelatory, since at its conclusion, it is the first time in the graphic novel that multiple panels produce one holistic reader viewpoint, with a close-up image of Jack's face fragmented across the bottom six panels of the twelve-panel page (Figure 7.1). The previous panels depict in straightforward comics fashion a back-and-forth conversation about overwork and

Figure 7.1 Initial fragmentation at the doctor's office (Lemire 2012, 41).

[186] *Comics and Cognition*

the stress of impending parenthood. Jack tries to share his hallucination with the doctor, but then seems to accept that "maybe you're right" and he just needs rest. The final half of the page, however, builds a complex, foreboding depiction of his mental state by breaking from the conventional depictions of distinct characters in a panel to a fragmented image of one character across multiple panels. This shift in depiction sets up and anchors metaphorical blends that continue to develop throughout the narrative.

Lemire establishes a metaphorical blend of figure and layout through pictorial fragmentation. Jack is depicted in a dejected, slumped posture with downward gaze. His doctor's optimistic statement—"I'm sure everything will be just fine"—seeks to build positive action, but is located in the bottom, dark edges of the page, and disembodied from the doctor. While conventionally suggesting that the voice is coming from another location in the storyworld, the coloration of the panel and Jack's posture foreshadow a darker, more troubled future instead. These more ominous elements of the panels are metaphorically reinforced through the fractured layout, which may be interpreted to reflect Jack's slumped mental state. The fractured figure leverages visual entailments of metaphors about self and knowledge to depict him as literally falling apart, suggesting that his mental state is also disintegrating. Such depictive strategies highlight the mental metaphorical notion that THE MIND IS A BODY (see Sullivan 2018, 75, 122), which allows readers to interpret bodily or physical states as reflective of mental states. Common expressions like "He can't keep himself together" or "He's falling to pieces" offer linguistic variations on this metaphor that reflect the viewpoint construal visually depicted in this example. As I will discuss, other metaphorical conceptualizations of self develop throughout the story through variations in layout fragmentations.[1]

The story continues to develop around Jack's distressed mental state when he returns to the mainland to recover, during which time he investigates some old documents and discusses his father's disappearance with his mother. Both his wife, Susan, and his mother encourage him to accept his father's passing as a presumed drunken drowning, but Jack refuses and pursues the death instead as a mystery that needs solving. He becomes so obsessed with memories of his father that he forgets to come home as promised, leaving his wife to build their baby's crib alone. When they argue about his obsessive behavior, Susan reprimands him:

> You just can't stop chasing him . . . chasing his big mysterious disappearance. / Well, I'll tell you something, Jack. There is no mystery. He was a drunk who got pissed one night and drowned. End of story. / And you know what . . . ? I'm right here. . . we're right here. But you're too busy chasing a ghost to notice! (94)[2]

She goes on to note how Jack is following his father's neglectful and drunk patterns of behavior, concluding that his obsession is the cause. He insists that that is not the case, but that there is "something out there" that he needs to find (95). She leaves. Poignantly, her slamming of the door is depicted with the same fragmented paneling seen at the doctor's office, emphasizing their psychic distance across the bedroom space with visual separation across several panels between Jack and the door, and with Susan's voice depicted coming through it after the slam: "We'll be fine without you!" (95). The fragmentation here illustrates the combination of psychic and social isolation that Jack has produced through his actions, and his inability to connect with his wife and unborn child.

The strategic use of fragmented paneling to signal psychologically loaded moments continues. Jack feels compelled to go back underwater to pursue the previously glimpsed watch. While on the seafloor, he again sees and grasps a watch. At this point, the visual fragmentation becomes much more extreme, with several full-page spreads depicting different variations of panel shapes and sizes arrayed in a disordered manner around Jack, with each containing images from his past. The panels then become smaller and more numerous, as seen in Figure 7.2, and begin radiating out along vertical and horizontal axes. Unlike conventional comic strips, the sequences

Figure 7.2 Underwater fragmentation (Lemire 2012, 112–13).

[188] *Comics and Cognition*

reflect no clear event structure, but are rather random objects and past images of his father and himself. After this page, the imagery shifts further to depict the panels as air bubbles rushing out from his agonized face. All of these images serve a similar function, to depict the self in crisis through a cacophony of images from his memory of recent and distant events and figures.

Figure 7.2 is particularly salient at illustrating Jack's mental turmoil. In this double-page spread, panels frame the central, crouching figure of Jack, and their alignment and size suggest a perspectival depth of field that highlights the isolated figure in the dark depths of the sea. Their radiation from him also seems to suggest that they indexically relate to him, as an embedded expression of his mental state. These framing panels do not relate casually, as one might expect for the depiction of a particular memory, but are jumbled fragments of mental imagery that suggest he has lost touch with his sense of his narrative self, of being a coherent, singular person through time (Gibbs 2006, 21).

Nonetheless, there is an organizing logic hinted at in the symmetric layout and the images along each axis. The parallel expressions between the left and right images, of his father and himself as a young boy, resonate with each other to present a historical focus and link between father and son along the horizontal axis. Each of the panels behind them reflects previously presented elements of Jack's memory of his childhood, distinguishing images associated with his father on the left axis, and himself on the right axis. Likewise, the panels that separate the top and bottom of Jack's underwater attire reflect images from very recent events and emphasize his wife's pregnant belly, and several resonant images from his recent story that reflect also the contextual images of lighthouses, pumpkins, and smoking that have informed both his distant and recent pasts. Both vertical and horizontal axes, therefore, present a contrast between the distant past and near present realities of Jack's life. As reflections of distinct temporal parameters, of the near and distant past, these sequences still connect to conventionalized notions of timelines and material anchors discussed in the previous chapter, but their disjointedness requires decompression of brief cues to make sense. Moreover, the organizational logic suggests that these two time frames are seemingly irreconcilable, contrasting across the cardinal directions of the page layout.

Nonetheless, the dominant images around the periphery and the lone figure at the center maintain a core to the seemingly intractable past and present jumble of panels, locating Jack at the center of the axis. In terms of cultural domain activation, perhaps his location at the center of a crossed structure also reflects a visualization of the idiomatic Christian phrase, "it was his cross to bear," blending the haunting loss of his father with a sense of suffering that must be shouldered until death. Such idiomatic and metaphorical content adds ontological and epistemic qualities to the pages' emergent meanings (see Kövecses and Szabcó 1996). The mutually pained expressions of the father and son across the horizontal axis heighten this sense of suffering with their screaming, bubbling mouths, and hands holding heads as though to encompass an explosive emotion. Such images might simulate as anguish, which typically develops a degree of empathy, developed in tandem and symmetrically for them both, blending father and son.[3] They also visualize the mental metaphor of EMOTION IS A CONTAINED FORCE (Górska 2019; El Refaie 2013; Sullivan 2018), which is verbally expressed in descriptive phrases like "he could barely contain his anger" or "he radiated love." Here, readers might simulate Jack's emotional state as reflecting a seemingly uncontainable anguish over the past that he cannot reconcile with. While the central figure is clearly still himself contained in his diving gear, the radiating yet non-sequential panels suggest that his feelings or mental viewpoint is in the process of exploding from him, rupturing aspects of his emotional state or sense of self, moving beyond coherent experience and dissolving into emotion.

Moreover, the imagery also evokes other emotion metaphors: his location at the bottom of the sea helps literalize such ideas as being overcome, awash, or drowning in emotion. Likewise, he might be in an oceanic "pit of despair," in which emotions are categorized in terms of light/dark schemas, in which darkness is coded through embodied metaphorical parameters as perceptually inhospitable or bad. Such emotion metaphors are a natural extension of the container metaphor of emotion as well, as it has now been ruptured and subsumes the subject that once sought to contain it, while he remains trapped in the literal container of the ocean. Simulating and blending these various pictorial and diagrammatic cues allow for a range of metaphorical understandings of Jack's emotional state.

There are important anomalies in perspective and features that may impact how readers simulate, blend, and interpret these elements as well. While the peripheral images blend father and son figures to build a coherent face that the reader might empathize with, the loan character on the seafloor is turned aside, presumably fixated on the watch floating above the seafloor in front of him. Viewers must mentally rotate the figure to align the panels with his face, and to unite this figure with the images that radiate out from him. This reorientation perceptually separates the figure from his thoughts, since readers need to decompress and reorient elements of the images in order to interpret them, creating mental projections that are literally disorienting. Moreover, the paneled figures are depicted as screaming underwater, without a respirator, unlike Jack at the center of everything, and the top panel shows the welder's equipment functioning regularly and dispelling bubbles outside. This dissonance between figures helps readers keep the different characters distinct, while only importing the relevant element of the mouth and its emotional expression into present-day Jack's viewpoint. The nonveridical aspect of the bubbles adds a metaphorical construal to the viewpoint by suggesting that the figures are drowning. Perhaps these are a visual metaphor that suggests that Jack feels so overwhelmed that he feels like he is suffocating. Other interesting adjustments and interpretations are also presented by the bubbles near the background figure of present-day Jack, which are depicted as coming more from the watch than from him. The bubbles, then, in their anomalous overabundance, present a blending and inferential opportunity for the reader because they connect multiple elements in the array of panels and images. Blending the screaming faces to the watch through their shared underwater bubbles suggests that they are somehow linked through affective resonances of distress or anguish. The watch's bubbles suggests that it has an unspoken or untapped role in the history that the other panels give glimpses of, foreshadowing a more significant role in the narrative ahead.

After his underwater crisis, Jack returns to the surface (Figure 7.3) in an even more fractured state. The page is not initially confusing: the landscape and figures seem to make a coherent scene. Yet, Lemire continues to mobilize the split self metaphor as a dominant visual motif, separating the character from his thoughts and from himself across space. Moreover, Jack moves through the page in a linear and scenically expected yet unconventional reading path, forcing readers to simulate him climbing up the page, rather than reading downward through the segmented page space. I have analyzed a similar pattern in Lemire's depiction of contrastive past and present viewpoints elsewhere (Borkent 2017), and arguably here there is a similar effect: when readers simulate a motion from the image that chafes against conventional reading paths and understandings of sequential narrative, this produces a sense of atemporality and discomfort or ominousness. In this case, the counter-flow of depicted motion is coupled to the split self metaphors that have been propagating throughout recent pages, reinforcing that Jack's distressed mental state is developing a troublingly distorted world. The next pages reinforce this readerly premonition, with Jack emerging into and living inside a dystopic vision of the oil rig and town, which are empty and broken. He emerges into a completely calm nightmare, emptied of his present, of his wife and mother, and only later is it revealed to be populated occasionally by his memories.

Figure 7.3 Multiple selves moving atypically (Lemire 2012, 123).

[192] *Comics and Cognition*

In this dystopic vision of his world, Jack slowly pieces together his memories of his father's troubling obsessions and struggles with alcoholism, including missed appointments, forgotten promises, and so on. Jack finally meets up with himself as a boy, engaging his past self in conversation, which literalizes and dramatizes the split-self metaphor into the narrative. Jack comes to realize that the watch at the center of his underwater visions was in fact a "treasure" his father had found and gifted to him. In reliving aspects of these memories, Jack comes to several revelations about himself and his father, and the history they shared (which I will not analyze in detail, so as not to spoil too much of the graphic novel). The imagery and scenes reinforce that his past and present had been at war in his head, actively fragmenting his psyche, and that only by reintegrating his sense of self and history could he reconcile with his past. This reintegration is even visualized in the narrative with a bird's-eye view of him walking through the town, as he moves from one memory to another. Following these reconnections, Jack returns to his sense of self and his love and affection for his wife and child, recognizing intrinsically that he is different from his father.

Jack's newfound, future-oriented viewpoint is visualized in a double-page spread (Figure 7.4). The scene silently depicts Jack rowing out to sea, to where he suffered his initial mental collapse, located below the derelict

Figure 7.4 Viewpoint reorientation and coherence (Lemire 2012, 196–97).

oil rig where he remerged. In this figure, small panels, similar to those in Figure 7.2, are arrayed in a coordinated timeline, looking into the future in a coherent manner, without alternative orientations and competing past and present axes. While he remains in his dystopia, he is finally moving toward the future, rather than fighting his past. He has agency, as he guides his boat (albeit in atypical, reverse rowing position) on the surface of the ocean, rather than being fragmented in its deepest depths.[4] This depiction metaphorically suggests Jack is in control rather than being subsumed and in emotional turmoil, and is looking forward to positive experiences with his wife and son in the future.

Through this contrastive image to Figure 7.2, Lemire represents Jack's viewpoint as reoriented and coherent, suggesting that through his time in his dystopic vision he has finally come to terms with his past and is able to focus on his future, he has become able to balance and rebuild his viewpoint, showing a resolution of the split self as optimally oriented toward the present and the future self. Here, the split-self metaphor comes to his aid, allowing him to separate his present self from his childhood self, distancing himself from his childhood trauma and misunderstandings of his father, in order to reorient his attentions to his present and future selves as separate from his father's influence. He is able to rebuild and heal his narrative self by reordering his psyche and placing distance between his childhood and his adulthood, which allows him to embrace his future. Of course, the image of the pocket watch, which only comes to prominence as a connection to his father, also acts as a literal instantiation of tracking time and reinforces that Jack's sense of self must realign with his understanding of time in order to heal by leaving the past behind.

7.3 SALIENCE AND MATERIALIZED NARRATIVE ANCHORS

All of the figures in this chapter have illustrated patterns of layout and image repetition (especially of water and watches) that help readers visualize and conceptualize the character viewpoint of Jack, adding and reinforcing metaphorical interpretations to his troubled expressions. However, the final figure also shows how salient aesthetic choices about embedded panels and layouts also serve as anchors for viewpoint comparisons, since it projects out into a future narrative that is otherwise never told, and in a way that aligns stylistically with the fragmented childhood memories that originally explode from him on the ocean floor. It is this repetition of the embedded paneling style, but with a difference in orientational layout, that allows the reader to reflect on the character's viewpoint re-orientation. This linking between elements of both imagery and layout across many pages of the story illustrates how narrative viewpoints on the nature of Jack's lived experience are developed through non-linear or more holistic mappings. Such weavings raise further questions about how the materiality of the page transcends panel and layout relationships to build broader coherences, a network of connections that Theirry Groensteen (2007) descriptively calls "braiding" across a comics' discourse space.

To locate what elements of a story braid together into a more general understanding of plot, character, and other narrative features requires attention to how elements become salient to readers in a way that prompts recursive mappings later on. Different types of perceptual experience lead to different interpretive possibilities. The conspicuousness of particular panels, layout patterns, and other choices helps build explicit attentional guidance and thereby perceptual salience on the page, which anchors that moment in the reader's memory in a way that can inform future storytelling moments. The fracturing of modalities and paneled components allows creators to strategically mobilize these experiences for various effects, much like a line break and caesura in poetry can highlight content even while the lines soon become blended through enjambment. Similarly, spatial logics of proximity and distance, as well as pattern and arrangement, are often perceived immediately at a gist level and can build rich perceptual cues that add to interpretations of characters and events as well as prompt (and anchor) broader mappings across the narrative. Thus, salient orchestrations of panels can push beyond sequentiality to build a sense of simultaneity or establish narrative connections and coherence.

Barbara Dancygier's analysis of narrative structures (2012) helps link these observations into the cognitive theory of mental space blending. She shows how understanding stories relies on recognizing different storytelling roles and values and the ability to ascribe new occurrences to their right place within this set of relations at the levels of character, narrator, and storyworld viewpoints as mental spaces are prompted, updated, and blended. Storytelling conventions are complex domain networks that are dependent upon cultural values, generic expectations, and so forth. They also align with different universal patterns of narration, such as the hero's journey or, in this case, anti-hero (Hogan 2003). In the previous chapter, I analyzed how vital relations surrounding characters in particular, as well as timeline assumptions, build event structures and viewpoint details by interpreting sequences as material anchors. Dancygier (2012) helpfully expands on the concept of the material anchor to address narratological interests through the notion of "narrative anchors." She argues that features of a narrative gain salience through their significance to character and epistemic narrative viewpoints, as well as through their repetition or incongruities to the wider narrative story space. Such salient features are highlighted for later activation through allusions or elaborations, which continue to develop or change that element, presenting opportunities to decompress viewpoints at strategic moments in the narrative. These dynamic qualities mean that "narrative anchors are difficult to define formally because they are not restricted to any specific aspect of narrativity which is typically discussed (plot, characterization, et cetera), but they may participate in all. They are best defined in terms of the processes they trigger which lead to the construction of the story" (Dancygier 2012, 42). Dancygier employs blending analyses of viewpoint constructions at different levels of written narrative to illustrate the complexity of narrative anchoring, and which I continue to develop here in relation to the multimodality of comics.

Narrative anchoring occurs in the previous figures through vital relations mappings between salient images and scenes from Jack's memory. The salient images serve as material anchors that compress until a new scene prompts their decompression and integration again in order to develop character and narratorial viewpoints. For much of the graphic novel, the anchors repeat while continuing to build the same motif of fragmentation, confusion, and affective dissonance. In the final figure, these anchors are reorganized and adjusted toward coherence and a future-oriented perspective. The anchors come to finally align along Jack's timeline. This overt reorientation resonates in contradistinction with his initial mental breakdown and the chains of repeated images that reinforced his fragmentation. As a clear reflection of the emerging healing and reformulating coherence to Jack's viewpoint, this full-page spread serves as a denouement for the crises that have driven the narrative, clarifying that he has come to understand himself as a father while leaving his past traumas behind, or at least reconciling with them.

While I have focused primarily on salience in layout and some imagery, there are other repeated multimodal elements that contribute to narrative coherence. The anchors gain salience through repetition in the earlier parts of the story, but become increasingly significant to the narrative as the story later reveals their significance to our understanding of Jack's memories of his father and sense of loss. Repetitions of aspects of the Halloween domain, for instance, reflect the day his father disappeared, as do repeated images of the pocket watch. The Halloween domain features in images of pumpkins and bats and other common festive figures. Likewise, characters occasionally reference it in conversation, such as, early on, when Jack's wife apologies for forgetting that it is Halloween as the explanation for Jack's glum demeanor. Through these repeated multimodal hints, the reader recognizes that Halloween is significant to the narrative long before understanding why. Multimodal cues surrounding water imagery and vocations work similarly. The multimodality of these cues showcases how domain activation develops a network of elements that can serve anchoring functions, such that the repetition does not need to be completely mimetic of a particular moment but simply associative with particular contextual elements. Nonetheless, while these elements of the story certainly help weave it together, the metaphorical layers and narrative anchoring and weaving of strategically salient layouts grounds their narrative functionality as they blend together.

7.4 CONCLUSION

The layout of comics pages act as material anchors that associate panels through the logic of perception to build resonance and connections. Schematic qualities suggest particular inferential logics about character and scenic qualities that in turn lead to narratively significant interpretations, including through mental metaphors of the self and time. As Dancygier (2012) has shown for literary texts, the setting up of mental spaces as narrative spaces further allows for particular elements to gain significance in terms of character and narrative epistemic viewpoints across long stretches of text. As I have shown, comics similarly prompt these different narrative spaces through multimodal cues, leveraging the affordances of diagrammatic, pictorial, and verbal modes to anchor and weave spaces together.

Material anchors transform into narrative anchors through repetition and highlighting of scenic and personal content and their metaphorical connections to senses of time, place, and character viewpoint developments. Here I have shown how strategic layouts of multimodal repetitions more broadly serves as a narrative and thematic anchor that enriches textual inferences through metonymic links and metaphorical resonances around the protagonist. Blending distal features allows for the compression and integration of mental spaces, completely or partially, as they relate to characters and events, to build cohesion and transformation of viewpoints. I argued in Chapter 6 that panels act as material anchors in sequences to build temporal logics. Here, I suggest that they also act as anchors for character, narrator, and narrative viewpoints with enriched thematic content. As such, any modality and feature of comics can function as an anchor that becomes compressed and linked into more composite blended outcomes.

CHAPTER 8
Abstraction and Experimentation in Comics

Improvisation and Meaning

8.1 THE PROBLEM OF ABSTRACTION AND SIMPLICITY

The cognitive approach I have developed in previous chapters has predominantly focused on examples with representational variation within the pictorial and verbal modalities, but all of which have been predominantly referential in interpretive potential. While choices in color, tone, and degrees of detail have varied, most have been relatively clear in their presentation of factual or fictional content. This chapter explores comics that push toward abstract and experimental limits of figuration and narration, which tests and expands the cognitive approach further to account for improvisational aspects of meaning-making.

McCloud has famously articulated comics as a communicative form grounded in abstraction, where simplification serves as a means to amplify key pictorial elements. In introducing the idea of abstraction, McCloud suggests that "when we abstract an image through cartooning, we're not so much eliminating details as we are focusing on specific details. By stripping down an image to its essential 'meaning,' an artist can amplify that meaning in a way that realistic art can't" (1993, 30). Moreover, they can produce a "universal identification" through the reader connecting abstracted images to themselves, to their "whole bodies" (36–37). Thus, McCloud focuses on how abstraction serves a perceptual function by focusing attention

Comics and Cognition. Mike Borkent, Oxford University Press. © Oxford University Press 2024.
DOI: 10.1093/oso/9780197509784.003.0008

on key qualities of an image that can align with embodied experiences, personalizing the imagery. Such observations do align in important ways with the model of embodiment and mental simulation I have developed over previous chapters.

McCloud generally lauds the use of simplification and abstraction in comics, but there are also reasons to be cautious because of the limits of modalities. As Anna Peppard notes, "amplifying the meaning of a body by simplifying it can mean very different things depending on whose body is being represented [. . .] Thus, while comics always simplify, such simplification is never simple; it is always knowing, purposeful and complicated" (2018, 61). Likewise, I would add that no text can be universally identified with, based on the varied embodied experiences of the reader engaging with these simplified prompts. Peppard analyzes how the simplification of black embodiment in early stories about Black Panther embeds stereotypes and problematic assumptions that serve white anxieties much more than the black liberatory agenda that the series also sought to develop. Clearly, the ways in which creators simplify and represent information, as one form of abstraction, comes with social and political implications.

McCloud goes on to attempt to model simplification and abstraction as a theory of meaning. He presents a pyramid of abstraction (1993, 52–53), which contrasts across its base a realist portrait from a photo-comic by Tom King against a simple face emoji and at the top basic geometric shapes as illustrative of the spectrum of abstraction. This raises some reasons to be hesitant with McCloud's model of abstraction through simplification. For instance, there is a latent logocentrism at root in this diagram, which suggests that "meaning" is located in more abstracted and symbolic realms in contrast to photo-realist imagery. Such a model obscures what might be meant by "meaning" by leaning into a commonly held assumption of Platonic ideals, which often align with old models of language, rather than recognizing the shifting qualities of meaning construal associated with different representational choices. Interestingly, Platonic logocentrism does not even align with McCloud's own preference for pictorial communication, but still serves to emphasize his notion of representational simplification as crucial to comics. However, the notions of simplification and abstraction are difficult to disentangle, especially in relation to the broad concept of "meaning," and as with the concept of temporality discussed in Chapter 6, here distinguishing between descriptions of text features and the experience of texture is crucial. McCloud's own description of perceptual engagement, and of complexification of meaning by creating opportunities for readers to imbue more personal nuances into the meaning of images, aligns with interpretive potentials of modalities. However, his diagram of abstraction focuses on features prior to meaning construction. As I discussed in Chapter 4, abstraction is a natural feature of cognition as part of memory formation and conceptual and categorical development. How modalities are activated within this cognitive context offers a means of better nuancing the conversation, where language and imagery can vary substantially in the construction of meaning.

Focusing on abstraction and simplification, and how they engage processes of meaning construction, offers an opportunity to engage experimental comics, sometimes also called abstract or art comics (Molotiu 2009, 2012), that push these notions to their extremes, fundamentally challenging questions of representation, reference, identification, and composition. Due to these challenges, they may be said to challenge readerly engagement. In which case, what happens to the cognitive framework developed so far? What happens to the nature of the meaning of the text when it becomes non-referential or asemic, where there is less overt "multimodal content" in the visual form? Do such excesses of abstraction or simplification skirt concerns with narrativity, agency, and social or political implications? How do readers think through such reductions in multimodal expression to come to some form of interpretation of this textuality? And, in terms of the major theories espoused in this book, how much perceptual and experiential information can really be simulated to build meaningful mental spaces from such sparse cues? In a sense, what does a cognitive theory of non-referential meaning look like? In this chapter, I expand the cognitive theory to engage with interpretive possibilities that are generated through improvisational qualities of cognition. I will show that even in abstract and experimental comics, modal and multimodal glimpses of agency offer opportunities to build meanings that explore the foundations of mediation and expressivity.

8.2 DYNAMIC FORMS AND NARRATIVE POTENTIALITIES

Abstract and experimental comics are genres that have developed around explorations of referential extremes and medial limitations. Such works generally fall into the broad category of "art comics." Andrei Molotiu (2016) offers a historical overview of such works and shows how they have consistently challenged accepted notions of depiction and narrative in comics. Thierry Groensteen surmises from several scholars that these types of comics highlight the skeletal machinery of the form (2013, 11). Molotiu has compiled a wide range of examples of such works in his anthology, *Abstract*

Comics (2009), which he frames as inspired by the history and philosophy of Modern experimentations with abstract art (n.p.). There he also loosely defines abstract comics as "sequential art consisting exclusively of abstract imagery" or that can "include those comics that contain some representational elements, as long as those elements do not cohere into a narrative or even into a unified narrative space" (n.p.). He documents in more detail elsewhere the definitional conundrums that abstract comics pose to previous scholarly works (Molotiu 2012), which often feature verbal, visual, and narrative requirements. Similarly Groensteen takes these abstract works as a liminal or border case of comic arts (2013, ch. 1) for the same reasons. He suggests that they work to highlight two key elements of comics: their visual content—"colors, lines, [and] forms organized into motifs"—and their "spatio-topical apparatus"—that is, "a space that is demarcated and compartmentalized, within which frames enter into spatial relationships and compose an organized reality" (12). He highlights that these qualities do not necessitate a sense of narrative, just "tabular" and "spatial relationships organizing a visual field" (13). Both Groensteen and Molotiu note how relationships between elements in an abstract comic can produce a sense of sequentiality and rhythm, but refuse a sense of narrative without a direct connection to referentiality. With regard to experimental comics, with more referential cues, bpNichol (discussed later) describes similar qualities, which he considered explorations of comics' "panelogic" (2002b).

Most critics accept these general definitions of abstract comics, working to elaborate on the effects of these representational limitations. Various critics have characterized the effects in a manner of ways, such as, for Molotiu (2009), as a sense of "transformation and interaction," "graphic dynamism," and "rhythm" (n.p.). Molotiu elaborates on these qualities as "sequential pleasure, [which is] achieved by putting the eye into motion, and by creating specific graphic paths, speeds of scanning, and graphic rhythms to enliven its aesthetic experience" (2012, 89). Similarly, he refers to "the panel-to-panel play of abstract shapes that creates potent formal dramas" (2009, n.p.). Kym Tabulo emphasizes the role of an illusion of temporality through visual connections and describes latent hints of narrativity that emerge from such qualities. Tabulo at the same time emphasizes the abstract nature of such qualities, which "focus on the medium and not the human" (2014, 35). Similarly, Daniel Worden suggests that abstraction and experimentation function as "a departure from the reader" (2015, 65) in his analysis of a comic by James Kochalka, which was included in Molotiu's anthology and reprinted in part here again (Figure 8.1). Worden also notes of the comic that "perhaps it is a study of line and ink, an exploration of

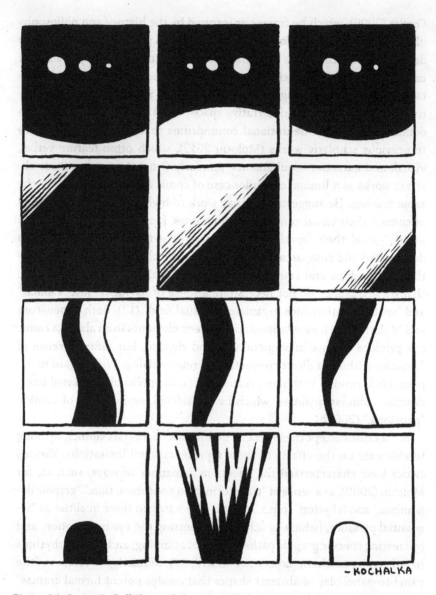

Figure 8.1 James Kochalka's untitled comic, included in *Abstract Comics* (Molotiu 2009, n.p.). Copyright: Kochalka 2009.

movement and organic-seeming shape, a tragedy, or even a comedy?" (63). What intrigues me about these various descriptions of the abstract comics is their emphasis on dynamicity, and how they often seem to focus on temporal and narrative qualities of the medium including dramatic categories, despite repeatedly refuting narrative as constitutive of abstract comics. Repeatedly the focus is on interactions, drives, rhythms, transformations, and illusions, and how these push through sequentiality toward narrative interests (drama, comedy, tragedy, etc.), despite the textual resistance of abstraction to clarify the content of the narrative.

All of these critics have characterized reader responses to perceptions of the abstract images, while simultaneously noting the focus on their resistance to representation or referentiality, and simultaneously gesturing to a narrativistic potential. As Worden states:

> The narrative and visual possibilities produced by the page engage the reader in a more radical process of imagining, one that brings to the fore questions about how meaning is made and what meanings are possible on the comics page. (2015, 63)

However, Worden does not elaborate on his reading of this comic beyond gesturing to these questions of meaning, nor on why he places emphasis on narrative genres as a way of describing dynamic connections. Groensteen similarly gestures to a reason for such interpretations by suggesting that the work of reading abstract comics "relies on making narrative hypotheses . . . to reduce the apparent incoherence of the strip" (2013, 19). Groensteen comes closes to describing a cognitive process prompted by abstract comics, which links to predictions about a text, but does not necessarily explain what structures these hypotheses and why particular forms of coherence may emerge. In this chapter, I seek to extend this discussion to begin to explain how these perceived connections and qualities emerge to produce the previous scholars' observations, which extend beyond Molotiu's emphasis on "sequential pleasure" to narrative hypotheses and dramatic qualities. I examine the reader's meaning-making processes to articulate how abstract and experimental comics structure and evoke interpretative and narrative possibilities.

Such experiments with the borders of expression in comics potentially challenge the model of cognition presented thus far, since it may seem difficult to analyze how perception, mental simulation, and blending come together in such abstracted situations. By elaborating on some of the central features of cognition outlined in Chapters 3 and 4, I show how a detailed focus on basic patterns of perception and their conceptual affiliations across domains in fact helps to isolate the interpretative parameters that readers draw on to improvise (hypothesize) salient connections to wider interests in temporality and narrative, including repetitions of dramatic narrative universals defined by Hogan (2003).[1] Moreover, by engaging abstract comics as improvisational invitations, I confirm the observations that abstract and experimental comics inject creativity and awareness into readerly experiences of comics form, and I show how this occurs through training readers to see and mobilize conventionalized and artistic patterns anew through the cognitive revitalization of meaning networks.

8.3 ABSTRACTION AND COGNITION

An emphasis on perception aligns nicely with Groensteen's (2007) and Cohn's (2013b) emphasis on panels operating as units of attention, discussed in more detail in Chapters 3 and 6. Abstract comics simplify this unit of composition, often reducing the multimodality of everyday comics to its visual and schematic modalities, and with language (or hints thereof) most often appearing solely as a descriptive title that frames the comic rather than being incorporated into panels. In a sense, abstract comics prioritize basic perceptual cues. This provides a valuable point of analytical entry, by engaging how readers likely perceive these forms in order to account for their effects, as well as the limited role that linguistic cues plays in their interpretation.

The complexity and variety of image compositions makes it difficult to designate how best to analyze them outside of the context of their expression. Therefore, qualitative experiences of dominant perceptual cues may serve as the best initial indicator of how readers work to interpret features in and between panels. After all, there are significant commonalities across human visual perception as a species, which focus on dominant qualities of shapes, color, orientations, perspective, organization, and other perceived connections between elements, which serve as reference points.

To describe these qualities and their interpretive possibilities with more cognitive relevance, I turn to the gestalt psychologically informed notions of abstraction, which help illustrate the central link between perception and conceptualization. As Rudolph Arnheim notes,

> The thought elements of perception and the perceptual elements of thought are complementary. They make human cognition a unitary process, which leads without break from the elementary acquisition of sensory information to the most generic theoretical ideas. The essential trait of this unitary cognitive process is that at every level it involves abstraction. (2004, 153)

Crucially, in his analysis of what abstraction is, and is not, Arnheim carefully maintains a connection between the perceptually grounded qualities of abstraction, so as to refute the notion that to be abstract is to be inaccessible or purely conceptual in some way (the problem with McCloud's pyramid of abstractions). Moreover, gestalts are important perceptual experiences of pattern, organization, and context, which lend themselves to specific conceptual developments, working to scaffold inferential and interpretive processes. Elsewhere, Arnheim considers abstraction in formal cues as a type of interpretive artistic choice in how perception is guided to produce effects in the viewer (2009, 156). Such an approach notices patterns of multimodal orchestration as "ceptual" in nature, as unifying both perceptual and conceptual aspects, based on combined gestalt patterns and formal details that have communicative effects.

I will now return to James Kochalka's comic (Figure 8.1) in order to expand on its perceptual qualities and their interpretive possibilities. Arguably, the comic prioritizes sequentiality, with each level or strip orchestrating around a shared visual theme. Gestalt perception of the top strip, for instance, traces the lines—solid and wavy along the bottom, as well as dotted across the top—across all three panels. These shared forms and their visual alignments unite the panels perceptually, despite their segmentation or sequentiality. In this sense, the panels operate as units of attention with discrete content (which itself has potentially dynamic qualities, based on the wavy formal cues), but also connect because of dominant perceptual similarities. This unified experience of a scene reflects Molotiu's concept of "iconostasis," which describes "the perception of the layout of a comics page as a unified composition" (2012, 91). In this sense, the strip acts like an art triptych of a dark landscape with abstract ghostly clouds.

On the other hand, the segmentation and sequentiality of the top strip could possibly reflect one space thrice represented. Blending and charting changing elements in mental simulations of cause and effect or change, the circles may be interpreted as pulsing white dots (stars or disco lights, perhaps?) floating over an undulating surface. In this way, as a comic strip, it reflects strongly the dynamic, rhythmic qualities described by the critics, while also maintaining that sense of "iconostasis" of the triptych paneling, within which dynamic elements like floating dots or broken lines are in tension with iconostatic qualities. So, how do these qualities emerge and suggest narrative interpretations, including Worden's comment about drama?

In what follows, I expand on several concepts that isolate key features of gestalt perception and abstraction through schemas, fictivity, and vital relations described in previous chapters. These perceptual cues develop fictive experiences of change and motion, which reflect the dynamic descriptions by critics. These fictive qualities of perception provide powerful parameters and possibilities for inferential improvisation that operate through mental simulation and blending. All of these cognitive components bring a focus onto the materiality and sensorial qualities that ground the relationship between comics and cognition.

8.3.1 Forms and Fictivity: Simulating Schemas and Fictive Transformations

Many general patterns of perception can be expressed through gestalt qualities of shapes, patterns, and object relations. Gestalts also provide important connection points between sensorimotor experiences and conceptualization processes (Arnheim 2004; Johnson 1987, 2007). This is particularly evident through analyses of schematic concepts that inform both images and language. As I described in Chapter 3, examples of schemas include MOTION, CONTAINMENT, FIGURE/GROUND, PATH, BALANCE, EMANATION, VERTICALITY, SCALARITY, and DIRECTIONALITY. These gestalt elements provide perceptual and inferential logics that are particularly salient for engaging abstract comics, since they reflect common formal qualities and symmetries, like the line and object-containment elements that compose Kochalka's comic. The first row of panels exhibits lines and contained circles above them, which group each set together and facilitating blends of their forms. The next row shows a variety of parallel lines that diagonally bisect the panel at several locations, seeming to traverse the panel space. As a series, they also offer a symmetrical balance of light and dark, with the dominant darkness of the opening panel becoming symmetrical in the middle, and inverted to lightness in the final panel, offering a balanced center panel as well as a sequential balancing of light and dark forms across a path. The third and fourth strips similarly presents lines or contained spaces in a range of forms that reflect and balance each other in various ways. It is these general perceptions that inform Worden's suggestion that "perhaps it is a study of line and ink, an exploration of movement and organic-seeming shape" (2015, 63). But why are these surface features of inked lines somehow moving, organic shapes?

Mental simulation and blending play a significant role in explaining how static cues can contribute to dynamic textual interpretations. Substantial evidence suggests that visual cues activate motion and action simulations. In representational works, implied motion in static images induces action responsivity in viewers (Kourtzi and Kanwisher 2000), including through visual instability or asymmetries in body postures (Osaka et al. 2010). At the same time, De Lucia (2016) shows how even abstract drawings can elicit motor action simulations in viewers. Similarly, Hoenen, Lübke, and Pause (2017) show how very abstract drawings, many non-representational, prompt motor simulations reflecting bodily actions that might produce a similar picture. Teenie Matlock (2010) reviews and extends prior research to show how "abstract motion" induces object and action simulations as well. As she suggests elsewhere, "mental simulation is ubiquitous" (2004, 1389) because it is involved in such a range of mental activities from understanding complex personal actions through to rotating abstract geometric shapes to interpreting statements of abstract transfers of intangible entities. Such research supports Gallese's and Freedberg's arguments[2] that simulation plays a crucial role in aesthetic engagements with visual art by activating embodied responses to both what is depicted *and* how it is produced (such as gestural traces), which can lead to affective and empathetic responses. The sensorimotor activations of simulation, which operate unconsciously across cultural and personal aspects of experience, seem capable of activations at both representational and non-representational levels of meaning, and are implicated in a range of synesthetic connections (Ramachandran and Hubbard 2001). In short, Kochalka's comic feels dynamic because of perceptual simulated responses to its forms.

Mental simulation of visual phenomena can inject fictivity into conceptualization, even in cases where one might think one is being factually straightforward. For instance, the wavy, dashed, and dotted lines in the first three strips, and even the fragmented lines of the middle panel in the final strip of Kochalka's comic, each adds dynamic qualities to their panels. This occurs in part by cognitively breaking the prototypical schematic concept of a LINE into a wavy, dotted, or fragmented representation. This discrepancy with the prototype sets up a sense of fictive change, because gestalt perception aligns them as elements of a formal unity that have been caught at a moment of breaking or shifting from their schematic sense of linearity. To be clear, fictive change is when something is perceived as a singularity that at the same time reflects potentialities of change or changeability: thus, there is a tendency to perceive a singular dotted line rather than multiple dots moving or arranged in space. Scanning across the lines also produces a sense of fictive motion as viewers conceptualize the duration of scanning a group of elements in space. Fictive motion is when something is conceptualized as moving when in actuality it is still, such as a road that "goes" or "runs" around a lake. Leonard Talmy (1996) offers a detailed analysis of many examples of fictive motion in language, suggesting that fictivity is one way that language correlates perception and conception to reflect a nexus point between the two which he calls "ception." Returning to the lake road: roads clearly cannot run or go anywhere, but the qualitative perceptual process of scanning the length of the road becomes imbedded in the language to develop a sense of perceptual duration that extends the mental simulated sense of the road's length. Thus, mental simulation incorporates aspects of real-world motion to inform conceptualizations (Fauconnier 1997), and is in turn impacted by fictive motion expressions (Matlock 2010), which include both language and arguably abstract depictions like those discussed here.

While language and pictures are not synonymous, the fictive qualities of perception and conceptualization nonetheless inform how viewers engage with and interpret abstract comics. Thus, through gestalt unity and scanning of their lengths, the lines of Kochalka's comic, especially the top one, seem to be dynamically changeable and moving, despite their factively static nature. John Miers (2014) describes this tension between representational form and perceived connections and implications as a tension between material "facture" and wider inferential connections, or between seeing and seeing-in. This was discussed in terms of representational nonveridicality that prompts alternative interpretations, including metaphorical or metonymic mappings, in Chapters 4 and 5, but functions similarly well in abstract comics as well, but at the schematic and diagrammatic level of fictivity. Here, the tensions between factive and fictive qualities continue to occur within panels and become increasingly dynamic as readers move through a series, sequence, and layout. Tracing how these dynamics activate and blend together into abstract scenarios helps to better isolate how and why critics describe such works in terms of temporality and narrative.

As I have argued and shown in previous chapters, blending serves as a helpful model to disentangle how simulations develop across a text to build complex understandings or interpretive potential. As readers blend elements from panel to panel in Kochalka's comic, especially combining the thematically linked strips, abstract scenarios arguably emerge. For instance, a person might read the top series as a singular wavy and dotted line, or a series of changing lines. Reading the panels as sequence builds in assumptions of causality or temporality by projecting the analogous forms onto each other and noting the similarities and differences. Blending the forms and charting the differences relies on vital relations that blend similar elements together (form to form) to build a mental simulation of these forms as changeable and changing throughout the sequence, linking sequences through the vital relation of causality. Importantly, within the panel fictive change and motion is cued within the forms, but when panels are blended, such changeability is experienced factively. Here, the sequential and recursive development of inferential reasoning about objects in space are simulated and blended in a way that shifts the aesthetic experience from inferred transformations to explicit ones. Thus, there is a tension within each strip between fictive and factive transformations, which Worden lists together as lines and movement, or which others have called rhythms and stasis. Such movements are fictively imbued through object simulations and panel blends.

8.3.2 Vital Relations and the Improvisation of Narrative

To move further toward narrative-like interpretations of drama, of tragedy or comedy, and of more explicit temporality beyond panel-to-panel changes, requires further blended simulations and knowledge activation from narrative domains. Chris Gavaler notes that changes to forms in successive panels can establish the forms themselves as characters through their perceived transformations and interactions (2017, 10–11), and as such, extending Postema's (2013) formal analysis of transitions, he suggests that "ordered recurrence" (19–20) becomes the basis for agentive attribution to abstract forms.[3] In short, readers personify the fictive and factive motions and changes within and between panels, activating object features and line traces as motivated communication and action, despite their abstracted, non-representational nature. Moreover, these agentive readings include not just the sense that the text is communicative (read representational) in some way, but that the forms are abstracted objects and characters whose changes and fictive interactions have some inherent meaning. In this sense, readers can never escape the cognitive bias toward intersubjective communication through textuality and discourse domains: since it looks (somewhat) like a comic, viewers likely presume it must have meaning. Analyzing the simulated blending networks in abstract comics can isolate how those presumed meanings are constructed.

To build up simulations of abstract action, readers blend repeated, similar, or analogous forms together, tracking their changes through space. The focus on recurrence and change reflects a core principle of blending theory, which focuses on the development and support of connections between mental spaces through vital relations. As discussed in previous chapters, vital relations include formal features, such as of identity, part-whole relations (object permanence), role, property, and similarity, as well as cognitive assumptions about agents and environments, such of as cause-effect, space, change, time, and intention (Fauconnier and Turner 2002, 93–102). Vital relations allow for connections to be built between mental spaces, including more nuanced activations of domains that share features. In abstract comics like Kochalka's, the simplicity of his images seems to help isolate properties or identities for the different forms, which in turn facilitate mappings between circles and lines across each strip. These mappings between similar elements further develops other relational qualities of change, which is strongly associated with basic notions of temporality and even causality or intentionality as well. These interpretive aspects of vital relations align formal features in a way that facilitates the more dynamic and intentional qualities in the critical readings.

Going further with Kochalka's comic, viewers might see formal alignments between panels, including through simulations of object qualities, that build a complex network of blends based largely on vital relations of identity, role, and change. For instance, the first row of panels might blend into an oscillating or waving line and pulsing dots. These dynamic qualities develop through a sense of role or identity of these forms based on fictive qualities and factive blends. The second row continues to trace transformations, as though the darkness is sliding down the page (relying on a sense of object permanence), which again maintains a sense of change, movement, and object identity. At the same time, the vital role of movement may prompt viewers to connect this sequence to the previous one, supporting an interpretation of this sequence as a close-up view of the wave motion of the first line. The third row of panels provides yet another focus on an undulating line, but this time with added transformations within it, suggesting perhaps a sense of either a rolling tube of mixed elements, or of an upward motion of a snake-like thing. The similar identifying features of undulating lines again connects this row to the top row, giving a sense of similar motion, but with an unclear viewpoint. Perhaps the third row is a more distant view of the oscillating first row. Throughout the first three rows of Kochalka's comics, a theme emerges of fictive and dynamic qualities of lines being repeated with hints of connections between rows based on analogous roles and identities.

In the final row, the comic seems to shift dramatically from this thematic approach, turning away from linear movements and toward a sense of object transformation. The first panel offers a dark blob. The second panel presents a somewhat diagrammatically expected representation of an explosion, which activates domains associated with explosions, such as parties, mining, and war. The third panel again presents the same shape as the first panel, but in white. As a sequence, readers might blend the first and last panel together, based on the shared identity of the recurring shape, while noticing the change in their coloration. Blending these with the middle panel suggests a cause-effect relationship, by which the explosion transforms the dark object into the light object. As such, this is the most directly temporal and narrativistic series of panels in the comic, and is arguably the ground for Worden's suggestion that this is a tragedy or comedy based on the domains associated with explosions, since they are associated with both war and slapstick. In a way, it is the diagrammatically informative icon that provides the narrative lens for this series, which then is backward projected to previous panels to inform how readers interpret them.

The explosive qualities continue to bleed back through formal affinities, including the web of connections between the roles of motion and transformation previously examined through each strip. Projecting back further, the oscillating white dots or dotted line, and the moving darkness of the first two rows, may also connect back to this explosive transformation, lending the serenity of the balance and circuity of those panels a potentially sinister quality. Or perhaps, this explosion really is a percussive finale to what has been a slow yet general transformation from dark to light dominance across the bottom three rows, establishing a sense of symmetry and balance in terms of overall coloration. Herein lies the drama of the comic, which hinges primarily on the recognition of a diagrammatic reference that is typically associated with agentive, intentional action. This sense of a viewpoint that seeks to affect causal transformations in some way then aligns with and gives an agentive and intentional drive to the dynamic qualities of lines and tensions between colors. This sense of intentional alteration mobilizes existing tensions between contrasting colors and their associated fictive and factive motions and changes to develop potential for narrative interpretation. It is unclear, however, how far such projections go, nor how significant this narrative element is to any given reader.

There are other formal relations and dynamics to also focus on in this comic that can go beyond these dramatic hints. The vital relation of identity can align other elements beyond lines, such as coloration and orientation. While I have focused on linear elements, the color and shape of the blobs, as well as of the previous lines, allows for further mappings between them, especially if readers mentally simulate object rotations of these abstract forms, which is quite likely.[4] It seems to me that the bottom of the tube in the third row aligns in both width and coloration to the blobs below, which suggests a vertical rather than horizontal mapping between contiguous panels as a hyperframe (see Figure 3.2). This formal resonance might prompt a ninety-degree reorientation from the third to the fourth row, wherein the fourth row presents an end view of the tube that is seen snaking up the page above. In this sense, the rotating and snaking tube in the third row gathers more energy, as it blends with the changing and exploding elements below, which might suggest that the fictive and factive motions are motivated with a more dramatic tension between white and black dominance within this object. Perhaps then, the dramatic tension ascribed to the alterations between light and dark elements could be further reconstrued to reflect a tension within a singular figure, rather than alternative forms, adding further interiority to a dynamic scene that lends itself toward narrativity.

Patrick Colm Hogan outlines a universal, schematic definition of narrative: "prototypical narratives have a telic structure including an agent, a goal, and a causal sequence connecting the agent's various actions with the achievement or nonachievement of the goal" (2003, 205). Critics describe abstract comics as non-narrative because they break away from this prototypical structure. However, as I have shown, readers can certainly still construct a sense of some of these elements. These reflect attributions of motivation to blended changes between forms. Such changes may be interpreted as transformations from one state to another, which may reflect a causal (sequential) move toward a goal, with the central figure being a schematic protagonist in the sequence. As such, abstract forms are personified, are imbued with agentive qualities because of their transformations and their dynamic qualities within and between panels. Beyond this sense of forms becoming animated as characters, readers might also recognize and ascribe common narrative patterns that can further structure their interpretations. Colm has again carefully documented three common cross-cultural narrative patterns of romance, tragedy, and comedy, each of which operates as an extremely abstract domain. Each story pattern comes with generic attributes, and it is telling that Worden draws on two of these as potential interpretational lenses for Kochalka's comic.

Noting the abstract patterns, fictive and factive changes, and potential iconographic cue (the explosion) provides readers with inferential and predictive parameters that lead toward narrative tropes and agentive attributions. The ambiguity of reference throughout makes it difficult to ascribe specific or detailed narrative coherence to the comic, despite hints of action. Rather, it is this fact that abstract comics remain locked in interpretive tensions that makes them so interesting, since they act as spaces of formal meditation, wherein the viewer is invited to navigate and interpret the basic formal features of and in the panel in whatever way they choose. Arguably, experiencing comics like this affirms a heightened awareness of the dynamic qualities inherent to mental simulation of even the most basic forms on paper.

At the heart of this meditative aspect is what I call cognitive improvisation, which emerges particularly strongly in response to vague and non-referential cues and encourages slow and recursive reading practices (see Borkent 2014b). It is a problem-solving disposition, as Groensteen rightly notes, that grasps at and blends various levels of perception and responsive simulations to develop an array of interpretive possibilities for elements within the compositional ecosystem of a text and its context. Kochalka's comic is particularly instructive in its seeming simplicity that nonetheless generates a complex sense of both coherence and tension across a range of features, fictive and factive. Narrative qualities emerge when predictive possibilities are thwarted and perception must lean more strongly on creative cognitive resources. This involves a questioning disposition that seeks out meaningful relations, improvising a sense of relevance and narrative potential from basic affinities and inferred transformations as well as abstract diagrammatic properties. These affinities and properties are not directly referential, but they are somewhat deictic to embodied patterns of interaction with a dynamic environment. Such cognitive improvisational patterns and processes of connection, inference, and interpretation through largely abstract simulations and blends undergird Worden's summative description of Kochalka's work, and others like it.

Fictive and factive qualities of simulations and blends are common through a range of abstract comic styles. It is important to note that cognitive improvisational patterns can respond to more gestural visual styles as well, not just to aesthetically clean comics like Kochalka's example. As a point of contrast to Kochalka's work, I will briefly examine a gestural comic by myself (Figure 8.2). While clearly exhibiting fictive motion and fictive change through its curved and scribbled lines, the gestural nature of the work heightens these effects through mental simulation of hand motions that might make them. Knowledge of mark-making heightens reader awareness of the dynamically constructed nature of this text, and of the creator who made it (Lefèvre 2016). While everything is factively static, perception again renders the lines dynamic. Similar to Kochalka's work, the mappings between lines blend into an ever-changing and developing scene in which more and more curved lines wind around each other to form a writhing mass that then coheres into a singular point. The marks may also take on a somewhat agentive or viewpointed quality by having the mass seem to slowly move or shrink away from the viewer across successive

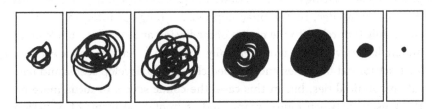

Figure 8.2 Untitled comic by author.

panels, becoming a small dot. All of these gestural and agentive qualities suggest a scene of growing chaos and transformation, suggesting aspects of a narrative arch when blended together, one that fits the dramatic mode of rising conflict and resolution.

When building alignments with domain knowledge about communication, there are several imagic and structural qualities that add nuance to the improvised narrative sense of these changing forms. Read as a complete series of panels, it seems like the comic presents a growing mass of gestural lines that are then becoming inscribed in a more dominant, technical mark that subsumes all other types of lines. The comic starts with overt gestural qualities of mark-making—the beginnings of potential communication through pen and paper—which are then subsumed to some degree into a more technological presence. While the dark mass is not a perfect circle, and therefore maintains a dynamic aspect through fictive change, the shift in register from multiplicity to singularity of marking suggest a shift in the scenario, in vital relations around figuration, roles, and values. These basic marks activate at the very least the domains of communication and technology. Within this context, viewers might improvise a reading from these abstract marks as setting up a scene that depicts a shift in possibilities of mark-making and expression through the impositions, or possibilities, of technology. In a sense, the technological conclusion erases the vibrant dynamicity of the previous panels, in which case the comic could be read as a tragedy, drawing on the roles and cultural values of the domains of expression and sociality in which individual expression is good, and a means of confining and controlling the message is not. It may also be establishing a metaphorical scene that reflects on the nature of mediated expression and its susceptibility to technological influence, reflecting in a way Marshall McLuhan's (1964) famous dictum that "The medium is the message." Of course, this possibility imbues the comic with irony, since it exploits the mediated space of the page, along with discourse conventions of comics, to show the erasure of individualized expressivity in comics themselves. Or, finally, the comic might be said to visualize or diagram a description like, "he rambled around for quite a while but finally made his point." By simulating the connections and possibilities of formal cues with domain knowledge, readers may improvise a range of interpretations of this comic that relate to the nature of mediation and convention in comics and in discursive spaces more generally. Like Kochalka, this comic exploits abstract formal fictivities and blended changes to develop scenic and narrative potentialities, but in this case, the comic seems to focus more on the tension between more organic and technological forms of depiction through and despite comics conventions.

Of course, there are many other ways in which mediated features of comics can be highlighted in abstracted ways. The gestural lines of the previous comic illustrate abstract sensorimotor simulations tied to artistic creation that play a role in how readers perceive these works. Such simulations impact the reception of most comics that are painted or drawn or overtly handmade in some way (and clearly, this is not just for abstract comics). Other texts that may be constructed through digital manipulations, computer algorithms, and other technological processes, including some forms of collage, will be simulated in a slightly different manner, as many are more distanced from embodied action, but they still derive meaning from the recognition of their constructional processes, their purposeful orchestration of elements, and related domain networks for inferred actions and potentialities. Often these constructed elements and domains hint at viewpointed aspects of attentional guidance and intervention, or through fictive change and motion imbue the transformations with a sense of agentive action.

Abstract comics vary greatly in compositional elements. This chapter does not seek comprehensive coverage, but to show how analysis of cognitive processes in response to cues can help unpack how readers come to ascribed meanings to them. At their core, abstract comics exhibit a formal playfulness, which in turn induces a mental playfulness in readers as they seek to improvise possible interpretations. Examining how such works exploit perception to impact mental simulation and blending processes shows how meanings emerge from seemingly meaningless marks.

8.4　EXPERIMENTATION AS METACOMMENTARY: POSSIBILITIES AND REFUSALS

8.4.1　bpNichol's Creative Possibilities

Such abstract playfulness within comics may consternate readers who expect a certain degree of recognizability and accessibility in their texts. Such works are not interested in these more conventional approaches to referential and propositional meaning. However, there are more communicative elements beyond pure abstract forms that are often included in discussions of abstract comics, or in slightly broader terms as avant-garde or experimental comics. In fact, nearly half of the comics in Molotiu's (2009) anthology of abstract comics include icons and representational elements that signal speech, and other recognizable references that help to ground interpretations. Such works strongly resemble purely abstract comics in the focus on pushing borders of meaning, and they also readily exploit fictive and factive qualities of perception, simulation, and blending, while obscuring narrative interpretations. These experimental works highlight conventionalized elements of comics beyond panels and rudimentary characterization. I call such works experimental comics because, unlike abstract comics, they include an increased sense of referentiality and can even include some text. Thus, they blur the border between various narrative genres and abstract comics. Like abstract comics, they tend to heighten reader perceptions of formal qualities of comics and their potential for improvisational readings and thwarted narrative and temporal clarity. The comics also relate to the idea of abstraction as simplification discussed at the beginning of this chapter, in particular to examine further social commentaries inherent in the erasure of reference and how this might impact the presentation of agentive and culturally significant messages.

The following brief examples illustrate how comics conventions and minimal language can be exploited to challenge readers, as abstract comics do, in a more representational manner that nonetheless pushes against narrative and showcases the edges of mediation. The works function as metacommentaries on visual communication and its ability to build connections or withhold them. These experimental comics maintain an interest in the borders and potentialities of communication, as is particularly clear in "Allegory #7" by Canadian author bpNichol (Figure 8.3), featuring

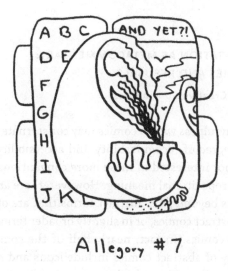

Figure 8.3 "Allegory #7" by bpNichol (1970b, n.p., used with permission of the Estate of bpNichol).

the author's alter ego Milt the Morph (the face behind the mask of Nichol's spoof superhero Captain Poetry; see Nichol 1970b). This work has many recognizable features of comics discourse—panels, sequences and layouts, figures, and narration boxes—but lacks a clear scenic or narrative coherence. Much like the abstract comics above, the work raises questions about how viewers might read and interpret it.

bpNichol published "Allegory #7" along with thirty-two other "allegories" in *Love: A Book of Remembrances* in 1970, all of which used comic-derived artistic styles and conventions to comment on language and meaning.[5] Brian Henderson contends that these allegories' "mandate is to shift the task of reading into the task of perception" by representing language and reality as "highly ambiguous. What kind of reality do they represent? [. . .] transformation and contradiction are the keys to this poetic play" (1989, 12). Henderson concludes that the series of allegories concern themselves with "transformation of the self and of the world through the agency of the word, both systematically and rationally as well as dramatically and intuitively" (15). Arguably, Nichol offers more than this. Beyond giving language agency, his comic exploits multimodal opportunities to shift the reader's perception of language and layers of representation to build mutually constitutive connections between language, the self, and the world. Language does not necessarily build the world, but is embodied and enmeshed in it.

Since bpNichol is well known as an experimental poet and less so as a cartoonist, readings of this work have tended to focus on the comic as an allegorical visual poem, attempting to locate it in a literary tradition and logocentric interests, including misreading comics conventions as lettristic elements. For instance, Jack David's analysis, which is widely cited and supported (Billingham 2000, 69; Scobie 1984, 49), reads:

> In "Allegory #7" [. . .] large printed letters—here, the capital *I* or possibly an *H*—are the framework. The two vertical *I*'s represent the two tablets of Moses: on one is written the letters A-L; on the other, "and yet?" Allegorically, the letters of the alphabet stand for the Ten Commandments. But the drawing gives another point of view. Here I might explain that the cartoon character is Captain Poetry [*sic*: Milt the Morph], Nichol's major persona, and one who signifies traditional poetry. In the drawing, the central image of Captain Poetry is melting into a pot, just as the Israelites melted their gold to produce the Golden Calf. Captain Poetry stands for the traditional uses of language, and his destruction is language's destruction. On the perimeter, another Captain Poetry is observing the melting, and his smile means possibly that he agrees with Nichol's view that language must be broken up in order to revivify it. (1977, 265)

David clearly prioritizes the religious and literary domains for his reading of the comic as allegory in a biblical form, rather than its more generic qualities of perceptual reorientation that Henderson describes. This extends to his misnaming of the character as Captain Poetry, rather than as Milt the Morph (short for Morpheme), who is the character behind the mask of Captain Poetry, and features prominently in bpNichol's comics as a trickster figure (Nichol 2002a). (Captain Poetry's attire, on the other hand, is hard to miss since it strongly resembles a chicken.[6]) While poetry is a grand genre, a morpheme is a much more rudimentary element of meaning construction, and one which aligns less with the biblical and literary reading David offers. Susan Billingham offers a slight expansion of David's reading of the allegory by highlighting its presentation of "language's destruction" and the "fragmentary and fragile nature of the subject" (Billingham 2000, 69). Similarly, Scobie suggests that there may be other readings, but does not elaborate. All of these literary critics reveal their bias toward lettristic and deconstructive mythopoeic approaches in these readings. This is not to dismiss them. Such analyses offer some important insights, especially since they reveal how reader background knowledges activate a range of domains for improvising meanings. At the same time, these readings tend to avoid discussion of the comics qualities that play a crucial role in the perceptual shifts that Henderson highlights as central to the role of allegory, a role that all of bpNichol's series of "allegories" explicitly visualize through the discourse of comics and cartooning.

There are reasons to be cautious with David's analysis, and the others that follow from it, because it does not attend to the comics form and conventions that are a part of its meaning-making structure. The comics-specific features at play in bpNichol's "Allegory #7" raise specific questions: why should readers assume that basic panels represent letters (I, H) and tablets, but not link to comics panels as attentional units, or as other formal cues (such as the crossed lines in a game of tic-tac-toe)? Reading the panels as tablets seems to motivate David's very biblical reading of twelve letters as ten commandments (a numerical mismatch) while sidestepping their nature as basic forms as potential morphemes for Milt *the Morph* no less. Moreover, why does the character of Milt repeat on the tablet, and does this literal frame shift also offer potential temporal, spatial, or viewpointed readings, as befits a sequence in a comic? How does the narratorial comment of "and yet?" add to possible interpretations? Similarly, in other readings, why should readers interpret this as depicting language's destruction, when such actions are at best implied and does not necessarily follow from the reading order? These readings reflect literary biases that prioritize deconstructive postmodern readings without addressing comics-specific qualities. The readings are not necessarily wrong, but are certainly impoverished by not reflecting the full compositional complexity of this comic.

By attending to the flows and fictivities of perception and possible improvisational constraints, other readings are possible and perhaps offer a more comprehensive engagement with the experimental comic. I begin with the attentional guidance of the panels and the perceptual dominance of the central figure of Milt the Morph, working through the perspectival layers of presentation. Arguably the comic is composed of five panels organized into three layers, with the central, partial figuration of Milt inhabiting an semi-framed space in front of two more layers of two panels each behind him, with his rounded body acting as a frame for his face and hand. The central figure of Milt is likely interpreted as dissolving or in some way interacting with, rather than being constituted by, the wavy lines due to the attentional bias to focus on faces and the Western cultural-linguistic bias of reading right to left, here reading from figure to lines. These wavy lines connect to key points of Milt's figure, thereby focusing the reader's attention on his drawn qualities and aligning them with the object in his hand, perhaps a sheet of paper. Moreover, competing fictive and factive motion simulations of the LINE or SOURCE-PATH-GOAL schemas reinforce a dynamic connection between his drawn face and the object in his hands. The focus on the hand and drawn lines likely helps to activate a domain simulation of drawing and other communicative domains that are mediated through their materiality.

The mapping between a figure and active spaces of making and mediation prompts the beginning of the allegorical reading, by blending the figure with his page through the active process of writing, left to right, top to bottom. The emergent structure of this blend prompts an experiential simulation of handwriting and its related metaphorical entailments around subjective expression. Here the lines visualize putting one's thoughts down (as objects) on paper. This visually enacts the CONDUIT metaphor, discussed in Chapter 4, through which people conceptualize words as objects that contain concepts and be transferred to someone else (see Reddy 1979).[7] Here, viewers might simulate some sense of the material essence of Milt being transferred to the page in his hand. In this emergent space, writing is fully and literally embodied, through the simulated material blending with its author. This highlights the actions within the writing domain, especially the popular, intersubjective notion that one places something of oneself on the page when writing. This comic depicts the SOURCE-PATH-GOAL schema inherent in the notion of transposing thoughts onto the page, but also constructs an allegorical reading of the letters as composed by the figure's body, not ink. In this allegorical visualization, material expression is literally embodied.

This initial allegorical blend of figure and the page is complicated and expanded in the next layer of two panels behind Milt. Here, the modalities of expression gain specificity, with the panels highlighting and contrasting two dominant modalities, language and images. In the first panel, the beginning of the alphabet prompts a metonymic simulation of the language domain, at the very least of the entire alphabet (a part-for-whole metonymy). Here is language in its most abstracted and basic form. Readers likely expect this modality to some extent, as it aligns closely with the CONDUIT metaphor blend enacted by the central figure. The second panel contrasts with the first through its shift in modality to pictographic representation, with the narrative box highlighting this contrast by asserting "And yet?!" Here, the imagery is also abstracted and basic, but much more communicative in its clear presentation of Milt on a beach with clouds and a bird behind him. The narratorial voice might seem to challenge reader assumptions that prioritize language by presenting the counter position of images, playing on traditional dualisms between pictographic and verbal modalities. By using extremely simple and abstracted cues, the two domains seem to come closer together and chafe against each other. The "And yet?!" seems to challenge the supremacy of language as a communicative domain, placing imagery in an equally sized panel with its own effective simplicity. This is important, since in terms of David's biblical allegorical reading, the truth of the Word would contrast with the idolatry of the Image (a dominant logocentric ideology of Western culture I discussed in Chapter 2). In my reading, this logocentric assumption is less assured, since Milt the Morph seems perfectly pleased with his beach-scape. Perhaps he has taken a vacation from language, and this is his postcard to the reader. Or perhaps he seeks to affirm another model of communication in which morphemes might be visually construed, perhaps suggesting something like Cohn's (2013a) visual morphology in comics. Here, the contrast between language and image is not an assured model, but a recognition of tensions, which aligns more with a deconstructive impulse (see Schmitt 1992) than an explicit message.

Another reading of this second layer could interpret the narratorial contrast differently. The dissolution of Milt into language in the first layer might lead viewers to read the letters in the first panel in the second layer as a representation of the page in his hand, reflecting his embodied re-presentation. The subsequent narratorial insertion then returns to his embodied presence in a more naturalistic environment, reaffirming his wholeness as a figure who has not disappeared. In this case, the narratorial interjection might challenge readers not to equate language with the figure, but to recognize that both exist as separate entities. Here, Nichol's comic pokes at the tension between writing as personal expression, and writing as inherently separate or separateable from the person. While being embodied, the "and yet?!" recognizes that materiality disembodies language in some ways as well.

There is yet another reading that might be improvised through the dynamics of these panels, and which may inform the previous ones, this time by focusing on viewpoint. The cyclic attentional path blends author and writing, moving the reader through linguistic pieces and abstraction back to the author. This process seems to dissolve the author into language, reflecting Billingham's assertion of fragmentation and fragility, but at the same time returns to him, happily surrounded by a picturesque scene in the world. Interestingly, the author moves, via fictive motion and fictive change, into and through letters to an enlarged perspective, since he remerges into a richer environment. In simulating this transformation, through the various fictive and iconic movements, the sequence suggests that engagement in the process of creation has widened Milt's viewpoint. Readers might simulate such a shift as an acknowledgment of the power of language to either expand perspectives or build evocative storyworlds (ironically, here depicted through pictorial imagery). Importantly, language is present or implied in the first three panels, not as a limitation but perhaps as a prompt for the process of building new meanings and perspectives. The panels thus construct an allegorical relation between language and life, showing an infusion of both into each other, focalized through the figure of Milt. The narratorial "and yet?!" acts to highlight this transformative tension through abstraction to an expanded character and narratorial viewpoint, where abstraction seems to add richness rather than take it away.

Moving down yet another level to the final two panels, several final observations can be made. The two panels are obscured by the previous contrastive panels. The perceptual process of object completion suggests these are two panels, nearly the same size as the previous two, but which have been rotated into a horizonal orientation. This perceptual quality enacts a fictive change in orientation, as readers blend these elements together based on their shared qualities. As attentional units, perhaps this suggests a change in viewpoint, a reorientation that follows from the contrastive logics of the previous panels. Importantly, the panels do not reveal any modalities, thereby leaving it to the reader to choose the allegorical conclusion to the tension in the previous panels. The blending of contrastive and reoriented panels and narratorial question opens up an improvisational simulation that raises questions about modalities and their role in communication. Does one become hierarchically superior to the other, as the panels place one over the other? Or perhaps does the inclusion of the narratorial box with Milt on the beach already suggest a blended rather than contrastive solution to the ancient tension between modalties?

In bpNichol's "Allegory #7," iconic and metonymic mappings, fictivity, and metaphors of writing motivate a cyclic movement into, out of, and beyond the domains of artistic and literary expression. Through such dynamic prompts, Nichol seems to posit a view of language that transcends the boundaries imposed upon it by tracing its interaction with broader experiences and modalities, not simply to destroy it, as some scholars describe. The comic seems to visualize a sense of an indivisible integration of body, language, and imagery in an intimate and mutually constitutive manner that reflects the embodied approach to communication described in Chapter 3. This view contests or expands the previous scholarly readings by affirming that instead of being composed through language, the body and experience compose it and are also enriched by it, thereby transforming the poststructuralist linearity of language making reality into a multimodal and dynamic circuity.[8] While biblical readings like David's are interesting, they draw heavily from cultural domains that are less relevant than the material, generic, and conventional elements of the comic itself.

bpNichol's comic builds up an array of possible allegorical meanings by placing a series of prompts in relation and inviting readers to navigate and improvise possible interpretations especially in relation to domain relevant ideas about authorship, modalities, and creativity. Here, the comic conventions build a space to think about representational modalities and their relation to background logocentric assumptions and hierarchies, as well as their role in reframing and informing creative experiences. Moreover, there is also a tension between the cyclical sequencing of the panels and iconostatic balance, which suggests an allegorical completeness through which these tensions are dynamically cohesive or inter-substantive within the space. The allegory pushes readers to question assumptions about modalities, but does so in a way that is both playful and balanced, rendering the somewhat accusatory "and yet?!" non-confrontational and open to improvisational possibilities. Such cognitive work is what "suggests exciting possibilities, the inherent potential for hidden contents, the revelation of something unexpected concealed within the ordinary" (Billingham 2000, 69). In this case, the comics conventions are part of both the ordinariness and unexpected revelations, all constructed through simulations of fictive transformations and abstracted modalities. bpNichol leverages the potentialities of the comics panel to present, obscure, contrast, and reorient content to develop these allegorical possibilities for relating authors, modalities, and experiences. "Allegory #7" uses the affordances and dynamicity of lines and panels to raise questions about connections, causality, characterization, and narrativization. It also serves as a metacommentary on the creative potential of modalities within comics conventions, as openings for both expression and interpretation. bpNichol's work illustrates the overlaps between perceived relationships and conceptual possibilities that emerge through improvisational processes in dialogue with a reader's background knowledge. bpNichol's work invites readers to engage fully with the multimodality of the comics page (see also Borkent 2019b).

8.4.2 Garneau's Decolonial Refusal

As the previous examples have shown, abstract and experimental comics often offer little referential clarity, but open up opportunities to think through aspects of mediated expression. They seek to obscure and challenge expected modes of expression and reception. Underneath such acts there seems to be an assumed assurance that should the author decide to represent things that they could, but they choose not to. The refusal of expression is a marked state, wherein expression is assumed as self-evidently present as the default mode. But access to forms of published expression have not always been assured for everyone, nor are they still, even with the rise of digital publications (after all, you still need a computer and internet access for that). Historically and presently many voices remain on the periphery or excluded from publication spaces, especially gendered, racialized, and otherwise marginalized voices. Therefore, while the assumption of potential expressivity undergirds many abstract and experimental works, that assumption is also problematic. As Sonnet L'Abbé (2019) shows through an examination of avant-garde poetry (including texts that are highly visual), avant-garde material practices of abstraction, fragmentation, and erasure, including through the appropriation of found texts, can certainly reinforce this fraught assumption. She traces a tradition of white and usually male poets who delight in being "Against Expression"—the title of a key anthology of the movement, the cover of which also reflects an abstract comic (Dworkin and Goldsmith 2011)—and shows how a delight in refusal in such work may also escape the fact that others still fight for expression. As such, one view of experimental works is that they inadvertently perform and reinforce social hierarchies and hegemonic norms. Such a critique could be leveled at abstract and experimental comics as well.

Importantly, L'Abbé goes on to show an "unprecedented shift" in the Canadian context to experimental practices that are increasingly being employed as revolutionary tactics to decolonize and retrofit discourses and perceptions for alternative Indigenous discourses. Such work of abstraction and perceptual manipulation for decolonial and revolutionary aims is also emerging in abstract comics.[9] A key example is David Garneau's painting "Aboriginal Curatorial Collective Meeting" (Figure 8.4), which derives its meaning from comics conventions of panels and speech balloons. This

Figure 8.4 David Garneau's "Aboriginal Curatorial Collective Meeting" (2012. Oil on canvas, 152x122 cm).

[224] *Comics and Cognition*

work uses its title to present the location, while variably colored panels, an empty narrator box, and many empty speech balloons fill the comic. The outlines of some speech balloons also vary, dripping and buzzing, to provide hints of emotional or sonic qualities (see Chapter 4, and Forceville, Veale, and Feyaerts 2010). The tails of many balloons point to shared points in the panel space, suggesting a location of conversation, and sometimes side conversations. One balloon also has multiple tails, presumably to suggest many voices speaking the same message in unison. Despite there being a cacophony of voices, readers are not able to access the conversation because none of the speech balloons include language. Moreover, the speakers are not depicted either, although the various skin-toned coloring of the speech balloons might suggest perhaps individualized and racialized viewpoints associated with them. Like other abstract comics, this comic rebuffs the reader's desire for scenic and narrative coherence, while giving a location through the title and a sense of some social dynamics through the tails and shapes of the speech balloons.

Garneau's comic purposefully refuses to document the content of the Aboriginal Curatorial Collective Meeting. As he writes, the work "is an attempt to picture my memory of an event without violating the privacy of those who were there" (2016, 21). He continues, "I hope viewers will read argument, agreement, frostiness, overlapping dialogue, shared and evolving ideas, and innumerable other things into these shapes and thereby get a sense of the scene. I also imagine that many will feel frustrated that their comprehension is restricted" (21). This frustration is crucial to the meaning of this comic. While frustration might be a general response to many abstract comics, here it is socially and politically motivated and directed. Worden observes that the "departure from the reader" (discussed at the beginning of this chapter) builds in a social or political aspect to abstraction, because "Only by seeing how we can no longer see [. . .] can we begin to imagine the possibility of another way of living" (2015, 65). Garneau's abstract work illustrates this alternative with more specificity, as it "visualize[s] Indigenous intellectual spaces that exist apart from a non-Indigenous gaze and interlocution. The idea is to signal to non-Indigenous spectators the fact that intellectual activity is occurring without their knowledge" (2016, 25). Such a perspective asserts a sovereignty to Indigenous representation that does not seek connection with a Western audience, but to signal and respect differences in interactive spaces, affirming autonomy here within the spaces of expression.

The inaccessibility based in abstraction does not take expression for granted, but documents how access cannot be assumed because representation is inherently inscribed through its intersubjective nature in political and social values and spaces. By refusing to give access, Garneau asserts the reality of Indigenous sovereignty and alternativity; he makes visible an Indigenous counter-discourse. Garneau's work is a powerful example that asserts that abstraction and experimentation in comics can be both formal and political, and can include and even protect marginalized voices. This visualization of resistance to the colonial gaze, which assumes access and control of Indigenous spaces, turns the tables on dominant domain assumptions about expression, refusing a particular form in favor of another. Garneau intercedes through abstraction into the white space of comics conventions, transforming assumptions and implications about expression. Interestingly, Indigenous voices are still silent in this comic, but now they are purposefully obscured rather than being silenced. The assertion of Indigenous autonomy and agency in this particular silence speaks volumes. As with other abstract comics in general, it "requires us to think politically, about how we and our social world produce meaning, identity, and value" (Worden 2015, 65). Here, the political action is to grant viewers limited access to a particular Indigenous social space, while respecting the privacy of specific practices and conversations. I have analyzed the significance of this comic elsewhere as it relates to the political work of conciliation in Canada, and so will not delve much more here into the politics (Borkent 2020). Suffice it to say, Garneau's work shows the potential of abstraction to function in favor of marginalized voices to invert common communicative assumptions about access and, along with other Indigenous comics, to "help the reader visualize and comprehend the path to a conciliatory future in Canada, which is grounded in Indigenous resilience and reclamation" (Borkent 2020, 281).

As has been discussed, abstraction and simplification are not necessarily devoid of politics, since what is abstracted or simplified can reflect a range of readerly assumptions. Such works shift the conversation from what is expressed to what is received. Readers improvise meanings, but are also invited by refusals and reconfigurations to interrogate why those meanings arose from abstracted prompts. Much like a Rorschach test, these works provide parameters for improvisation, but also open up room for rumination over why particular conclusions may arise. For instance, Garneau's work might frustrate or delight the viewer, and the reasons why are revelatory. His work invites readers to improvise meanings that include interrogating assumptions about who speaks and who listens, and why these roles are necessary. Such questions force readers to potentially reconfigure colonial logics at work in their unconscious. Garneau's comic acts as revolutionary refusal, as well as material metacommentary, asserting autonomy and multiplicity in expression as well as decolonial opportunities in reception.

8.5 CONCLUSION

As has been seen in the examples of abstract and experimental comics in this chapter, abstraction and simplification can be a useful tools to explore the borderlands of expression and reception. Playfulness with conventions and abstracted domains allow for a reinterpretation of their components, in part through the improvisational capacities inherent in mental simulation and blending, which allow for predictions to be updated and reinterpreted. The repeating refrain in this chapter is that even at the extremes of abstraction, basic comics conventions, including simple panels and lines, become animated through simulation and blending of schematic perceptual knowledge into active, meaningful qualities that readers use to improvise further temporal, agentive, narrative, and political interpretations. In a sense, such works rebuff the reader in order to force them to cognitively play within the confines of material and formal possibilities in comics. Rather than seeking to express a message, such works develop metacommentaries on the materials of expression in comics, perhaps serving as art manifestoes for creativity in comics and their perception.

It is crucial to keep in mind the political implications of abstraction and experimentation while enjoying the border-pushing dynamics of experimental works, so as not to lose out on their potential for revolutionizing how readers read and interpret comics. While intersubjective assumptions about communicative forms, including a sense of a right to accessibility and comprehension, inform the reception of comics in general, abstract and experimental comics push back against these assumptions to explore formal qualities, assumptions about compositionality, and political complexities.

CHAPTER 9
Conclusions and Extensions

Expanding Multimodal Cognitive Poetics through Digital Comics

9.1 CONCLUSIONS

This book has focused on the multimodal cues typically found in the comics form, and the layers of perception and interpretation, both conscious and unconscious, that inform how readers engage them. I have analyzed levels of abstraction in figuration, attentional guidance, viewpoint construction and construal, metonymy and metaphor, and layout, as well as experimentation amid all of these elements. I focused on key cognitive parameters, such as schemas, mental metaphors, and domains, and cognitive processes as modeled through the theories of blending and mental simulation. This approach helps to isolate the linkages between perception and conceptualization, including elements of prediction, inference, and comprehension, and places the reader's embodied experiences and their activation as a crucial facet of reception. I sought to show how these elements provide a set of scientifically substantiated views into reader comprehension, thereby providing empirically valid tools to ground literary and cultural analysis, and an explanatory framework for the diversity of responses to comics.

My proposed multimodal cognitive poetics has by no means been exhaustive in its presentation of the comics form, comics creators and readers, nor of second generation (4E) cognitive sciences. I have sought to bring together areas of research in order to lay the groundwork for an integrated interdisciplinary approach to multimodal textuality. I freely admit that much more can be said about all of the topics engaged in the previous chapters, and I hope that the framework benefits others who can extend the research further to address any gaps. It is hoped that, in good comics fashion, the gaps inspire further creativity and improvisation.

9.2 DIGITAL ALTERATIONS AND EXPANSIONS OF MULTIMODALITY

One particularly salient area that was only addressed at times and deserves further mention is the materiality of comics and how this informs multimodal resources and reader interactions with the text. Throughout the previous chapters, I focused almost exclusively on print productions (including mentions of page turns and such). However, the innovations in particular through digital practices of production, distribution, and reception complicate and extend the cognitive perspective in important ways. I cannot provide a detailed cognitive analysis of digital and webcomics in this final chapter, since that is worth a book unto itself. However, I will review key aspects of digital engagement and their extension or impact on cognitive processes as a means of turning to a more complicated future for the multimodal cognitive poetic approach started in this book.

The advent of digital and webcomics in relatively recent comics history has had a profound impact on comics writing, reading, and distribution. This has become a complex space where texts are being purposefully composed for digital consumption only, and others are adapted to it from print; some are created by hand and others through other digital technologies; some are short cartoons and comic strips (such as *Dinosaur Comics*, *xkcd*, and *Saturday Morning Breakfast Cereal*) and others long narratives (such as *Lavender Jack* on WebToons); some stay digital, and others become printed collections (such as *Hark! A Vagrant* [Beaton 2011] or *The Private Eye* [Vaughan, Martin, and Vicente 2015], which are both also still available online). Moreover, many online comics gather various diverse and global readerships because of the wider access available through online distribution, and they often offer merchandising such as book reprints, calendars, original art, games, memorabilia, and t-shirts, all of which are easily linked into websites to produce a multimedia and transmedia experience coalescing around an initiating comics product, a storyworld that facilitates transmedial convergences (Ryan and Thon 2014) that also provides multiple revenue streams for the comics creator (Johnston 2015).

This has strong parallels with other merchandising practices around print comics, which move online as well (especially through comics apps) and are of course adapted to films and videogames too. At the same time, the shift in medium and accessibility, and whether or not webcomics transition back to printed forms, has a range of possible impacts on the medium-oriented practices of fan cultures (Woo 2011, 2012). While the flows between material and digital productions seem to go both ways, the impacts on reader and fan practices will vary depending on how and what comics-specific elements are translated or transition between media, all of which inform aspects of textual reception.

The online realm offers a broader array of new communicative factors to consider, which this chapter cannot encapsulate fully. Others, like Kashtan (2018), provide a much more comprehensive view of this array of engagements. Here, I seek to briefly capture the most dominant of these different aspects with regard to their enriched array of communicative modalities and affordances. Ryan (2014) argues that the modalities and affordances of new media alter the narrative potential of their communication in ways that open up new readerly opportunities. Similarly, Hayles (2004) has noted the need for medium-specific approaches to criticism in order to engage with each artifact in terms of its own affordances, rather than by importing assumptions from previous forms. In this case, digital and print comics operate in separate media, because the affordances for communication are fundamentally altered and diversified, despite sharing many features that import the conventions of print comics into the online space. The digital space has the potential to alter every aspect of comics, in terms of both production and reception. These changes in terms of potential modalities and intractability expand what is meant by perception and conceptualization of such comics, drawing in a wider array of the sensorium.

9.2.1 Digital Productions

Digital technologies for creating images, such as programs for drawing, image manipulation, text editing, and so on, all facilitate the production of online comics. These align closely to print productions, where such technologies also play a role in the development of many comics. Nonetheless, digital productions offer affordances, that is environmental or actional opportunities (Gibson 1979; Greeno 1994), that a print comic may or may not have access to.

Perhaps one of the most ubiquitous aspects of digital technologies is the ability to copy, at times as virtual simulacrum, and at others simply as repetition. The increased ease of reproducing and repurposing a given image, which underpins memes and a range of other intermedial and material cultural products, has been expertly exploited for many years in Ryan North's long-running series *Dinosaur Comics*. In it, a few basic images and a consistent boxy layout are repeated between comics, but the role of language alters the content substantially (as speech, thought, and narratorial insertions). The associated content developments, including viewpoint and content construal, transform the inferences about the images, much like in memes (Dancygier and Vandelanotte 2017). While not a particularly far stretch from printed media, the digital ability to directly copy the images and layout subtly shifts the function of the image. North's copied repetition might seem to downplay in some ways the power of the image to communicate novel information. However, his creative use of language to build a huge array of scenarios and ideas illustrates the co-productive usefulness of the images, since they continue to construe actions, emotions, and conversational content. North's work highlights the reproducibility of digital media, creating a world on repeat but always with a twist. While the repetition of simple images might seem banal, the strips are almost always insightful and hilarious, and their reliance on the image in fact illustrates the multifunctionality of the image to ground linguistic variations and to build up character viewpoints across time.

9.2.2 Digital Spatializations

The digital production of interface space allows for a range of possibilities for creation and distribution. As Aaron Kashtan (2018) observes at several points, the printed page continues to play a significant role as a domain for conceptualizing digital space, as well as delimiting how it might function. Many Western webcomics continue to use the tabular style of the page, including mimicking the page turn with click-through functions. Such functions maintain a very close relationship between the printed page and digital screen, and they do not necessarily exploit the possible affordances of the digital space.

Such functional parallelism is not necessarily a bad thing. The reproducibility of digital comics in print also serves important economic and accessibility functions. For instance, *The Private Eye* project (Vaughan, Martin, and Vicente 2015) expressly used the close relation between print and screen to crowdfund a printed book from the online comic at the onset of its creation. The comic remains online as a "name your price" PDF download purchase,[1] but has now been published in print as well. In this way, the creators were able to combine the open-access qualities of the internet with fan interests in print collections as well. Maintaining a clear pathway to remediate from digital to printed production allows for a more viable economic model for creators (Kashtan 2018; Kleefeld 2020).

While the printed page can serve as a constraining concept for digital projects, expanded spatial perceptions of digital interfaces allow for increased interactive qualities. For instance, in his long-running series *Saturday Morning Breakfast Cereal*, Zach Weinersmith uses hover text and a red-button popup bonus panel/window to adds layers of commentary or extended content to each cartoon (North uses hover text in *Dinosaur Comics* similarly). This content is hidden from view, unless the reader knows how to interact with the cartoon and website in particular ways. Such commentary is not accessible in the print medium in the same way, but would need to be transposed and perhaps hidden through pop-up flaps or some other material approximation in order to be remediated. This interaction with the digital space adds perceptual and conceptual content to the initial image, often reconstruing it. The hidden content also often includes metacommentary about the creator's skills or a call-out to readers, which adds yet another layer of meaning and possible interpretations. Weinersmith has a community of followers who host reddit threads as well, so this metacommentary functions as hidden content that builds relationships with those fans both through its insider interactability and through more specific call-outs to the specialized knowledge of particular reader groups.

The digital page also offers more dramatic possibilities by expanding the frame of an image into different-sized and -shaped screen-scapes that can be navigated through scrolling and zooming, rather than simply being perceived or even layered. Scott McCloud calls the spatial adjustments of digital interfaces the possibility of the "infinite canvas" (2009). This concept actively engages the affordances of digital imagery to amend perceptions of the properties of the pictorial modality by rendering an image any size and locating the reader at any location and perspective within it through some simple coding. This fundamentally alters the immediacy of gestalt perceptions of the image (discussed in Chapter 3) and scanning patterns throughout it, because it delimits the area to be scanned as less than the whole, and not in relation to other images. This shift in relation to pictorial modalities and the segmentarity of comics alters how space and time are perceived, transforming the image into a multitemporal narrative space of exploration that may later interact with other inputs, adjusting some ideas presented in Chapter 6 (see Goodbrey 2013a). This means that readers may only see a part of the whole image and need to scroll sideways, or up and down, to explore and comprehend the content as a broader mosaic of screens, shifting how metonymy works on a micro- and macro-level within the comic (see Chapter 5). Kashtan (2018) analyzes this functionality in an *xkcd* comic that invites readers to explore around a landscape in order to comprehend the comic's message. The multidirectional scroll is richly personal, as readers control both speed and direction of exploration. Perhaps the wood box design of layout in Michael Nicoll Yahgulanaas' *Red* or Chris Ware's diagrammatic layouts in *Building Stories* (both discussed in Chapter 6) might be considered somewhat analogous print versions of an exploratory reading style. However, Yaghlanaas does not rely on the background carved layout for story-level comprehension, and Ware's work still includes gestalt perception and diagrammatic qualities to help guide mappings between elements and panel sequences. The digital interface provides a rich array of exploratory movements within visualized space that go beyond these printed delimitations.[2]

While both horizontal and vertical axes are possible for navigation, vertical scrolling has perhaps become the most dominant feature of digital comics, which likely reflects the role of smartphones as the predominant interface.[3] For example, *Out the Door* by E. M. Carroll (2010)[4] scrolls predominantly downward, occasionally including a short horizontal sequence that shifts the location of vertical panels to literally follow the movements of a character through a house and down into a dark basement. Many comics seem to only scroll vertically, shifting how sequentiality is perceived and minimizing other contributions from layout, as discussed in Chapters 6 and 7. When scrolling, the size of panels impacts a sense of proximity and frequency, which can continue to produce a sense of rhythm and temporality, but also negate any non-sequential perceptions that may arise in broader layouts. At the same time, scrolling produces a pacing between panels that can transition quickly or larger gaps between panels can produce delays, such as to produce a strong sense of suspense as the visual silence produces a longing for or fear about upcoming content (a strategy also used by Carroll).

Since scrolling can produce a scanning motion controlled by the reader, it can smooth transitions as well and lead to somewhat cinematic effects. Works like *Lavender Jack* by Dan Schkade (2022)[5] exploits this potential by including long images that, when scrolled through, produce a slow panning effect, as seen in the opening segment of the series. In that segment, the opening image introduces the city as readers slowly scroll downward from the sky, settling into the mayor's office and the location of a conversation. Nothing is animated, but rather gestures to common introductory segments in cinema through the movement produced by the reader's scrolling. Unlike cinema, then, the reader takes a slightly more active role in the cinematography by creating the panning speed and can even reverse it to pause and reconsider elements, while still being directed downward by the art and the interface.

Such works more directly link the eye and the hand, beyond the printed versions, wherein there is a stronger aspect of tracing the action and making it happen. In this way, the scrolling function acts somewhat like gestural reinforcement to content, and may even facilitate comprehension, as gestures do (Narayan 2012), especially through feedback loops between speeding up or slowing down engagements. It is difficult to say whether these perceptual qualities will have significant impacts on broader narratological or conceptual aspects of meaning construction, since it is difficult to quantify how substantially they alter multimodal cues, but it is clear that they impact spatial and temporal qualities of engagement and shift tactile and gestural qualities of textual experience as well. These qualities certainly reinforce the reader's connection to the text through feedback loops within perceptual systems that extend the mind into the environment. I would suggest that the heightened degree of interaction with the interface, even just through scrolling, may increase subtle affective resonances with the action by aligning the readers' embodied actions with the viewpoints and developments of the story.

9.2.3 Dynamic Expansions

Digital spaces not only allows for expanded interactive options with modalities, but also expands the types of modalities available for creation. The discussion of scrolling, for instance, naturally leads to thinking about other types of dynamic multimodality, such as animation, sound, or video. Adding modalities to the list discussed in Chapter 2 alters the nature of the comics form, as defined from a print perspective, and opens up potentialities for new narrative developments and forms of engagement and comprehension. In terms of cognition, further dynamicity opens up more domains and avenues for simulation and blending, which does not exceed the bounds of the approach, but complicates it, including the kinds of literacies and backgrounds that might inform interpretations.

With regard to animations, Chow and Harrell describe these as "elastic anchors" that "embody sensation and meaning in flexible forms" (Chow and Harrell 2013, 423). Elastic anchors function similarly to material and narrative anchors, but often integrate motor feedback or environmental dynamics from perception to build a richer visceral quality to mental imagery and comprehension. Chow and Harrell's analysis focuses on interface animations, but could be modified to apply to scrolling as well. Either way, animations offer a dynamical flexibility in modalities that contrasts to the way static forms prompt meaning construction, because they continue to change and highlight particular elements of a storyworld, forcing a responsivity from the reader that goes beyond the control of scrolling and interaction with static images. Animations transform the comics world into a space of dynamic responsivity, adding real-time, rather than reader timed, engagement with shifting modalities.

Animations in digital comics typically are momentary intrusions of action or change, rather than a longer animated story. They maintain a fidelity with the segmentary nature of the comics form, which keeps the comics from becoming synonymous with animated films. Rather, works can integrate animation and scrolling in ways that amend or complement the comics-based storytelling. For instance, *Hobo Lobo of Hamelin* by Stevan Živadinović (2011) blends the infinite canvas of scrolling horizontally through sequences of interwoven panels with a flipbook-styled quality of animation along the "page" that makes up each episode (with seven pages or episodes in total). Readers click numbered buttons at the top of the screen to change from scene to scene (see Figure 9.1), with the transitions animating aspects of the sliding static images in a flip-book style, strategically drawing the reader's attention through dynamic changes and intrusions into the reading environment. These animated elements add

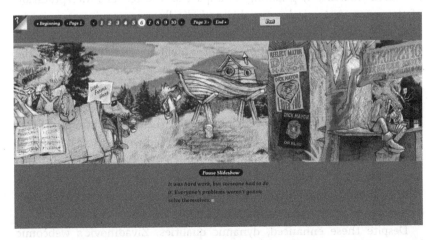

Figure 9.1 Screen shot from *Hobo Lobo of Hamelin* by Stevan Živadinović (2011).

further visual content about various figures and actions to construe them in subtle ways, while literally moving the story along. The flip-book style of this comic emphasizes changes within the images by adding elements from the center-right of the screen, which aligns with the embodied direction of reading, even though the text boxes are below the images (seen in the figure too) and change along with each transition. Thus, the modalities are separated for the purposes of reading, but both follow the logic of linguistically encoded reading directions (which is different from the example by Carroll, or many digital comics on WebToons, which directs the image reading path vertically).

The imagery of the comic is further complicated through layering. The images are stacked into three static layers—in the foreground, mid-ground, and background—to create an animated rendition of the pseudo-three-dimensionality of flip and slide books. As the figure shows, the layers, and natural breaks between images, maintain a sense of sequentiality that moves both in and out of as well as along the screen. Through this technique, the notion of the infinite canvas becomes three-dimensional, which complements and expands the discussion of sequentiality, causation, and temporality in Chapter 6. The layers are also sometimes subtly or overtly animated, with some images changing or even cycling among several different images in a spot, such as to emphasize Hobo Lobo's skills at developing solutions to community needs, seen in this figure.

Finally, further dynamic aspects also construct the comic. Animation of elements is integrated into the static images, such as a swirling fortune teller's crystal ball in the first episode. The animation of a portion of an image construes the content by drawing increased attention to the animated element, heightening its impact on the reader's interpretation of the scene. A musical score also periodically accompanies an episodic page, such as the third episode's dramatic soundscape to accompany an increasingly dramatic surrealist experience (I will not give it away), and the final episode's more melodic conclusion. These sonic additions present an affective tone or mood that underscores or blends across a sequence of images and animations: there is a consistent sonic affect that amends and construes the sequential movement through the story. Batinić includes Živadinović's work in his discussion of "enhanced webcomics" because of these layered and animated qualities (Batinić 2016, 83), which might also be considered a "hypercomic" for these same qualities (Goodbrey 2013a, 2013b). The notion of enhancement is crucial here since the work retains a comic-ness that the dynamic features support and improvise around.

Despite these enhanced, dynamic qualities, Živadinović's webcomic also maintains a connection to the materiality and tactility of print comics through its style of presentation. While adding dynamicity through sound and animated elements, the images seek to arrest the reader as they perceive the new scenes. There is a tactility and immediacy to these changes that punctuates the scrolling motion with a perceptual pause that aligns with the emergence of the short text boxes, which includes dialogue and narration (seen also in the figure). The webcomic exhibits a particularly strong bifurcation of image and text by emphasizing and literalizing a predominantly verbal and visual track. It also maintains a strong fidelity to the page-space metaphor of print culture, by describing each strip as a "page" while the navigation buttons at the top of the screen link to other pages and elements of the story. The sketchy style of the art also enhances a simulated sense of tactility and embodied expression. Thus, there is an interesting tension in this webcomic, which highlights the dynamical and interactive qualities of digital space, while maintaining a strong connection to print culture and embodied expression.

9.2.4 Cross-genre Connections

Another way that digital comics can complicate the ways that images and text function is through cross-genre features. For example, *Aztec Empire*, written by Paul Guinan and illustrated by David Hahn (2023),[6] presents a deeply researched and engaging historical account of the fall of the Aztec empire to the Spaniards at the start of Latin American colonization. The story is composed in a realist style and with a font size that requires a large screen to read. As such, it falls into the category of a more traditional rather than enhanced webcomic. What I want to focus on here, however, is the use of conspicuously un-comic elements that frame each episode: a cover page with very pixelated font and imagery reminiscent of old videogames and to some extent Aztec art and extensive notes at the end. While conspicuous, as a historical graphic narrative, the end notes make sense as knowledge-expanding historical grounding (i.e. domain enrichment) for those who wish to see how the graphic history was developed. However, the opening page is out of step with the following story in both story type (historical story versus video game) and visual style (exaggeratedly pixelated versus realism). There seems to be a disjuncture between the story and its cover.

I would suggest that the opening page is strategically operating on several different levels to appeal to a broad audience and to construe how readers view the story. Rather than presenting the story as such, it works to appeal to a comics and gaming subculture by connecting to an engaging digital genre. It therefore uses one digital genre to appeal to a broader readership, but then shifts into a separate storytelling genre to engage colonial history, an area often ignored by many. The game domain also relates to the comic content. The action-adventure game reflects the bloody battles and intrigue that feature in the story, and it perhaps suggests that the battles and strategies illustrated in the story are part of the war games or strategies and tactics of domination exhibited through colonization. This is somewhat problematic, if one assumes that the reader is then invited to see history as a violent story told for their amusement, or that somehow colonization is just a game. However, since the comic tells an empathetic and detailed historical story, I would also suggest that the creators are perhaps using the video-game domain to draw attention to the history (including by using Aztec art styles and glyphs in a the pixelated opening page), and to open up a meta-narrative viewpoint for construing how the reader should engage the comic.

The opening page prompts a range of interpretive options that offer a metacommentary on the history, building a meta-narrative viewpoint construal. It may invite a metaphorical blend that reflects the mentality of the Spanish Conquistadors who viewed Aztec lives as expendable, much like a video gamer lacks concern for their digital victims. It may also foreground the bloody history and power dynamics that drove colonial actions of dehumanization and subjugation. The game domain also includes puzzles and challenges, which may construe the story as a puzzle of history that needs to be put together, which aligns with the extensive historical notes that append the story. The game domain reconstrues the story of history as a puzzle that contemporary readers are invited to work through with the creators of the comic, to try and put together a history from its remaining pieces. Such metaphorical extensions of the domains of games and history open up opportunities to consider such a metacommentary, which is only prompted because of the seemingly out-of-place video-game style of the opening page. The blend of two digital genres, and their associated visual styles, build a broad introductory narrative viewpoint of metacommentary on the historical events that appeals to a digital audience while opening up questions about historical reconstruction and viewpoints. Webcomics may be particularly well suited for historical engagements, due to their multimodal qualities, since these expand what others have analyzed as the embodied engagements for historicism that are further highlighted through genre choices and changes (Hart 2004; Kukkonen 2019; Richardson 2004). *Aztec Empire* shows one way that historical and new medial connections, including endnotes and other additions, can build appealing and creative opportunities for critical engagement with historicity and offers often underrepresented stories to a wide online readership.

The brief analysis in these previous sections has shown how digital space reconfigures how comics function and might be defined in a new media environment. There is much more to explore in terms the affordances of modalities that blur the boundaries between genres and forms in this new space. The impact of new perceptual and interactive qualities of digital comics changes how readers respond to the cues, such as by taking more control of movements by scrolling through the text, and at others reacting to new animations moving the story along in front of them. Other digital-specific domain features can prompt different storytelling styles that bridge genres to build alternative construals of the content. These shifts in interaction and response have cognitive implications for the analysis of prediction and inference patterns and how these relate to the construction of viewpoints and narrative elements that I have only touched on here, and that others have also explored in relation to transmedial narratology (Jin 2015; Kukkonen 2011). Digital affordances certainly add much to a multimodal complexity of cognitive poetics, and digital comics offer an important space to engage these changes in storytelling practices.

Much of this discussion has focused on the transformation of print comics conventions as they shift into a new medium, including their transformation through the addition of new affordances, modalities, and genres within that space. Of course, film and animation adaptations have parallels to this discussion, especially through the multimodal expansion and animation of the medium. However, there is still a significant difference between comics and film that is maintained even when comics move to the digital screen. This difference is maintained through the focus on material anchoring and interactive qualities that are diminished in a motion-focused medium. As several scholars including Bukatman (2014) have asserted, film removes the participatory qualities of comics reading to become more prescriptive and immersive. There is less control over when to pause or return, which removes the "ruminative" potential of the comic. In film, the anchoring of meaning becomes more than "elastic" (as described here for brief animated prompts) becoming even more dynamic and immersive. This is a fundamentally different conversation about mediation and response. Cognitive research, including much that has been considered here, such as relating to attentional guidance, perception, gesture, viewpoint, and genre, also offers much to the study of film (see Gallese and Guerra 2012; McConachie and Hart 2006; Plantinga and Smith 1999; Shimamura 2013). Such transmedial experiences of storyworld convergences and elaborations offer even more to consider (Ryan and Thon 2014), but which I cannot unpack here.

9.3 TOWARD A DYNAMICAL MULTIMODAL COGNITIVE POETICS

The participatory and dynamical qualities of scrolling, clicking, animating, scoring, and other functions expand the possible features of comics creation and reception through digital space. This space also build in broader personal and intersubjective experiences that can add to a sense of community surrounding the comic. All of these aspects can maintain, adapt, or refute the multimodal and spatial assumptions of the page on the screen in ways that can prompt subtly different inferences and interpretations. They can perceptually expand the cognitive network and its simulated conceptual developments, and integrate texts and artifacts across multiple spaces. These medium-specific changes fundamentally impact the cognitive processes associated with comics as they have been discussed in the previous chapters, by activating or emphasizing new aspects of the embodied and extended (4E) cognitive network, in particular by altering states of perception and interaction, rendering them more elastic and dynamic through the flexibilities of digital space. New literacies will be necessary for nuanced digital-specific engagements, since not all comics will mobilize the same dynamical qualities afforded them. Digital comics expand further the reader's opportunities to construct and improvise meanings, which calls for an even broader dynamical multimodal cognitive poetics. Extending the cognitive approach to the complexity of digital comics is a crucial next step in the future of a more comprehensive and dynamical multimodal cognitive poetics of comics.

NOTES

CHAPTER 1
1. I prefer and use the term cognitive poetics, but other terms are also relevant and commonly used for similar and overlapping areas of research, including cognitive literary studies, cognitive cultural studies, cognitive stylistics, cognitive rhetoric, cognitive aesthetics, and cognitive semiotics. Not all of these fields have internal nor interdisciplinary consistency about what they mean by "cognitive" and often blend first- and second-generation cognitive science. While some research transcends the generational shift, much does not, since the first sees cognition as universal, amodal, and computational, while the second sees cognition as contextual, embodied, simulated, and constructional. I unpack this in future chapters.
2. The social semiotic approach to multimodality offers many helpful analyses that may align well with the cognitive poetic approach presented here, but it offers an incomplete theoretical framework, since it does not delve sufficiently into the cognitive underpinnings of meaning. As a situated, usage-based approach, cognitive linguistics can account for this research, since it also engages the social qualities of communication, but it connects these to a wider array and levels of cognitive embodiment and engagement (Gibbs 2006a; Verhagen 2005). As Karen Kukkonen (2013a) argues, an embodied cognitive model addresses deficiencies in semiotic models of comics.

CHAPTER 2
1. All of the following quotations come from the same broadcast of *Canada Reads*, Day 1 (CBC 2011a).
2. Bateman rightly critiques this approach as lacking specificity and in which the term "'medium' is being made to do a range of quite different tasks" (Bateman 2017, 161).
3. I am stating this somewhat forcefully. There is some legitimacy to the concerns about comic book content being too easily accessible by young children (especially the horror, detective, and Western genres) and so age ratings (like with movies) were a good innovation. Unfortunately, rather than age ratings, content moderation or criminalization was the response in the United States and Canada respectively for quite some time. As Beaty (2005) argues, both the leaders of the moral panic around comics, and the publishers and creators who pushed back against criticisms, overstated their positions to the detriment of all.

4. I should note that Wertham was focused primarily on delinquency, not literacy, and so, one should be cautious in attributing too much import to him in terms of linguistic theory. Rather, he helped propagate a powerful popular distrust of comics as a storytelling medium, which easily connected to the already common cultural prioritization of language and distrust of images.
5. Importantly, this distinction between literacy and other modes of communication contributed (and contributes) to colonial ideas that make a hard distinction between civilization and savagery as well (see LaRocque 2010). This helped promote religious and educational programs that sought to eradicate Indigenous cultures across North America and other colonized regions that often use more multimodal means of communication.
6. This model also connects to how thought is conceptualized, since one can weigh and balance ideas against each other. Thoughts and words become objects to help people conceptualize the notion of manipulation and augmentation that often goes with thought. Interestingly, the object manipulation and transformation model is not often applied to printed language itself, except in experimental literatures like visual poetry in which the materiality of visible media exploits and plays with the conduit metaphor of language (see Borkent 2010, 2014b).
7. This table integrates several versions of terminology for each modality that are often used in comics studies and derive from different analytical streams. Some might quibble with the conflations, but I would argue that the dominant, general connections are more productive for the purposes of aligning like-minded scholarship in a productive manner than in arguing for the merits of one particular set of terms over another.

CHAPTER 3

1. It is important to note that Cartesian dualism has often been mobilized to construe gendered and racialized identities by aligning them with either the presumed qualities of the body or of the mind. For example, misogynistic culture ascribes rationality or mental acuity to men in contrast to purportedly hysterical, unregulated, and emotional women. The dualism validates an unrealistic polarization of emotion, thought, and action based on presumed embodied differences, which are not in fact about emotional control or rationality but about a groups control of power, autonomy, and voice. Similarly, colonists have long self-justified their actions of genocide and ethnocide by presenting Indigenous peoples as beastly, savage, mentally inferior, or effeminate, in contrast to the rational, civilized conquerors. Again, the dualism fallaciously ascribes value to those with power at the expense of those with differences (of bodies, cultures, etc.).
2. Lakoff and Johnson extensively document (and refute) how the first cognitive revolution was a "project within a hybrid Cartesian-formalist philosophy" (1999, 470), which sees concepts as fundamentally universal and amodal symbols in the mind (that is, they are divorced from sense modalities). The disassociation of concepts from percepts further equated cognition with an innate linguistic-computational model. Such an approach assumes that "mathematical elegance" equates with "empirical verification" (Tomasello 1995, 134). Unfortunately for this approach, languages are way too diverse to be simple variations on core algorithms of amodal symbols in the mind (Evans and Levinson 2009).

3. Several texts offer important reflections on the second revolution approach and emphasis on semantics, rhetoric, and pragmatics (Bateman 2014; Bergen 2012; Hiraga 2005; Lakoff and Johnson 1980, 1999; Oakley 2009; Talmy 2000).
4. It has been and remains to some extent quite popular to build analogies to "language" and "grammar" in order to analyze other modalities; thus, there are discussions of "visual language" or the "language of music." Some of these approaches derive their analytic approach from the grammatical principles of first generation cognitive science and parallel dualist traditions in formalist semiotics. Such models helpfully emphasize the communicative value of non-linguistic modalities by legitimating them as types of quasi-literacy (reflecting the shift to a multiple literacies perspective discussed in the previous chapter) and promote the detailed examination of their communicative functions. This has benefited immensely the study of multimodality generally.

    However, such analogies can also confuse rather than clarify each modality's unique contributions to meaning construction and can include universalist assumptions grounded in earlier models of cognition that impoverish their capacity to analyze multimodal connections comprehensively and in a way that reflects the nuances of usage contexts and readerly backgrounds because of the search for universals. Since the mind does not operate and make meaning through a universal, amodal "language" or mentalese, other modalities cannot be equated to it either. Such projections of language structures onto other modalities are, rather, acts of "linguistic imperialism" (Bateman and Wildfeuer 2014, 180–81). Meaning is "more than words and deeper than concepts" (Johnson 2007, ch. 2; Oakley 2009, 61–62), and so the cognitive theory needs to be pushed further.

    Neil Cohn is one scholar who has worked hard to update the grammatical approach with his model of "visual language" in comics (2013b), which he claims to ground primarily in the recent cognitive linguistic work on construction grammar (2018) since it sees form as discursively and contextually informed. I draw from his empirical research throughout this book, but remain somewhat hesitant to fully endorse his model for the present purposes, in part because it is rather unwieldly when applied to literary criticism. More importantly, I wish to emphasize broader synthetic patterns of mental processes, whereas he is primarily interested in teasing apart fine-grained form-meaning connections in visual cues. Unlike what is suggested in the argument between Cohn (2018) and Bateman and Wildfeuer (2014), this is not an argument for or against the grammatical model, but rather a preference for a particular level of analysis. They can indeed be theoretically commensurate perspectives. Cohn takes a fine-grained approach to pictographic depiction (focused on what he refers to as their grammatical and lexical elements), which aligns with other works by comics theorists like Forceville (2005, 2013). However, Bateman and Wildfeuer's critique that a pragmatic, semantics-level focus better accounts for the construction of meaning in multimodal texts remains valid (Bateman and Wildfeuer 2014; see also Bateman 2014). I follow scholars like Bateman (2014), Herman (2010, 2011, 2016), and Kukkonen (2013a) in taking a more general semantic approach to analysis that aligns more productively with the narratorial and rhetorical readings more commonly found in literary, historical, and cultural comics studies. Furthermore, the critical frameworks of conceptual integration and simulation theory have been shown to function across these levels of analysis, suggesting that this work will help build a bridge between the high- and low-level analyses of other scholars.

5. Philosophers that reflect and promote the embodied perspective include the phenomenologist Maurice Merleau-Ponty and pragmatist John Dewey. Similarly, psychologists like James Gibson, William James, Jean Piaget, and Lev Vygotsky also promoted a more holistic and perceptually grounded approach. For more connections between recent cognitive science and non-dualistic traditions of philosophy, see Freeman (2004), Hart (2004, 2006), Johnson (1987, 2007), Johnson and Rohrer (2007), Gallese (2005), Gallese and Lakoff (2005), Gibbs (2006a), Oakley (2009, 77–123), Rohrer (2001), Slingerland (2008, 24–25, 240–47), Varela et al. (1991), and Zlatev (2010).

6. Johnson (1987, 2007) also explores important connections of embodiment and development with philosophical concerns.

7. While human cultures are extremely diverse, this diversity is still grounded in complex and pervasive cognitive processes and biases. While there is obviously distinct cross-cultural variation in communicative practices and types of knowledge, these develop within embodied and evolutionary constraints and processes (Kimmel 2013; Tomasello 2008). These constraints are what lead to similarities in response to texts by diverse readers or listeners. For instance, it has recently been shown that listeners even exhibit correlated heart rate patterns linked to conscious responses to narrative stimuli (Pérez et al. 2021). Nancy Easterlin (2012) argues for a "bio-cultural" perspective that engages both relatively universal cognitive processes and contextual and culturally specific features. This book develops such a bio-cultural approach for Western Anglophone comics by examining pervasive cognitive patterns within this sociocultural context of expression.

8. There is a relatively long tradition of research in the psychology of art, language, and perception that supports this abstracting quality of cognition. For recent developments and summaries, see: Arnheim (Arnheim 2015, 2009), Barsalou (1999, 2008, 2009), Johnson (1987, 2007), Lakoff (1987), and Oakley (2009).

9. The rabbit-duck illusion was originally published on October 23, 1892 in the German magazine *Fliegende Blätter*.

10. While cross-cultural and cross-linguistic research has affirmed many of the pervasive patterns of thought that I present here, my selection of multimodal texts is limited primarily to Anglophone works in North America (and some from the United Kingdom), and as such, this study would benefit from a complicating parallel, cross-cultural project that I am not equipped to do.

11. Aislin is the *nom de plume* of Terry Mosher, a Canadian political cartoonist who works primarily with the *Montreal Gazette*.

12. (Image) schemas, and mental metaphors (also called cognitive or conceptual metaphors), which are discussed in more detail shortly, are conventionally referred to in small capitals, to mark them as general cognitive structures rather than specific expressions in a given modality.

13. Mark Johnson's book *The Body in the Mind* (1987) remains to me one of the most extensive and accessible analyses of image schematic reasoning. Research into the various types and roles of image schemas continues, of course, especially in psychology and linguistics (see Clausner and Croft 1999; Gibbs 2008; Grady 2005; Hampe 1987; Zlatev 2005), as well as increasingly in the arts (see Coëgnarts and Kravanja 2012; Forceville 2017; Mittelberg 2013; Potsch and Williams 2012).

14. Importantly, while these metaphors are relatively pervasive and consistent, there is subtle variation within how they are used and responded to based on differences in embodiment. Casasanto (and various co-authors) describes variations in metaphor construction as the "bodily relativity hypothesis" in which he has shown differences in use and understanding of metaphorical expressions based on handedness (left is usually bad, but sometimes good) or verticality (Casasanto 2009; Casasanto and Henetz 2012; Casasanto and Chrysikou 2011; Willems and Casasanto 2011).
15. Domains are also referred to as "frames" in cognitive linguistics, but these terms are almost completely synonymous (Cienki 2007). I use only domain, instead of frame, to avoid any confusion between the structure in comics and the structure of cognition.
16. Frames and domains are in many ways compatible with Bourdieu's conceptualization of *habitus*, as a "system of dispositions—a present past that tends to perpetuate itself into the future by reactivation in similarly structured practices" (1990, 6). They are both systems of constrained relations and values that are inherited from cultural and educational experiences and that afford degrees of agentive creativity, but see Slingerland (2008, 94–96) for some problems with this connection as well.
17. Theory of Mind (ToM) research initially focused on autism (Baron-Cohen 1991, 1995), but has branched out substantially to focus on other social and attentional concerns like anxiety and depression. It has also directly informed some work in cognitive literary studies (see Tobin 2009; Zunshine 2006), but its contribution to cognitive approaches to the Arts may be somewhat obscured by the use of analogous terms like focalization and viewpoint as well (see Dancygier and Sweetser 2012; Dancygier, Lu, and Verhagen 2016).
18. For example, Scott McCloud popularized a seven-type classification scheme that attempts to sketch out the variety of image-text interactions: word-specific; picture-specific; duo-specific; additive; parallel; montage; and inter-dependent (McCloud 1993, 153–55). While impressionistically descriptive, this classification does not apply consistently in practice.
19. Affordances, originally described by visual psychologist James Gibson (1979), are structural analogies or creative extensions that a form suggests to the perceiver (Barsalou 1999; Johnson 2007, 46–49; Slingerland 2008, 162–66).
20. See note 3.

CHAPTER 4

1. While this version is translated by Alexis Siegel, I will not address this role in the English-language production of this graphic memoir beyond this note for the sake of brevity and to focus on the collaborative dynamic between Lefèvre, Guibert, and Lemercier, between photographer and visual artists, which plays a more central role in viewpoint construction.
2. The mirror-neuron system plays an important role in how people interpret the actions and possible intentions of others (Freedberg and Gallese 2007; Gallese 2005; Iacoboni 2008), but there are other aspects of higher-order thinking that also inform how inferences are made about particular cues that go beyond mirror neurons (Barrett 2017; Hickok 2010, 2014). As such, mental simulation of bodies activates more than mirror neurons in a wide array of complex conceptual and attentional systems.

3. Herman (2009b) seeks to align images in comics with cognitive analyses of gestures in spoken storytelling, but does not elaborate on the gestural qualities of specific bodily postures in comics but rather their multimodal construction of characterization. Similarly, Forceville (2011) focuses on extra indexical flourishes called "runes" that add emotional valences to expressions, but do not necessarily depict emotions themselves nor connect to bodily gestures. Other texts that focus on more holistic approaches to the communicative structures of comics (and whose observations align with aspects of my cognitive approach) do not include explicit engagement with gesture, but tend to treat it as mostly self-evident, including works by Paul Fisher Davies (2019) and Neil Cohn (2013).
4. Much can be said just about typographic meanings and innovations in contemporary literatures (Borkent 2010, 2014b, 2016; Bringhurst 2004; Drucker 1994; Gibbons 2012b; McGann 1991, 1993) and right back to medieval rubricated manuscripts (Phillips 2013), and how such features lead to textural and interpretive possibilities. Here, I focus on just a few of the most dominant and illustrative manipulations of text in comics as they relate to embodied qualities of expression and interpretation.
5. I should note that Bechdel occasionally includes small labels with arrows to draw the reader's attention to particular aspects of a scene, such as to clarify that "one of my brothers" is holding up a Christmas tree (11). This is an example of a relatively rare narratorial intrusion into the panel that functions like a narrator speech balloon. Notably, the block-ish style of these intrusions maintains the conventional use of narrative boxes, with the addition of an arrow to direct attention.

CHAPTER 5

1. Dancygier and Sweetser prefer the term "frame" rather than domain, but recall the previous chapter's discussion of domains and frames as synonymous terms for cognitive networks of knowledge. I have chosen to use *domain* to avoid confusion in this book with the common use of "frame" to denote the line (shown or implied) around a panel.
2. Matt Madden is a master of the creative use of mimetic style and genre markers. This is particularly evident in his experimental work *99 Ways to Tell a Story: Exercises in Style* (2005), in which he repeats the same one-page story in ninety-nine different styles and genres. The variety of possibilities he explores reveals important metonymic connections to a range of cultures and histories, thereby linking style and construal through domain and category metonymies. For the sake of brevity, I have focused on a single cartoon of his, but a similar revealing analysis could be performed on this entire book.
3. Visual blends like this are particularly powerful as well in graphic medicine, that is, the presentation of medical stories through graphic narratives that often build bodily metaphors to construe the experience of illness and medical intervention (Williams 2012, 2013).
4. From an embodied model of cognition, it is not surprising that vision and light metaphors are particularly dominant due to their prominence as a sense modality in human experience and cognitive architecture.

CHAPTER 6

1. Groensteen considers this the "internal duration" of a panel (2007, 133), grounded in the length of captions, rather than the more immediate

perception of figures and actions. I do not like this definition, since it assumes that the language directs the temporal texture of the panel, which is not necessarily given.
2. Much of the initial metaphorical data and analysis of time-space metaphoricity was based on English speakers, but there is emerging cross-linguistic evidence for a fair degree of universality to these concepts with some minor culturally specific variation (see Cooperrider and Núñez 2013).
3. There are some documented cases of an inversion of this metaphor, which is grounded in the same orientational axis but construes the perception of experience differently. The most commonly known case of this inversion is from the Aymara people in the Andes, who conceptualize time (in both language and gesture) in terms of the know-able past in front of them and the unknowable future behind them (Núñez and Sweetser 2006).
4. While McCloud equates space and time in a universal manner, he is not alone in thinking this way. Cognitive scientists (Jackendoff and Aaron 1991 cited in Gibbs 2006) have also attributed abstract connections between space and time that are divorced from cultural and communicative contexts. Gibbs (2006, 187–90) reviews several studies which contradict this view through an embodied, context-sensitive (or "situated") view of mental metaphors.
5. This form-meaning connection is reminiscent of the conduit metaphor (Reddy 1979) of linguistic communication and its fallacious entailments presented in the previous chapter. It follows from the same metaphorical understanding of meaning being contained and transported by forms.
6. I am grateful for a blog post by Wilson and Hopkins (2010) that reminded me of these connected pages.
7. Some critics suggest *Baddawi* is reminiscent of and informed by Marjane Satrapi's *Persepolis* (Reyns-Chikuma and Lazreg 2017). I am hesitant to align Abdelrazaq's work too strongly with Satrapi's, considering Kelp-Stebbins' (2018) persuasive analysis of the Orientalist inclinations of grouping art from the Middle East, by women, and in black and white, simply because of these parallels. Kelp-Stebbins documents how parallels between Satrapi and another Middle Eastern author Zeina Abirached are fraught because of how the many differences of publication and life histories inform these connections, all of which I cannot delve into at this point. Needless to say, authorial histories, motivations, and associations all inform how these works are produced, and how they are received, which limits the value of aligning them together too strongly.
8. This is an overt anthropomorphizing of the bee, blending the bee with a traditional domestic view of gender roles (putting aside, for instance, that in fact worker bees are female, as is the entire hive for much of the year). This blend obviously misrepresents the bee, but serves the narrative function of adding viewpoint and domain qualities that build empathy and connection to a non-human creature.

CHAPTER 7

1. Lakoff and Johnson offer an exhaustive exploration of metaphors about the self (Lakoff and Johnson 1999, 267–89). I find their list helpful, but difficult to operationalize in analysis, so I have opted for more colloquial expressions of their analysis, which grounds my thinking here.
2. Since the quote is compiled across several panels, the forward slash indicates breaks between panels. Ellipses are all part of the original text.

3. Cardoso (2016) documents a similar focus on facial depictions of suffering (and the power of the associated gaze) in Lemire's series *Sweet Tooth*, but for different aims.
4. Here Jack rows in a reverse position to how one typically rows a boat. However, this position helps reinforce his viewpoint alignment with his visions of the future in the panels.

CHAPTER 8

1. My approach offers an important shift in the treatment of perception in abstract comics. Groensteen, for instance, distinguishes between "mere *percepts*" and the "symbolic structure" of the concept (2013, 14). Such a view asserts a representational delimitation to conceptualization, whereas I am developing the notion that perception includes cognition and opportunities for propositional inference and meaning construction, and that all representational choices are depictive and activate simulative predictions and interpretations (for more on communication as depiction, see Clark 2016).
2. Key articles on simulation and aesthetics include Freedberg (2017), Gallese (2003, 2005, 2017), and Freedberg and Gallese (2007).
3. Gavaler employs Cohn's notion of visual grammar and the mental schema of narrative tree structures (defined by Orienter, Peak, and Release elements) to illustrate how minimalist and abstract comics may contain these elements as well. However, his analysis is hindered by a largely unacknowledged reliance on the framing language of the title of his sample abstract comic, which establishes much of the interpretational logic for the forms and unfortunately obscures how ideas about viewpoint, character, and plot emerge from the work. The less clear notions of visual grammar aside, Gavaler's orchestration of past approaches and his insights about the features of abstract comics and narrative remain largely relevant to this discussion, including his typological suggestion of six types of comics ranging from representational and abstract versions of narratives, arrangements, and non-sequiturs.
4. Presumably people will differ in their proficiencies at manipulating abstract forms, much like they do with general spatial abilities and object manipulation (see Hegarty and Waller 2005; Hegarty 2004), including as these relate to spatial perception and other abilities (Voyer and Jansen 2017). Nonetheless, the formal affinities in the comic are worthy of comment, even if they are not noticed by all readers, and with the knowledge that most readers likely develop some degree of awareness and simulation of these elements.
5. bpNichol explored comics regularly in his work, including expanding upon their material and allegorical potential, which I discuss (2019b) in more detail in relation to avant-garde and postmodern interests.
6. Captain Poetry is the superhero guise for Milt the Morph, as revealed in bpNichol's small-press, comic-book-sized release of *The Captain Poetry Poems Complete* (Nichol 1970).
7. I have analyzed the significance of the conduit metaphor and fictivity in relation to other forms of visual enactment in visual poetry (Borkent 2010, 2014b, 2016), which is relevant to comics studies with regard to the presentation of linguistic presence in sound effects, emphasis, and other typographic conventions.
8. See Edward Slingerland's (2008) helpful and strident critique of poststructuralist and postmodern models of meaning from an embodied cognitive perspective.

9. Increasingly comics creators are manipulating comics conventions in order to decolonize and Indigenize comics, in particular in alternative comics (see Aldama 2020; Borkent 2020; Harrison 2016; Spiers 2014).

CHAPTER 9

1. For the online interface for this comic see: http://panelsyndicate.com/comics/tpeye.
2. Both Kashtan (2018) and Kleefeld (2020) argue that the infinity of the digital screen has not been particularly enthusiastically embraced, as McCloud (2000) suggested it would, because it prohibits the webcomic from being possibly remediated into a printed version, and is therefore economically disincentivized.
3. A quick review of the many comics available on the popular digital comics website WebToon indicates the emerging medial constraint for vertical scrolling in a way that works particularly well on smartphones.
4. Carroll also uses a range of other digital affordances, including directional arrow buttons and click through mosaics to provide controls and choices to readers on when and how to navigate her stories (see https://emcarroll.com/).
5. This comic, published on WebToons, began on June 25, 2018, and was completed on December 19, 2022. As of July 12, 2023, the comic had 5.6 million views and 118,408 followers.
6. The graphic narrative series began in 2019 and as of July 2023, eight chapters have been published online.

REFERENCES

Abdel-Raheem, Ahmed. 2017. "Decoding Images: Toward a Theory of Pictorial Framing." *Discourse & Society* 28 (4): 327–52. https://doi.org/10.1177/0957926517702978.

Abdelrazaq, Leila. 2015. *Baddawi*. Charlottesville, VA: Just World.

Abel, Jessica, and Matt Madden. 2008. *Drawing Words, Writing Pictures: Making Comics from Manga to Graphic Novels*. New York: First Second.

Abel, Jessica, and Matt Madden. 2012. *Mastering Comics: Drawing Words and Writing Pictures Continued, a Definive Course in Comics Narrative*. New York: First Second.

Aislin, [Terry Mosher], and McCord Museum. 1997. "M2000.79.59 | Who Hasn't Fantasized . . . ?" McCord Museum Collections. http://collections.musee-mccord.qc.ca/en/collection/artifacts/M2000.79.59.

Aldama, Frederick Luis. 2009. *Your Brain on Latino Comics from Gus Arriola to Los Bros Hernandez*. Austin: University of Texas Press.

Aldama, Frederick Luis. 2010. *Multicultural Comics: From Zap to Blue Beetle*. Austin: University of Texas Press.

Aldama, Frederick Luis, ed. 2020. *Graphic Indigeneity: Comics in The Americas and Australasia*. Jackson: University Press of Mississippi.

Arnheim, Rudolf. 1999. "On the Integration of Gestalt Theory." *Gestalt Theory* 21 (3): 178–80.

Arnheim, Rudolf. 2009. *Art and Visual Perception: A Psychology of the Creative Eye the New Version*. Expanded. Berkeley: University of California Press.

Arnheim, Rudolf. 2015. *Visual Thinking*. 35 anniver. Berkeley: University of California Press.

Ball, David M., and Martha B. Kuhlman, eds. 2010. *The Comics of Chris Ware: Drawing Is a Way of Thinking*. Jackson: University Press of Mississippi.

Banita, Georgiana. 2010. "Chris Ware and the Pursuit of Slowness." In *The Comics of Chris Ware: Drawing Is a Way of Thinking*, edited by David M. Ball and Martha B. Kuhlman, 177–90. Jackson: University Press of Mississippi.

Barcelona, Antonio. 2002. "Clarifying and Applying the Notions of Metaphor and Metonymy within Cognitive Linguistics: An Update." In *Metaphor and Metonymy in Comparison and Contrast*, edited by René Dirven and Ralf Pörings, 207–77. Berlin: Mouton de Gruyter.

Barcelona, Antonio. 2003. "Metonymy in Cognitive Linguistics: An Analysis and a Few Modest Proposals." In *Motivation in Language: Studies in Honor of Günter*

Radden, edited by Hubert Cuyckens, Thomas Berg, Rene Dirven, and Klaus-Uwe Panther, 223–55. Philadelphia: John Benjamins.

Barnden, John A. 2010. "Metaphor and Metonymy: Making Their Connections More Slippery." *Cognitive Linguistics* 21 (1): 1–34. https://doi.org/10.1515/COGL.2010.001.

Baron-Cohen, Simon. 1991. "Precursors to a Theory of Mind: Understanding Attention in Others." In *Natural Theories of Mind: Evolution, Development and Simulation of Everyday Mindreading*, edited by Andrew Whiten, 233–51. New York: Blackwell Publishing.

Baron-Cohen, Simon. 1995. *Mindblindness: An Essay on Autism and Theory of Mind*. Cambridge, MA: MIT Press.

Barrett, Lisa Feldman. 2006. "Are Emotions Natural Kinds?" *Perspectives on Psychological Science* 1 (1): 28–58. https://doi.org/10.1111/j.1745-6916.2006.00003.x.

Barrett, Lisa Feldman. 2017. *How Emotions Are Made: The Secret Life of the Brain*. New York: Houghton Mifflin Harcourt.

Barry, Lynda. 2017. *One! Hundred! Demons!* Montreal: Drawn & Quarterly.

Barsalou, Lawrence W. 1999. "Perceptual Symbol Systems." *Behavioral and Brain Sciences* 22 (4): 577–609; discussion 610–60.

Barsalou, Lawrence W. 2008. "Grounded Cognition." *Annual Review of Psychology* 59: 617–45.

Barsalou, Lawrence W. 2009. "Simulation, Situated Conceptualization, and Prediction." *Philosophical Transactions of the Royal Society B* 364: 1281–89.

Bateman, John A. 2014. *Text and Image: A Critical Introduction to the Visual/Verbal Divide*. New York: Routledge.

Bateman, John A., Francisco O. D. Veloso, and Yan Ling Lau. 2021. "On the Track of Visual Style: A Diachronic Study of Page Composition in Comics and Its Functional Motivation." *Visual Communication* 18 (2): 1–39. https://doi.org/10.1177/1470357219839101.

Bateman, John A., and Janina Wildfeuer. 2014. "A Multimodal Discourse Theory of Visual Narrative." *Journal of Pragmatics* 74: 180–208. https://doi.org/10.1016/j.pragma.2014.10.001.

Bateman, John A. 2017. "Triangulating Transmediality: A Multimodal Semiotic Framework Relating Media, Modes and Genres." *Discourse, Context & Media* 20: 160–74. https://doi.org/10.1016/j.dcm.2017.06.009.

Bateman, John A, Annika Beckmann, and Rocío Inés Varela. 2018. "From Empirical Studies to Visual Narrative Organization: Exploring Page Composition." In *Empirical Comics Research: Digital, Multimodal, and Cognitive Methods*, edited by Alexander Dunst, Jochen Laubrock, and Janina Wildfeuer, 128–53. New York: Routledge.

Batinić, Josip. 2016. "'Enhanced Webcomics': An Exploration of the Hybrid Form of Comics on the Digital Medium." *Image & Narrative* 17 (5): 80–91.

Bazerman, Charles. 2012. "Genre as Social Action." In *Routledge Handbook of Discourse Analysis*, edited by James Paul Gee and Michael Handford, 252–64. New York: Routledge.

Beaton, Kate. 2011. *Hark! A Vagrant*. Montreal: Drawn & Quarterly.

Beaton, Kate. 2022. *Ducks: Two Years in the Oil Sands*. Montreal: Drawn & Quarterly.

Beaty, Bart. 2005. *Fredric Wertham and the Critique of Mass Culture*. Jackson: University Press of Mississippi.

Beaty, Bart. 2012. *Comics versus Art*. Toronto: University of Toronto Press.

Beaty, Bart, and Benjamin Woo. 2016. *The Greatest Comic Book of All Time: Symbolic Capital and the Field of American Comic Books*. New York: Palgrave Macmillan.

Bechdel, Alison. 2006. *Fun Home: A Family Tragicomic*. Boston: Houghton Mifflin.

Becher, Tony. 1994. "The Significance of Disciplinary Differences." *Studies in Higher Education* 19 (2): 151–61. https://doi.org/10.1080/03075079412331382007.

Bechlivanidis, Christos, Marc J. Buehner, Emma C. Tecwyn, David A. Lagnado, Christoph Hoerl, and Teresa McCormack. 2022. "Human Vision Reconstructs Time to Satisfy Causal Constraints." *Psychological Science* 33 (2): 224–35. https://doi.org/https://doi.org/10.1177/09567976211032663.

Bell, John. 2006. *Invaders from the North: How Canada Conquered the Comic Book Universe*. Toronto: Dundurn.

Bergen, Benjamin. 2003. "To Awaken a Sleeping Giant: Cognition and Culture in September 11 Political Cartoons." In *Language, Culture, and Mind*, edited by Michel Achard and Suzanne Kemmer, 1–12. Stanford, CA: CSLI Publications.

Bergen, Benjamin. 2005. "Mental Simulation in Literal and Figurative Language Understanding." In *The Literal and Nonliteral in Language and Thought*, edited by Seana Coulson and Barbara Lewandowska-Tomaszczyk, 255–78. Berlin: Peter Lang.

Bergen, Benjamin. 2012. *Louder than Words: The New Science of How the Mind Makes Meaning*. New York: Basic Books.

Bertoux, Maxime, Harmony Duclos, Marie Caillaud, Shailendra Segobin, Catherine Merck, Vincent de La Sayette, Serge Belliard, Béatrice Desgranges, Francis Eustache, and Mickaël Laisney. 2020. "When Affect Overlaps with Concept: Emotion Recognition in Semantic Variant of Primary Progressive Aphasia." *Brain* 143 (12): 3850–64. https://doi.org/10.1093/brain/awaa313.

Billingham, Susan E. 2000. *Language and the Sacred in Canadian Poet bpNichol's The Martyrology*. Queenston, ON: Edwin Mellen.

Bonnet, Claude, Carlos Paulos, and Christelle Nithart. 2005. "Visual Representations of Dynamic Actions from Static Pictures." *Perception* 34 (1973): 835–47. https://doi.org/10.1068/p5039.

Borkent, Mike. 2010. "Illusions of Simplicity: A Cognitive Approach to Visual Poetry." *English Text Construction* 3 (2): 145–64. https://doi.org/10.1075/etc.3.2.02bor.

Borkent, Mike. 2014a. "Carving Texts." *Canadian Literature* 223: 186–87. http://canlit.ca/article/carving-texts/.

Borkent, Mike. 2014b. "Visual Improvisation: Cognition, Materiality, and Postlinguistic Visual Poetry." *Visible Language* 48 (3): 4–27.

Borkent, Mike. 2015. "Cognitive Ecology and Visual Poetry: Toward a Multimodal Cognitive Poetics." Vancouver: University of British Columbia. https://doi.org/10.14288/1.0166140.

Borkent, Mike. 2016. "At the Limits of Translation? Visual Poetry and Bashō's Multimodal Frog." *Translation and Literature* 25 (2): 189–212. https://doi.org/10.3366/tal.2016.0246.

Borkent, Mike. 2017. "Mediated Characters: Multimodal Viewpoint Construction in Comics." *Cognitive Linguistics* 28 (3): 539–63.

Borkent, Mike. 2019a. "Anarchist Fantasies: A Cognitive Analysis of Fantasy to Promote Anarchism and Cultural Reformulation in Therefore Repent! A Post-Rapture Graphic Novel." *Inks: The Journal of the Comics Studies Society* 3 (2): 147–70.

Borkent, Mike. 2019b. "Post/Avant-Comics: BpNichol's Material Poetics and Comics Art Manifestoes." In *Avant-Canada: Artists, Prophets, Revolutionaries*, edited by Gregory Betts and Christian Bök, 95–115. Waterloo, ON: Wilfrid Laurier University Press.

Borkent, Mike. 2020. "Seeing Histories, Building Futurities: Multimodal Decolonization and Conciliation in Indigenous Comics from Canada." In *Graphic Indigeneity: Comics in The Americas and Australasia*, edited by Frederick Luis Aldama, 273–98. Jackson: University Press of Mississippi.

Bourdieu, Pierre. 1990. *The Logic of Practice*. Translated by Richard Nice. Stanford, CA: Stanford University Press.

Bredehoft, Thomas A. 2006. "Comics Architecture, Multidimensionality, and Time: Chris Ware's Jimmy Corrigan: The Smartest Kid on Earth." *Modern Fiction Studies* 52 (4): 869–90. https://doi.org/10.1353/mfs.2007.0001.

Bringhurst, Robert. 2004. *The Elements of Typographic Style*. 3rd ed. Point Roberts, WA: Hartley & Marks.

Bukatman, Scott. 2014. "Sculpture, Stasis, the Comics, and Hellboy." *Critical Inquiry* 40 (3): 104–17. https://doi.org/10.1086/677334.

Burke, Michael. 2001. "Iconicity and Literary Emotion." *European Journal of English Studies* 5 (1): 31–46.

Cánovas, Crisobal Pagán, and Max Flack Jensen. 2013. "Anchoring Time-Space Mappings and Their Emotions: The Timeline Blend in Poetic Metaphors." *Language and Literature* 22 (1): 45–59.

Cardoso, André Cabral de Almeida. 2016. "Apocalypse and Sensibility: The Role of Sympathy in Jeff Lemire's Sweet Tooth." *Transatlantica. Revue d'études Américaines. American Studies Journal* 2: 0–21.

Carrier, David. 2000. *The Aesthetics of Comics*. University Park: Pennsylvania State University Press.

Carroll, E.M. 2010. *Out the Door*. http://emcarroll.com/comics/outthedoor.html

Carroll, P. J., J. R. Young, and M. S. Guertin. 1992. "Visual Analysis of Cartoons: A View from the Far Side." In *Eye Movements and Visual Cognition: Scene Perception and Reading*, edited by Keith Rayner, 444–61. New York: Springer. https://doi.org/10.1007/978-1-4612-2852-3_27.

Casasanto, Daniel. 2009. "Embodiment of Abstract Concepts: Good and Bad in Right- and Left-Handers." *Journal of Experimental Psychology: General* 138 (3): 351–67. https://doi.org/10.1037/a0015854.

Casasanto, Daniel. 2011. "Different Bodies, Different Minds: The Body Specificity of Language and Thought." *Current Directions in Psychological Science* 20 (6): 378–83.

Casasanto, Daniel. 2013. "Development of Metaphorical Thinking: The Role of Language." In *Language and the Creative Mind*, edited by Mike Borkent, Barbara Dancygier, and Jennifer Hinnell, 3–18. Stanford, CA: CSLI Publications.

Casasanto, Daniel. 2017. "Relationships between Language and Cognition." In *Cambridge Handbook of Cognitive Linguistics*, edited by Barbara Dancygier, 19–37. Cambridge: Cambridge University Press.

Casasanto, Daniel, and Roberto Bottini. 2014. "Mirror Reading Can Reverse the Flow of Time." *Journal of Experimental Psychology: General* 143 (2): 473–79. https://doi.org/10.1037/a0033297.

Casasanto, Daniel, and Evangelia G. Chrysikou. 2011. "When Left Is 'Right.'" *Psychological Science* 22 (4): 419–22. https://doi.org/10.1177/0956797611401755.

Casasanto, Daniel, and Tania Henetz. 2012. "Handedness Shapes Children's Abstract Concepts." *Cognitive Science* 36 (2): 359–72.

Castellucci, Cecil, and Jose Pimienta. 2017. *Soupy Leaves Home*. Milwaukie, OR: Dark Horse Books.

CBC. 2011a. "Canada Reads 2011: Debates—Day One." Canada: Canadian Broadcast Corporation. https://www.cbc.ca/player/play/1797326533.

CBC. 2011b. "Canada Reads 2011 People's Choice Poll." CBC Books. 2011. http://www.cbc.ca/books/canadareads/2011/canada-reads-2011-peoples-choice-poll.html.

CBC. 2016. "CBC Books Announces Canada Reads 2017 Theme, Host and Longlist." CBC Media Centre. 2016. http://www.cbc.ca/mediacentre/press-release/cbc-books-announces-canada-reads-2017-theme-host-and-longlist.

CBC. 2023. "Mattea Roach, championing *Ducks* by Kate Beaton, wins Canada Reads 2023." CBC Books. 2023. https://www.cbc.ca/books/canadareads/mattea-roach-championing-ducks-by-kate-beaton-wins-canada-reads-2023-1.6795030.

Chandler, Daniel. 2007. *Semiotics: The Basics*. 2nd ed. New York: Routledge.

Chaney, Michael A. 2011. "Animal Subjects of the Graphic Novel." *College Literature* 38 (3): 129–49.

Chemero, Anthony. 2009. *Radical Embodied Cognitive Science*. Cambridge, MA: MIT Press.

Chomsky, Noam. 1965. *Aspects of the Theory of Syntax*. Cambridge MA: MIT Press.

Chow, Kenny K. N., and D. Fox Harrell. 2013. "Elastic Anchors for Imaginative Conceptual Blends: A Framework for Analyzing Animated Computer Interfaces." In *Language and the Creative Mind*, edited by Mike Borkent, Barbara Dancygier, and Jennifer Hinnell, 427–44. Stanford, CA: Centre for the Study of Language and Information.

Chute, Hillary. 2008. "Comics as Literature? Reading Graphic Narrative." *PMLA* 123 (2): 452–65.

Chute, Hillary. 2010. *Graphic Women: Life Narrative and Contemporary Comics*. New York: Columbia University Press.

Cienki, Alan. 2007. "Frames, Idealized Cognitive Models, and Domains." In *The Oxford Handbook of Cognitive Linguistics*, edited by Dirk Geeraerts and Hubert Cuyckens, 170–87. New York: Oxford University Press.

Clark, Herbert H. 2016. "Depicting as a Method of Communication." *Psychological Review* 123 (3): 324–47. https://doi.org/10.1037/rev0000026.

Clausner, Timothy C., and William Croft. 1999. "Domains and Image Schemas." *Cognitive Linguistics* 10 (1): 1–31.

Clowes, Daniel. 1998. *Ghost World*. Seattle: Fantagraphics Books.

Coëgnarts, Maarten, and Peter Kravanja. 2012. "Embodied Visual Meaning: Image Schemas in Film." *Projections* 6 (2): 84–101. https://doi.org/10.3167/proj.2012.060206.

Cohn, Jesse. 2007. "Breaking the Frame: Anarchist Comics and Visual Culture." *Belphégor: Littérature Populaire et Culture Médiatique* 6 (2): Web. http://hdl.handle.net/10222/47735

Cohn, Neil. 2010a. "The Limits of Time and Transitions: Challenges to Theories of Sequential Image Comprehension." *Studies in Comics* 1 (1): 127–47.

Cohn, Neil. 2010b. "Extra! Extra! Semantics in Comics!: The Conceptual Structure of Chicago Tribune Advertisements." *Journal of Pragmatics* 42 (11): 3138–46. https://doi.org/10.1016/j.pragma.2010.04.016.

Cohn, Neil. 2013a. "Navigating Comics: An Empirical and Theoretical Approach to Strategies of Reading Comic Page Layouts." *Frontiers in Psychology* 4: 1–15. https://doi.org/10.3389/fpsyg.2013.00186.

Cohn, Neil. 2013b. *The Visual Language of Comics: Introduction to the Structure and Cognition of Sequential Images*. New York: Bloomsbury.
Cohn, Neil. 2013c. "Visual Narrative Structure." *Cognitive Science* 37 (3): 413–52. https://doi.org/10.1111/cogs.12016.
Cohn, Neil. 2014. "The Architecture of Visual Narrative Comprehension: The Interaction of Narrative Structure and Page Layout in Understanding Comics." *Frontiers in Psychology* 5: 1–9. https://doi.org/10.3389/fpsyg.2014.00680.
Cohn, Neil. 2018. "In Defense of a 'Grammar' in the Visual Language of Comics." *Journal of Pragmatics* 127: 1–19. https://doi.org/httpps://doi.org/10.1016/j.pragma.2018.01.002.
Cohn, Neil. 2021. *Who Understands Comics? Questioning the Universality of Visual Language Comprehension*. New York: Bloomsbury Academic. https://doi.org/10.5040/9781350156074.ch-007.
Cohn, Neil, Jessika Axnér, Michaela Diercks, Rebecca Yeh, and Kaitlin Pederson. 2019. "The Cultural Pages of Comics: Cross-Cultural Variation in Page Layouts." *Journal of Graphic Novels and Comics* 10 (1): 67–86. https://doi.org/10.1080/21504857.2017.1413667.
Conard, Sébastien, and Tom Lambeens. 2012. "Duration in Comics." *European Comic Art* 5 (2): 92–113. https://doi.org/10.3167/eca.2012.050206.
Cooperrider, Kensy, and Rafael Núñez. 2013. "The Tangle of Space and Time in Human Cognition." *Trends in Cognitive Sciences* 17 (5): 220–29. https://doi.org/10.1016/j.tics.2013.03.008.
Coulson, Mark. 2004. "Attributing Emotion to Static Body Postures: Recognition Accuracy, Confusions, and Viewpoint Dependence." *Journal of Nonverbal Behavior* 28 (2): 117–39. https://doi.org/10.1023/B:JONB.0000023655.25550.be.
Coulson, Seana, and Cristobal Pagán Cánovas. 2009. "Understanding Timelines: Conceptual Metaphor and Conceptual Integration." *Cognitive Semiotics* 5 (1–2): 198–219.
Coulson, Seana, and Teenie Matlock. 2005. "Cognitive Science." In *Handbook of Pragmatics*, edited by Jef Verschueren and Jan-Ola Östman, 1–30. Philadelphia: John Benjamins Publishing Co.
Coulson, Seana, and Todd Oakley. 2003. "Metonymy and Conceptual Blending." In *Metonymy and Pragmatic Inferencing*, edited by Klaus-Uwe Panther and Linda L. Thornburg, 51–80. Philadelphia: John Benjamins Publishing Co.
Croft, William. 2002. "The Role of Domains in the Interpretation of Metaphors and Metonymies." In *Metaphor and Metonymy in Comparison and Contrast*, edited by René Dirven and Ralf Pörings, 161–205. Berlin: Mouton de Gruyter.
Culler, Jonathan. 1981. *The Pursuit of Signs: Semiotics, Literature, Deconstruction*. Ithaca, NY: Cornell University Press.
Culler, Jonathan. 2007. *The Literary in Theory*. Stanford, CA: Stanford University Press.
Dancygier, Barbara. 2012. *The Language of Stories: A Cognitive Approach*. New York: Cambridge University Press.
Dancygier, Barbara, ed. 2017. *The Cambridge Handbook of Cognitive Linguistics*. New York: Cambridge University Press.
Dancygier, Barbara. 2019. "Reported Speech and Viewpoint Hierarchy." *Linguistic Typology* 23 (1): 161–65. https://doi.org/10.1515/lingty-2019-0004.
Dancygier, Barbara, Wei-Lun Lu, and Arie Verhagen. 2016. *Viewpoint and the Fabric of Meaning: Form and Use of Viewpoint Tools across Languages and Modalities*.

Edited by Barbara Dancygier, Wei-Iun Lu, and Arie Verhagen. Berlin: Walter de Gruyter.

Dancygier, Barbara, and Eve Sweetser, eds. 2012. *Viewpoint in Language: A Multimodal Perspective*. New York: Cambridge University Press.

Dancygier, Barbara, and Eve Sweetser. 2014. *Figurative Language*. New York: Cambridge University Press.

Dancygier, Barbara, and Lieven Vandelanotte. 2016. "Discourse Viewpoint as Network." In *Viewpoint and the Fabric of Meaning: Form and Use of Viewpoint Tools across Languages and Modalities*, edited by Barbara Dancygier, Wei-Iun Lu, and Arie Verhagen, 13–40. Berlin: Walter de Gruyter.

Dancygier, Barbara, and Lieven Vandelanotte. 2017a. "Internet Memes as Multimodal Constructions." *Cognitive Linguistics* 28 (3): 568–98.

Dancygier, Barbara, and Lieven Vandelanotte. 2017b. "Multimodal Artefacts and the Texture of Viewpoint." *Journal of Pragmatics* 122: 1–9. https://doi.org/10.1016/j.pragma.2017.10.011.

David, Jack. 1977. "Visual Poetry in Canada: Birney, Bissett, and Bp." *Studies in Canadian Literature* 2: 252–66.

Davies, Paul Fisher. 2019. *Comics as Communication: A Functional Approach*. London: Palgrave Macmillan.

Davis, Guy. 2009. *The Marquis: Inferno*. Milwaukie, OR: Dark Horse Books.

Denis, Michel. 2017. "Arrows in Diagrammatic and Navigational Spaces." In *Representations in Mind and World: Essays Inspired by Barbara Tversky*, edited by Jeffrey M. Zacks and Holly A. Taylor, 65–84. New York: Routledge.

Deroy, Ophelia, Charles Spence, and Uta Noppeney. 2016. "Metacognition in Multisensory Perception." *Trends in Cognitive Sciences* 20 (10): 736–47. https://doi.org/10.1016/j.tics.2016.08.006.

Devitt, Amy J. 1993. "Generalizing about Genre: New Conceptions of an Old Concept." *College Composition and Communication* 44 (4): 573–86.

Devitt, Amy J. 2004. *Writing Genres*. Carbondale: Southern Illinois University Press.

Devitt, Amy J. 2021. "Genre for Social Action: Transforming Worlds Through Genre Awareness and Action." In *Genre in the Climate Debate*, edited by Sune Auken and Christel Sunesen, 17–33. Warsaw: De Gruyter Open Poland.

Dorrell, L., D. Curtis, and K. Rampal. 1995. "Book Worms without Books? Students Reading Comic Books in the School House." *Journal of Popular Culture* 29: 223–34.

Doucet, Julie. 1995. *My Most Secret Desire*. Montreal: Drawn & Quarterly.

Drucker, Johanna. 1994. *The Visible Word: Experimental Typography and Modern Art, 1909–1923*. Chicago: University of Chicago Press.

Drucker, Johanna. 2008. "Graphic Devices: Narration and Navigation." *Narrative* 16 (2): 121–39. https://doi.org/10.1353/nar.0.0004.

Duchowski, Andrew T. 2002. "A Breadth-First Survey of Eye-Tracking Applications." *Behavior Research Methods, Instruments, & Computers* 34 (4): 455–70.

Duchowski, Andrew T. 2007. *Eye Tracking Methodology: Theory and Practice*. 2nd ed. London: Springer-Verlag.

Dukewich, Kristie R., Raymond M. Klein, and John Christie. 2008. "The Effect of Gaze on Gaze Direction While Looking at Art." *Psychonomic Bulletin & Review* 15 (6): 1141–47. https://doi.org/10.3758/PBR.15.6.1141.

Duncan, H.F. 1973. "A Study of Pictorial Perception among Bantu and White Primary School Children in South Africa." Johannesburg: Witwatersrand University Press.

Dworkin, Craig, and Kenneth Goldsmith, eds. 2011. *Against Expression: An Anthology of Conceptual Writing*. Evanston IL: Northwestern University Press.

Easterlin, Nancy. 2012. *A Biocultural Approach to Literary Theory and Interpretation*. Baltimore: Johns Hopkins University Press.

Eisner, Will. 2008a. *Comics and Sequential Art*. Revised. New York: W.W. Norton.

Eisner, Will. 2008b. *Expressive Anatomy for Comics and Narrative*. New York: W.W. Norton.

Eisner, Will. 2008c. *Graphic Storytelling and Visual Narrative*. New York: W.W. Norton.

Ekman, Paul. 2003. *Emotions Revealed*. New York: Henry Holt.

Elkins, James. 2008. *Visual Literacy*. New York: Routledge.

Evans, Nicholas, and Stephen C. Levinson. 2009. "The Myth of Language Universals: Language Diversity and Its Importance for Cognitive Science." *Behavioral and Brain Sciences* 32 (5): 429–48; discussion 448–94.

Fabry, Regina E. 2017a. "Predictive Processing and Cognitive Development." In *Philosophy and Predictive Processing*, edited by T. Metzinger and W. Wiese, 1–18. Frankfurt am Main: MIND Group. https://doi.org/10.15502/9783958573147.

Fabry, Regina E. 2017b. "Transcending the Evidentiary Boundary: Prediction Error Minimization, Embodied Interaction, and Explanatory Pluralism." *Philosophical Psychology* 30 (4): 391–410. https://doi.org/10.1080/09515089.2016.1272674.

Fabry, Regina E., and Karin Kukkonen. 2019. "Reconsidering the Mind-Wandering Reader: Predictive Processing, Probability Designs, and Enculturation." *Frontiers in Psychology* 9: 2648. https://doi.org/10.3389/fpsyg.2018.02648.

Fauconnier, Gilles. 1997. *Mappings in Thought and Language*. New York: Cambridge University Press.

Fauconnier, Gilles, and Mark Turner. 1998. "Conceptual Integration Networks." *Cognitive Science* 22 (2): 133–87.

Fauconnier, Gilles, and Mark Turner. 1999. "Metonymy and Conceptual Integration." In *Metonymy in Language and Thought*, edited by Uwe Panther and Gunter Radden, 77–90. Philadelphia: John Benjamins.

Fauconnier, Gilles, and Mark Turner. 2000. "Compression and Global Insight." *Cognitive Linguistics* 11 (3/4): 283–304.

Fauconnier, Gilles, and Mark Turner. 2002. *The Way We Think: Conceptual Blending and the Mind's Hidden Complexities*. New York: Basic Books.

Fauconnier, Gilles, and Mark Turner. 2008. "Rethinking Metaphor." In *Cambridge Handbook of Metaphor and Thought*, edited by Raymond W. Gibbs Jr., 53–66. New York: Cambridge University Press.

Fein, Ofer, and Asa Kasher. 1996. "How to Do Things with Words and Gestures in Comics." *Journal of Pragmatics* 26: 793–808. https://doi.org/10.1016/S0378-2166(96)00023-9.

Feng, Dezheng, and Kay L O'Halloran. 2012. "Representing Emotive Meaning in Visual Images: A Social Semiotic Approach." *Journal of Pragmatics* 44 (14): 2067–84. https://doi.org/10.1016/j.pragma.2012.10.003.

Fillmore, Charles. 1982. "Frame Semantics." In *Linguistics in the Morning Calm*, edited by the Linguistics Society of Korea, 111–37. Seoul: Hanshin.

Fischer, Craig, and Charles Hatfield. 2011. "Teeth, Sticks, and Bricks: Calligraphy, Graphic Focalization, and Narrative Braiding in Eddie Campbell's *Alec*." *SubStance* 40 (1): 70–93. https://doi.org/10.1353/sub.2011.0010.

Fodor, Jerry. 1983. *The Modularity of Mind: An Essay on Faculty Psychology*. Cambridge MA: MIT Press.

Forceville, Charles. 2005. "Visual Representations of the Idealized Cognitive Model of Anger in the Asterix Album La Zizanie." *Journal of Pragmatics* 37 (1): 69–88. https://doi.org/10.1016/j.pragma.2003.10.002.

Forceville, Charles. 2008. "Metaphor in Pictures and Multimodal Representations." In *The Cambridge Handbook of Metaphor and Thought*, edited by Raymond W. Gibbs Jr., 462–82. New York: Cambridge University Press.

Forceville, Charles. 2011. "Pictorial Runes in Tintin and the Picaros." *Journal of Pragmatics* 43 (3): 875–90.

Forceville, Charles. 2013. "Creative Visual Duality in Comics Balloons." In *Creativity and the Agile Mind*, edited by Tony Veale, Kurt Feyaerts, and Charles Forceville, 253–73. Berlin: Walter de Gruyter.

Forceville, Charles. 2017. "From Image Schema to Metaphor in Discourse: The FORCE Schemas in Animation Films." In *Metaphor: Embodied Cognition and Discourse*, edited by Beate Hampe, 239–56. Cambridge: Cambridge University Press. https://doi.org/10.1017/1108182324.http.

Forceville, Charles, and Eduardo Urios-Aparisi, eds. 2009. *Multimodal Metaphor*. New York: Mouton de Gruyter.

Forceville, Charles, Tony Veale, and Kurt Feyaerts. 2010. "Balloonics: The Visuals of Balloons in Comics." In *The Rise and Reason of Comics and Graphic Literature: Critical Essays on the Form*, edited by Joyce Goggin and Dan Hassler-Forest, 56–73. Jefferson, NC: McFarland.

Foulsham, Tom, Dean Wybrow, and Neil Cohn. 2016. "Reading Without Words: Eye Movements in the Comprehension of Comic Strips." *Applied Cognitive Psychology* 30: 566–79. https://doi.org/10.1002/acp.3229.

Freedberg, David. 2017. "From Absorption to Judgment: Empathy in Aesthetic Response." In *Empathy: Epistemic Problems and Cultural-Historical Perspectives of a Cross-Disciplinary Concept*, edited by Vanessa Lux and Sigrid Weigel, 139–80. London: Palgrave Macmillan. https://doi.org/10.4324/9781315856506.

Freedberg, David, and Vittorio Gallese. 2007. "Motion, Emotion and Empathy in Esthetic Experience." *Trends in Cognitive Sciences* 11 (5): 197–203. https://doi.org/10.1016/j.tics.2007.02.003.

Freeman, Margaret H. 2020. *The Poem as Icon: A Study in Aesthetic Cognition*. New York: Oxford University Press.

Freeman, Margaret H. 2004. "Crossing the Boundaries of Time: Merleau-Ponty's Phenomenology and Cognitive Linguistic Theories." In *Linguagem, Cultura e Cognição: Estudos de Linguística Cognitiva*, edited by Augusto Soares da Silva, Amadeu Torres, and Miguel Gonçalves, 643–55. Coimbra, Portugal: Almedina.

Freeman, Margaret H. 2007. "Poetic Iconicity." *Annual Review of Cognitive Linguistics*, edited by Wladyslaw Chlopicki, Andrzej Pawelec, and Agnieszka Pokojska, 472–501. Kraków: Tertium.

Fryer, Louise, Jonathan Freeman, and Linda Pring. 2014. "Touching Words Is Not Enough: How Visual Experience Influences Haptic–Auditory Associations in the 'Bouba–Kiki' Effect." *Cognition* 132 (2): 164–73. https://doi.org/10.1016/j.cognition.2014.03.015.

Fuhrman, Orly, and Lera Boroditsky. 2010. "Cross-Cultural Differences in Mental Representations of Time: Evidence from an Implicit Nonlinguistic Task." *Cognitive Science* 34 (8): 1430–51.

Fuller, Danielle. 2007. "Listening to the Readers of 'Canada Reads.'" *Canadian Literature* 193: 11–34.

Gabilliet, Jean-Paul. 2009. "Comic Art and Bande Dessinée: From the Funnies to Graphic Novels." In *The Cambridge History of Canadian Literature*, edited by Coral Ann Howells and Eva-Marie Kröller, 460–77. New York: Cambridge University Press.

Gabilliet, Jean-Paul. 2010. *Of Comics and Men: A Cultural History of American Comic Books*. Edited by Bart Beaty and Nick Nguyen. Jackson: University Press of Mississippi.

Gallagher, Shaun. 2005. *How the Body Shapes the Mind*. New York: Clarendon Press.

Gallagher, Shaun, Sergio F. Martínez, and Melina Gastelum. 2018. "Action-Space and Time: Towards an Enactive Hermeneutics." In *Place, Space and Hermeneutics*, edited by Bruce B. Janz, 83–96. Cham, Switzerland: Springer International. https://doi.org/10.1007/978-3-319-52214-2_7.

Gallese, Vittorio. 2003. "A Neuroscientific Grasp of Concepts: From Control to Representation." *Philosophical Transactions of the Royal Society of London. Series B, Biological Sciences* 358 (1435): 1231–40.

Gallese, Vittorio. 2005. "Embodied Simulation: From Neurons to Phenomenal Experience." *Phenomenology and the Cognitive Sciences* 4: 23–48.

Gallese, Vittorio. 2017. "The Empathic Body in Experimental Aesthetics—Embodied Simulation and Art." In *Empathy: Epistemic Problems and Cultural-Historical Perspectives of a Cross-Disciplinary Concept*, edited by Vanessa Lux and Sigrid Weigel, 181–99. London: Palgrave Macmillan. https://doi.org/10.4324/9781315856506.

Gallese, Vittorio, and Michele Guerra. 2012. "Embodying Movies: Embodied Simulation and Film Studies." *Cinema: Journal of Philosophy and the Moving Image* 3: 183–210.

Gallese, Vittorio, and George Lakoff. 2005. "The Brain's Concepts: The Role of the Sensory-Motor System in Conceptual Knowledge." *Cognitive Neuropsychology* 22 (3): 455–79.

Gardner, Jared. 2011. "Storylines." *SubStance* 40 (1): 53–69.

Garneau, David. 2016. "Imaginary Spaces of Conciliation and Reconciliation: Art, Curation, and Healing." In *Arts of Engagement: Taking Aesthetic Action in and beyond the Truth and Reconciliation Commission of Canada*, edited by Keith Martin, Dylan Robinson, and David Garneau, 21–32. Waterloo, ON: Wilfrid Laurier University Press.

Gavaler, Chris. 2017. "Refining the Comics Form." *European Comic Art* 10 (2): 1–23. https://doi.org/10.3167/eca.2017.100202.

Gegenfurtner, Andreas, Erno Lehtinen, and Roger Säljö. 2011. "Expertise Differences in the Comprehension of Visualizations: A Meta-Analysis of Eye-Tracking Research in Professional Domains." *Educational Psychology Review* 23: 523–52. https://doi.org/10.1007/s10648-011-9174-7.

Gentner, Dedre, and Brian Bowdle. 2008. "Metaphor as Structure-Mapping." In *The Cambridge Handbook of Metaphor and Thought*, edited by Raymond W. Gibbs Jr., 109–28. New York: Cambridge University Press.

Gibbons, Alison. 2012a. "Multimodal Literature and Experimentation." In *The Routledge Handbook of Experimental Literature*, edited by Joe Bray, Alison Gibbons, and Brian McHale, 420–34. New York: Routledge.

Gibbons, Alison. 2012b. *Multimodality, Cognition, and Experimental Literature*. New York: Routledge.

Gibbs, Raymond W. Jr. 2000. "Making Good Psychology out of Blending Theory." *Cognitive Linguistics* 11 (3/4): 347–59.

Gibbs, Raymond W. Jr. 2006a. *Embodiment and Cognitive Science*. Cambridge University Press.
Gibbs, Raymond W. Jr. 2006b. "Metaphor Interpretation as Embodied Simulation." *Mind & Language* 21 (3): 434–58.
Gibbs, Raymond W. Jr. 2008. "Images Schemas in Conceptual Development: What Happened to the Body?" *Philosophical Psychology* 21 (2): 231–39.
Gibbs, Raymond W. Jr. 2011. "Evaluating Conceptual Metaphor Theory." *Discourse Processes* 48 (8): 529–62. https://doi.org/10.1080/0163853X.2011.606103.
Gibbs, Raymond W. Jr., and Herbert L. Colston. 2012. *Interpreting Figurative Meaning*. New York: Cambridge University Press.
Gibbs, Raymond W. Jr., and Teenie Matlock. 2008. "Metaphor, Imagination, and Simulation: Psycholinguistic Evidence." In *The Cambridge Handbook of Metaphor and Thought*, edited by Raymond W. Gibbs Jr., 161–76. New York: Cambridge University Press.
Gibbs, Raymond W. Jr., and Markus Tendahl. 2006. "Cognitive Effort and Effects in Metaphor Comprehension: Relevance Theory and Psycholinguistics." *Mind & Language* 21 (3): 379–403. https://doi.org/10.1111/j.1468-0017.2006.00283.x.
Gibson, James J. 1979. *The Ecological Approach to Visual Perception*. Boston: Houghton Mifflin.
Gibson, Mel. 2015. "Who Does She Think She Is? Female Comic-Book Characters, Second-Wave Feminism and Feminist Film Theory." In *Superheroes and Identities*, edited by Mel Gibson, David Huxley, and Joan Ormrod, 135–46. New York: Routledge.
Goldberg, Adele E. 2013. "Constructionist Approaches." In *The Oxford Handbook of Cognitive Grammar*, edited by Thomas Hoffmann and Graeme Trousdale, 15–31. New York: Oxford University Press.
Gombrich, E. H. 1959. *Art and Illusion: A Study in the Psychology of Pictorial Representation*. Oxford: Phaidon Press.
Gombrich, E. H. 1973. "Illusion and Art." In *Illusion in Nature and Art*, edited by Richard Langton Gregory, 193–243. London: Duckworth.
Goodale, M. A., and G. K. Humphrey. 1998. "The Objects of Action and Perception." *Cognition* 67 (1–2): 181–207. http://www.ncbi.nlm.nih.gov/pubmed/9735540.
Goodbrey, Daniel Merlin. 2013a. "Digital Comics–New Tools and Tropes." *Studies in Comics* 4 (1): 185–97.
Goodbrey, Daniel Merlin. 2013b. "From Comic to Hypercomic." In *Cultural Excavation and Formal Expression in the Graphic Novel*, edited by Jonathan C. Evans and Thomas Giddens, 291–302. Oxford, UK: Brill.
Górska, Elżbieta. 2018. "A Multimodal Portrait of Wisdom and Stupidity: A Case Study of Image-Schematic Metaphors in Cartoons." In *New Insights into the Language and Cognition Interface*, edited by Rafał Augustyn and Agnieszka Mierzwińska-Hajnos, 98–117. Newcastle upon Tyne: Cambridge Scholars Publishing.
Górska, Elżbieta. 2019. "Spatialization of Abstract Concepts in Cartoons: A Case Study of Verbo-Pictorial Image Schematic Metaphors." In *Current Approaches to Metaphor Analysis in Discourse*, edited by Ignasi Navarro i Ferrando, 279–94. Berlin: De Gruyter Mouton.
Grady, Joseph. 1998. "The 'Conduit Metaphor' Revisited: A Reassessment of Metaphors for Communication." In *Discourse and Cognition: Bridging the Gap*, edited by Jean-Pierre König, 1–16. Stanford, CA: Centre for the Study of Language and Information.

Grady, Joseph. 2005a. "Image Schemas and Perception: Refining a Definition." In *From Perception to Meaning: Image Schemas in Cognitive Linguistics*, edited by Beate Hampe, 35–55. New York: Mouton du Gruyter.

Grady, Joseph. 2005b. "Primary Metaphors as Inputs to Conceptual Integration." *Journal of Pragmatics* 37 (10): 1595–1614. https://doi.org/10.1016/j.pragma.2004.03.012.

Gray, Brenna Clarke. 2016. "Border Studies in the Gutter: Canadian Comics and Structural Borders." *Canadian Literature* 228/229: 170–87.

Greeno, James G. 1994. "Gibson's Affordances." *Psychological Review* 101 (2): 336–42.

Grennan, Simon. 2017. *A Theory of Narrative Drawing*. London: Palgrave Macmillan.

Groensteen, Thierry. 2007. *The System of Comics*. Translated by Bart Beaty and Nick Nguyen. Jackson: University Press of Mississippi.

Groensteen, Thierry. 2013. *Comics and Narration*. Translated by Ann Miller. Jackson: University Press of Mississippi.

Guillory, Rob. 2019. *Farmhand*, Volume 1: *Reap What Was Sown*. Portland: Image Comics.

Guinan, Paul, and David Hahn. 2023. *Aztec Empire*. https://www.bigredhair.com/books/aztec-empire/about/.

Hagmann, Carl Erick, and Neil Cohn. 2016. "The Pieces Fit: Constituent Structure and Global Coherence of Visual Narrative in RSVP." *Acta Psychologica* 164: 157–64. https://doi.org/10.1016/j.actpsy.2016.01.011.

Hamburger, Jeffrey F. 2011. "The Iconicity of Script." *Word & Image: A Journal of Verbal/Visual Enquiry* 27 (3): 249–61.

Hampe, Beate. 1987. *Image Schemas in Cognitive Linguistics: Introduction*. Berlin: Mouton du Gruyter.

Harrison, Richard. 2016. "Seeing and Nothingness: Michael Nicoll Yahgulanaas, Haida Manga, and a Critique of the Gutter." *Canadian Review of Comparative Literature / Revue Canadienne de Littérature Comparée* 43 (1): 51–74.

Hart, Christopher, and Javier Marmol Queralto. 2021. "What Can Cognitive Linguistics Tell Us about Language-Image Relations? A Multidimensional Approach to Intersemiotic Convergence in Multimodal Texts." *Cognitive Linguistics* 32 (4): 529–62. https://doi.org/10.1515/cog-2021-0039.

Hart, F. Elizabeth. 2004. "Embodied Literature: A Cognitive-Poststructuralist Approach to Genre." In *The Work of Fiction: Cognition, Culture, and Complexity*, edited by Alan Richardson and Ellen Spolsky, 85–106. Burlington, VT: Ashgate.

Hart, F. Elizabeth. 2006. "Performance, Phenomenology, and the Cognitive Turn." In *Performance and Cognition*, edited by F. Elizabeth Hart and Bruce McConachie, 29–51. New York: Routledge.

Harvey, Robert. 1996. *The Art of the Comic Book: An Aesthetic History*. Jackson: University Press of Mississippi.

Hatfield, Charles. 2005. *Alternative Comics: An Emerging Literature*. Jackson: University Press of Mississippi.

Hatfield, Charles. 2008. "How to Read A . . . " *English Language Notes* 46 (2): 129–49.

Hatfield, Charles. 2009. "Defining Comics in the Classroom; or, The Pros and Cons of Unflexibility." In *Teaching the Graphic Novel*, edited by Stephen E. Tabachnick, 19–27. New York: Modern Language Association of America.

Hayles, N. Katherine. 2004. "Print Is Flat, Code Is Deep: The Importance of Media-Specific Analysis." *Poetics Today* 25 (1): 67–90.

Hegarty, Mary. 2004. "Mechanical Reasoning by Mental Simulation." *Trends in Cognitive Sciences* 8 (6): 280–85. https://doi.org/10.1016/j.tics.2004.04.001.

Hegarty, Mary, and David A. Waller. 2005. "Individual Differences in Spatial Abilities." In *The Cambridge Handbook of Visuospatial Thinking*, edited by Priti Shah and Akira Miyake, 121–69. New York: Cambridge University Press. https://doi.org/10.1145/2662253.2662334.

Heimermann, Mark. 2017. "The Grotesque Child: Animal-Human Hybridity in *Sweet Tooth*." In *Picturing Childhood: Youth in Transnational Comics*, edited by Mark Heimermann and Brittany Tullis, 234–50. Austin: University of Texas Press.

Henderson, Brian. 1989. "New Syntaxes in McCaffery and Nichol: Emptiness, Transformation, Serenity." *Essays on Canadian Writing* 37: 1–29.

Herman, David. 1997. "Scripts, Sequences, and Stories: Elements of a Postclassical Narratology." *PMLA* 112 (5): 1046–59.

Herman, David, ed. 2003. *Narrative Theory and the Cognitive Sciences*. Stanford CA: CSLI Publications.

Herman, David. 2009a. *Basic Elements of Narrative*. Chichester, UK: Wiley-Blackwell.

Herman, David. 2009b. "Word-Image/Utterance-Gesture: Case Studies in Multimodal Storytelling." In *Narrative and Multimodality: New Perspectives and Practices*, edited by Ruth Page, 78–98. New York: Routledge.

Herman, David. 2010. "Multimodal Storytelling and Identity Construction in Graphic Narratives." In *Telling Stories: Language, Narrative, and Social Life*, edited by Deborah Schiffrin, Anna De Fina, and Anastasia Nylund, 195–208. Washington, DC: Georgetown University Press.

Herman, David. 2011. "Storyworld/Umwelt: Nonhuman Experiences in Graphic Narratives." *SubStance* 40 (1): 156–81. https://doi.org/10.1353/sub.2011.0000.

Herman, David. 2016. "Hermeneutics beyond the Species Boundary: Explanation and Understanding in Animal Narratives." *Storyworlds: A Journal of Narrative Studies* 8 (1): 1–30.

Hickok, Gregory. 2010. "The Role of Mirror Neurons in Speech and Language Processing." *Brain and Language* 112 (1): 1–2. https://doi.org/10.1016/j.bandl.2009.10.006.

Hickok, Gregory. 2014. *The Myth of Mirror Neurons: The Real Neuroscience of Communication and Cognition*. New York: W.W. Norton.

Hiraga, Masako. 2005. *Metaphor and Iconicity: A Cognitive Approach to Analysing Texts*. New York: Palgrave Macmillan.

Hoenen, Matthias, Katrin T. Lübke, and Bettina M. Pause. 2017. "Sensitivity of the Human Mirror Neuron System for Abstract Traces of Actions: An EEG-Study." *Biological Psychology* 124: 57–64. https://doi.org/10.1016/j.biopsycho.2017.01.010.

Hoffmann, Thomas. 2017. "Multimodal Constructs—Multimodal Constructions? The Role of Constructions in the Working Memory." *Linguistics Vanguard* 3 (1): 1–10. https://doi.org/10.1515/lingvan-2016-0042.

Hoffmann, Thomas. 2018. "Construction Grammars." In *The Cambridge Handbook of Cognitive Linguistics*, edited by Barbara Dancygier, 310–29. New York: Cambridge University Press.

Hoffmann, Thomas, and Alexander Bergs. 2018. "A Construction Grammar Approach to Genre." *CogniTextes* 18. https://doi.org/10.4000/cognitextes.1032.

Hoffmann, Thomas, and Graeme Trousdale, eds. 2013. *The Oxford Handbook of Construction Grammar*. New York: Oxford University Press.

Hogan, Patrick Colm. 2003. *The Mind and Its Stories: Narrative Universals and Human Emotion*. Cambridge: Cambridge University Press. https://doi.org/10.1017/CBO9780511499951.

Hogan, Patrick Colm. 2008. "Of Literary Universals: Ninety-Five Theses." *Philosophy and Literature* 32 (1): 145–60. https://doi.org/10.1353/phl.0.0002.

Holsanova, Jana, Nils Holmberg, and Kenneth Holmqvist. 2009. "Reading Information Graphics: The Role of Spatial Contiguity and Dual Attentional Guidance." *Applied Cognitive Psychology* 23: 1215–26. https://doi.org/10.1002/acp.

Hutchins, Edwin. 1995. "How a Cockpit Remembers Its Speeds." *Cognitive Science* 19 (3): 265–88.

Hutchins, Edwin. 2005. "Material Anchors for Conceptual Blends." *Journal of Pragmatics* 37 (10): 1555–77.

Hutchins, Edwin. 2010. "Cognitive Ecology." *Topics in Cognitive Science* 2 (4): 705–15.

Iacoboni, Marco. 2008. *Mirroring People: The New Science of How We Connect with Others*. New York: Farrar, Straus, and Giroux.

Iacoboni, Marco. 2009. "Imitation, Empathy, and Mirror Neurons." *Annual Review of Psychology* 60 (January): 653–70.

Jackendoff, Ray, and David Aaron. 1991. "Review Article of Lakoff and Turner's More than Cool Reason." *Language* 67 (2): 320–38.

Jacobs, Dale, and Greg Paziuk. 2016. "The Chance of Life: Jeff Lemire's Essex County Trilogy, Canadian Identit, and the Mythos of Hockey." *Canadian Review of Comparative Literature / Revue Canadienne de Littérature Comparée* 43 (1): 75–86.

Jastrow, Joseph. 1899. "The Mind's Eye." *Popular Science Monthly* 54: 299–312.

Jewitt, Carey. 2008. "Multimodality and Literacy in School Classrooms." *Review of Research in Education* 32: 241–67.

Jin, Dal Yong. 2015. "Digital Convergence of Korea's Webtoons: Transmedia Storytelling." *Communication Research and Practice* 1 (3): 193–209. https://doi.org/10.1080/22041451.2015.1079150.

Johnson, Mark. 1987. *The Body in the Mind: The Bodily Basis of Meaning, Imagination, and Reason*. Chicago: University of Chicago Press.

Johnson, Mark. 2007. *The Meaning of the Body: Aesthetics of Human Understanding*. Chicago: University of Chicago Press.

Johnson, Mark, and Tim Rohrer. 2007. "We Are Live Creatures: Embodiment, American Pragmatism and the Cognitive Organism." In *Body, Language and Mind*, Volume 1: *Embodiment*, edited by Tom Ziemke, Jordan Zlatev, and Roslyn M. Frank, 17–54. Berlin: Walter de Gruyter.

Johnston, Paddy. 2015. "Bad Machinery and the Economics of Free Comics: A Webcomic Case Study." *Networking Knowledge* 8 (4): 1–12.

Jonauskaite, Domicele, Ahmad Abu-Akel, Nele Dael, Daniel Oberfeld, Ahmed M. Abdel-Khalek, Abdulrahman S. Al-Rasheed, Jean Philippe Antonietti, et al. 2020. "Universal Patterns in Color-Emotion Associations Are Further Shaped by Linguistic and Geographic Proximity." *Psychological Science* 31 (10): 1245–60. https://doi.org/10.1177/0956797620948810.

Kannenberg, Gene Jr. 2007. "The Comics of Chris Ware: Text, Image, and Visual Narrative Strategies." In *The Language of Comics: Word and Image*, edited by Robin Varnum and Christina T. Gibbons, 174–98. Jackson: University Press of Mississippi.

Kashtan, Aaron. 2018. *Between Pen and Pixel*. Columbus: Ohio State University Press.

Kelp-Stebbins, Katherine. 2012. "Hybrid Heroes and Graphic Posthumanity: Comics as a Media Technology for Critical Posthumanism." *Studies in Comics* 3 (2): 331–48.

Kelp-Stebbins, Katherine. 2018. "Global Comics: Two Women's Texts and a Critique of Cultural Imperialism." *Feminist Media Histories* 4 (3): 135–56.

Kendon, Adam. 2004. *Gesture: Visible Action as Utterance*. New York: Cambridge University Press.

Khng, Desiree L. 2016. "Philosophising Gender Politics in *Y: The Last Man*." *Journal of Graphic Novels and Comics* 7 (2): 167–77. https://doi.org/10.1080/21504 857.2015.1093518.

Kimmel, Michael. 2013. "The Arc from the Body to Culture: How Affect, Proprioception, Kinesthesia, and Perceptual Imagery Shape Cultural Knowledge (and Vice Versa)." *Integral Review* 9 (2): 300–348.

Kirtley, Clare, Christopher Murray, B. Vaughan, and Benjamin W. Tatler. 2018. "Reading Words and Images: Factors Influencing Eye Movements in Comic Reading." In *Empirical Comics Research: Digital, Multimodal, and Cognitive Methods*, edited by Alexander Dunst, Jochen Laubrock, and Janina Wildfeuer, 264–83. New York: Routledge.

Kleefeld, Sean. 2020. *Webcomics*. New York: Bloomsbury Academic.

Köhler, Wolfgang. 1929. *Gestalt Psychology*. New York: Horace Liveright.

Køhlert, Frederik Byrn. 2012. "Female Grotesques: Carnivalesque Subversion in the Comics of Julie Doucet." *Journal of Graphic Novels and Comics* 3 (1): 19–38. https://doi.org/10.1080/21504857.2012.703883.

Kourtzi, Zoe, and Nancy Kanwisher. 2000. "KourtziKanwisher-Activation_VisualMotionSimulation.Pdf." *Journal of Cognitive Neuroscience* 12 (1): 48–55.

Kövecses, Zoltán. 2010. *Metaphor: A Practical Introduction*. New York: Oxford University Press.

Kövecses, Zoltán. 2013. *Metaphor and Emotion: Language, Culture, and the Body in Human Feeling*. Cambridge: Cambridge University Press.

Kövecses, Zoltán, and Péter Szabcó. 1996. "Idioms: A View from Cognitive Semantics." *Applied Linguistics* 17 (3): 326–55. https://doi.org/10.1093/applin/17.3.326.

Kress, Gunther. 2009. "What Is Mode?" In *The Routledge Handbook of Multimodal Analysis*, edited by Carey Jewitt, 54–67. New York: Routledge.

Kress, Gunther. 2010. *Multimodality: A Social Semiotic Approach to Contemporary Communication*. New York: Routledge.

Kress, Gunther, and Theo Van Leeuwen. 1996. *Reading Images: The Grammar of Visual Design*. London; New York: Routledge.

Kuipers, Christopher M. 2011. "The New Normal of Literariness: Graphic Literature as the next Paradigm Genre." *Studies in Comics* 2 (2): 281–94.

Kukkonen, Karin. 2008. "Beyond Language: Metaphor and Metonymy in Comics Storytelling." *English Language Notes* 46 (2): 89–98.

Kukkonen, Karin. 2011. "Comics as a Test Case for Transmedial Narratology." *SubStance* 40 (1): 34–52.

Kukkonen, Karin. 2013a. *Contemporary Comics Storytelling*. Lincoln: University of Nebraska Press.

Kukkonen, Karin. 2013b. "Form as a Pattern of Thinking: Cognitive Poetics and New Formalism." In *New Formalisms and Literary Theory*, edited by Verena Theile and Linda Tredennick, 159–76. London: Palgrave Macmillan.

Kukkonen, Karin. 2013c. "Space, Time and Causality in Graphic Narratives: An Embodied Approach." In *From Comic Strips to Graphic Novels: Contributions on the Theory and History of Graphic Narrative*, edited by Daniel Stein and Jan-Noël Thon, 49–66. Berlin: DeGruyter.

Kukkonen, Karin. 2014. "Presence and Prediction: The Embodied Reader's Cascades of Cognition." *Style* 48 (3): 367–84.

Kukkonen, Karin. 2016. "Fantastic Cognition." In *Cognitive Literary Science*, edited by Michael Burke and Emily T. Troscianko, 151–67. New York: Oxford University Press.

Kukkonen, Karin. 2017. "Narrative Adventures in Duck-Rabbitry: Multistable Elements of Graphic Narrative." *Narrative* 25 (3): 342–58.

Kukkonen, Karin. 2019. *4E and Eighteenth-Century Fiction: How the Novel Found Its Feet*. New York: Oxford University Press.

Kukkonen, Karin. 2020. *Probability Designs: Literature and Predictive Processing*. New York: Oxford University Press.

Kunzle, David. 1973. *The Early Comic Strip: Narrative Strips and Picture Stories in the European Broadsheet from c.1450 to 1825*. Berkeley: University of California Press.

Kuzmičová, Anežka. 2014. "Literary Narrative and Mental Imagery: A View from Embodied Cognition." *Style* 48 (3): 275–93.

L'Abbé, Sonnet. 2019. "Erasures from the Territories Called Canada: Sharpening the Gaze at White Backgrounds." In *Avant-Canada: Artists, Prophets, Revolutionaries*, edited by Gregory Betts and Christian Bök, 197–222. Waterloo, ON: Wilfrid Laurier University Press.

Lakoff, George. 1987. *Women, Fire, and Dangerous Things: What Categories Reveal about the Mind*. Chicago: University of Chicago Press.

Lakoff, George. 1993. "The Contemporary Theory of Metaphor." In *Metaphor and Thought*, edited by Andrew Ortony, 202–51. New York: Cambridge University Press.

Lakoff, George, and Mark Johnson. 1980. *Metaphors We Live By*. (2nd edition 2003). Chicago: University of Chicago Press.

Lakoff, George, and Mark Johnson. 1999. *Philosophy in the Flesh: The Embodied Mind and Its Challenge to Western Thought*. New York: Basic Books.

Langacker, Ronald. 1990. *Concept, Image, and Symbol: The Cognitive Basis of Grammar*. New York: Mouton de Gruyter.

Langacker, Ronald. 2008. *Cognitive Grammar: A Basic Introduction*. New York: Oxford University Press.

LaRocque, Emma. 2010. *When the Other Is Me: Native Resistance Discourse, 1850–1990*. Winnipeg: University of Manitoba Press.

Layman, John, and Rob Guillory. 2013. *Chew: The Smorgasbord Edition*, Volume 1. Berkeley: Image Comics.

Lefèvre, Didier, Emmanuel Guibert, and Frédéric Lemercie. 2009. *The Photographer: Into War-Torn Afghanistan with Doctors Without Borders*. Translated by Alexis Siegel. New York: First Second.

Lefèvre, Pascal. 2016. "No Content Without Form: Graphic Style as the Primary Entrance to a Story." In *The Visual Narrative Reader*, edited by Neil Cohn, 67–87. New York: Bloomsbury.

Lemire, Jeff. 2009. *The Complete Essex County*. Atlanta: Top Shelf Productions.

Lemire, Jeff. 2010. *Sweet Tooth: Out of the Woods*. Collected. New York: DC Comics.

Lemire, Jeff. 2011. *Sweet Tooth: Animal Armies*. New York: DC Comics.

Lemire, Jeff. 2012. *The Underwater Welder*. Atlanta: Top Shelf Productions.

Lemke, Jay. 2004. "Metamedia Literacy: Transforming Meanings and Media." In *Visual Rhetoric in a Visual World: A Critical Sourcebook*, edited by Carolyn Handa, 71–93. Boston: Bedford/St. Martin's.

Lessing, Gotthold Ephraim. 1874. *Laocoon*. Edited by Robert Phillimore. London: Macmillan.

Levenston, Edward. 1992. *The Stuff of Literature: Physical Aspects of Texts and Their Relation to Literary Meaning*. Albany: State University of New York Press.

Littlemore, Jeannette. 2017. "Metonymy." In *The Cambridge Handbook of Cognitive Linguistics*, edited by Barbara Dancygier, 407–22. New York: Cambridge University Press.

Locher, Paul J. 2015. "The Aesthetic Experience with Visual Art 'At First Glance.'" In *Investigations into the Phenomenology and the Ontology of the Work of Art: What Are Artworks and How Do We Experience Them?*, edited by Peer F. Bundgaard and Frederik Stjernfelt, 75–88. Cham: Springer. https://doi.org/10.1007/978-3-319-14090-2_5.

Lopes, Dominic McIver. 2016. *Four Arts of Photography*. Hoboken, NJ: John Wiley & Sons. https://doi.org/10.1002/9781119053194.

Loschky, Lester C., John P. Hutson, Maverick E. Smith, Tim J. Smith, and Joseph P. Magliano. 2018. "Viewing Static Visual Narratives through the Lens of the Scene Perception and Event Comprehension Theory (SPECT)." In *Empirical Comics Research: Digital, Multimodal, and Cognitive Methods*, edited by Alexander Dunst, Jochen Laubrock, and Janina Wildfeuer, 217–38. New York: Routledge.

Lucia, Natascia De, Luigi Trojano, Vincenzo Paolo Senese, and Massimiliano Conson. 2016. "Mental Simulation of Drawing Actions Enhances Delayed Recall of a Complex Figure." *Experimental Brain Research* 234 (10): 2935–43. https://doi.org/10.1007/s00221-016-4696-3.

Lupton, Ellen. 2004. *Thinking with Type: A Critical Guide for Designers, Writers, Editors, and Students*. New York: Princeton Architectural Press.

Madden, Matt. 2005. *99 Ways to Tell a Story: Exercises in Style*. New York: Chamberlain Bros.

Madden, Matt. 2012. "A History of American Comic Books in Six Panels." *Matt Madden*. http://mattmadden.com/2012/08/08/a-history-of-american-comic-books-in-six-panels/.

Magnussen, Anne. 2000. "The Semiotics of C. S. Peirce as a Framework for the Understanding of Comics." In *Comics and Culture: Analytical and Theoretical Approaches to Comics*, edited by Anne Magnussen and Hans-Christian Christiansen, 193–208. Copenhagen: Museum Tusculanam Press.

Malaby, Mark, and Melissa Esh. 2012. "Nice Cape, Super Faggot! Male Adolescent Identity Crises in Young Adult Graphic Novels." *Journal of Graphic Novels and Comics* 3 (1): 39–53. https://doi.org/10.1080/21504857.2012.701443.

Malik, Rachel. 2008. "Horizons of the Publishable: Publishing in/as Literary Studies." *English Literary History* 75: 707–35. https://doi.org/10.1353/elh.0.0016.

Mar, Raymond A., and Keith Oatley. 2008. "The Function of Fiction Is the Abstraction and Simulation of Social Experience." *Perspectives on Psychological Science* 3 (3): 173–92.

Marrone, Daniel. 2016. "Seth's Ironic Identities: Forging Canadian History." *Canadian Review of Comparative Literature / Revue Canadienne de Littérature Comparée* 43 (1): 166–79.

Matlock, Teenie. 2004. "Fictive Motion as Cognitive Simulation." *Memory & Cognition* 32 (8): 1389–1400. http://www.ncbi.nlm.nih.gov/pubmed/15900932.

Matlock, Teenie. 2010. "Abstract Motion Is No Longer Abstract." *Language and Cognition* 2 (2): 243–60. https://doi.org/10.1515/langcog.2010.010.

McCloud, Scott. 1993. *Understanding Comics: The Invisible Art*. New York: HarperPerennial.

McCloud, Scott. 2000. *Reinventing Comics: How Imagination and Technology Are Revolutionizing an Art Form*. New York: Perennial.

McCloud, Scott. 2006. *Making Comics: Storytelling Secrets of Comics, Manga and Graphic Novels*. New York: Harper.

McCloud, Scott. 2009. "The 'Infinite Canvas.'" *Scottmccloud.Com*. http://scottmccloud.com/4-inventions/canvas/.

McConachie, Bruce, and F. Elizabeth Hart, eds. 2006. *Performance and Cognition: Theatre Studies and the Cognitive Turn*. London: Routledge.

McGann, Jerome. 1991. *The Textual Condition*. Princeton, NJ: Princeton University Press.

McGann, Jerome. 1993. *Black Riders: The Visible Language of Modernism*. Princeton, NJ: Princeton University Press.

McKegney, Sam, and Sarah Henzi. 2016. "Indigenous Literatures and the Arts of Community: Editors' Afterword." *Canadian Literature* 230/231: 238–48.

McLuhan, Marshall. 1964. *Understanding Media: The Extensions of Man*. New York: McGraw-Hill.

McNeill, David. 1992. *Hand and Mind: What Gestures Reveal about Thought*. Chicago: University of Chicago Press.

McNeill, David. 2005. *Gesture and Thought*. Chicago: University of Chicago Press.

Medley, Stuart. 2010. "Discerning Pictures: How We Look at and Understand Images in Comics." *Studies in Comics* 1 (1): 53–70. https://doi.org/10.1386/stic.1.1.53/1.

Medley, Stuart, and Hanadi Haddad. 2011. "The Realism Continuum, Representation and Perception." *International Journal of the Image* 1 (2): 145–56.

Megías-Robles, Alberto, María José Gutiérrez-Cobo, Rosario Cabello, Raquel Gómez-Leal, Simon Baron-Cohen, and Pablo Fernández-Berrocal. 2020. "The 'Reading the Mind in the Eyes' Test and Emotional Intelligence." *Royal Society Open Science* 7 (9): 201305. https://doi.org/10.1098/rsos.201305rsos201305.

Mellette, Justin. 2021. "Of Men and Mongrels: Myth and Queer Representation in Brian K. Vaughan's Y: The Last Man and Saga." *Journal of Graphic Novels and Comics* 13 (2): 225–40. https://doi.org/10.1080/21504857.2021.1901756.

Menary, Richard. 2013. "Cognitive Integration, Enculturated Cognition and the Socially Extended Mind." *Cognitive Systems Research* 25–26: 26–34.

Menary, Richard. 2015. "Pragmatism and the Pragmatic Turn in Cognitive Science." In *The Pragmatic Turn: Toward Action-Oriented Views in Cognitive Science*, edited by Andreas K. Engel, Karl J. Friston, Bernhard Hommel, Danica Kragic, Julia Lupp, Paul F. M. J. Verschure, and Gottfried Vosgerau, 215–34. Cambridge, MA: MIT Press. https://doi.org/10.7551/mitpress/9780262034326.003.0013.

Merleau-Ponty, Maurice. 1962. *Phenomenology of Perception*. New York: Humanities Press.

Meskin, Aaron. 2007. "Defining Comics?" *Journal of Aesthetics and Art Criticism* 65 (4): 369–79.

Miers, John. 2014. "Depiction and Demarcation in Comics: Towards an Account of the Medium as a Drawing Practice." *Studies in Comics* 6 (1): 145–56. https://doi.org/10.1386/stic.6.1.145.

Mignola, Mike. 2009. *Hellboy: Conqueror Worm / Strange Places*. 1st librar. Milwaukie, OR: Dark Horse Books.

Millard, Elaine, and Jackie Marsh. 2001. "Sending Minnie the Minx Home: Comics and Reading Choices." *Cambridge Journal of Education* 31 (1): 25–38.

Miller, Frank, Klaus Janson, and Lynn Varley. 2002. *Batman: The Dark Knight Returns*. New York: DC Comics.

Miodrag, Hannah. 2013. *Comics and Language: Reimagining Critical Discourse on the Form*. Jackson: University Press of Mississippi.

Mitchell, W. J. T. 2002. "Showing Seeing: A Critique of Visual Culture." *Journal Of Visual Culture* 1 (2): 165–81.

Mitchell, W. J. T. 2008. "Visual Literacy or Literary Visualcy." In *Visual Literacy*, edited by James Elkins, 11–29. New York: Routledge.

Mitchell, W. J. T. 2012. "Image X Text." In *The Future of Image and Text: Collected Essays on Literary and Visual Conjunctures*, edited by Ofra Amihay and Lauren Walsh, 1–11. Newcastle upon Tyne: Cambridge Scholars Publishing.

Mittelberg, Irene. 2013. "Balancing Acts: Image Schemas and Force Dynamics as Experiential Essence in Pictures by Paul Klee and Their Gestural Enactments." In *Language and the Creative Mind*, edited by Mike Borkent, Barbara Dancygier, and Jennifer Hinnell, 325–46. Stanford, CA: CSLI Publications.

Mittelberg, Irene. 2017. "Embodied Frames and Scenes: Body-Based Metonymy and Pragmatic Inferencing in Gesture." *Gesture* 16 (2): 203–44. https://doi.org/10.1075/gest.16.2.03mit.

Mittelberg, Irene. 2018. "Gestures as Image Schemas and Force Gestalts: A Dynamic Systems Approach Augmented with Motion-Capture Data Analyses." *Cognitive Semiotics* 11 (1): 1–21. https://doi.org/10.1515/cogsem-2018-0002.

Molotiu, Andrei, ed. 2009. *Abstract Comics: The Anthology, 1967–2009*. Seattle: Fantagraphics Books.

Molotiu, Andrei. 2012. "Abstract Form: Sequential Dynamism and Iconostasis in Abstract Comics and in Steve Ditko's Amazing Spider-Man." In *Critical Approaches to Comics: Theories and Methods*, edited by Matthew J. Smith and Randy Duncan, 84–100. New York: Routledge.

Molotiu, Andrei. 2016. "Art Comics." In *The Routledge Companion to Comics and Graphic Novels*, edited by Frank Bramlett, Roy Cook, and Aaron Meskin, 119–27. New York: Routledge.

Moore, Alan, and Dave Gibbons. 1986. *Watchmen*. New York: DC Comics.

Morais, Jose, and Regine Kolinsky. 2005. "Literacy and Cognitive Change." In *The Science of Reading: A Handbook*, edited by Margaret J. Snowling and Charles Hulme, 188–203. New York: Blackwell.

Moss, Laura. 2004. "Canada Reads." *Canadian Literature* 182: 6–10.

Müller, Cornelia. 2007. "A Dynamic View of Metaphor, Gesture and Thought." In *Gesture and the Dynamic Dimensions of Language: Essays in Honor of David McNeill*, edited by Susan D. Duncan, Justina Cassell, and Elena Levy, 109–16. Philadelphia: John Benjamins Publishing Company.

Mullins, Katie. 2014. "Embodiment, Time, and the Life Review in Jeff Lemire's *Ghost Stories*." *English Studies in Canada* 40 (4): 29–54.

Munroe, Randall. 2011. "Never Do This." *Xkcd*. 2011. https://xkcd.com/860/.

Murray, Chris. 2000. "Popaganada: Superhero Comics and Propaganda in World War Two." In *Comics and Culture: Analytical and Theoretical Approaches to Comics*, edited by Anne Magnussen and Hans-Christian Christiansen, 141–56. Copenhagen: University of Copenhagen.

Nänny, Max, and Olga Fischer, eds. 1999. *Form Miming Meaning: Iconicity in Language and Literature*. Philadelphia: John Benjamins Publishing Co.

Narayan, Shweta. 2012. "Maybe What He Means Is He Actually Got the Spot: Physical and Cognitive Viewpoint in a Gesture Study." In *Viewpoint in Language: A*

Multimodal Perspective, edited by Barbara Dancygier and Eve Sweetser, 113–35. New York: Cambridge University Press.

Newall, Michael. 2011. *What Is a Picture? Depiction, Realism, Abstraction.* New York: Palgrave Macmillan.

Nichol, bp. 1970. *The Captain Poetry Poems Complete.* New ed., 2011. Toronto: BookThug.

Nichol, bp. 2002a. *bpNichol Comics.* Edited by Carl Peters. Vancouver, BC: Talonbooks.

Nichol, bp. 2002b. *Meanwhile: The Critical Writings of bpNichol.* Edited by Roy Miki. Vancouver, BC: Talonbooks.

Nodelman, Perry. 1988. *Words about Pictures: The Narrative Art of Children's Picture Books.* Athens: University of Georgia Press.

Nodelman, Perry. 2012. "Picture Book Guy Looks at Comics: Structural Differences in Two Kinds of Visual Narrative." *Children's Literature Association Quarterly* 37 (4): 436–44.

Noë, Alva. 2004. *Action in Perception.* Cambridge Mass.: MIT Press.

Noë, Alva. 2009. *Out of Our Heads: Why You Are Not Your Brain, and Other Lessons from the Biology of Consciousness.* 1st ed. New York: Hill and Wang.

Núñez, Rafael E., and Eve Sweetser. 2006. "With the Future Behind Them: Convergent Evidence From Aymara Language and Gesture in the Crosslinguistic Comparison of Spatial Construals of Time." *Cognitive Science* 30 (3): 401–50.

Nyberg, Amy Kiste. 1998. *Seal of Approval: The History of the Comics Code.* Jackson: University Press of Mississippi.

O'Regan, J. 2011. *Why Red Doesn't Sound like a Bell: Understanding the Feel of Consciousness.* New York: Oxford University Press.

Oakley, Todd. 2009. *From Attention to Meaning: Explorations in Semiotics, Linguistics, and Rhetoric.* New York: Peter Lang.

Oatley, Keith. 1999. "Why Fiction May Be Twice as True as Fact: Fiction as Cognitive and Emotional Simulation." *Review of General Psychology* 3 (2): 101–17.

Oberman, Lindsay M., Piotr Winkielman, and Vilayanur S. Ramachandran. 2010. "Embodied Simulation: A Conduit for Converting Seeing into Perceiving." In *Social Psychology of Visual Perception*, edited by Emily Balcetis and G. Daniel Lassiter, 201–21. New York: Psychology Press.

Osaka, Naoyuki, Daisuke Matsuyoshi, Takashi Ikeda, and Mariko Osaka. 2010. "Implied Motion Because of Instability in Hokusai Manga Activates the Human Motion-Sensitive Extrastriate Visual Cortex: An FMRI Study of the Impact of Visual Art." *NeuroReport* 21 (4): 264–67. https://doi.org/10.1097/WNR.0b013 e328335b371.

Pederson, Kaitlin, and Neil Cohn. 2016. "The Changing Pages of Comics: Page Layouts across Eight Decades of American Superhero Comics." *Studies in Comics* 7 (1): 7–28. https://doi.org/10.1386/stic.7.1.7.

Pedri, Nancy. 2011. "When Photographs Aren't Quite Enough: Reflections on Photography and Cartooning in Le Photographe." *ImageText: Interdisciplinary Comics Studies* 6 (1): n.p.

Peirce, Charles Sanders. 1940. "Logic as Semiotic: The Theory of Signs." In *The Philosophy of Peirce: Selected Writings*, edited by Justus Buchler, 98–119. London: Routledge & Kegan Paul.

Peppard, Anna F. 2018. "'A Cross Burning Darkly, Blackening the Night': Reading Racialized Spectacles of Conflict and Bondage in Marvel's Early Black Panther Comics." *Studies in Comics* 9 (1): 59–86. https://doi.org/10.1386/stic.9.1.59.

Pérez, Pauline, Jens Madsen, Leah Banellis, Başak Türker, Federico Raimondo, Vincent Perlbarg, Melanie Valente, et al. 2021. "Conscious Processing of Narrative Stimuli Synchronizes Heart Rate between Individuals." *Cell Reports* 36: 109692. https://doi.org/10.1016/j.celrep.2021.109692.

Phillips, Noelle. 2013. "Seeing Red: Reading Rubrication in Oxford, Corpus Christi College MS 201's Piers Plowman." *The Chaucer Review* 47 (4): 439–64.

Pinker, Steven. 1994. *The Language Instinct*. New York: W. Morrow and Co.

Plantinga, Carl, and Greg M. Smith, eds. 1999. *Passionate Views: Film, Cognition, and Emotion*. Baltimore: Johns Hopkins University Press.

Postema, Barbara. 2013. *Narrative Structure in Comics: Making Sense of Fragments*. Rochester, NY: RIT Press.

Potsch, Elisabeth, and Robert F. Williams. 2012. "Image Schemas and Conceptual Metaphor in Action Comics." In *Linguistics and the Study of Comics*, edited by Frank Bramlett, 13–36. New York: Palgrave Macmillan.

Prinz, Jesse. 2004. *Gut Reactions: A Perceptual Theory of Emotion*. New York: Oxford University Press.

Prinz, Jesse. 2007. *The Emotional Construction of Morals*. New York: Oxford University Press.

Purvey, Diane, and John Douglas Belshaw. 2011. *Vancouver Noir*. Vancouver: Anvil Press.

Radden, Günter. 2003. "How Metonymic Are Metaphors?" In *Metaphor and Metonymy in Comparison and Contrast*, edited by René Dirven and Ralf Pörings, 407–34. New York: Mouton de Gruyter.

Ramachandran, V. S., and E. M. Hubbard. 2001. "Synaesthesia—A Window Into Perception, Thought and Language." *Journal of Conciousness Studies* 8 (12): 3–34.

Reddy, Michael. 1979. "The Conduit Metaphor." In *Metaphor and Thought*, edited by A. Ortony, 284–324. Cambridge: Cambridge University Press.

Refaie, Elisabeth El. 2009. "Multiliteracies: How Readers Interpret Political Cartoons." *Visual Communication* 8 (2): 181–205. https://doi.org/10.1177/1470357209102113.

Refaie, Elisabeth El. 2013. "Cross-Modal Resonances in Creative Multimodal Metaphors: Breaking out of Conceptual Prisons." *Review of Cognitive Linguistics* 11 (2): 236–49. https://doi.org/10.1075/rcl.11.2.02elr.

Reyns-Chikuma, Chris, and Houssem Ben Lazreg. 2017. "Marjane Satrapi and the Graphic Novels from and about the Middle East." *Arab Studies Quarterly* 39 (1): 758–76.

Richardson, Alan. 2004. "Studies in Literature and Cognition: A Field Map." In *The Work of Fiction: Cognition, Culture, and Complexity*, edited by Alan Richardson and Ellen Spolsky, 1–29. Burlington, VT: Ashgate Publishing.

Rohrer, Tim. 2001. "Pragmatism, Ideology and Embodiment: William James and the Philosophical Foundations of Cognitive Linguistics." In *Language and Ideology: Cognitive Theoretical Approaches*, edited by Rene Dirven, Bruce Hawkins, and Esra Sandikcioglu, 49–81. Amsterdam: John Benjamins.

Rohrer, Tim. 2007. "Embodiment and Experientialism." In *Oxford Handbook of Cognitive Linguistics*, edited by Dirk Geeraerts and Hubert Cuyckens, 25–47. New York: Oxford University Press.

Rose, Steven. 2005. *The Future of the Brain: The Promise and Perils of Tomorrow's Neuroscience*. New York: Oxford University Press.

Ryan, Marie-Laure. 2014. "Narration in Various Media." In *Handbook of Narratology*, edited by Peter Hühn, Jan Christoph Meister, John Pier, and Wolf Schmid, 468–88. Berlin: de Gruyter.

Satrapi, Marjane. 2003. *Persepolis: The Story of a Childhood*. New York: Pantheon.

Schkade, Dan. 2022. *Lavender Jack*. https://www.webtoons.com/en/super-hero/lavender-jack/list?title_no=1410&page=1.

Schmitt, Ronald. 1992. "Deconstructive Comics." *Journal of Popular Culture* 25 (4): 153–61.

Schweppe, Judith, and Ralf Rummer. 2014. "Attention, Working Memory, and Long-Term Memory in Multimedia Learning: An Integrated Perspective Based on Process Models of Working Memory." *Educational Psychology Review* 26: 285–306. https://doi.org/10.1007/s10648-013-9242-2.

Scobie, Stephen. 1984. *bpNichol: What History Teaches*. Vancouver, BC: Talonbooks.

Seth. 2009. *George Sprott, 1894–1975*. Montreal: Drawn & Quarterly.

Shea, Ammon. 2014. *Bad English: A History of Linguistic Aggravation*. New York: Perigee.

Shimamura, Arthur P., ed. 2013. *Psychocinematics: Exploring Cognition at the Movies*. New York: Oxford University Press.

Shimojo, Shinsuke, and Ladan Shams. 2001. "Sensory Modalities Are Not Separate Modalities: Plasticity and Interactions." *Current Opinion in Neurobiology* 11 (4): 505–9. http://www.ncbi.nlm.nih.gov/pubmed/11502399.

Simons, Daniel J., and C. F. Chabris. 1999. "Gorillas in Our Midst: Sustained Inattentional Blindness for Dynamic Events." *Perception* 28 (9): 1059–74.

Simons, Daniel J., and Daniel T. Levin. 1998. "Failure to Detect Changes to People during a Real-World Interaction." *Psychonomic Bulletin & Review* 5 (4): 644–49.

Singer, Marc. 2018. *Breaking the Frames: Populism and Prestige in Comics Studies*. Austin: University of Texas Press.

Slingerland, Edward. 2008. *What Science Offers the Humanities: Integrating Body and Culture*. New York: Cambridge University Press.

Smith, Barbara Herrnstein. 1995. "Value/Evaluation." In *Critical Terms for Literary Study*, edited by Frank Lentricchia and Thomas McLaughlin, 2nd ed., 177–85. Chicago: University of Chicago Press.

Smolderen, Thierry. 2014. *The Origin of Comics: From William Hogarth to Winsor McCay*. Translated by Bart Beaty and Nick Nguyen. Jackson: University Press of Mississippi. https://muse-jhu-edu.ezproxy.library.ubc.ca/book/30852.

Solso, Robert L. 1994. *Cognition and the Visual Arts*. Cambridge, MA: MIT Press.

Sousanis, Nick. 2015. *Unflattening*. Cambridge, MA: Harvard University Press.

Spiegelman, Art. 1997. *The Complete Maus*. New York: Pantheon Books.

Spiers, Miriam Brown. 2014. "Creating a Haida Manga: The Formline of Social Responsibility in *Red*." *Studies in American Indian Literatures* 26 (3): 41–61. https://doi.org/10.1353/ail.2014.0026.

Stockwell, Peter. 2002. *Cognitive Poetics: An Introduction*. New York: Routledge.

Stockwell, Peter. 2009. *Texture: A Cognitive Aesthetics of Reading*. Edinburgh: Edinburgh University Press.

Sullivan, Karen. 2017. "Conceptual Metaphor." In *The Cambridge Handbook of Cognitive Linguistics*, edited by Barbara Dancygier, 385–406. New York: Cambridge University Press.

Sullivan, Karen. 2018. *Mixed Metaphors: Their Use and Abuse*. New York: Bloomsbury.

Sweetser, Eve, and Gilles Fauconnier. 1996. "Cognitive Links and Domains: Basic Aspects of Mental Space Theory." In *Spaces, Worlds and Grammars*, edited by Eve Sweetser and Gilles Fauconnier, 1–28. Chicago: University of Chicago Press.

Szczepaniak, Angela. 2011. "Minding the Gaps: A Cannulated Reading Process Developed through the Works of bpNichol, Chris Ware, and Art Spiegelman." Buffalo, NY: State University of New York.

Szép, Eszter. 2020. *Comics and the Body: Drawing, Reading, and Vulnerability*. Columbus: Ohio State University Press.

Tabulo, Kym. 2014. "Abstract Sequential Art." *Journal of Graphic Novels and Comics* 5 (1): 29–41. https://doi.org/10.1080/21504857.2013.803994.

Talmy, Leonard. 1996. "Fictive Motion in Language and 'Ception.'" In *Language and Space*, edited by Paul Bloom, Mary A. Peterson, Lynn Nadel, and Merrill F. Garrett, 211–76. Cambridge, MA: MIT Press.

Tamaki, Jillian. 2015. *Supermutant Magic Academy*. Montreal: Drawn & Quarterly.

Taub, Sarah. 2001. *Language from the Body: Iconicity and Metaphor in American Sign Language*. New York: Cambridge University Press.

Tobin, V. 2009. "Cognitive Bias and the Poetics of Surprise." *Language and Literature* 18 (2): 155–72. https://doi.org/10.1177/0963947009105342.

Tomasello, Michael. 1995. "Language Is Not an Instinct." *Cognitive Development* 10 (1): 131–56.

Tomasello, Michael. 1999. *The Cultural Origins of Human Cognition*. Cambridge, MA: Harvard University Press.

Tomasello, Michael. 2008. *Origins of Human Communication*. Cambridge, MA: MIT Press.

Turner, Mark. 1999. "A Mechanism of Creativity." *Poetics Today* 20 (3): 397–418.

Turner, Mark. 2006. "Compression and Representation." *Language and Literature* 15: 17–27.

Turner, Mark. 2014. *The Origin of Ideas: Blending, Creativity, and the Human Spark*. New York: Oxford University Press.

Varela, Francisco J., Evan Thompson, and Eleanor Rorsch. 1991. *The Embodied Mind: Cognitive Science and Human Experience*. Cambridge, MA: MIT Press.

Vasseleu, Cathryn. 1998. *Textures of Light: Vision and Touch in Irigaray, Levinas and Merleau Ponty*. New York: Routledge.

Vaughan, Brian K., and Pia Guerra. 2003. *Y: The Last Man—Cycles*. New York: Vertigo/DC Comics.

Vaughan, Brian K., Marcos Martin, and Muntsa Vicente. 2015. *The Private Eye*. Berkeley: Image Comics.

Verhagen, Arie. 2005. *Constructions of Intersubjectivity: Discourse, Syntax, and Cognition*. Toronto: Oxford University Press.

Voyer, Daniel, and Petra Jansen. 2017. "Motor Expertise and Performance in Spatial Tasks: A Meta-Analysis." *Human Movement Science* 54: 110–24. https://doi.org/10.1016/j.humov.2017.04.004.

Ware, Chris. 2002. *Jimmy Corrigan: The Smartest Kid on Earth*. Pantheon Books.

Ware, Chris. 2012. *Building Stories*. New York: Pantheon Books.

Watterson, Bill. 1986. *Calvin and Hobbes*. Kansas City: Andrews McMeel.

Wertham, Fredric. 1955. *Seduction of the Innocent: The Influence of Comic Books on Today's Youth*. London: Museum Press.

Whitlock, Gillian. 2006. "Autographics: The Seeing 'I' of the Comics." *MFS Modern Fiction Studies* 52 (4): 965–79. https://doi.org/10.1353/mfs.2007.0013.

Willems, Roel M., and Daniel Casasanto. 2011. "Flexibility in Embodied Language Understanding." *Frontiers in Psychology* 2: 116. https://doi.org/10.3389/fpsyg.2011.00116.

Williams, Ian C. M. 2012. "Graphic Medicine: Comics as Medical Narrative." *Medical Humanities* 38 (1): 21–27. https://doi.org/10.1136/medhum-2011-010093.

Williams, Ian C. M. 2013. "Graphic Medicine: The Portrayal of Illness in Underground and Autobiographical Comics." In *Medicine, Health and the Arts: Approaches to the Medical Humanities*, edited by Victoria Bates, Alan Bleakley, and Sam Goodman, 64–84. New York: Routledge.

Wilson, Austin, and David Hopkins. 2010. "Paying Too Much Attention: Panel Progression and Design." Hideous Energy. http://hideousenergy.blogspot.ca/2010/10/paying-too-much-attention-panel.html.

Wilson, Deirdre, and Dan Sperber. 2004. "Relevance Theory." In *The Handbook of Pragmatics*, edited by Laurence R. Horn and Gregory L. Ward, 606–32. Malden, MA: Blackwell.

Wilson, Margaret. 2002. "Six Views of Embodied Cognition." *Psychonomic Bulletin & Review* 9 (4): 625–36.

Wilson, Nicole L., and Raymond W. Gibbs Jr. 2007. "Real and Imagined Body Movement Primes Metaphor Comprehension." *Cognitive Science* 31 (4): 721–31.

Witek, Joseph. 2009. "The Arrow and the Grid." In *A Comics Studies Reader*, edited by Jeet Heer and Kent Worcester, 149–56. Lincoln: University Press of Mississippi.

Woo, Benjamin. 2011. "The Android's Dungeon: Comic-Bookstores, Cultural Spaces, and the Social Practices of Audiences." *Journal of Graphic Novels and Comics* 2 (2): 125–36. https://doi.org/10.1080/21504857.2011.602699.

Woo, Benjamin. 2012. "Understanding Understandings of Comics: Reading and Collecting as Media-Oriented Practices." *Participations* 9 (2): 180–99. http://www.participations.org/Volume 9/Issue 2/12 Woo.pdf.

Worden, Daniel. 2015. "The Politics of Comics: Popular Modernism, Abstraction, and Experimentation." *Literature Compass* 12 (2): 59–71.

Yahgulanaas, Michael. 2009. *Red: A Haida Manga*. Vancouver: Douglas & McIntyre.

Živadinović, Stevan. 2011. *Hobo Lobo of Hamelin*. http://hobolobo.net/.

Zlatev, Jordan. 2005. "What Is a Schema? Bodily Mimesis and the Grounding of Knowledge." In *From Perception to Meaning: Image Schemas in Cognitive Linguistics*, edited by Beate Hampe, 313–42. Berlin: Walter de Gruyter.

Zlatev, Jordan. 2010. "Phenomenology and Cognitive Linguistics." In *Handbook of Pragmatics and Cognitive Science*, edited by Shaun Gallagher and Dan Schmicking, 415–46. Dordecht: Springer.

Zunshine, Lisa. 2006. *Why We Read Fiction: Theory of Mind and the Novel*. Columbus: Ohio State University Press.

Zunshine, Lisa. 2010. *Introduction to Cognitive Cultural Studies*. Baltimore: Johns Hopkins University Press.

Zwaan, Rolf A. 1996. "Toward a Model of Literary Comprehension." In *Models of Understanding Text*, edited by Bruce K. Britton and Arthur C. Graesser, 241–55. Lawrence Erlbaum.

Zwaan, Rolf A. 2008. "Time in Language, Situation Models, and Mental Simulations." *Language Learning* 58 (1): 13–26.

Zwaan, Rolf A. 2009. "Mental Simulation in Language Comprehension and Social Cognition." *European Journal of Social Psychology* 39 (7): 1142–50.

Zwaan, Rolf A., Gabriel A. Radvansky, Amy E. Hilliard, and Jacqueline M. Curiel. 1998. "Constructing Multidimensional Situation Models during Reading." *Scientific Studies of Reading* 2 (3): 199–220. https://doi.org/10.1207/s153279 9xssr0203_2.

Zwaan, Rolf A., and Richard H. Yaxley. 2003. "Spatial Iconicity Affects Semantic Relatedness Judgments." *Psychonomic Bulletin Review* 10 (4): 954–58.

Zwaan, Rolf A. 2004. "The Immersed Experiencer: Toward an Embodied Theory of Language Comprehension." In *The Psychology of Learning and Motivation: Advances in Research and Theory*, edited by Brian H. Ross, 35–62. Boston: Academic Press.

INDEX

For the benefit of digital users, indexed terms that span two pages (e.g., 52–53) may, on occasion, appear on only one of those pages.

Tables, figures and endnotes are indicated by t, f, and n following the page number.

Abdelrazaq, Leila, 168–71, 180
abstraction
    and comics (*see* comics)
    and domains (and categories), 55, 58–59
    and genre, 72–76, 117
    and identity, 199, 223–27
    and mental metaphors, 52–53, 81, 119–20, 146, 149–50
    and metaphorical constructions, 119–20, 125
    and metonymy, 111, 220
    and schemas, 34, 38–39, 42, 51–52, 82–84, 205–7, 227
    and simplification and meaning, 24, 25t, 40–41, 50–51, 55, 61–62, 70, 198–200, 201–16, 226–27
    and simulation and improvisation, 58, 62–63, 215, 227
    and synesthesia, 100, 103–5
    and viewpoint, 66, 70–76, 93, 136, 170–71, 209–10, 212, 221
affect. *See* emotion
affordances, 2–3, 22, 36–37, 67–68, 184, 185–86, 197, 222–23, 230, 239
agentive, or agentivity
    and abstraction, 82, 209–10, 211–12
    and blending, 64, 65f, 153–54, 157, 227
    and metaphor, 52–53, 119–20

    and viewpoint, 47, 51–52, 56, 60, 75, 76–97, 128, 162–63, 174, 176, 213–15
Aislin, 45–50, 51–68
anchor
    cognitive, 140–41
    elastic, 234–35
    material, 140–41, 151–54, 168, 181–82, 185, 189, 195–97, 239
    narrative, 140–41, 162–63, 168, 181–82, 185, 194–97, 234–35
Arnheim, Rudolf, 2–3, 15–16, 38–39, 71, 204–5, 206
attention. *See* perception

Baddawi. *See* Abdelrazaq, Leila
balloon
    speech, 24–25, 25t, 26, 43f, 44–45, 47, 67–68, 77–78, 85–86, 88–89, 93, 95–96, 98–106, 109, 116–17, 130–36, 166, 224–25
    as synesthetic constructions, 98–105
    as text or narrative box, 25t, 44, 98–106, 109, 130–36
    thought, 25t, 47, 98–105, 133
Barrett, Lisa Feldman, 53–54, 58, 70, 88–91
Barry, Lynda, 118
Barsalou, Lawrence W, 33, 36–37, 39–40, 57–58, 59–60

Bateman, John, 2–3, 21–16, 24, 67–68, 183–84
Beaton, Kate, 10–11, 229–30
Beaty, Bart, 11–12, 45, 241n.3
  and Benjamin Woo, 11, 19–20, 27–28
Bechdel, Alison, 26–27, 105–7, 118
Bergen, Benjamin, 36–37, 45, 50, 58, 61, 110–11, 112–13, 141
Bergs, Alexander. *See* Hoffmann, Thomas
bias
  in cognition, 30–31, 36, 37–44, 46–48, 62–63, 76–78, 82–88, 103, 143, 145, 159–60, 180–82, 209
  linguistic or literary, 13, 19–20, 27–28, 46–47, 218–19
blending
  biases in, 159–60
  cascades, 66, 158–59
  as closure or gap-filling, 44, 140–41, 167, 179–80, 185, 195–96, 205, 235–36
  compression, 63, 135, 160–67, 197
  decompression or in-filling, 71–72, 112, 126, 154–67
  definition, 62–66
  and fictivity, 206–15
  and gesture (*see* gesture)
  and improvisation (*see* improvisation)
  and intertextuality, 113–19, 130–33, 217–19
  and metaphor and metonymy, 61, 80–81, 98–100, 103–5, 111–12, 115–30, 135–37, 185–94, 219–20
  as model of creativity, 3, 63, 68, 177
  and second cognitive revolution, 34–35
  and semantic, pragmatic, and aesthetic analysis, 67–68, 70, 150–51, 183–84, 208–9
  as synesthesia, 100–5, 130–31
  and temporality, 145–47, 151–54, 155, 160–67, 180–82, 236
  and viewpoint construction, 72–73, 76, 78–82, 86–87, 105–6, 108–9, 121–24, 125–30, 132–33, 135–36, 155, 162–63, 166, 168–71, 177–80, 185–94, 221–22, 238
  and vital relations and mappings (*see* vital relations)
body schema, 79–80, 82–83, 90, 92–93, 108–9
bubble. *See* balloon

Calvin and Hobbes. *See* Watterson, Bill
Canada Reads (CBC), 5–7, 10–11, 13, 18–20
Captain America. *See* Lee, Stan; Kirby, Jack
Carroll, E M, 233
cartoons, defined 45, 65–66, 112–13, 232
Castellucci, Cecil, 133–36, 164–66. *See also* Pimienta, Jose
category, 50–51, 52, 53–58, 59, 74, 79–80, 90, 97, 111–15, 117–19, 132, 160, 190, 200–1, 237
change blindness. *See* perception
Chew. *See* Layman, John; Guillory, Rob
Chomsky, Noam. *See* cognitive revolutions
closure. *See* blending
cognitive metaphor. *See* mental metaphor
cognitive revolutions, 32–54
cognitive science interdisciplinarity, 1–2, 24, 50
Cohn, Neil, 243–44n.5, 15–16, 19–20, 30, 34, 40–41, 44, 83, 93, 141, 145–46, 151, 183–84, 204, 220
colonial, 178–79, 237–38, 242n.1, 242n.5. *See also* decolonial; Indigenous
comics, definitions of, 26–29, 30, 200–1
conceptual integration theory. *See* blending
conceptual metaphor. *See* mental metaphor
conduit metaphor. *See* mental metaphor
Cooperrider, Kensy, 140, 146, 148–51

Dancygier, Barbara, 1–2, 16–17, 30–31, 98, 99–100, 185, 195–96, 197
  and Eve Sweetser, 52–53, 64–65, 95–96, 110–13, 245n.17
  and Lieven Vandelanotte, 2, 64–65, 231
Davis, Guy, 91–93
decolonial, 26, 179–80, 223–27. *See also* colonial; Indigenous
Dinosaur Comics. *See* North, Ryan

domain
    definition, 53–57
    See also genre
Doucet, Julie, 85–88

Eisner, Will, 21–22, 26–27, 37, 44, 76, 88–89, 93, 95–97, 139
Ekman, Paul, 89–90
El Refaie, Elisabeth, 45, 65–66, 87, 110–11, 190
embodiment
    and cognitive poetics, 35–36
    defined, 3, 33–35
emotion
    defined, 25t, 58, 88–91
    embodied depictions of, 76–97
    metaphors of, 88–89, 96–97, 103–5, 189–90
Essex County. See Lemire, Jeff
experimental comics. See comics
extended cognition. See embodiment
eye-tracking. See perception

facial expression, 60, 76, 88–94. See also gesture
fallacy
    Cartesian dualism, 32–33, 36–37
    conduit or transmission metaphors, 13–14, 16–18, 105, 246–47n.1 (*see also* mental metaphor: conduit)
    logocentrism, or linguistic imperialism, 217
    pictorial immediacy, transparency, or totality, 15–16
    visual turn, 14–15
Fauconnier, Gilles, 207–8
    and Eve Sweetser, 54–55
    and Mark Turner, 36–37, 54–55, 62–64, 119–21, 151–52, 153, 159–60, 209–10. See also blending
fictive change. See perception
fictive motion. See perception
fictivity. See perception
figurative meaning, 119–30. See also mental metaphor: and figurative metaphors
    and blending
Fillmore, Charles, 53–54. See also domain
film, 12, 18–21, 139, 229–30, 235–36, 239

focalization. See viewpoint
Fodor, Jerry. See cognitive revolutions
Forceville, Charles, 47, 96–97, 99, 103–5, 110–11, 119–20, 157, 224–25, 243n.3
frame, 43f, See also domain; Fillmore
Fun Home: A Family Tragicomic. See Bechdel, Alison

Gallese, Vittorio. See mental simulation
gaps. See gutter.
Garneau, David, 26, 223–27
genre
    and cognition, 55–56, 70, 71–76, 86–87, 113–15, 117–18, 132, 195–96, 215–16, 237–39
    and competition, 5–7
    and literacy, 18–19, 21–22, 27–28, 85, 180, 200–1, 222
    and social and material situatedness, 21–24, 56–57, 67, 71, 75–76, 118, 183–84
George Sprott, 1894–1975. See Seth
gestalt (and gist). See perception
gesture. See also facial expression
    defined, 95–97
    and mental simulation, 59, 76, 90–91, 107–8, 143, 157
    and multimodality, 21, 36, 98
Gibbons, Alison, 2, 20–21, 35–36, 98, 99, 119–20, 246n.4
Gibbons, Dave, 113–14, 115–16, 130–31. See also Moore, Alan
Gibbs, Raymond W Jr., 12, 33–36, 38–40, 50, 52–53, 54–55, 59–60, 61–62, 95–96, 189, 241n.2. See also embodiment
Gibson, James J. See affordances
Gombrich, E H, 15–16, 38–41, 71–72
Goodbrey, Daniel Merlin, 232–33, 236
Grady, Joseph, 52–53, 63, 98–99
graphic medicine, 246n.3
Groensteen, Thierry, 17–18, 27–28, 43f, 44, 138, 154, 162–63, 185, 194–95, 200–1, 203, 204, 212–13, 246–47n.1, 248n.1
Guerra, Pia. See Vaughan, Brian K, and Pia Guerra
Guibert, Didier. 72–76. See also Lefèvre, Emmanuel; Lemercier, Frédéric.

Guillory, Rob. 83–85, 127–30. *See also* Layman, John
gutter, and gap, 43f, 138–46, 151, 156, 157, 177–80, 233. *See also* closure; blending

hand drawn. *See* line style
handwriting, 100, 219–20. *See also* typography
Harvey, Robert, 26–27, 45
Hatfield, Charles, 13, 26–28, 29, 30–31, 45, 118, 149
Hellboy. *See* Mignola, Mike
Herman, David, 2, 54, 70, 243n.3
Hickok, Gregory. *See* mental simulation
Hobo Lobo of Hamelin. *See* Živadinović, Stevan
Hoffmann, Thomas, 33–34, 50, 58–59, 63–64
 and Alexander Bergs, 74
Hogan, Patrick Colm, 2, 23, 195–96, 203–4, 212
Hutchins, Edwin, 34–35, 36, 59, 152
hybrid art, 10, 11–12, 15, 19–21, 26–27, 28–29. *See also* hybridity
hybridity, 121–24, 160, 184–85

Iacoboni, Marco, 90–91, 245n.2
image schema. *See* schema
immersion, 148–51, 239
improvisation, 4, 140–41, 146, 198, 200, 203–4, 205–6, 209–16, 218–19, 221–23, 226–27, 240
Indigenous (representation, space, resistance), 178–79, 224–26
infinite canvas, 232–33, 235–36
intersubjective (and intersubjectivity), 2, 16–17, 39–40, 59–60, 75–76, 77–78, 87, 90–91, 93, 95, 100, 103–4, 109, 118, 119–20, 137, 143, 157, 181, 209, 225–26, 227, 240
intertextual, 61–62, 71, 113–19, 130–33, 160

Johnson, Mark, 1–2, 16–17, 33–34, 35–36, 38–39, 51–53, 120–21, 147–49, 206

Kashtan, Aaron, 230, 231–33
Kelp-Stebbins, Katherine, 123, 184–85, 247n.8

Kendon, Adam, 95, 96
Kirby, Jack, 18–19, 85, 141, 147–48
Kochalka, James, 201–3, 205, 206–14
Kress, Gunther, 2
 and Theo Van Leeuwen, 15–16, 21, 46–47
Kukkonen, Karin, 2, 34–36, 39, 50, 53–54, 55–56, 69–72, 74, 88–89, 110–12, 115–16, 131–33, 145–46, 239

Lakoff, George, 1–2, 16–17, 33–35, 52–53, 55, 59–60, 120–21, 147–49
Langacker, Ronald, 1–2, 34, 58
Lavender Jack. *See* Schkade, Dan
Layman, John, 127–30. *See also* Guillory, Rob
layout, diagram of comics page, 42–44, 43f
Lee, Stan, 141, 147–48
Lefèvre, Didier. 72–76. *See also* Guibert, Emmanuel; Lemercier, Frédéric.
Lemercier, Frédéric, 72–76. *See also* Lefèvre, Didier; Guibert, Emmanuel
Lemire, Jeff
 Essex County, 5–13, 18–21
 Sweet Tooth, 121–24, 160–64, 248n.3
 Underwater Welder, The, 4, 183–97
Lemke, Jay, 18–19
lettering. *See* typography
line style, 18–19, 26, 27–28, 71, 92–93, 213–14
literacy
 definitions, 10–11, 12–13, 16–19, 240
 and education or background, 5–6, 12, 40–42, 59, 149–50, 234
 and values 11, 13–16, 18–21
logocentrism, or linguistic imperialism, 2–3, 12, 199–200, 217, 220

Madden, Matt, 113–19
 and Jessica Abel, 37
margin, 42–44
materiality, 23–24, 25t, 29, 30, 95, 151–52, 172, 194–95, 205–6, 219, 220–21, 229, 236–37, 242n.6
Maus. *See* Spiegelman, Art
McCloud, Scott, 2–3, 21–22, 26–27, 29–30, 39–40, 42–44, 43f, 89–92, 138–41, 145, 146–49, 151–52, 153–54, 198–200, 204, 232–33, 245n.19

McLuhan, Marshall, 21, 214
McNeill, David, 96
media, and medium, 12, 15, 20–29, 36, 41–42, 200–1, 223, 225, 229–32, 239. *See also* transmedia
　and cognitive engagement, 58, 70, 214, 219–20, 238–39
　and gesture, 95–96
　and metaphor, 99, 130–31, 214
mental metaphor. *See also* blending
　and the conduit metaphor and conduit fallacy, 16–18, 98–100, 219–20, 247n.6
　defined, 52–53
　of emotion, 96–97, 189–90
　and figurative metaphors, 119–20, 121–24
　of knowledge, 81, 98–99, 105, 120, 127–30, 135–36, 156, 247n.4
　of life and journeys, 135–36, 157–40
　of morality, 80–81
　and schemas, 51–53, 79–80
　of self, 80–81, 87–88, 122–23, 185–94, 247n.1
　of time, 119–20, 135–36, 146–51, 152, 153–54
　and viewpoint, 80–81
mental simulation, defined regarding
　emotion and empathy, 58–51, 59–61, 65–66, 88–91, 96–97, 189–90
　fictivity and abstraction, 205, 206–9, 211–12
　general features, 3, 50, 57–62, 76
　gesture, 95–96
　mental spaces and blending, 62–63, 66
　metonymy and metaphor, 61–62, 80–81, 111–12
　style, 71–72, 100, 215
　synesthesia and multimodality, 100, 103–5, 130
　temporality, 141–43, 145–46
　viewpoint, 60, 69–70, 73–79, 100
metacommentary, 116–17, 159, 168–71, 215–27, 232, 238
metaphor. *See also* blending
　defined, 119–20
metonymy. *See also* blending
　defined, 111–12
Mignola, Mike, 100–1, 102f
Miodrag, Hannah, 27–28

mirror neurons, 245n.2, *See also* mental simulation
Mitchell, W J T, 12, 14–15, 18–21
Mittelberg, Irene, 76, 95–96, 244n.13
modalities
　defined, 24, 25t
　and digital comics, 230, 234
　multimodality, defined 2, 21
mode. *See* modalities
Molotiu, Andrei, 184, 200–3, 205, 215–16
Moore, Alan, 113–14, 115–16, 130–31. *See also* Gibbons, Dave
moral panic, 9–10
Müller, Cornelia, 95, 96
multimodality. *See* modalities
Munroe, Randall, 126–27

narrative anchor. *See* anchor: narrative
Nichol, bp, 24, 25t, 105–6, 200–1, 215–23
Noë, Alva, 16, 35, 39–40, 82–83
North, Ryan, 229–30, 231, 232
Núñez, Rafael
　with Cooperrider, Kensy, 140, 146, 148–51
　and Sweetser, Eve, 119–20

Oatley, Keith, 59, 61–62
onomatopoeia, 100–1

panel. *See also* anchor: material
　as attentional window, 44
　functions of, 17–18, 29, 42–45
　and "ghost" panels, 156
Peppard, Anna F, 199
perception. *See also* panel: as attentional window; synesthesia
　and attentional guidance, eye tracking, and scanning, 41–50, 98–104, 106–8, 137, 145–46, 174–75, 195, 198–99, 207–8
　and attentional or change blindness, 40–41, 82–88
　and background knowledge and biases, 18–20, 27–28, 36, 37–38, 39–42, 77–78, 82–83, 217, 224–25
　and conception, 2–3, 23–24, 32–33, 36–37, 204, 234, 240
　defined, 38–39

Index [281]

perception (*cont.*)
   and fictivity, fictive motion, and fictive change, 207–8, 213–14
   and gestalts and gist, 47–48, 51–52, 79–80, 153–54, 190–91, 204–6, 232–33 (*see also* schema)
   and illusion/multistability, 39
   and object and pattern completion, 70, 79–80, 103, 111–12, 221–22
   of objects and events, or space and time, 119–20, 147–51, 204
   and simulation, 57–58 (*see also* simulation *and* emotion)
   as visual thinking, 2–3, 16, 38–39, 130
Persepolis. *See* Satrapi, Marjane
perspective. *See* viewpoint
Photographer, The. *See* Guibert, Didier; Lefèvre, Emmanuel; Lemercier, Frédéric.
Pimienta, Jose, 133–36, 164–66. *See also* Castellucci, Cecil.
Pinker, Steven. *See* cognitive revolutions
Postema, Barbara, 17–18, 29–30, 138–39, 209
posture, 76, 78–80, 88–89, 95, 96–97, 108–9, 126–27, 135, 141–43, 162–63, 170–71, 187, 206–8, 212. *See also* gesture
Prinz, Jesse, 61–62, 88–89, 90–91. *See also* emotion
prototypical or prototype, 50–51, 72, 76–77, 79–80, 92–93, 114–15, 160, 164, 207–8

Red: A Haida Manga. *See* Yahgulanaas, Michael Nicoll
Reddy, Michael, 16–17, 98–99, 219–20
relevance, 39–40, 55–56, 60, 118, 181, 212–13

Satrapi, Marjane, 83–84, 124–25, 247n.8
scanning. *See* perception: attentional guidance, eye tracking, and scanning
schema, defined, 50–53, 244n.12, *See also* abstraction; body schema; mental metaphor
Schkade, Dan, 233–34
semiotics, 21, 24, 241n.1

sequentiality. *See* time *and* stasis
Seth, 166–67
Singer, Marc, 21–22, 27–28
situated cognition, 2, 19–21, 23, 34–35, 88–89, 95, 123, 149–50
Slingerland, Edward, 35, 38–40, 104–5, 130
Smolderen, Thierry, 45
Soupy Leaves Home. *See* Castellucci, Cecil; Pimienta, Jose.
Sousanis, Nick, 2
Spiegelman, Art, 106–8, 113–14, 118
stasis (and static), 15–16, 39–44, 71–72, 76, 96–97, 100–1, 126–27, 145, 160–67, 182, 184, 205–9, 213–14, 222–23, 234–36
Stockwell, Peter, 1–2, 35–38, 71–72
Sullivan, Karen, 120, 187, 189–90
Super Mutant Magic Academy. *See* Tamaki, Jillian
Sweetser, Eve. *See also* Dancygier, Barbara
   and Fauconnier, Gilles, 54–55
   and Núñez, Rafael E, 119–20
Sweet Tooth. *See* Lemire, Jeff
synesthesia, or synesthetic, 98, 100–1, 103–5, 109, 129–31, 206–7. *See also* blending

Talmy, Leonard, 36–37, 207–8, 243n.3
Tamaki, Jillian, 157–59
Taub, Sarah, 24, 104–5
Terry Mosher. *See* Aislin
text box. *See* balloons
texture, 1–2, 3, 36–38, 59, 63, 71–72, 199–200
Theory of Mind (ToM), 59–60, 69–70
time, or temporality. *See also* mental metaphor: of time
   and asynchronicity between modalities, 94, 141–45
   as emergent property, 139–40
   and sequentiality, 145–46
Tomasello, Michael, 12, 33, 90–91, 242n.2
tone. *See* emotion
transmedia, 229–30, 239
transmission model. *See* mental metaphor: conduit

Turner, Mark, 63. *See also* Fauconnier, Gilles
typography and lettering, 37, 98–105, 217–21. *See also* hand writing; line style; synaesthesia; onomatopoeia

Understanding Comics: The Invisible Art. *See* McCloud, Scott
universal cognitive features and abilities, 2, 19–20, 23, 32–35, 40–42, 88–90, 104–5, 195–96, 198–99, 203–4, 212

Van Leeuwen, Theo. *See* Kress, Gunther
Vaughan, Brian K
   and Marcos Martin and Muntsa Vicente, 229–30, 231–32
   and Pia Guerra, 77–82
Verhagen, Arie, 241n.2, 245n.17, *See also* intersubjective
visual turn. *See* fallacy: visual turn
vital relations. *See also* blending
   defined, 63–64, 120–21, 153–54

and time lines and sequentiality, 151–54, 155–57, 196, 208–9

Ware, Chris, 113–14, 151, 172–77, 179–80, 184, 232–33
Watchmen. *See* Moore, Alan; Gibbons, Dave
Watterson, Bill, 154–57, 159
WebToons, 229–30, 235–36, 249n.5
Wertham, Fredric, 10–11, 14
Woo, Benjamin, 27–28, 229–30. *See also* Beaty, Bart
Worden, Daniel, 201–3, 206, 208–9, 210–11, 212–13, 225–26

xkcd. *See* Munroe, Randall

Y: The Last Man. *See* Vaughan, Brian K: and Pia Guerra
Yahgulanaas, Michael Nicoll, 177–80, 232–33

Živadinović, Stevan 235–37
Zunshine, Lisa, 35–36, 59
Zwaan, Rolf A, 24, 50, 54, 59